Business-to-Business Marketing

We work with leading authors to develop the
strongest educational materials in business and marketing,
bringing cutting-edge thinking and best
learning practice to a global market.

Under a range of well-known imprints, including
Financial Times Prentice Hall, we craft high quality
print and electronic publications which help readers
to understand and apply their content, whether
studying or at work.

To find out more about the complete range of our
publishing, please visit us on the World Wide Web at:
www.pearsoned.co.uk

Business-to-Business Marketing

Relationships, Systems and Communications

Chris Fill
University of Portsmouth

Karen E. Fill
University of Southampton

FT Prentice Hall
FINANCIAL TIMES

An imprint of **Pearson Education**
Harlow, England • London • New York • Boston • San Francisco • Toronto • Sydney • Singapore • Hong Kong
Tokyo • Seoul • Taipei • New Delhi • Cape Town • Madrid • Mexico City • Amsterdam • Munich • Paris • Milan

Pearson Education Limited
Edinburgh Gate
Harlow
Essex CM20 2JE
England

and Associated Companies throughout the world

Visit us on the World Wide Web at:
www.pearsoned.co.uk

ISBN 0 273 68279 2

British Library Cataloguing-in-Publication Data
A catalogue record for this book is available from the British Library

Library of Congress cataloging-in-Publication Data
A catalog record for this book is available from the Library of Congress

10 9 8 7 6 5 4 3 2 1
09 08 07 06 05

Typeset in 9/12pt Stone Serif by 35
Printed and bound by Ashford Colour Press Ltd, Gosport

The publisher's policy is to use paper manufactured from sustainable forests.

Contents

Part B B2B marketing management   47

Part C Marketing channels and networks   177

This book is dedicated to
LVB

Preface

Overview

B2B Marketing: relationships, systems and communications is an academic textbook written largely from a marketing management perspective. Unlike other books presented in this subject area, this book attempts to consider the subject through two primary themes. The first theme concerns the interorganisational relationships which organisations develop in order to deliver their business and marketing goals. The second main theme reflects the increasing impact of information systems and technology (IS&T) on organisational performance. Much of contemporary business-to-business (B2B) marketing is influenced by the application of digital technology and this book provides readers with a basic understanding of the principal IS&T concepts. In addition, throughout the book, there are examples of the different ways in which technology is applied by organisations to improve the effectiveness and efficiency of their various B2B marketing activities.

This book reflects the integration of relationships and technology that characterise contemporary B2B marketing practice.

The nature and theme of the book

Since the early 1990s the relationship marketing paradigm has gained credence. At the same time the IS&T revolution has accelerated and spawned a growing number of eCommerce, eBusiness and digital media-related books. With increasing focus now on B2B, this book seeks to integrate ideas about interorganisational relationships and the use of IS&T to support and advance marketing activities in this significant sector.

Apart from considering the nature and characteristics of B2B communications, this book provides an important, though often neglected, bridge between marketing and information systems concepts, within the context of interorganisational relationships. The application of IS&T is explored in some depth, so that readers may better understand its role in B2B marketing.

The book is orientated to the UK and European markets, although some examples are drawn from other regions of the world in order to reflect good practice and the wider global perspective.

This is an applied book, in the sense that the theory and concepts of business marketing are interpreted in the light of business practice. This is an important structural feature of the book with each chapter containing a number of relatively brief examples of business practice that demonstrate marketing theory in action. A range of organisations are used to illustrate practice, from the large multi-national blue chip organisations to small and medium-sized companies with relatively scarce resources, and from the commercial and private companies to the not-for-profit and public sector organisations.

Target market

A high proportion of graduates enter organisations which operate within the B2B sector. The book is intended to help students and lecturers explore this aspect of marketing and to provide an important counterbalance to the mainly consumerist perspective adopted by the majority of marketing educators, their courses and the available resources.

In particular, this book is aimed at both postgraduate and final year undergraduate students. The former may be studying Marketing, Marketing with eCommerce, Media and Multimedia Marketing, eBusiness and MBA programmes in particular. Final year undergraduates will also find the book useful if studying Marketing, Business Studies, Business Information Systems, eCommerce and degree programmes with business-related units such as those increasingly found in Engineering and Social Studies-based programmes.

Students following the Chartered Institute of Marketing's Professional Diploma module, Marketing Communications, will also benefit from this textbook. There are a number of stand-alone professional B2B Marketing programmes that will find the book supportive.

Book structure and organisation

The book consists of twelve chapters, presented in four parts. Therefore, it could form the basis of a complete taught unit or module, delivered over a term or a 12-week semester. This structure enables tutors to deliver in sequence particular chapter topics in class. They can also set any necessary further reading and exercises, such as coursework assessments or independent learning vehicles, based on material from across the book.

The book is intended to be a single source for tutors, although other resources, for example, newspapers, websites, journal papers and edited readers, will be required to supplement and enhance student learning. Each chapter has a complete set of aims and learning objectives, examples, discussion questions, navigation aids and a summary to help readers develop their understanding in a structured and logical manner. The book is presented in four parts, each building on the other.

Part A: Introduction

This part consists of two chapters that introduce the two main themes of the book: business-to-business (B2B) marketing and information systems and technology (IS&T). These chapters are designed to provide a thematic platform on which the rest of the book builds.

Chapter 1 introduces the fundamental characteristics of B2B markets and considers the nature, size and dynamics of the sector. Reference to the consumer market is made to highlight both the differences and similarities between the two fields and approaches. The main objective of this chapter is to set out the essential characteristics and importance of B2B marketing, the pivotal aspects of value creation and interorganisational relationships. This enables readers unfamiliar with the B2B market to become conversant with topics that are developed and explored in subsequent chapters of the book.

Chapter 2 introduces fundamental IS&T concepts to ensure that readers have a basic appreciation of business information systems and related technologies. It is written in a style sympathetic to those readers who neither have, nor need, a particularly technical background in order to come to some understanding of how systems can be used to support marketing operations.

The main content of this chapter relates to core functional systems, data management, digital communications, interactive and multimedia technologies. The knowledge and vocabulary acquired, or consolidated, by reading this chapter is intended to help readers better understand the implementation and integration of systems approaches to support B2B marketing, and appreciate the application examples that are provided throughout the book.

Part B: B2B marketing management

The purpose of this part of the book is to explore the nature and dynamics of some of the principal marketing management issues associated with the B2B sector. It is not designed to lead readers through a full B2B marketing planning process. We believe that such an instrumental and hierarchical approach to the subject is covered more than adequately in many other marketing texts, where marketing planning and strategic development issues are explored at depth.

Chapter 3 considers issues concerning different approaches to segmenting B2B markets. It develops conventional approaches and explores issues around the implementation and practicalities of B2B segmentation. It concludes by discussing ways in which organisations can use different positioning, once segments and target markets are agreed. This provides the first core reference to marketing communications, a topic explored in Part D.

Chapter 4 then examines the nature and features of B2B products, services and pricing. These constitute some of the essential elements through which organisations develop value-based propositions for their customers. Product market portfolios, including the product and technology life cycles, new product development processes and various B2B pricing issues and techniques are investigated.

Organisational buyer behaviour and the various issues about how organisations determine which products and services to buy are examined in Chapter 5. Again, the importance of relationships emerges and this focus is continued into Chapter 6, where interorganisational relationships, relationship marketing ideas and more advanced concepts associated with networks and groups of interacting organisations are discussed. Appropriate examples of IS&T applications within the B2B sector are integrated throughout these chapters.

Part C: Marketing channels and networks

The focus of this part of the book is on marketing channels, supply chains and networks. It examines their roles, purposes and structures and explores the issues and challenges of managing interorganisational relationships. This section thus builds on and develops theories about relationships considered previously.

Chapter 7 examines the different types and purposes of marketing channels and considers related concepts about service output theory, channel flows and the main roles that channel participants assume. This chapter is also concerned with notions of independence/interdependence and cooperation/autonomy, introduced before examining the different roles and functions performed by intermediaries. Service output theory is used to consider the customer perspective on channel purpose, structure and design.

Chapter 8 builds on this to consider the variety of structures that exist in marketing channels. Supply chains are examined and differentiated from marketing channels, and the impact of technology on these two value chain constructs is illustrated. The main goal of this chapter is to review different channel structures and contemporary multi-channel approaches. Readers are encouraged to consider the application of digital technologies, new electronic trading formats and some of the resulting structural changes such as disintermediation and reintermediation. The chapter concludes with a review of ideas about competition and collaboration in terms of both individual organisations and networks of enterprises.

Concerns arise from these chapters about the behaviour of channel members and network partners and the management of interorganisational relationships. Therefore,

Chapter 9 discusses some of the key managerial issues such as power and conflict, trust, commitment and satisfaction. This chapter is important as it provides a consideration of popular concepts such as trust and commitment, typically Morgan and Hunt (1994) but it also examines these from a channel and network perspective, for example the work of Achrol (1997). In addition, the contemporary use of technology is explored and used to challenge some of the established interpretations of interorganisational models.

Part D: B2B marketing communications

The final part of the book considers interorganisational marketing communications. It draws on the technological facilities, relationship marketing characteristics and behavioural concepts developed earlier in the book.

The main thrust of Chapter 10 is to examine some of the roles and strategic issues associated with interorganisational marketing communications. The core characteristics and roles of marketing communications are examined before considering the key marketing communication strategies that can be pursued by organisations. Attention is given to the influences and features of marketing communications in the marketing channels. The chapter concludes with a consideration of the nature of agency/client relationships and ways in which technology can be used to improve the performance of agencies.

Chapter 11 examines the nature and characteristics of the individual communication tools and media of the B2B promotional mix. Attention is given to the importance of personal selling and direct marketing in this sector, but also to the characteristics and usage of exhibitions, sponsorships, public relations and the role of the Internet within B2B marketing communications. Reference is also made to the different ways in which the promotional mix can be configured, based on the key strengths of the particular tools.

The importance of personal selling in the B2B promotional mix is highlighted, as this is the focus of Chapter 12. Here, an examination of the role and characteristics of this promotional tool is followed by a consideration of the variety of structural issues that concern the management of the personal selling resource. The chapter reflects upon a number of different ways in which the sales force can be organised and supported. It also explores how technology can be used to improve the effectiveness of the sales force. To conclude this chapter, issues concerning key account management are explored, looking at the work of leading authors in the area such as Millman and Wilson (1995) and McDonald (2000). Throughout this final part of the book, and this chapter in particular, significant attention is given to the importance of managing relationships.

Teaching support and learning resources

This book is supported by a range of teaching and learning resources. An instructor's manual is available for those who decide to adopt the text. This contains PowerPoint overheads of figures and diagrams from the book, lecture plans and teaching notes along with ideas for assessment and in-class study.

A website designed to support the book is available at www.booksites.net/fill for both tutors and students. At this site there are instructor teaching-support facilities, including all the materials outlined above, as well as other cases studies, examples and a range of hyperlinks to sites of interest and value to help students develop their knowledge and understanding of this exciting and important subject.

References

Achrol, R.S. (1997). 'Changes in the theory of interorganisational relations in marketing: toward a network paradigm', *Journal of the Academy of Marketing Science*, 25, 1, pp. 56–71.

McDonald, M. (2000). 'Key account management – a domain review', *Marketing Review*, 1, pp. 15–34.

Millman, T. and Wilson, K. (1995). 'From key account selling to key account management', *Journal of Marketing Practice: Applied Marketing Science*', 1, 1, pp. 9–21.

Morgan, R.M. and Hunt, S.D. (1994). 'The commitment-trust theory of relationship marketing', *Journal of Marketing*, 58 (July), pp. 20–38.

Acknowledgements

Many people have contributed to the development, research, writing and production of this book. They have sought and provided information, granted permissions, answered phone calls, returned emails and tolerated our persistence. Others have reviewed drafts, made constructive and insightful comments and provided moral support and encouragement. To all of you we extend our warmest thanks.

In particular we should like to thank all the reviewers:

Wim G. Biemans – University of Groningin, Holland
Ross Brennan – Middlesex University
Nick Ellis – Leicester Business School
Adriana Dredge – London Institute
Steve Mitchell – University of Gloucestershire
Albert Schofield – University of Lancashire
Peter Stoney – University of Liverpool

In addition, the following people and organisations have provided material which has enabled us to impart depth, clarity and a little sparkle to the book through the snapshots of B2B marketing practice:

Andrew Burrell	CXO Media
Angela Campbell	Jeld-wen
Simon Campbell	XM London
Steve Cooper	Argos
Debbie Cranston	prospectswetenhams
John Dawson	Exel
AJ Dent	Nicholl Food Packaging
Katya Danilova	Kanda Software
Jan van Dongen	International Service for National Agricultural Research
Alexander Dries	BBDO Consulting
Enrique Flores	Alfa
Helen Gunter	TUI
Alex Karpousky	Kanda Software
Louise Kettle	IBM UK
Cronan MacMahon	BUPA Direct

Mike Moran   Kanatsiz
Judy Nokes   Her Majesty's Stationery Office
Peter Nyquist   SCA
Amy Orford   Canon UK
Jenni Osbaldeston   Chartered Institute of Marketing
Martin Owen-Brown   Aroplus
Adrian Payne   Cranfield
Niklas Pettifor   Grayling
Shauna Roolvink   Brandhub
Adam Southam   Reshare Corporation
Kristina Schurr   BOC
Diana Siler   DoveBid
John Wallace   Association of Exhibition Organisers
Else Warmbier   Institut for Transportstudier

Other organisations:

American Marketing Association
Chartered Institute of Marketing
EMAP Glenigan
Fisher Marketing
Ford UK
Gotmarketing
Harley Davidson
Inbox
Kent Express
Opt-in News

This book would not have been possible without the contributions of a large number of researchers, academics, authors and practitioners whose work has advanced our understanding of B2B marketing. Some of their ideas have been incorporated in this book and to them all we offer our thanks.

Finally we would also like to thank our editorial team at Pearson Education, and in particular Thomas Sigel, Peter Hooper and Georgina Clark-Mazo who between them have supported and steered us in the production of this book.

Publisher's acknowledgements

We are grateful to the following for permission to reproduce copyright material:

Snapshot 3.5 from Renting Lists of ProspectSwetenhams in Website (formerly known as The Prospect Shop); Figure 1.2 from *Competitive Advantage: Creating and Sustaining Superior Performance*, publisher The Free Press (Porter M., 1985); Figure 1.4, G.S. Day, in *Journal of Academy of Marketing Science* (Winter), pp. 24–31, 2000, from *Managing Marketing Relationships*, reprinted by permission of Sage Publications Inc.; Figures 3.2

and 3.3 and Table 3.2, Anderson, Rolph E., *Personal Selling*, copyright © 2004 by Houghton Mifflin Company, used with permission; Figure 3.4 from 'A new research agenda for business segmentation', in *European Journal of Marketing*, pp. 252–71, published with permission, Emerald Publishing Group (Goller, S., Hogg, A. and Kalafatis, S.P., 2002); Figure 4.1 from *The Brand Leadership Matrix™*, *The Brand Leadership®* (2003 BrandHub Pte Ltd. All rights reserved); Figure 4.4 from 'Managing supplier involvement in new product development: a portfolio approach', in *European Journal of Purchasing and Supply Management*, 6,1 (March), pp. 49–67, published with permission from Elsevier (Wynstra F. and ten Pierick E., 2000); Figure 4.6 in *Crossing the Chasm: Marketing and Selling Technology Products to Mainstream Customers*, copyright © 1995 by Geoffrey A. Moore Consulting, Inc., reprinted with permission of HarperCollins Publishing Inc.; Figure 5.3 from 'Global account management: a supply side managerial view', in *Industrial Marketing Management*, 32, 7 (October) pp. 563–71, with permission from Elsevier (Harvey, M.G., Novicevis, M.M., Hench, T. and Myers, M., 2003); Figure 5.4 from 'Web-based B2B portals', in *Industrial Marketing Management*, 32, pp. 15–23, with permission from Elsevier (Clarke III, I. and Flaherty, T.B., 2003); Figure 5.5 from 'Organisational risk perception and reduction: a literature review', in *British Journal of Management*, 4, pp. 115–33, publisher Blackwell Publishing (Mitchell, V.M., 1995); Figure 6.1 and Table 6.2 from *Relationship Marketing: Creating Stakeholder Value*, publisher Pearson Education (Bruhn M., 2003); Figure 6.3 from *Relationship Marketing: Creating Stakeholder Value*, M. Christopher, A. Payne and D. Ballantyne, 2002, with permission from Elsevier; Figure 6.4 and Table 6.1 from 'Capabilities for managing a portfolio of supplier relationships', pp. 79–88, reprinted with permission from *Business Horizons*, 45, 6 (November–December) 2002, copyright 2002 by the Trustees at Indiana University, Kelley School of Business; Figure 6.5 from 'The commitment–trust theory of relationship marketing', in *Journal of Marketing*, 58 (July), pp. 20–38, publisher American Association of Marketing (Morgan, R.M. and Hunt S.D., 2002); Figure 6.6 from 'A strategic framework for CR in draft working document', publisher Cranfield School of Management, Cranfield University, (Payne, A.F.T.); Figure 8.3 reprinted with permission of *Harvard Business Review* from 'E-hubs: the new B2B marketplaces', by S. Kaplan and M. Sawhney (2000), 78, 3, pp. 97–103; Figure 9.1 from *Understanding Channel Conflict*, published by Reshare Corporation (A.G. Southern); Figure 9.3 from 'Electronic marketplaces and supply chain relationships', in *Industrial Marketing Management*, 32–3 (April), pp. 199–210 (T. Skjott-Larsen, H. Kotozab and M. Grieger, 2003), with permission from Elsevier; Figure10.1 and Table 10.1 from 'Towards a model of marketing communications effects', in *Industrial Marketing Management*, 26, pp. 15–29 (D.I. Gilliland and W.J. Johnston, 1997), with permission from Elsevier; Figure 10.9 and Table 10.4 from 'Communication strategies in marketing channels', in *Journal of Marketing* (October) pp. 36–51, publisher American Association of Marketing (J. Mohr and J.R. Nevin 1990); Figure 12.3 from 'Examining the antecedents of sales organisation effectiveness: an Australian study', in *European Journal of Marketing*, 33, 9/10 pp. 945–57, published with permission, Emerald Publishing Group (K. Grant and D.W. Cravens, 1999); Figure 12.4 from 'A conceptual model for building and maintaining relationships between manufacturers' representatives and their principals', in *Industrial Marketing Management*, 30, 2 (February), pp. 165–81, with permission from Elsevier (D.H. McQuiston, 2001); Table 1.1 in *Purchasing and Supply Chain Management: Analysis, Planning and Practice*, publisher Thomson Learning, London (A.J. van Weele, 2002); Table 3.3 from 'Market segmentation: diagnosing and treating the barriers', in *Industrial Marketing Management*, 30, 8 (November), pp. 609–25, with permission from Elsevier (S. Dibb and L. Simkin, 2001); Table 4.4 from 'Creating project plans to focus product development', S.C. Wheelwright and K.B. Clark, March/April 1992, *Harvard Business Review*; Table 4.5 from 'The effect of project and process characteristics on product development cycle time', in *Journal of Marketing Research*, 34 (February), pp. 24–35, with permission from Elsevier (A. Griffin, 1997); Tables 7.5 and 9.1, Coughlan, Anderson, Stern, El-Ansary, *Marketing Channels*, 6th edn, © 2001, adapted by permission of Pearson Education, Inc., Upper Saddle River, NJ; Table 8.1 from *Using the Balanced Scorecard to Measure Supply Chain Performance*, Vol. 21, Edition 1, pp. 75–95, published by The Council of Logistics Management; Table 10.6 from 'Key criteria for agency/client portals', publisher Kanda Software Inc.; Table 10.7 from 'Features and benefits of using a portal within an advertising agency', publisher Kanda Software Inc.; Table 12.6 from *Journal of Personal Selling and Sales Management*, 22, 3 (Summer 2002), copyright © 2002 Pi Sigma Epsilon, Inc., reprinted with permission of M.E. Sharpe, Inc.; Table 12.7 from 'Technology and the sales force: increasing acceptance of sales force automation', in *Industrial Marketing Management*, 30, 5 (July), pp. 463–72 (A.J. Morgan and S.A. Inks, 2001), with permission from Elsevier.

Her Majesty's Stationery office for the extracts adapted from www.parliament.the-stationery-office.co.uk and www.statistics.gov.uk; Elsevier for extracts from the articles 'Strategic use of the Internet and e-commerce: Cisco Systems', by Kraemer and Dedrick, published in *Journal of Strategic Information Systems*, 11 (2002) and 'Market segmentation: diagnosing and treating the barriers', by Dibb and Simkin, published in *Industrial Marketing Mangement*, 30, 8 (2001); BASF for an extract adapted from 'BASF Annual Report 2002', published on www.berichte.basf.de; Prospect Swetenhams for an extract adapted from the article 'Database Information at Prospect Swetenhams', published on www.prospectswetenhams.com; ASME and Trygve Dahl for two extracts adapted from the article 'The evolution of the pump business in the information age', by Trygve Dahl, published on www.intelliquip.com; Jupitermedia Corporation for an extract from the article 'Embrace the gatekeeper', by Belbey and Gedney, published on www.clickz.com © Jupitermedia Corporation 2004; Bearing Point for an extract from www.bearingpoint.com; Reed Business Information for an extract from the article 'Sainsbury's boosts supplier collaboration', by Daniel Thomas, published on www.computerweekly.com, 24 October 2003; Times Newspapers Limited for an extract adapted from the article 'Mobile phone minnow snaps up trade from the giants', by P. Durman, published on www.timesonline.co.uk, 10 August 2003, © The Times 2003; VNU Business Publishers Ltd for an extract adapted from the article 'Cisco gets its channels sorted out', by Karl Flinders, published on www.vnunet.com; ECT News Network for an extract adapted from the article 'Site launched to settle B2B disputes online', by Ken Cimino, published on www.ecommercetimes.com, 13 July 2001; Midland Communications for extracts adapted from the articles 'Charity: Video conferencing helps Actionaid' and 'Manufacturing: coutant Lambda', published on www.midlandcomms.co.uk; Argos Business Solutions for an extract adapted from the article 'Kent Express' published on www.argos-b2b.co.uk; and Cofunds Ltd for an extract adapted from the article 'An overview of Cofunds', published on www.cofunds.co.uk.

In some instances we have been unable to trace the owners of copyright material and we would appreciate any information that would enable us to do so.

Part A
Introduction

This part consists of two chapters that introduce the two main themes of the book: business-to-business (B2B) marketing and information systems and technology (IST). These chapters are designed to provide a thematic platform on which the rest of the book builds.

Chapter 1 introduces the fundamental characteristics of B2B markets and considers the nature, size and dynamics of the sector. The main objective of this chapter is to set out the essential characteristics and importance of B2B marketing, the pivotal aspects of value creation and interorganisational relationships. This enables readers unfamiliar with the B2B market to become conversant with topics that are developed and explored in subsequent chapters of the book.

Chapter 2 introduces fundamental IST concepts to ensure that readers have a basic appreciation of business information systems and related technologies. The main content covered in this chapter relates to core functional systems, data management, digital communications, interactive and multimedia technologies. The intention is to help readers understand the implementation and integration of systems approaches to support B2B marketing, and to appreciate the application examples that are provided throughout the book.

Chapter 1

An introduction to business-to-business marketing

Chapter overview

This chapter discusses the principal characteristics used to define business markets. It establishes the key elements of business-to-business (B2B) marketing and makes comparisons with the better-known business-to-consumer (B2C) sector. This leads to consideration of appropriate definitions, parameters and direction for the book.

After setting out the main types of organisations that operate in the B2B sector and categorising the goods and services that they buy or sell, the chapter introduces ideas about value, supply chains, interorganisational relationships and relationship marketing.

This opening chapter lays down the vital foundations and key principles which are developed subsequently in the book.

Chapter aims

The aim of this chapter is to introduce and explore the characteristics and dimensions of business-to-business (B2B) marketing.

Objectives

The objectives of this chapter are to:

1 Consider the nature and scope of business markets.

2 Identify the different types of organisational customers and categorise the goods and services that are sold and bought in the sector.

3 Explore the characteristics of B2B marketing.

4 Show familiarisation with the value and supply chain concepts.

5 Introduce the importance of relationships in B2B marketing.

Introduction

The market for goods and services bought and sold between businesses is huge. Far larger than the consumer market, the business market comprises many types and sizes of organisations that interact selectively and form relationships of varying significance and duration with one another. Although these organisations are often structurally and legally independent entities, a key characteristic is that they are also interdependent. That is, they have to work with other organisations to varying degrees in order to achieve their goals.

Imagine the complicated, multi-player chain of buying and selling for all the component parts that Airbus Industries needs in order to build an aeroplane. The operational complexity is enormous and the value of the total materials, components, labour and energy involved far exceeds consumer spending in either the confectionery or clothing markets. Regardless of whether they sell their products and services to consumers or to other organisations, all businesses buy and sell items in

SNAPSHOT 1.1

THE BRITISH AIRWAYS LONDON EYE

The construction of the London Eye, the giant observation wheel on the banks of the Thames opposite the Houses of Parliament, involved major components that were built in a number of European countries:

Holland fabricated the steel structure.

Italy supplied the cables and the glass for the capsules.

Germany manufactured the bearings.

France built the capsules.

The Czech Republic built the spindle and the hub.

The United Kingdom supplied the electrical components and the steel (for Holland).

The intricate and complex supply chains required to build the £75 million 'Eye' illustrate the huge range of business-to-business relationships. Furthermore, the project was a notable consumer success. The 3.2 million passengers who enjoyed the London Eye in its first year compares favourably with the forecast demand of 2.2 million passengers.

The sixteen-month project time required not only the project partners to design, manufacture, assemble and erect the wheel, but also a whole raft of suppliers and subcontractors to source parts and subassemblies in order to fulfil their commitments to the main contractors and the project. The coordination, collaboration and sharing of ideas and information necessary to meet these tight deadlines bear testimony to the relationships that developed between the members of the project team.

Source: Adapted from Mann *et al.* (2001).

order to create their own offerings. In recognition of their added value, other businesses may then buy these products to use, to create other products or to sell as finished items to consumers.

B2B marketing is fundamentally different from consumer goods or services marketing because buyers do not consume the products or services themselves. Unlike consumer markets, where goods and services are consumed personally by the people who buy them, the essence of business markets is that individual organisations undertake the act of consumption. This book is developed around this important principle which has critical implications for the marketing strategies and associated programmes that are used to satisfy organisational buyers.

Before looking at the characteristics of business markets and B2B marketing, it is important to note that, although there are several vital differences to consumer marketing, organisations which have a market orientation, regardless of the sector in which they operate, share at least two key similarities:

1 Both have a customer orientation and work backwards from an understanding of customer needs.

2 Both need the ability to gather, process and use information about customers and competitors in order to achieve their objectives.

This market orientation is an essential foundation upon which to begin exploring the exciting and dynamic world of business markets and the contribution of B2B marketing.

This chapter introduces various fundamental aspects of B2B marketing. It is designed to provide an overview and to set out the parameters for exploring the subject. It is not intended to provide an in-depth analysis or understanding, but to outline issues and concepts that are covered in detail in later chapters.

The characteristics of business markets

Business markets are characterised by a number of factors, the main ones being the nature of demand, the buying processes, international dimensions and, perhaps most importantly, the relationships that develop between organisations in the process of buying and selling. These are now considered from an introductory point of view.

The nature of demand

One of the key factors is the nature of demand in business markets. Three aspects of demand are considered: derivation, variance and elasticity.

Demand is derived in business markets. It is derived from consumers. With respect to the Airbus example, consumers (and business travellers) determine, through the number of flights they make and what they are prepared to pay, the number of aircraft that airlines make available. However, each aircraft is the product of hundreds of organisations interacting with one another. Air passengers stimulate demand.

Demand is variable in business markets. Simply because it is derived, fluctuations develop according to changes in consumer preferences and behaviour. This means that organisations should monitor and anticipate demand as cycles emerge. Note the decline in the demand for air travel following the events of 9/11 and the subsequent impact on airlines, support services, aircraft manufacturers and the whole array of suppliers and subcontractors in the commercial aviation market.

Demand is inelastic in business markets. Once a manufacturer has incorporated a differentiated product into its processes, unforeseen and uncontrollable supplier price increases have to be absorbed until a revised or redesigned product can be developed, eliminating the original materials or part. On the basis that manufacturers are generally reluctant to let their customers down by a delayed or failed delivery while searching for new suppliers, these price increases have to be incorporated, at least over the short to medium term, hence the inelasticity or low price sensitivity (Brassington and Pettitt, 2003).

Buying processes

Another major aspect of B2B marketing concerns the buying processes used to purchase goods and services. In consumer markets, decisions are made relatively quickly, the level of risk is low, at least for everyday items, and the focus is primarily on the emotional aspects attaching to a purchase.

In B2B markets the potential risk is often quite large so decisions take much longer and involve considerably more people. Consequently, the nature and form of interaction between organisations is based on an understanding of individual business customers' needs and a willingness to provide and share information.

SNAPSHOT 1.2

B2B BUYING MOTIVATIONS

The decision making unit for an engineering company considering the purchase of solar energy may consist of the following, all of whom will have different criteria when selecting suitable suppliers.

Senior Management	Reduce costs, use and be seen using latest technology.
Purchasing Manager	Get value for money, increase own credibility and colleague satisfaction.
Plant Engineer	Use modern equipment and provide cover for power breakdown.
Production Manager	Reduce operating costs and improve reliability.
Consultants	Improve plant efficiency, improve staff working conditions.

In consumer markets purchases are generally made, and often consumed, individually. Purchasing in B2B markets is essentially a group activity, with the composition and size of the group changing according to the significance of the item being purchased. The group is referred to as the Decision Making Unit (DMU) or Buying Centre. Consumption, or product usage, is an organisational activity.

International aspects

Increasingly B2B organisations are engaging in international markets. Advances in technology, most notably the Internet, have enabled organisations to do business more or less anywhere. In comparison to consumer markets, international business is easier. In B2C markets there are a wide range of issues concerning the culture and values that consumers hold, and how products and promotional activities need to be adapted to accommodate colour, ingredient, style, buying processes, packaging and language requirements to ensure success. By contrast, B2B organisations benefit from a lower diversity in product functionality and performance. This is partly because of the inherent nature of the products and materials but also due to various trading associations across the world agreeing standards relating to content and performance. For example, the steel, plastic, chemicals and paper industries all have common agreed standards which facilitate the interorganisational exchange process. Thus, B2B organisations are able to work together to help shape their trading environment.

Relationships

A fundamentally key characteristic of business marketing concerns the significance of relationships. In B2C markets relationships between manufacturer and consumer, or reseller and consumer have been regarded, at least in the past, as relatively weak and unimportant. Although many organisations have now recognised the importance of developing these relationships, the nature of the products, their perceived value to consumers, and competitive factors, particularly in the fast-moving consumer goods (FMCG) markets, suggests that such relationships will remain difficult and costly to establish and maintain.

In B2B markets, by contrast, the development and maintenance of positive relationships between buying and selling organisations is pivotal to success. Collaboration and partnership over the development, supply and support of products and services is considered a core element of B2B marketing. Indeed, Morgan and Hunt (1994) recognise this when they refer to relationship marketing and the importance of marketing activities that seek to establish, develop and maintain successful exchanges with customers. Unlike consumer markets, where relationships are often considered to revolve around an active seller and a passive buyer, understanding of relationships in B2B markets now encompasses networks of relationships in which participants are regarded as interactive. This means that both buyers and sellers are actively involved in initiating and maintaining relationships. All parties to a network have the capability to influence a wide range of relationships, either directly or indirectly.

The importance of this aspect of B2B marketing cannot be underestimated nor should it be understated. This book adopts a relationship-based marketing perspective and seeks to explore and establish ways in which technology is used by organisations to enhance their relationships with key stakeholders.

Types of organisational customers

Business-to-business marketing was previously referred to as industrial marketing, but this phrase failed to recognise the involvement of a range of other, non-industrial enterprises. For example, governments and the not-for-profit sector also contribute a significant amount of commercial activity. Think about the economic transactions necessary to support the prison and military services. The sheer volume and value of pharmaceutical and medical supplies necessary to provide adequate health services, alone represent a major slice of the B2B sector. In addition, charities and institutions generate a substantial level of economic transactions. Therefore, the term **organisational marketing** has been adopted for this book and encompasses all these activities and types of organisation.

One way of characterising organisations is by size, to differentiate between the very large and the very small. For example, there are a number of differences between global and national organisations, the public sector, small and medium-sized enterprises (SMEs) and small office/home office (SOHOs) not least in the ways they specify products and services (Macfarlane, 2002). Although this approach based on size and structure may be suitable for market research purposes, it is not entirely appropriate for understanding different purchasing procedures and buyer needs.

The approach presented here considers three broad types of organisation yet encompasses a number of sub-sections all based on their roles within marketing channels. These are **commercial, government** and **institutional** organisations (see Figure 1.1).

Figure 1.1 Types of B2B organisations

Commercial organisations

There are four main sectors in commercial B2B, all characterised by the different ways in which they use products and services. They share common buyer behaviour characteristics and associated communication needs. These four commercial organisational types are:

- distributors;

- original equipment manufacturers;

- users;

- retailers.

Distributors

These organisations are sometimes referred to as intermediaries. The most common types are **wholesalers**, **distributors/dealers** and **value added resellers**. Their role is to facilitate the transfer of products through the marketing channel and to add value, perhaps by providing credit facilities, storage or service support. Ownership and physical possession of the goods often pass from one distributor to another, but there are occasions when this might not always be true. For example, the involvement of an agent in negotiations may mean that ownership passes over, rather than through, it to the next intermediary or customer.

Distributors fulfil a vital service. As middlemen they enable manufacturers to reach customers who do not require sufficient quantities to buy directly from them. This **breaking bulk** concept is an important principle and is examined further in Chapter 7. It allows manufacturers to concentrate on their core activities and leave the skills associated with distribution to others, namely the dealers and distributors.

Value added resellers are a relatively recent type of intermediary. Their role is to bring together a variety of software and hardware products to design customised systems solutions for their business customers. They provide integrated systems by drawing on a network of providers and in doing so create a value network, at the business customer level.

Distributors/Dealers supply both end-user business customers and original equipment manufacturers. They take full title to the industrial goods they purchase for resale and fulfil the important role of providing a wide range of products from a number of different manufacturers, offering easy access to them for their customers. In addition dealers and distributors provide advice, repair and credit facilities where necessary.

Original Equipment Manufacturers (OEMs)

OEMs purchase materials that are subsequently built into the products that they market to their customers. These materials may take many forms, such as parts, finished and partly finished goods, and even sub-assemblies which have been outsourced.

For example, a number of car manufacturers buy in radio components and assemble their own branded car radios. They source light bulbs directly from a range of authorised manufacturers and tyres from a variety of suppliers all of whom meet specific quality and performance standards. Thus in a finished Ford car, for example, the tyres may be identified as Michelin, the radio will be branded Ford, and it will not be possible to identify the manufacturer(s) of the various light bulbs.

Users

Users are organisations that purchase goods and services to support their production and manufacturing processes. Users consume these materials, they do not appear in the final offering but contribute to its production.

Ford will purchase many support materials; for example, machine tools, electrical manufacturing equipment, vending machines, office furniture and stationery. None of these can be identified within the cars they manufacture.

Retailers

Technically, retailers are intermediaries, but their role is different. A retailer's customer is an end-user, the consumer. Retailers need to purchase goods in order to offer them to consumers but the buying processes, although similar, are not always as complex or as intricate as those in the DMU.

Recognition of the role and significance of retailers is an important aspect of B2B marketing. Organisations need to sell into retailers and understand the needs of this market and accommodate them accordingly. Retailing is a specialist activity and, although the roles and tasks of retailers are considered in Chapter 7, it does not form a major part of this book.

In all of the situations described above, organisations are involved in the buying of products and only in the last are consumers at all involved. The nature and form of cooperation, and the interorganisational relationships that develop from the various exchange transactions, influence the type of marketing activities used. The degree of cooperation between organisations will vary, and part of the role of marketing is to develop and support the relationships between partner organisations.

Government

Governments, and related institutions, are responsible for a huge volume and enormous value of business purchases. Health, environmental protection, education, policing, transport, national defence and security are just some of the areas that attract funding and sellers.

The procedures and guidelines relating to buying behaviour in a government context are in many ways radically different from those encountered in commercial organisations. However, despite many of the differences outlined below, the principle remains that a continual focus on customer needs is paramount. Suppliers that fail on a regular basis to win government business might well be too product-orientated. Many of the larger projects that concern governments and associated ministries are massive, complex and involve a huge number of stakeholders. It is unsurprising that many run way over their original budgets and planned timescales (see Snapshot 1.3).

SNAPSHOT 1.3

GOVERNMENT PROJECTS

A considerable number of government-funded projects have run beyond their original targets and/or exceeded their budgets.

One of a large number of building projects in this category, the UK's Millennium Dome in London, was built on time but overran its original budget by at least £300 million. The cost of building the Scottish Parliament building rose from £40 million to £430 million. The refurbishment of the European Commission's headquarters building was reported to have exceeded the original £270 million by at least 12 per cent. Various hospital and prison construction projects have also been subject to delay and cost overruns.

UK government-funded information technology based projects have also overrun. For example, the 1999 project to install a new computer system at the United Kingdom Passport Agency resulted in delays and public inconvenience, and increased the unit cost of producing a passport to an estimated £15.50, compared to the target of £12. The new air traffic control centre at Swanwick in Hampshire was originally due to open in 1996 but, due to software difficulties, the opening was delayed until 2002. This project cost approximately £700 million, double the original estimate. Other information systems projects to cause difficulties involve various Inland Revenue, Benefit Fraud and Jobseekers projects, to name but a few.

Other examples include the Eurofighter project and the building of the Channel Tunnel, both of which considerably exceeded their original budgets and completion times.

Source: www.parliament.the-stationery-office.co.uk/pa/cm199900/cmselect/cmpubacc/65/6509.htm for more information. (Accessed 25 March 2004.)

Of the many differences between government and private commercial purchasing, van Weele (2002) cites the following as the more prominent: political objectives, budget policies, accountability and EC directives.

Political objectives

The balance between meeting different goals can be difficult in the public sector. The drive to meet efficiency targets might not accord with the need to satisfy political or social goals. For example, Portsmouth City Council faced difficulties when developing the Spinnaker Tower. There was a political need to be seen using the Lottery funding that had already been awarded to them and a community need to be using local council taxpayers' money wisely and efficiently. These had to be balanced against the project's social goals as part of the 'Renaissance of Portsmouth', and economic imperatives to attract tourism, increase jobs and raise the overall reputation of the city. The degree to which these various stakeholder needs were met depend largely upon an individual's political perspective.

Budget policies

All government spending is bounded and constrained by central government policy and, in that sense, priorities are predetermined and generally immovable. For example, budgets associated with projects to build or extend the road network may be modified on a change of government (and road transport policy) or subject to serious down-grading, even withdrawal, should the overall economy move into recession such that spending has to be reduced or switched into other areas.

Government budgeting techniques and policies are very different from those in the private commercial sector. Government budgets are subject to public scrutiny and, as a result, some decisions regarding major projects are deliberated for a considerable time. Procedures are normally detailed and protracted, involving a large number of people. The Department of Health in the United Kingdom publicises its purchasing policy, as required by EC regulations. Interested readers can review it at the website www.doh.gov.uk/purchasing/policy.htm.

If the allocated funding is not spent within the prescribed budget period, any underspend (or saving) may not be retained. Indeed, the budgeting process might have to be started again, causing delay, frustration and possibly a decrease in the amount of money made available.

Some projects are funded by a number of different budgets, further complicating procedures, not just for the administration but for sellers trying to win business. Pan European publicly funded projects such as those for the troubled Eurofighter (now renamed 'Typhoon') demand transparent budgeting and approval processes. In this case where the 20-year project requires collaboration among four main countries/companies: Alenia in Italy, BAE Systems in the United Kingdom, EADS-CASA in Spain and EADS-DASA in Germany, the cost has escalated as environmental and political influences have changed and as the desired specification has altered to accommodate future technological developments (Lake, 2003).

Accountability

The hierarchical nature of government institutions means that purchasing procedures are invariably slow as each manager is required to give authorisation. The root cause is that these managers are spending public money and they are accountable for the money they authorise. As a result the whole system becomes bureaucratic, with an emphasis placed on procedure rather than the quality of the purchase itself.

Associated with the notion of accountability is the practice of contract management, quite common in many countries. Under this approach, contracts are awarded to con-tractors when both parties are fully aware that the actual cost will be far in excess of that originally agreed. This process leads to a failure to implement significant and con-sistent purchasing procedures, resulting in inefficiency and inappropriate spending of public money.

Partly in response to these failings the UK government introduced the Office of Government Commerce (OGC) in order to improve the purchasing procedures. Readers particularly interested in this aspect of business-to-business purchasing should visit the OGC website at www.ogc.gov.uk.

One of the more recent initiatives by the UK government has been the Private Finance Initiative (PFI). This involves partnership between the public and private sec-tors in order to access the skills and expertise of the private sector in providing public services and facilities. It is about the financing of capital investments and exploiting the full range of private sector management, commercial and creative skills.

SNAPSHOT 1.4

PFI IN THE HEALTH SERVICE

In the health sector, the NHS continues to be responsible for providing high quality clinical care to patients. But, where capital investment is required, there is a role for a private sector partner in the provision of facilities.

Major PFI schemes are typically DBFO (design, build, finance and operate). This means that the private sector partner is responsible for:

■ designing the facilities (based on the requirements specified by the NHS);

■ building the facilities (to time and at a fixed cost);

■ financing the capital cost (with the return to be recovered through continuing to make the facilities available and meeting the NHS's requirements);

■ operating the facilities (providing facilities management and other support services).

Risks in each of these areas is assumed by the PFI partner which, it is believed, will be strongly incentivised to continue to perform well throughout the life of the contract because capital is at stake.

NHS Trusts remain the employers of clinical staff but the PFI is intended to ensure that the facilities in which they work are as modern, efficient and cost effective as possible by placing responsibility for their provision on specialist managers who are expert at providing them. The NHS can then concentrate upon the provision of health care.

Typically, for a large scheme, the private sector partner will be a consortium whose members may include a construction company and a facilities management provider, amongst others. The private sector partner obtains finance for the project, constructs the hospital, and provides services to the NHS Trust as specified in the contract agreed between the NHS Trust and the private partner. The terms of the contract set out the range of services to be provided and the performance standards required of the consortium.

No payments are made by the NHS until services are provided to the agreed standard. Thereafter, the standard must be maintained to ensure full payment.

Source: Adapted from Department Health PFI Overview at www.doh.gov.uk/pfi/overview.htm (Accessed January 2004.) Used with permission.

These schemes promote the development of new partnerships and relationships and, of course, new ways of purchasing products and services for the public sector. There is debate about whether these schemes are in the best interests of the public and, in particular, public sector employees. However, this new approach is expected to be the model for government financing of major capital projects.

EC directives

The European Commission has tried to regularise purchasing and contract procedures throughout member countries. The detail concerning procedures is beyond the scope of this book. Interested readers could start by visiting the portal at www.ojec.com. However, the EC directives that have evolved attempt to achieve two main aspects. One is to specify who and what is covered by any directive, and the second is to regularise or standardise the procedures by which public expenditure on contracts worth over 200,000 euro are communicated, tendered, suppliers selected and contracts, including the technical specifications, are prepared, awarded and managed.

Just as individual countries have purchasing procedures, policies and guidelines, so the European Commission also has a set of purchasing directives and procedures. Table 1.1 sets out the three types of procedure that are available for the award of public supply contracts.

Institutions

There are a range of other organisations, which are neither entirely governmental nor private and commercial in nature. For example, there are not-for-profit organisations such as churches and charities, there are government-related organisations such as hospitals, schools, museums, libraries and universities and there are community-based organisations such as housing associations. This brief list serves to demonstrate the breadth and variety of institutional markets and the impact that these types of organisations can have on the overall B2B market. All these organisations need to buy a range of goods, materials and services as part of their drive to satisfy their customers' needs.

In many respects, these organisations adopt some of the characteristics associated with both commercial and government markets. Purchasing in some institutional markets can be significantly constrained by political influences (for example, schools under the direct control of local education authorities) while in others the drive for corporate efficiency is an over-riding influence.

One of the main characteristics of this market is the willingness of organisations to unite to form large buying groups. The primary advantage of group purchasing is the

Table 1.1 Three types of procedure for the award of public supply contracts

Procedure	Explanation
The open procedure	This involves the submission of tenders from a huge variety of suppliers, most of whom will not be known to the government.
The restricted procedure	This involves only those suppliers previously invited (and vetted) by the contracting organisation to tender for the work.
Negotiated procedure	Subject to special conditions, specified by the EC, the contracting authority may choose five suppliers and enter into negotiations with them, as long as, among other things, all parties are treated fairly.

Source: Adapted from van Weele (2002).

ability to command increased discounts based upon volume purchases. For example, local health services combine and agree a list of drugs and medicines from which all doctors must prescribe. This enables discounts and hence lower costs and better value for the public they serve. This 'formulary list' both constrains the range of suppliers and items purchased and also provides improved efficiencies. Supplier organisations must adapt their marketing approaches, as the processes and personnel associated with group purchasing can be very different to individual institutional buying procedures. With group purchasing, members of the purchasing team may be motivated by needs that differ from those of personnel responsible for purchasing at individual institutions. Therefore, relationships will need to be determined and developed, communications adapted, and price will inevitably be paramount while delivery and support is required at individual group member level.

Finally, the impact of multiple buying influences in institutional markets can be strong. In service-based institutions, for example schools and hospitals, the primary provision is delivered by professionals such as teachers, lecturers and doctors. It has been known for their purchasing departments to impose restrictions on certain supplies or materials or to deny access to particular products. This can lead to resentment and conflict between those in 'administration' and the professional staff. From a marketing perspective, supplier organisations need to be aware of this potential conflict and communicate with all parties.

Types of business goods and services

Following the above examination of market characteristics and customers in the B2B sector, this section highlights the variety and complexity of the goods and services that are bought and sold.

If the production process is adopted as the template it is possible to discern three main categories of goods. These are input goods, equipment goods and supply goods (see Table 1.2).

Table 1.2 A categorisation of business market goods

Type of Goods	Explanation
Input goods	Raw materials and semi-manufactured parts, which become part of the finished item.
Equipment goods	Capital items that are not part of the finished item but necessary to enable production process to take place (e.g. land and buildings).
Supply goods	Materials necessary to keep the production process running (e.g. electricity and oil).

Input goods

Input goods become part of the finished item. There are two main types, **raw materials** and **semi-manufactured parts**.

Raw materials have been subject to minimal processing and enter the production process in their natural state. For example, copper, iron ore, coffee and oranges.

Semi-manufactured parts have undergone some processing before entering the main manufacturing process. For example, car manufacturers buy in sheet metal and cloth for the interior, previously prepared by other organisations. Components such as pistons, headlights and radios are bought in and physically unchanged. They are assembled into the finished product.

In addition to this there are **finished goods**. Retailers and resellers buy finished products and physically add very little, if anything to them. For example, mobile phone manufacturers, such as Nokia and Motorola, may offer carry cases and hands-free attachments as additional items but these are made by specialist suppliers and bought in as required.

Equipment goods

Items that are purchased to enable the production of finished goods, yet are not part of the finished product, are referred to as **equipment**, **capital** or **investment goods**. They are depreciated in value over time because they are not consumed immediately. For example, land and buildings, computer systems and machine tools are all necessary to support the production process, but are not an integral part of the finished product.

Supply goods

Each production process requires consumable materials to keep it running. These are not assets and are not depreciated. They appear as an expense item. Sometimes these are referred to as **maintenance**, **repair and operating materials** (or MRO items). For example, lubricants, paint, screws and cleaning materials may all be necessary to maintain a firm's operations.

In addition to MROs are **services**. Normally managed on a contract basis with a third-party organisation, services are necessary for the smooth running of the organisation. For example, computer servicing is necessary to maintain operations and to avoid down time, while accounting audits are a legal requirement.

Developments in technology have led to an increase in IT and related services, for example, website design organisations and eCommerce/eBusiness providers of hosting facilities. All these services have to be outsourced when organisations do not have sufficient internal skills or expertise. They often do not want to hire and develop these skills internally because they prefer to concentrate on their core business activities.

SNAPSHOT 1.5

INPUT GOODS AT SCA

SCA is a Swedish organisation operating across 40 countries, manufacturing hygiene, packaging and forest-based products. It recently embarked upon a strategy to coordinate the purchase of many of its input goods. The organisation realised that it stood to lose large amounts of money if it failed to coordinate its purchases and also if its purchasing procedures were not implemented correctly.

One of the more usual approaches is to centralise purchasing and drive volume discounts. However, this does not always work, especially in the medium to long term, as invariably there is a loss of business flexibility and central purchasing departments do not always reach the most profitable agreements.

SCA saw advantages in group-wide purchasing using cooperative programmes to drive down costs and also ensure that the group collective knowledge is available whenever it is needed. This approach enables the organisation to identify solutions and improvement opportunities that can also be implemented quickly in the operations of other plants.

Network cooperation has been used to purchase input goods such as machine parts and chemicals. For example, peroxide is used in large volumes at the group paper mill and at the major pulp plant. It is also used, in much smaller amounts, in some of the plants operated by SCA Packaging and SCA Hygiene Products. Through programmes of cooperation between directly involved units, they are able to create significant purchasing synergies, when acquiring peroxide as a group, in terms of both know-how and price advantage.

Source: Adapted from text by Björn Lyngfelt, www.sca.com/default.asp?/career/scapeople/ interview_kenneth-feb03.asp (Accessed 4 December 2003.) Used with permission.

The characteristics of B2B marketing

So far in this chapter, the characteristics of the business market, the different types of products and services and the variety of customers have been considered. What do these factors contribute to an understanding of B2B marketing?

Overall, the marketing of goods and services between organisations is not the same as consumer goods marketing and, because there are a number of fundamentally different characteristics, diverse marketing strategies and operations need to be implemented to meet the needs of business customers.

However, many products and services are targeted at both consumers and organisations. Products such as office furniture, software and cellular phones can be sold into consumer and business markets. Business marketing is distinguished from consumer marketing by two main ideas: first, the intended customer, which is an organisation; second, the intended use of the product to support organisational objectives. As a result, different marketing programmes are required to reach and influence organisational buyers as

Table 1.3 The main differences between B2B and consumer marketing

	Key characteristics	
	Consumer markets	**B2B markets**
Purchase orientation to satisfy	Individual or family needs	Organisational needs
Nature of markets		
Number of decision makers	Small	Large
Length of decision time	Short and simple	Long and complex
Size of purchase	Small quantities	Large in value and volume
Consequence of poor purchase	Limited	Potentially critical
Nature of product/service	Standard range of products	Customised packages
Channel configuration	Complex and long	Simple and short
Promotion focus	Psychological benefits	Economic/utilitarian benefits
Primary promotional tool	Advertising	Personal selling
Supplier switching costs	Limited	Large

opposed to consumers. In order better to understand B2B marketing it is useful to compare and contrast it with consumer marking. Table 1.3 sets out the main differences. Although there are many differences, there are also many similarities. Indeed it is possible to identify an increasing number of areas where the two markets converge. These will be examined in greater depth in Chapters 3 and 6.

In the business sector, organisations buy a range of products and services either to make new products or to enable the production or added value process to operate successfully. Defined processes and procedures are used to buy products and services, and the decisions attached to securing the necessary materials very often involve a large number of people. Fuller details about these characteristics can be found in Chapter 5. However, central to an understanding of organisational purchasing is the decision making unit and the complexities associated with a variety of people and processes. There are pivotal implications for suppliers in terms of timescales and the communication mix and messages necessary to reduce the levels of risk inherent in these buying situations. These issues are examined in the next section and throughout the rest of this book.

B2B marketing management approaches

For a long time now, the **marketing mix** concept has been equally applicable in B2B markets as in B2C. The main differences concern the nature of the individual variables and the way the mix is deployed. Some of the broad points concerning the traditional interpretation of the marketing mix (McCarthy, 1960), namely the 4Ps, are introduced here. However, this idea has been challenged by a more contemporary perspective, termed **relationship marketing**. This is based on the principle that, first and foremost, an organisation must manage a series of relationships with a variety of organisations. The two different approaches are briefly considered here.

The marketing mix

Products

In consumer markets products are traditionally made available with limited opportunities for adaption or customisation. Increasingly, manufacturers are seeking ways in which customers feel they can customise the product. For example, some cars can be ordered via a dealer showroom directly from the production unit. This enables customers to specify the interior and exterior finishes, grade of in-car entertainment and perhaps a range of other cosmetic touches. However, the norm is to provide relatively little flexibility within different product ranges.

In the B2B market the entire offering (product and service components) can often be reconfigured to meet a customer's particular requirements. It is quite usual for more technical products to be developed and specified through joint negotiations and partnership arrangements. The result is an offering that is unique to the buying organisation.

Pricing

Price is a measure of the value that both parties assign to their contribution to an exchange. In consumer markets, list prices are usually the norm and limited discounts applied to them, especially for more expensive items. Hire purchase and credit-based schemes are designed to spread the financial risk, make purchase more accessible for a greater number of consumers and so increase the perceived value to a consumer. Negotiation is not usually a feature of pricing in consumer markets, the exceptions being cars and houses.

In business markets the designated value is likely to increase as a relationship becomes more collaborative and partnership-orientated. Therefore, prices associated with transaction exchanges will be based largely on list prices, quantity discounts and competitive bidding. As exchanges become more relational, so price becomes an integral part of the design, specification, development, trial and finishing processes. Discounts and allowances become more varied and complicated and reflect the risks and opportunities faced by the two parties. Negotiation becomes an important aspect of pricing in B2B markets. Large projects and intricate technical offerings often require complex financing arrangements, while pricing for international markets introduces new risks and financial uncertainties.

Place

In consumer markets intermediaries provide utility in terms of reducing the complexity of the range of goods consumers are offered, by providing a level of specialisation and support (advice) and enabling consumer expectations to be met. Consumer preferences in terms of location, the quantity of items that need to be purchased and the ease with which they can be acquired are deemed to be of value to consumers and so effort is concentrated in satisfying consumer needs in these areas and enhancing the level of perceived value. However, these services still need to be aggregated and provided on a group basis.

In B2B markets the utility principles are similar but the main difference lies in the length of the channels and the number of intermediaries deemed necessary to deliver the level of functionality required. Individual attention and customisation of product offerings, plus the need to deliver in the quantities and at the time required by the buyer, result in a shortening of the marketing channel. This leads to direct relationships and new dimensions in terms of the way in which offerings are made available.

Promotion

In consumer markets advertising has long been regarded as the focal point of the marketing communications mix. Some of the reasons for this concern the need to reach large, widely dispersed audiences, with relatively simple messages relating to awareness, interest and beliefs. Feedback is minimal and relationships between reseller and consumer are more commonly temporary and not very close. In recent years increased use of the other tools in the mix has reduced the high reliance on advertising, but it remains the focal part of a consumer organisation's promotional strategy.

Advertising is a relatively impotent marketing communications tool in B2B markets because of the need to provide more detailed, often technical information. Audiences are small in number and can be more closely defined and easily targeted with less wastage. Messages need to provide means of differentiation, reinforcement and persuasion. Feedback is important in B2B and so the emphasis is traditionally placed on personal selling. This helps the development of both a dialogue and also a relationship. Relationships between organisations in business markets are expected to be close and their duration much longer than in consumer markets.

Direct marketing is also important in B2B markets and, in some situations, can be used effectively to support the personal selling effort. Technology can be used to support all aspects of an organisation's marketing communications strategy and some applications are considered in the last section of this book.

Relationship marketing

In the twenty-first century, the above interpretation of the marketing mix is both outdated and, by and large, inappropriate to organisational marketing needs. B2B marketing is now based on a wide range of factors, mostly rooted in people and the interaction between individuals representing their respective organisations. For example, Gummesson (2002) has suggested that the marketing mix should consist of 30Rs since organisations have potentially 30 different types of relationships. These are divided into two categories, **Market** and **Non-market** relationships (see Table 1.4). Market relationships are those between suppliers, customers, competitors and all those who contribute to a market's operations. Non-market relationships involve all the other organisations that indirectly influence market relationships. Not all relationships are applicable to all organisations and every context but, in principle, an organisation must manage a portfolio of relationships. Issues concerning relationship marketing are explored in greater depth in Chapter 6 and constitute a major theme throughout the book.

Table 1.4 Gummesson's four groups of relationships

Relationships	Participants
Classic	Concerned with the supplier–customer, supplier–customer–competitor and relationships with the physical distribution network. A market relationship.
Special	Concerned with particular aspects of the classic Rs. For example, the interaction in the service encounter or the customer within loyalty programmes. A market relationship.
Mega	Concerned with supporting market relationships. Lobbying and political initiatives together with social relationships such as friendships and ethnic bonds. A non-market relationship.
Nano	Concerned with intraorganisational relationships and internal activities that influence external relationships. A non-market relationship.

Source: Adapted from Gummesson (2002).

Understanding value and supply chains

The concept of value and the importance of providing it for customers has become an increasingly significant aspect of business and marketing strategy. It has long been understood that customers buy benefits not features. They buy products that enable them to do what they want to achieve. Consumers do not buy toothpaste just because it has a red stripe or a minty taste. What they do buy is a clean mouth, fresh breath or white gleaming teeth, depending upon their segment characteristics. The same principle applies to organisational marketing. Business customers buy solutions to business problems not just stand-alone products. These benefits and solutions constitute **added value** for the customer, and represent the reason why one offering is selected in preference to another. For both consumers and business customers, value is determined by the net satisfaction derived from a transaction, not the costs to obtain it.

Another way of viewing these solutions and benefits is to consider them as (customer) needs. Customers seek to satisfy their needs through their purchase of products and services. The satisfaction of needs therefore is a way of delivering value. Kothandaraman and Wilson (2001) argue that the creation of value is dependent upon an organisation's ability to deliver high performance on the benefits that are important to the customer and this in turn is rooted in their competency in technology and business processes, or core competences. Doyle (2000) regards the creation of customer value to be based on three principles. These are:

1 Customers will choose between alternative offerings and select the one that (they perceive) will offer them the best value.

2 Customers do not want product or service features, they want their needs met.

3 It is more profitable to have a long-term relationship between a customer and a company rather than a one-off transaction.

Value is the customer's estimate of the extent to which a product or service can satisfy their needs. However, there are normally costs associated with the derivation of benefits such that a general model of value would identify the worth of the benefits received for the price paid (Anderson and Narus, 1998). Thus, value is relative to customer expectations and experience of competitive offerings within a category. Value can be derived from sources other than products, such as the relationships between buyers and sellers (Simpson *et al.*, 2001). Indeed, the creation and the sharing of value is a critical aspect of buyer–seller relationships (Anderson, 1995). This is important when considering marketing channel relationships which are an integral and critical aspect of B2B marketing.

SNAPSHOT 1.6

CISCO ADD VALUE

Cisco Systems, said to be the world's largest manufacturer and supplier of networking equipment, has created a virtual organisation designed to provide added value and efficiencies in the value chain, for all business partners, suppliers and customers. Part of this strategy has been accomplished through its use of web-based applications that focus on Internet, Intranet and Extranet applications, designed to link all aspects of its value network.

For example, the company openly encourages its customers' engineers to solve their technical problems through use of Cisco's self-help web-based Technical Support pages and network Configurator. By making these facilities easy to use, not only are Cisco better placed to manage their staffing (time and costs) required for technical support but are also encouraging customers to become more involved in Cisco applications and better placed to reduce their own organisation's systems difficulties. As a result customer organisations are able to share technical knowledge and through their satisfaction provide positive word-of-mouth referrals.

Source: Adapted from Kraemer and Dedrick (2002) and www.cisco.com

---

The value chain

Customers choose among competitive offerings on the basis of their perceptions of the relative value they will derive from each supplier. Each selling organisation competes for business by trying to offer enhanced value which is developed, internally, through a coordinated chain of activities. These activities include product design, production, marketing, delivery and support. Porter (1985) referred to these activities as the **value chain** (see Figure 1.2).

The value chain was devised as a tool to appraise an organisation's ability to create what Porter terms **differential advantage**. It consists of nine activities, five primary and four support, all of which incur costs but together can (and should) lead to the creation of value.

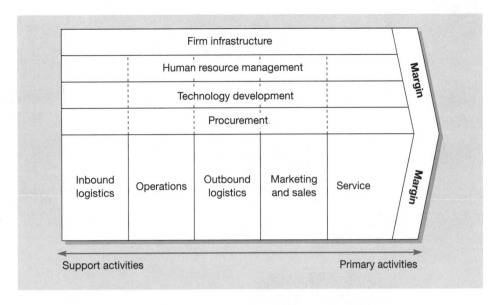

Figure 1.2 The value chain

The **primary activities** are those direct actions necessary to bring materials into an organisation, to convert them into final products or services, to ship them out to customers and to provide marketing and servicing facilities. **Support activities** facilitate the primary activities. For example, the purchase of parts and materials, the recruitment of suitably trained personnel and the provision and maintenance of suitable technology are important support activities. Management should attempt to create value by reducing costs or improving the performance of each of the activities. However, real value is generated by linking together these activities through processes and in such a way that customers perceive they are getting superior value. Doyle refers to three processes:

1 Innovation processes to generate a constant stream of new products and hence ability to maintain margins.

2 Operations processes to deliver first-class performance and costs.

3 Customer creation and support processes to provide a consistent and positive cash flow.

The processes used by an organisation become a critical part of the way in which they can add value. Customers, however, lie at the heart of the value chain. Only by understanding particular customer needs and focusing value chain activities on satisfying them, can superior value be generated. This has implications for B2B segmentation strategies and is explored further in Chapter 3.

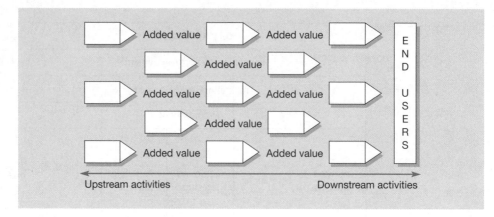

Figure 1.3 The supply chain concept

SNAPSHOT 1.7

BASF SUPPLYING VALUE

Car manufacturers have for a long time faced many problems associated with paint finishes. Difficulties occur with evenness of the finish, colour matching and toning plus issues concerning preparation and application processes and technologies and all associated costs.

BASF add value for their customers by overcoming the problems associated with paint finishes. BASF developed a paint-free film moulding process which enables the production of exterior car body parts that no longer require painting. Coated or coloured plastic films ensure that exterior car bodies are an identical shade. Films of special BASF plastics are moulded exactly into the shape specified by the customer and then insert-moulded using specially developed plastics. For the roof of the Smart car, for example, BASF were able to develop the first large exterior body part in which areas of glass and plastic components appear to be made in one piece, demonstrated by the way the black-tinted sunroof sits perfectly in the surrounding high-gloss plastic film.

Launched in partnership with DaimlerChrysler in Rastatt, Germany, in 1997, the system has been adopted by other car manufacturers. For example, VW, Audi, Ford and Renault are involved and have appointed BASF to take process responsibility with regard to materials and stock management as well as coordination of external and internal logistics. Furthermore, BASF inspect incoming goods, organise and supervise suppliers, and are responsible for colour management, quality control of materials and processes and analyses.

BASF not only add superior value by overcoming many of the paint-associated technical problems experienced by car manufacturers' but have also reduced their customers' material and process costs, improved quality and now contribute by managing their customers' logistics and material handling requirements.

Source: Adapted from www.berichte.basf.de/en/2002/jahresbericht/wertschaffen/?id=V00-oFhpw4O0xbir.x- (Accessed 19 January 2004.) Used with permission.

Supply chains

So far the value chain has been considered within an internal context. However, organisations do not exist in isolation but combine with others in order to provide a consistent stream of resources. Therefore, organisations join their value chains together and form **supply chains** (see Figure 1.3). The operation of the overall supply chain helps generate sustainable value for each business. Issues concerning supply chains and marketing are explored in more detail in Chapter 8.

The concepts of value and the value chain are important because they provide a reminder of basic principles. First, customers buy superior value, which means that the creation of profits can only be through the delivery of value that customers want. Trimming costs to save money and to improve the bottom line may result in removing the value that customers actually desire, and which represent their reason to buy. Many organisations cut back on aspects of their offerings in times of recession or economic difficulty. The objective is to save costs and improve profits but this short-term approach can damage the long-term prospects if it dispenses with a crucial part of the value that customers perceive to be important.

Second, value can be perceived in many ways, for example by providing associations with prestige (exclusivity or membership), reliability, modular formats, ease and speed of servicing, stock and delivery flexibility, ease of customisation and access to new markets, to name a few. Therefore, the whole of an organisation's activities must be considered and their contribution to the generation of superior value appraised. Among other things, this means looking at pre- and post-purchase customer support, pricing, communications, distribution and logistics and positioning.

The development of new technology and the increasing breadth and depth of business applications has provided new value creation opportunities for organisations. Advances in Information, Systems and Technology (IST) can lead to new forms of value being created. Apart from the obvious impact on speed and accuracy of information transfer between organisations, value can be enhanced through product development and customisation, production and manufacturing, supply chain management, marketing communications and, of course, closer interorganisational understanding and relationships (Sharma *et al.*, 2001).

Part of the approach adopted for this book is to explore and understand the role IST can play in creating and maintaining superior value and organisational relationships in a B2B Marketing context.

SNAPSHOT 1.8

THE SUPPLY CHAIN

Shell Chemical has embraced web-based technologies to strengthen its relationships with downstream customers and upstream suppliers. With the aid of SIMON, a particular software package, Shell has been able to identify the cycle of customer product usage and as a result make more accurate production forecasts and so reduce stock and work in progress on behalf of others in the supply chain. Costs fall, profits increase and supply chain relationships become closer.

Source: Adapted from Marcolin and Gaulin (2001).

The importance of B2B relationships

Following on from the introduction to value and value chains, the supply chain concept raises interesting points about the nature and scope of the relationships that exist between supplier and buyer organisations. Organisations interact with other organisations in order to provide superior value for their customers. However, it should come as no surprise to read that the quality, duration and level of interdependence between organisations in the supply chain can and does vary considerably. The reasons for this variance are many and wide-ranging but at the core are perceptions of value shared by both parties. The value that organisations offer each other can be visualised as a continuum (see Figure 1.4).

At one end of the continuum are **transactional or market exchanges**, characterised by short-term, commodity or price-orientated exchanges, between buyers and sellers coming together for one-off exchanges independent of any other or subsequent exchanges. Both parties are motivated mainly by self-interest. Movement along the continuum represents increasingly valued relationships. Interactions between parties are closer and stronger. The focus moves from initial attraction to retention and mutual understanding of each other's needs.

At the other end of the continuum are **relational exchanges** or what Day (2000) refers to as **collaborative exchanges**. These are characterised by a long-term orientation, where there is complete integration of systems and processes and the relationship is motivated by partnership and mutual support. Trust and commitment underpin these relationships and these variables become increasingly important as relational exchanges become established.

B2B marketing is characterised by a variety of relationships that all need managing. Some relationships are price-orientated and some are fully collaborative, while the large majority fall somewhere between the two. Organisations manage a portfolio of relationships. This book seeks to explore B2B marketing by taking into account the rich variety of interdependent activities that occur between organisations. In addition, attention is given to the way in which new technology influences B2B marketing and relationships.

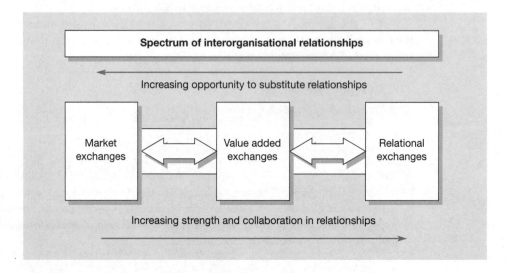

Figure 1.4 A continuum of value-orientated exchanges
Source: Adapted from Day (2000).

Summary

This aim of this chapter was to introduce B2B marketing by first exploring some of the distinguishing characteristics of business markets. There are a range of organisations that comprise the business market and these were classified as commercial, government and institutional. These organisations buy products and services to make goods for resale to their customers but they also consume items that are required to keep their offices and manufacturing units functioning. The items sold through business markets were categorised as input, equipment and supply goods.

The methods used by organisations in the B2B sector to purchase goods and services reflect the level of risk inherent in their trading activities and the importance of the specific items being purchased. Apart from group purchasing activities one of the other ways in which organisations manage this aspect of their operations is to develop closer, long-term relationships with suppliers.

B2B marketing is concerned with the identification and satisfaction of business customers' needs. The anticipation and satisfaction of these needs requires that all stakeholders benefit from the business relationship and associated transactions. Customers derive satisfaction by purchasing goods and services that are perceived to provide them and/or their organisations with particular value. B2B marketing managers must understand these needs and develop marketing programmes which include a set of goods and services that provide unique solutions, and hence value, for customers. Many suppliers have recognised the benefit of developing long-term relationships with buyers, acting collaboratively and in partnership in order to deliver enhanced value.

This book will revisit many of these topics in the chapters that follow. However, at the heart of B2B marketing are the interorganisational relationships that businesses develop either implicitly or deliberately. These form the basic platform for examining B2B marketing.

Discussion questions

1 Identify the key characteristics associated with B2B markets and suggest how they might impact on B2B marketing activities.

2 Discuss the key differences between B2B and B2C marketing. What are the similarities?

3 Describe the different types of organisations that make up the business market.

4 Draw the value chain as depicted by Porter (1985) and include the nine constituent elements.

5 Using organisations that form part of a supply chain in an industry of your choice, critically appraise their contribution to the industry value chain.

6 Examine the contention that the traditional concept of the marketing mix (4Ps) is now redundant and should be replaced by a relationship-centred approach to marketing activities.

References

Anderson, J. (1995). 'Relationships in business markets: exchange episodes, value creation and their empirical assessment', *Journal of the Academy of Marketing Science*, 23, 4, pp. 346–50.

Anderson, J.C. and Narus, J.A. (1998). 'Business marketing: understand what customers value', *Harvard Business Review*, 76 (June), pp. 53–65.

Brassington, F. and Pettitt, S. (2003). *Principles of Marketing*, 3rd edn, Harlow: Pearson Education.

Day, G.S. (2000). 'Managing market relationships', *Journal of Academy of Marketing Science*, 28, 1 (Winter), pp. 24–31.

Doyle, P. (2000). *Value Based Marketing*, Chichester: Wiley.

Gummesson, E. (2002). *Total Relationship Marketing. Rethinking Marketing Management: From 4Ps to 30Rs*, Oxford: Butterworth-Heinemann.

Kothandaraman, P. and Wilson, D. (2001). 'The future of competition: value creating networks', *Industrial Marketing Management*, 30, 4 (May), pp. 379–89.

Kraemer, K.L. and Dedrick, J. (2002). 'Strategic use of the Internet and e-commerce: Cisco Systems', *Journal of Strategic Information Systems*, 11, pp. 5–29.

Lake, D. (2003). 'Eurofighter – weapon of mass construction: future proofing', www.open2.net/eurofighter/(Accessed 30 January 2004.)

Lyngfelt, B. (2003). 'SCA People'. www.sca.com/default.asp?/career/scapeople/interview_kenneth-febø3.asp/ (Accessed 4 December 2003.)

Macfarlane, P. (2002). 'Structuring and measuring the size of business markets', *International Journal of Market Research*, 44, 1 (Winter), pp. 7–31.

Mann, A.P., Thompson, N. and Smits, M. (2001). 'Building the British Airways London Eye', *Proceedings of ICE, Civil Engineering, 14 May 2001*, pp. 60–72, www.iceknowledge.com/images/preview/2001.pdf (Accessed 19 November 2003.)

Marcolin, B. and Gaulin, B. (2001). 'Changing the eCommerce value chain: a modular approach', *Ivey Business Journal*, 65, 6 (July), pp. 23–32.

McCarthy, E.J. (1960). *Basic Marketing: A Managerial Approach*, Homewood, IL: Irwin.

Morgan, R.M. and Hunt, S.D. (1994). 'The commitment-trust theory of relationship marketing', *Journal of Marketing*, 58 (July), pp. 20–38.

Porter, M.E. (1985). *Competitive Advantage: Creating and Sustaining Superior Performance*, New York, NY: The Free Press.

Sharma, A., Krishman, R. and Grewal, D. (2001). 'Value creation in markets: a critical area of focus for business-to-business markets', *Industrial Marketing Management*, 30, 4 (May), pp. 341–402.

Simpson, P.M., Sigauw, J.A. and Baker, T.L. (2001). 'A model of value creation: supplier behaviors and their impact on reseller-perceived value', *Industrial Marketing Management*, 30, 2 (February), pp. 119–34.

van Weele , A.J. (2002). *Purchasing and Supply Chain Management: Analysis, Planning and Practice*, 3rd edn, London: Thomson Learning. www.cisco.com (Accessed 8 August 2003.)

Chapter 2
Introduction to business information systems

Chapter overview

This chapter introduces basic information systems concepts and terminology.

The history of business use of computer and communications technology is briefly described. Six snapshots, drawing on personal experience of working in both business and education, illustrate the changes in the field over the last 30 years.

Current technology and business information systems are then described, with particular attention to specific B2B applications.

Finally, possible future directions in information systems and technology are considered, together with their implications for B2B marketing.

Chapter aims

The aim of this chapter is to give a broad introduction to Business Information Systems (BIS), defining common terms and the context within which specific B2B marketing applications will be explored throughout the book. Innovative use of BIS underpins some interesting approaches to B2B marketing and the reader will benefit from understanding the background to these.

Objectives

The objectives of this chapter are to:

1   Introduce basic systems concepts.
2   Outline the history of information systems and technology in business.
3   Provide an overview of modern BIS.
4   Consider current technology and directions.
5   Give specific examples of B2B applications.

Basic systems concepts

For the purposes of this book, readers need to be comfortable with the following basic systems concepts.

- **Computers** are machines which, via a combination of hardware and software, are capable of receiving data (*input*), *processing* data, *storing* data and reproducing both data and information (*output*).

- **Communication networks** connect computers, enabling the transfer of data and information between them.

- **Technology** is the equipment and methods; it determines *how* things are done.

- **Information** is the result of collecting and processing data; it determines *why* things are done.

Most importantly, **Business Information Systems (BIS)** involve both technology and people. People decide what data to collect and input, how it should be processed to produce meaningful information, and how it should be stored, output, used and communicated. A vital element in any system is **feedback** which can come from inside the system (internal) or from its environment (external). Adjusting to feedback is **adaptation**.

There are numerous books and other resources that describe the hardware and software involved in transferring, accepting and processing data. They make worthy attempts to explain the current (when written) technology and terminology. For students of business-related subjects, they are often not particularly easy or interesting to read and they date rapidly because of technological progress.

Much more interesting is how Information Systems and Technology (IST) are used by people to do things differently in all walks of life. From the earliest days of science and engineering applications, often developed with an initial military purpose, human ingenuity has both built on and expanded the boundaries of the technology.

In this book we are concerned with IST to support B2B marketing. This chapter starts with a brief look at the history and evolution of business information systems, in order to understand why we are where we are today. It also considers current technology and directions in order to think a bit about possible future developments. Specific B2B examples are used to illustrate the main concepts.

A brief history of business information systems

Figure 2.1 shows a timeline from 1950 to 2000 and indicates when certain technologies, methods and business information systems were introduced.

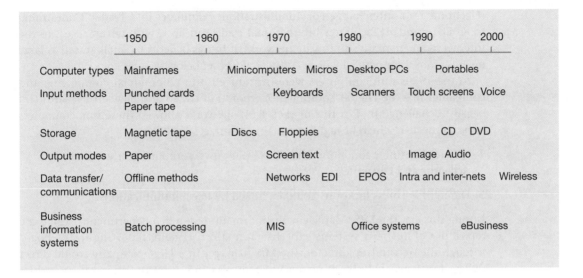

	1950	1960	1970	1980	1990	2000
Computer types	Mainframes		Minicomputers Micros	Desktop PCs	Portables	
Input methods	Punched cards Paper tape		Keyboards	Scanners	Touch screens Voice	
Storage	Magnetic tape	Discs	Floppies		CD DVD	
Output modes	Paper		Screen text		Image Audio	
Data transfer/ communications	Offline methods		Networks EDI	EPOS	Intra and inter-nets	Wireless
Business information systems	Batch processing		MIS		Office systems	eBusiness

Figure 2.1 BIS timeline

Readers interested in the detailed history of IST should refer to O'Leary and Williams (1989, Appendix A) or Turban *et al.* (1999, T1 and T2) or similar texts. Naughton (2000) offers a fascinating, and very readable, account of the origins and development of the Internet.

The first 'mainframe' computers to be used commercially were the UNIVAC and the IBM 650 in 1954. The operating mode was 'batch processing', so called because both data and programs were submitted in batches. These were fed into the computer by an operator, processed, and the resulting output was returned later to the users. By and large, in these early days, the commercial company mainframe was used for primary business purposes, plus accounting and payroll.

In the 1960s some large companies began to transfer order, shipping and invoice data between their computers via telephone connections. This was the beginning of Electronic Data Interchange (EDI). Data formats varied from company to company and by the late 1960s organisations were beginning to work on standards to simplify and increase the effectiveness of EDI. The principal standards still in use today are ASC X12 from the American National Standards Institute (ANSI) and the UN-sponsored EDIFACT

SNAPSHOT 2.1

KF personal experience: I first got involved in computing in 1972, working as a technical assistant in an engineering company that was part of the GEC Marconi group. Part of my job involved submitting batches of punched cards, together with programs on paper tape, for processing by an IBM mainframe and collecting the printed output for the engineers. The program performed mathematical calculations on the data. If there were errors in the data or program, the engineer would indicate changes to be made to the cards or paper tape and I would make them. It was all so fascinating that I asked to go on a course of 'Computer Studies', during which I learnt to program in 'machine code' – representing every letter and number as a series of binary digits, that is 0s and 1s.

(Electronic Data Interchange For Administration, Commerce and Trade). Conforming to an EDI standard facilitates international trade and now, with cheap access to the Internet as an alternative to private networks, it brings benefits to small as well as large organisations. Internet EDI will be considered further below.

In the 1970s minicomputers were introduced into commercial computing, and companies like the Digital Equipment Corporation (DEC) and Hewlett Packard (HP) began to challenge IBM in this market. Early networks allowed these minicomputers to be connected, which brought two main advantages for BIS:

1 Different business functions could have their own computer (for example, Accounts and Personnel).

2 Different business locations could be linked by telecommunications.

During this era, the MIS (Management Information Systems) department became the repository of business systems expertise and effort. Usually reporting to the board through the Accounting director, the MIS manager in a large company would direct teams of systems analysts, computer programmers and operators. In small companies one or two people would combine all these functions, which involved the activities described below.

Systems analyst: charged with understanding user requirements and designing systems applications which would satisfy them; liaising with the programmers to produce and test the programs; training the users (unless specialist trainers were employed); evaluating the success of applications to improve business processes.

Computer programmer: writing and testing programs in a quasi-natural language such as COBOL (Common Business Oriented Language); debugging (i.e. finding and correcting errors in the programs), modifying and documenting programs.

Computer operator: scheduling and running programs.

SNAPSHOT 2.2

KF personal experience: In 1979, by now with a degree in Computing and Management Science, I joined a snack food manufacturer, Smith's Crisps, as an analyst/programmer. The company had just decided to change from using a central mainframe to a network of distributed minicomputers. I visited factories and distribution depots to find out the data-processing and information requirements of staff in these locations, and worked with the head office MIS team to design and develop appropriate programs. Programming was done in COBOL (Common Business Oriented Language) that was closer to natural language than machine code and therefore much easier to 'debug'.

An early example of 'mobile computing' was the use of dataloggers by Smith's van drivers who called on small retailers. These rather bulky, handheld, devices were used to record stock sold, or remaining, and on-the-spot replenishment figures, which were then transmitted from the van to the depot minicomputer.

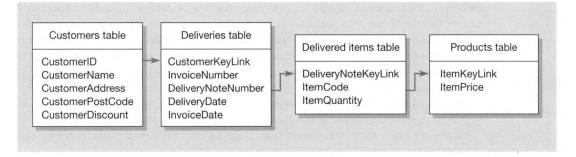

Figure 2.2 An example of linked database tables

On the data storage and retrieval front, the late 1970s saw the introduction of *databases* and early Database Management Software (DBMS). Put simply, a database holds records in tables that are accessed via key fields. Creation of the database tables, input, retrieval and updating of records is facilitated by the DBMS and is much faster than was previously possible with ordinary files. **Relational databases** contain multiple tables linked by common key fields (see Figure 2.2) and are very flexible information resources.

In the late 1970s and early 1980s, office systems, such as wordprocessing, memo and diary applications, were beginning to be developed on minicomputers and made available online to appropriate staff, such as senior secretaries, via 'dumb' terminals (i.e. terminals with no processing power or storage). These applications quickly migrated to the personal computers (PCs) that were about to transform the user end of computing.

SNAPSHOT 2.3

KF personal experience: in 1982, working as a business systems analyst in Hewlett Packard's UK head office, I developed an early B2B marketing application. Based on the requirements of sales administrators, I designed a database and user interface that allowed them to enter the particulars of business customers and record details of literature sent out, sales representative calls made and resulting sales. This was a 'bespoke' system, programmed to run on an in-house minicomputer, with an online user interface (as opposed to batch input) to enter and update details and schedule reports.

The Apple II Plus (1979) and the IBM PC (1981) revolutionised business computing. It is difficult for people who did not experience the pre-PC era to appreciate the radical impact of computing power on the desk and a local printer. As the 'early adopters' got into their stride, they bypassed the MIS department, and started developing their own applications. One of the resulting headaches was that multiple versions of company data began to proliferate and were not synchronised. Think about the implications of an innovative district sales manager setting up product/price data on a local PC, but not having any method to keep it up to date other than manually keying in changes gleaned from the latest paper-based price list sent out quarterly from head office.

In the early 1980s, a version of the 'Oracle' DBMS was released that ran on mainframes, minicomputers and PCs. This was an important step towards overcoming the problems of data synchronicity. However, it was the ability to connect computers to each other that enabled automatic, two-way updating of databases. Early connectivity was by means of point-to-point cable, that is, wiring within a building and/or telephone lines between buildings. The advantages in terms of interpersonal and business communications were soon apparent and both hardware and software developers invested heavily in network innovations.

> The late 1990s is witnessing a massive growth in computer networks [which] involve computers communicating with other computers or peripheral devices either by means of cabling, of which there are various types such as optic fibre, or through microwave or satellite links.
>
> (Cleary, 1998, p. 80)

This explosion in networks, based on sophisticated telecommunications, facilitating both public and private networks, has had a tremendous impact on many areas of personal and working life, including B2B processes.

SNAPSHOT 2.4

KF personal experience: working for a housing association in the mid-1990s, I was able to use my desktop computer to obtain information on council waiting lists, fair rents legislation, and other government policies via telecomms links to outside organisations. Updates I made to the association's databases were immediately available to housing officers at their desks in head office or remotely, and we could all avail ourselves of one high-quality laser printer thanks to internal cabling.

Electronic data interchange (EDI) via public networks, including eventually the Internet, is one of the most commonly cited advances of the 1980–90s in this field. EDI, the direct transmission between different companies' computer systems of data relating to business transactions, works effectively because it is based on agreed standards. There is, or should be, no need for human intervention such as the re-entering of product codes because one company uses a different style or length of code from others with which it does business. In the early days of EDI, it was suggested that there would be significant cost savings for companies who adopted EDI. However as Swatman and Swatman (1991, p. 3) declared:

> Surveys and case studies undertaken in the U.S. (…) indicate that the real benefits available from EDI are qualitative in nature – the *direct* financial gains from EDI tend to be small and rather unimpressive (…) major benefits arise *indirectly*, that is, they lie in the areas of inventory control and improved trading partner relationships.

Another business enhancing application on early networks was Electronic Point of Sales (EPOS). Primarily this involves computerised tills linked back to a company's central computer(s). The data transmitted back from every retail sale facilitates sales and inventory management and, in a marketing context, can be used to better understand customer demand and buying behaviour. As networks, including the Internet, have extended to connect multiple businesses in the supply chain, sophisticated point of sale data has enabled collaborative marketing. An example is Sainsbury's system which enables selected suppliers to 'find out information such as the repeat purchase rate of individual products, profiles of customers purchasing particular products and the most appropriate tools to attract customers' (Thomas, 2003).

The global network we now know as the Internet had its beginnings in the Information Processing Techniques Office of the American Advanced Research Projects Agency (ARPA) in the early 1960s. Recently, it has had a massive impact on business communications, both with suppliers and service organisations in terms of procurement, and with purchasing departments, retailers and customers with respect to marketing, sales and after-sales activities. Electronic commerce, based on Internet communications, was initiated by the early adopters in the mid-1990s and really began to take off in the late 1990s. It is worth bearing in mind that, at the time of writing, this was only five years ago.

De Boer *et al.* (2002, p. 3) define six, Internet-enabled, electronic procurement forms that are 'quite well-defined and relatively well-developed':

- e-MRO;

- web-based ERP;

- e-sourcing;

- e-tendering;

- e-reverse auctioning;

- e-informing.

All of these will be considered in more detail throughout the rest of the book (see in particular Chapter 4 – Technological applications and the PLC); Chapter 5 – eProcurement and the impact of IST on OBB; Chapter 6 – Systems impact on inter-organisational relationships; Chapter 7 – Impact of technology on marketing channels; Chapter 8 – Principles of supply chain management; Electronic channels).

The Internet has also had a significant impact on both B2C and B2B marketing, sales and service activities. Internet-enabled marketing communications' tools that will be covered in more detail throughout this book include:

- corporate websites;

- specialist portals;

- auctions;

- email;

- search engines.

Along with the expanding capabilities of Internet-enabled commerce came very real concerns about data protection, privacy, piracy and aggressive hacking. Countering these has involved sophisticated technological solutions including:

- data encryption;

- digital certificates;

- secure browser protocols, for example Secure Sockets Layer (SSL);

- firewalls;

- virtual private networks (VPN).

Detailed technical discussions of these and other measures are beyond the scope of this book. Interested readers are referred to Stallings (2002).

SNAPSHOT 2.5

NETWORKS

Networking then. KF personal experience: in 1984, as a technical support manager at Hewlett Packard, I was responsible for the smooth operations of a network of five regional mini-computers linked by dedicated private telephone lines. One of the applications running on the network provided regularly updated sales and marketing information to regional managers and customer support officers. I do not recall there being any concerns about 'hacking' by competitors or anybody else.

Networking now. With increasing use of the Internet to enable access to such information, technical managers in similar positions today have to be constantly aware of the potential damage that can be caused by 'hackers' and 'crackers'. Denial-of-service (DOS) attacks, worms and viruses in email attachments are just the tip of the iceberg. Increasingly, online competitors or criminals are finding ways to break into networks and steal data about customers, products and transactions. This has led to some organisations setting up enterprise portals, extranets or private exchange networks. An example of the latter is the Australian Automotive Network eXchange (AANX) which is used by vehicle manufacturers, suppliers, dealers, other related businesses and government agencies. It uses Internet technology, enhanced with additional hardware and software security measures, to facilitate communications and transactions between trading partners. Similar projects are underway in Europe (*see* www.enxo.com/), Japan and Korea. The Australian pioneers are optimistic about future networking on a global scale.

Source: Adapted from www.noie.gov.au/publications/NOIE/ITOL_CS/Auto/ (Accessed 23 September 2003.)

Specific B2B examples of the use of intranets and extranets are discussed in Chapters 5, 8, 10 and 11.

Portable computers first came on the scene in the early 1980s. The Compaq portable released in 1983 was compatible with IBM PCs, which endeared it to the business community. Even though it was relatively expensive at US$3,590 and heavy at 12.7 kilograms, 53,000 were sold in the first year (*source*: www.oldcomputers.net; accessed 23 September 2003). The first IBM portable released the following year was even more expensive, US$4,225 and slightly heavier, 13.6 kilograms. In late 2003 an IBM laptop, the TPR31, could be bought in the United Kingdom for £550 (US$909) and weighs 2.6 kilograms. So 20 years on, we can pay a quarter of the price to carry a device that is 80 per cent lighter and, of course, packs many times more processing punch than in the early days.

The big advantage of portables in the B2B context, whether they be laptops, tablets or the palm-helds (palms) that are the latest technology at the time of writing, is the access to company and customer information they can provide to marketing and sales staff who are working away from the office. This may be at exhibitions, conferences, seminars, presentations or face to face with a current or potential customer. B2B applications of portable computers, including laptops and palms are considered in more detail in Chapters 7 and 12.

The late 1990s also saw increasing use of multimedia systems, the integration of text, audio, and images to enhance the user interface with computer-based applications. On

SNAPSHOT 2.6

KF personal experience: updating my skills on a Masters degree course in 2003, I researched the field of services marketing and produced a multimedia CD-ROM for a supplier of online education and training. This used audio and images to promote and describe the courses on offer and, of course, had a link which, when clicked, initiated Internet connection and took the user to the supplier's website for more extensive information and registration of learners. If time and money had permitted, it could have been enhanced by embedded video clips.

the software side, sophisticated 'authoring' packages, such as Macromedia's Director, facilitate the production of such systems. Hardware and communications technology are evolving to cope with the complexity, processing, storage and transmission requirements; for example, the 'streaming' of video and audio over the Internet.

Modern business information systems

In September 2003, IBM made the following declaration on its eBusiness page:

Today's technology has the ability to make any business a truly global one. Supply chains can be integrated across borders, employees can work wirelessly from outposts far from their desks, and no one can know where competition will come from next in a truly world-wide marketplace.

Source: www-3.ibm.com/e-business (Accessed 29 September 2003.)

One aspect of this global market is some concern in the United Kingdom and western Europe about the out-sourcing of jobs – in many sectors – to countries where rates of pay are much lower, for example, India and the Far East. However, it also gives all businesses, regardless of provenance, size or physical location, opportunities to sell their products or services worldwide. On the other hand, competition may come from any country, and may not be regulated or bound by conventional constraints.

The products and services IBM lists are similar in nature to those of other IT solutions providers, such as HP and Dell. These offerings are summarised in Table 2.1. Readers should refer to textbooks such as Bocij *et al.* (2003) or O'Brien (2003), or use the Internet, to look up products about which they would like to have more technical detail.

Website design, hosting and operation is a significant area of investment, expertise and continuing improvement, especially with respect to dynamic web pages, client/server applications, on-line databases, accessibility issues and security/privacy. Others include data repositories, data warehousing and data mining; decision support, knowledge-based and expert systems; artificial intelligence applications – including simulations and intelligent agents.

In small, medium and large enterprises data from within and without can be captured relatively easily. Modern BIS enable this and facilitate fast availability of

Table 2.1 Current BIS products and applications

Hardware	Software	Applications
Handhelds	Operating systems	Office and personal
Notebooks	Database & data management	productivity
Desktops	Office systems	Procurement & sourcing
Printers	Networking/webservers/portals	Product lifecycle management (PLM)
Scanners	Personal & enterprise messaging	Customer relationship
Work stations	Host transaction processing	management (CRM)
Mainframes	Document/digital asset	Enterprise resource planning
Storage (disks, tapes)	management	(ERP)
Servers	Security	Supply chain management (SCM)
Communication/network	Software development	eCommerce
controllers	Storage management	Business intelligence
Point of sale kiosks &		
peripherals		

information, derived from the data, to staff, customers, suppliers, the media and government organisations.

Current B2B applications

In this section, **generic B2B applications** are described, in the categories listed in the third column of Table 2.1, in order to set the general context and serve as a reference point as you read the other chapters. From Chapter 3 onwards, you will find many specific examples of systems used to enhance **B2B Marketing**.

Office and personal productivity

Computer-based applications in this area enable the production and sharing of documents and information. Documents, such as budgets, reports, project plans and brochures, as well as letters and memos, may be just text or combined with numbers, tables, still images and, increasingly, audio or video multimedia clips. Document and information sharing may be facilitated by email, file transfer, shared servers, groupware, portals, web pages and conferencing applications. In the B2B arena these applications can speed up and cut the costs of most transactions and collaborative efforts.

Procurement and sourcing

Commonly used procurement systems facilitate the purchase of essential business supplies, often referred to as MRO (maintenance, repair and operations) items, for example, office furniture and stationery. They may be based on online catalogues from, or portals to, preferred suppliers. Inbuilt authentication methods and spending authorisation levels help to speed up procurement processes, ensure use of preferred suppliers and cut transaction costs. Online auctions are also proving popular sources for MRO purchases. Increasingly too, organisations are implementing integrated systems which mesh with other strategic systems such as Enterprise Resource Planning (ERP) and Supply Chain Management (SCM) (see below).

> E-procurement can complement B2B exchanges, which are emerging as a significant force in organizational sales and purchasing activities. E-procurement is also an important component of a larger supply chain strategy to reduce cycle times and lower costs.
>
> *Source*: www-1.ibm.com/services/feature/procurement_systems.html (Accessed October 2003.)

Product lifecycle management (PLM)

PLM systems are used to manage all stages of a product's 'life', from initial idea, through design, development, production, introduction to the market, service, ongoing improvements and withdrawal. At their best, they provide an 'integrated environment that ensures all people involved in product development, manufacturing, and service have quick and secure access to current information' (www.sap.com/solutions/plm/, October 2003).

Further, as noted in a recent online newsletter, *PLM Perspective*, the information available from such systems can be analysed to suggest future directions for 'leveraging and building on a company's intellectual capital … PLM is ultimately a strategy for delivering continuous innovation, and innovation is one of today's key business drivers, regardless of industry' (www.eds.com/products/plm/newsletters/perspective/2003_october/index.shtml).

Customer relationship management (CRM)

CRM systems may be simple analysis and reporting from a customer database, or as complex as fully integrated call centre management of both sales and service processes. In order to understand a customer's behaviour and manage the, hopefully ongoing, relationship, an organisation may choose to collect all or some of the following data:

- demographics – for example, location, age, gender, spending power;
- responses to marketing campaigns;
- purchases – products and dates;
- service requests;
- accounts.

Analysis of these factors results in information that can be used to improve many processes, including product design, sales and marketing, support and service.

Enterprise resource planning (ERP)

Complete ERP systems attempt to integrate all business processes across an organisation's accounting, manufacturing, sales and human resource departments. The original SAP software which has led the way in this field since the early 1970s is well described in Turban *et al*. (1999, p. 373). Nowadays, SAP employs over 20,500 people in more than 50 countries (www.saptech.8m.com/erp_history.htm) and their ERP products like many others have been adapted to run on modern networks, including the Internet.

Equant, a service provider in this area, describes ERP systems implemented in 2002 for Sylvania Lighting International (SLI), a European manufacturer of commercial and consumer lighting products. The application runs on computers in London, Madrid, Erlangen, Paris and Brussels and supports the finance, manufacturing, sales ordering and logistics functions. The new intranet serves workers in those locations and 'more than 1,000 mobile and remote users' (www.equant.com/content/ xml/press_sylvania_case_study.xml; accessed October 2003).

Supply chain management (SCM)

The ultimate goal of SCM systems is to help organisations balance the supply and demand for their products or services. Ilford, a UK–based supplier of photographic materials and services, have been using a customised SCM application since June 2001 to optimise inventory, control customer service levels, and manage product rollovers and launches (www.finechain.com/article/overview/86; accessed October 2003).

Increasingly sophisticated SCM systems extend beyond purchase ordering and inventory management to encompass elements of MRO, PLC, ERP and CRM. Indeed, Radjou (2003, p. 25) refers to **supply network processes**, which encompass the following categories:

- collaborative product life cycle management;
- supply management;
- enterprise asset management;
- production network management;
- continuous demand management;
- order fulfilment and distribution management;
- aftermarket service management.

eCommerce

The European Commission defines electronic commerce as 'any transaction that involves an on-line commitment to purchase or to sell a good or service, and that results in the import or export of this good or service' (europa.eu.int/ information_society/topics/ebusiness/ecommerce/1welcome/what_is_ecommerce/ind ex_en.htm; accessed October 2003). As such, of course, it encompasses both B2C and B2B processes. Many readers of this book will have direct, personal experience of on-line purchasing and an understanding of many of the issues in the B2C sector: access via the Internet, connection speeds, availability of selected goods or services, payment security, delivery times, returns.

In the B2B sector, without the need for mass access and, especially where private networks are used, transaction speeds and security are generally less of a problem. However, aligning data formats and systems is still challenging. The Queensland Information Industries Bureau describes a B2B eCommerce pilot involving a transport company and two of its customers. Instead of telephoning through consignment details, the two business customers transferred them electronically. While noting the demands for higher accuracy placed on personnel entering data to the system, the study concluded that B2B eCommerce:

> has tremendous potential to save transport companies money while improving the standards of customer service. It introduces new requirements for the standards of data quality and alignment between the participating companies' methodologies, yet delivers returns far in excess of simply reducing data entry effort.
>
> *Source*: www.iib.qld.gov.au/using/Ecommerce-Case_Study.htm (Accessed October 2003.)

Business intelligence

Business intelligence (BI) systems are concerned with the analysis of an organisation's data to address and direct strategic initiatives. They can be based on conventional database management tools or use sophisticated data-mining and modelling techniques. Modern BI applications are building on and extending the techniques developed in earlier On-Line Analytical Processing (OLAP) systems, including Decision Support Systems (DSS) and Executive Information Systems (EIS). A common feature is a graphical interface facilitating many views of the underlying data. Browser-based interfaces are often used when the data needs to be retrieved from networked computers.

Information Builders, a New York-based global consultancy in this field, describes using its BI product 'WebFOCUS' to help First Hawaiian Leasing reduce bad payments by 46 per cent and improve information flows to account handlers and senior management (www.informationbuilders.com/applications/first_haw.html; accessed October 2003).

Finally in this chapter, we look towards the future in both the general area of BIS and then specifically at possible B2B applications.

Future directions for BIS

The original list drawn up for this section read:

- technologies – wireless, speech recognition/response;

- systems – knowledge-based, semantic web, intelligent agents;

- databases – multimedia, privacy issues.

The 7th International Conference on Business Information Systems, held in Poland, in 2004, included contributions on those items and much else besides. Some of the more 'future-looking' topics are listed below:

- multimedia information retrieval and filtering (IRaF);

- multilingual and cross-lingual IRaF;

- adaptive and collaborative filtering;

- portal technology;

- semantic web for decision support;

- time granularities in document collections, databases, and the web; temporal reasoning;

- standards for legal information interchange, interactive and 'intelligent' legal services on the web;

- political and societal implications of e-Government.

Sociological issues are evident here in the multilingual, legal and political topics; psychological concerns in the adaptive and semantic ones. It seems reasonable to postulate that business information systems will draw on advances that support ever-more sophisticated utilisation of the data available in web-enabled databases.

Wireless applications are already doing away with office cabling and enabling remote systems access for mobile personnel via cell phones and PDAs (Personal Digital Assistants). Elliott (2003) distinguishes between 'push' and 'pull' mobile applications:

- push – mobile device user requests information;

- pull – data is sent to a mobile device without any previous user request.

There is great scope here for B2B applications, in particular for new approaches to marketing.

Speech recognition and response technologies are also gaining commercial credibility and momentum (Lamont, 2001). Largely concentrating on improving response to customer calls to sales and service centres currently, it remains to be seen if there will be useful applications for other business processes.

In the area of information search and retrieval it seems likely that intelligent agents (software, not people!) will be used increasingly to trawl the web for the best deals when businesses are buying, the likeliest purchasers when they are selling and the most effective collaborators for survival and success in the global marketplace.

One of the possible issues here is conflict resolution in the online world. Interested readers are referred to the American Arbitration Association's website (www.adr.org). One of its focus areas is eCommerce, and a 'B2B eCommerce Dispute Management Protocol' has been promoted on the website since 2001.

Future B2B applications

Apart from innovative use of new technologies, such as speech recognition, mobile messaging and new 'intelligent' software to seek and synthesise information, the immediate future will surely see the convergence of current B2B applications. Already the edges are blurring, the overlaps are irksome and the field is ripe for an overhaul that integrates the best of systems that have been adopted over the past 20 or so years. Radjou's list of separate vendors in the different categories (2003, p. 25) seems likely to be of limited validity.

Integrated systems encompassing all the supply chain, production, sales and service processes, scaleable for small, medium and large businesses, with appropriate networking for effective communications inside and outside an organisation, are both desirable and achievable. Multimedia technologies will foster visual and audio alternatives to text-based interfaces. There are challenges with respect to privacy, security and interoperability which must be resolved if these systems are really to foster collaboration.

Finally, it is very important to keep in mind that the systems technology, however sophisticated, is nothing more than the infrastructure on which much of modern business is, or can be, based.

E-business (Electronic Business) is the convergence of communication and information processing technology within core business process and culture. It is an enabling *business* process made possible with technology that provides more information and faster information delivery. It is neither a separate technology for business nor a separate business process. To most people, E-business incorrectly conjures an umbrella of radical initiatives for doing business on the Internet – rather than for efforts at enabling business as usual and extending marketing, sales, and support opportunities merely through a new channel.
Nemzow (2000)

Summary

The evolution of information systems and technology since the 1950s has been astonishing in its speed and creativity. In the sphere of business information systems, as in so many others, IST applications have mainly been used to good effect, especially when care has been taken to analyse and understand user requirements and match them with good design and training. Innovations continue at a pace. This chapter represents a snapshot at the beginning of the twenty-first century. Rather than learn by rote the current acronyms and underlying technologies, readers are encouraged to think creatively about how IST does, and will, support commercial enterprise, including B2B applications.

Discussion questions

1 Identify and explain the four basic system concepts outlined at the beginning of the chapter.

2 You are preparing to give a presentation to some colleagues on the evolution of information systems and technology to support business processes. Write brief notes outlining the structure and basic content of your presentation.

3 Explain the nature and significance of computer networks and the benefits they offer to business organisations.

4 Visit four websites of BIS suppliers and compare their products and services based on the information presented online. Can you identify any significant gaps in their provision?

5 Find examples of supply chain management systems for small, medium and large companies and categorise common and differing characteristics.

6 Discuss possible future uses of mobile computing to support business people and tasks.

References

Bocij, P., Chaffey, D., Greasley, A. and Hickie, S. (2003). *Business Information Systems: Technology, Development and Management for the e-business*, 2nd edn, Harlow: Pearson Education.

Cleary, T. (1998). *Business Information Technology*, London: Financial Times Management.

De Boer, L., Harink, J. and Heijboer, G. (2002). 'A conceptual model for assessing the impact of electronic procurement', *European Journal of Purchasing and Supply Management*, 8, 1, pp. 25–33.

Elliott, G. (2003). 'The wireless Internet: an international comparison of mobile commerce products, services, technologies and business systems applications', *Proceedings of the IS One World Conference 2003*, Las Vegas, NV, pp. 23–5. OHP slides available online at www.scism.sbu.ac.uk/~elliotgd/ISoneWorld03-Presentation03.ppt (Accessed 21 October 2003.)

Lamont, I. (2001). 'Speech recognition technology will hear you now', CNN.com/SCI-TECH, www.cnn.com/2001/TECH/industry/06/06/auto.speech.idg/ (Accessed 21 October 2003.)

Naughton, J. (2000). *A Brief History of the Future*, London: Phoenix.

Nemzow, M. (2000). 'The E-Business Agenda', *Journal of Internet Banking and Commerce*, 5, 1, www.arraydev.com/commerce/JIBC/0001-02.htm (Accessed 21 October 2003.)

O'Brien, J.A. (2003). *Introduction to Information Systems: Essentials for the E-Business Enterprise*, 11th edn, New York, NY: McGraw-Hill Higher Education.

O'Leary, T. J. and Williams, B.K. (1989). *Computers and Information Systems*, 2nd edn, Redwood City, CA: Benjamin/Cummings Publishing.

Radjou, N., (2003). 'Supply chain processes replace applications: 2003 to 2008', pp. 24–8 in Mulani, N. (ed.), *Achieving Supply Chain Excellence Through Technology*, San Francisco, CA: Montgomery Research.

Stallings, W. (2002). *Network Security Essentials*, 2nd edn, Englewood Cliffs, NJ: Prentice Hall. See also williamstallings.com/NetSec2e.html for useful links posted by the author.

Swatman, P.M.C. and Swatman P.A. (1991). 'Electronic Data Interchange: Organisational Opportunity, Not Technical Problem', www.uni-koblenz.de/~swatmanp/pdfs/dbis91.pdf (Accessed 25 October 2002.)

Thomas, D. (2003). 'Sainsbury's boosts supplier collaboration', *ComputerWeekly.com*, Friday 24 October 2003, www.computerweekly.com/articles/ (Accessed 10 November 2003.)

Turban, E., McLean, E. and Wetherbe, J. (1999). *Information Technology for Management*, 2nd edn. New York, NY: Wiley.

Part B
B2B marketing management

The purpose of this part of the book is to explore the nature and dynamics of some of the principal marketing management issues associated with the B2B sector. It is assumed that readers will have prior knowledge of certain aspects of marketing planning, for example marketing audits and marketing research, so these topics are not covered here. The focus is on issues about selecting markets, developing added value, understanding buyer behaviour and the importance of interorganisational relationships.

Chapter 3 considers issues concerning different approaches to segmenting B2B markets. It develops conventional approaches and explores issues around the implementation and practicalities of B2B segmentation. It concludes by discussing ways in which organisations can use different positioning, once segments and target markets are agreed.

Chapter 4 examines the nature and features of B2B products, services and pricing. These constitute some of the essential elements through which organisations develop value-based propositions for their customers. Product market portfolios, including the product and technology life cycles, new product development processes and various B2B pricing issues and techniques are investigated.

Chapter 5 explores various issues relating to organisational buyer behaviour. In particular, it reviews the processes by which, and key influences on how, organisations determine which products and services to buy. Attention is given to aspects of interorganisational risk and the significance of relationships is established.

Chapter 6 is concerned with the nature and characteristics of interorganisational relationships. This chapter establishes important background information underpinning the development of relationship marketing and introduces more advanced concepts associated with networks and groups of interacting organisations.

Appropriate examples of IST applications within the B2B sector are integrated throughout these chapters.

Chapter 3
B2B market segmentation and positioning

Chapter overview

In addition to describing the elements associated with market segmentation, this chapter focuses on the traditional approaches to segmenting B2B markets and supplements them with ideas and processes concerning the relationship needs of business customers.

Segmentation is presented as a less than perfect form of marketing management, and the chapter deals with inherent problems associated with choosing between segments and implementing the whole process successfully. In particular, the barriers to segmentation are examined and systems solutions to some of these problems are explored.

The chapter concludes with an examination of positioning and how businesses should determine particular positioning strategies. Just as optimal target markets should be derived in the light of customer needs and seller resources and strategies, so positioning needs to take into account the requirements of all parties to a marketing relationship.

Chapter aims

The aim of the chapter is to examine current issues concerning the development and implementation of segmentation processes in B2B markets.

Objectives

The objectives of this chapter are to:

1   Examine the bases for segmenting business markets.
2   Consider the breakdown and build-up approaches to market segmentation in B2B markets.
3   Explore some of the processes used to select target markets.
4   Evaluate the practice of segmentation in business markets.
5   Consider the role of positioning (and strategies) in the segmentation, targeting and positioning (STP) process.
6   Indicate and illustrate helpful systems approaches and tools.

Introduction

The principles of market segmentation have been established for a long time and there is widespread agreement that they form an important foundation for successful marketing strategies and activities (Wind (1978), Hooley and Saunders (1993), Dibb and Simkin (2001)).

Generally, segmentation is a technique for dividing a mass market into identifiable subunits, in order that the individual needs of buyers and potential buyers can be more easily satisfied. Traditionally it is about the division of a mass market into distinct groups that have common characteristics, needs and similar responses to marketing stimuli.

Wind and Cardozo (1974) referred to market segmentation in B2B markets as the identification of 'a group of present or potential customers with some common characteristic which is relevant in explaining (and predicting) their response to a supplier's marketing stimuli'. However, B2B market segmentation has not been as well researched and documented as that in consumer markets (Bonoma and Shapiro, 1983). Abratt (1993) and Weinstein (1994) sought to extend our understanding, the latter making comparisons of both markets' characteristics. Recalling the simple principle that 80 per cent of profits are usually delivered by just 20 per cent of customers, there is a significant need to segment markets and create precisely targeted marketing programmes.

The intricacies involved in business market segmentation are said to make it a more exacting activity than in consumer markets. Griffith and Pol (1994) argue this point on the basis of multiple product applications, greater customer variability and problems associated with the identification of the key differences between groups of customers. However, there have been numerous attempts to define and describe business segmentation, using a variety of variables ranging from product-specific to customer-specific attributes. Readers are advised to read Mitchell and Wilson (1998) for a deeper account of various segmentation proposals.

The overall process associated with target marketing is referred to as the Segmentation, Targeting and Positioning process (STP) (see Figure 3.1).

The first task is to identify the mass market and then identify the various segments within the overall market using a variety of criteria. The second task is for organisations to select and target the particular segments which appear to represent the strongest marketing opportunities and match most closely the resources available to the organisation.

Having selected particular target markets, the final activity is to position products and/or services in such a way that buyers can clearly differentiate what is being offered from the prevailing competition. Distinct marketing programmes can be developed for each market selected. For example, Albert (2003) shows how segmentation analysis can be used for developing targeted communication strategies within marketing channels.

This brief overview is both a simplified and understated summary of what is a complex and hard to implement marketing management activity. The following sections explore each of these phases in turn.

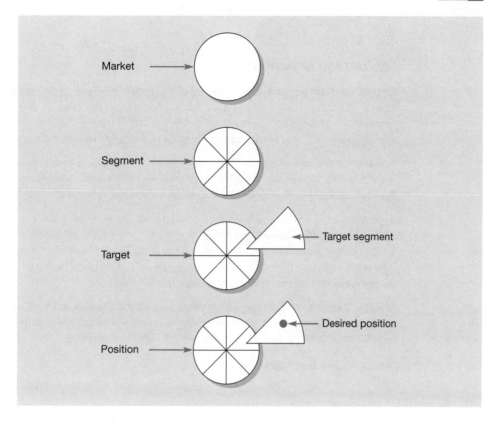

Figure 3.1 The STP process of target marketing

The process of segmenting B2B markets

The justification for segmentation is that groups of customers, or potential buyers, who share similar needs and buying characteristics are more likely to respond to an organisation's marketing programmes in similar ways. As Beane and Ennis (1987) suggest, this enables organisations to focus resources more efficiently and deliver more targeted marketing programmes in order better to meet customer needs. Instead of reaching out to a mass audience, the selection of particular submarkets concentrates activities and leads, in theory, to improved profitability. Dibb and Simkin (2001) also point out additional benefits in terms of improving market intelligence, being customer-orientated and competitor aware, which leads to improved targeting and positioning programmes.

There are two main approaches to segmenting B2B markets. The first adopts the view that the market is considered to consist of businesses (and buyers) that are essentially the same, so the task is to identify groups that share particular differences. This is referred to as the **breakdown method**. The second approach considers a market to consist of businesses that are all different, so here the task is to find similarities. This is known as the **build-up method**.

RBS AND B2B SEGMENTATION

One of the business activities undertaken by the Royal Bank of Scotland (RBS) is invoice financing. This involves banks lending companies the value of their debts, and represents a growing and strategically significant part of RBS's business. Recently however, response rates to RBS's mailing activities had fallen to less than 1 per cent.

In response to this situation, the first action by the bank was to clean, enhance and segment the 600,000-strong database. Approximately 40 financial fields were determined from a database which contained 2 million UK companies.

Eight unique groups with names that indicated their characteristics such as 'small independents', 'steady Eddies' and 'large corporates' were isolated before generating a series of individual profiles of decision makers within each of the eight main segments. This was completed through the use of both internal and external lifestyle databases. It is a classic example of the breakdown approach to segmentation.

Mailings then resumed, ensuring that the right product, channel and tone were used in each communication. As a result, response rates rose from 0.5 per cent to 3 per cent, with £290,000 saved on mailing costs through improved targeting.

Source: Adapted from Acland (2003).

The breakdown approach is perhaps the most established and well recognised. Some of the first advocates were Wind and Cardozo (1974) with their **Macro-Micro** method and Bonoma and Shapiro (1983) who promoted a **Nested** method. Both methods try to establish the general case and then seek individual clusters of businesses that share common differences.

According to Freytag and Clarke (2001) the build-up approach seeks to move from the individual level where all businesses are different, to a more general level of analysis based on the identification of similarities. The build-up method is customer-orientated as it seeks to determine common customer needs.

The debate however, should not be about the direction but the content of the segmentation approach. Many of these ideas about segmentation were developed at a time when transactional marketing was the overriding marketing orientation and the allocation of resources to achieve the designated marketing mix goals was paramount. Contemporary B2B market segmentation should not be solely about the allocation of resources, but concerned with buyer needs and relationship requirements. Even back in 1985, Plank believed that B2B segmentation should involve an analysis of buyers' attitudes towards relationships, attitudes towards each seller and a greater understanding of the reasons and ways in which organisations use products and services. More recently, a McKinsey report echoed these thoughts. Due to changes in technology, buyer attitudes and increased levels of competition, it argued that it is even more important to:

uncover the deep, unique consumer insights that will form the basis of a differentiated market strategy and pave the way to profitable growth. Whether formulating B2B or B2C strategies, marketers must identify something deep within the consumer psyche that can help them better meet marketplace needs.

McKinsey (2000)

Freytag and Clarke (2001) quite rightly identify that market segmentation is not a static concept and that the process should reflect current market conditions. Some organisational exchanges are purely transactional, while others are rooted within complex relationships. Indeed, it could be argued that the development of electronic data interchange (EDI) and eCommerce processes sought to routinise a large part of organisational commercial activities. In that sense, transactional marketing is encouraged when eCommerce is implemented. Indeed, Whitely (2000, p. 6) defines eCommerce in solely transactional terms as 'formulating commercial transactions at a site remote from the trading partner and then using electronic communications to execute that transaction'.

To be fully successful, the process and development of market segmentation activities should reflect a continuum between those organisations that only seek purely transactional marketing activities and those for whom the management and development of complex relationships is essential. All customers' needs are important; some are very different, even unique to the particular context in which the stakeholders operate.

When considering purely transactional situations the **breakdown** method would appear to be most appropriate. If relationship marketing issues dominate a business, or businesses, then the **build-up** approach seems more appropriate, simply because of the customer focus and the detailed information that is required when managing relationships.

Thus, the segmentation process will vary according to the prevailing conditions and needs of the parties involved, not just the needs of the selling organisation. Relationships concern the interaction of stakeholders, very often multiple stakeholders, and it is the needs of the interrelationship(s) that should dominate any segmentation activity. For example, an analysis of the relationship potential and buyer attitudes towards the supplier and other related stakeholders might provide a useful means of segmenting a market to the advantage of all relevant stakeholders.

As indicated above, target marketing is the process whereby specific segments are selected and marketing programmes are then developed to satisfy the needs of the potential buyers and other stakeholders, including the selling organisation, in the chosen segments. The development, or rather identification, of segments can be perceived as opportunities – as Beane and Ennis (1987, p. 20) suggest, 'a company with limited resources needs to pick only the best opportunities to pursue' – but can also be seen as a means of recognising and determining the nature and form of relationships between stakeholders (Freytag and Clarke, 2001).

For any segmentation approach to work, a basis by which markets are to be analysed has to be appreciated and applied before any meaningful analysis can commence.

Bases for segmenting business markets

The bases for segmenting consumer markets are well documented (Dibb and Simpkin, 2001; Kotler, 2003). Although similar principles apply, the bases used to segment

Table 3.1 Bases for segmenting B2B markets

Main segment variables	Explanation
Market characteristics	Based on organisational size and location variables.
	Used primarily where there is transactional marketing and the breakdown approach predominates.
Buyer characteristics	Based on the decision making process and associated variables.
	Used primarily where collaborative relationships and the build-up approach predominates.

business markets are different. Indeed, there is no fixed way of simply identifying business segments, mainly because the needs of business markets vary considerably.

There are two main groups of variables used to segment B2B markets, and they are interrelated. The first set of variables involves **market characteristics**, such as organisational size and location. Those seeking to segment markets where transactional marketing and the **breakdown** approach dominates would be expected to start with these variables. The second group is based upon the characteristics surrounding the decision making process employed within each of the organisational segments, and this is referred to as the **buyer characteristics**. Those organisations seeking to establish and develop particular relationships would normally be expected to start with these variables, and **build-up** their knowledge of their market and customer base (see Table 3.1).

Segmenting by market characteristics

These factors concern the buying organisations that make up a business market. There are a number of criteria that can be used to cluster organisations but size, market served, value, location, usage rate and purchase situation characteristics are some of the more common methods used.

Size

By segmenting organisations by size it is possible to identify particular buying requirements. Large organisations may have particular delivery or design needs, while purchasing activities in smaller organisations may be heavily influenced by key individuals, such as owners or managing directors.

Market served

Very often organisations buy a particular part of a supplier's range of products. This may reflect their business activity. For example, a road construction company may only purchase particular size diggers and rollers. Opportunities exist to determine new users in the same business area, develop new products and services for the sector, or communicate the whole of the current range more effectively to existing road construction companies.

SNAPSHOT 3.2

MARKETS SERVED BY CISCO

Part of the original structure at Cisco Systems was based on lines of product. This changed in 1993 to one orientated towards customer markets. These were:

■ service providers (large telecommunications companies);

■ enterprises (large Fortune 1000-type companies);

■ small and medium businesses (companies that need their internal networks linked to wide area networks to enable electronic commerce);

■ Cisco later added the home market as it saw opportunities emerging to network not only computers in homes but also to network home appliances.

Source: Adapted from Kraemer and Dedrick (2002)

Value

Similar to the usage rate factor, this aims to divide markets according to the value they represent to the selling organisation. This value (high, medium or low) may be based on sales revenue or, more appropriately, on profit contribution or to some softer factors – such as strategic access to new markets – or on terms of production efficiencies.

Location

Targeting by geographic location is one of the more common methods used to segment B2B markets, and is often used by new or small organisations attempting to establish themselves. However, the use of the Internet and websites means that location need not always be an important factor.

Usage rates

By grading existing customers and category users according to their rate of product and/or service consumption, it may be possible to isolate low, light, medium and heavy user segments. The goal would then be to encourage some medium users to become heavy users by changing some aspect of the marketing mix variables.

Purchase situation

There are three factors associated with the purchase situation. First, the structure of the buying organisation's purchasing procedures; is it centralised, decentralised, flexible or inflexible? Second, what type of buying situation is present; new task, modified rebuy or straight rebuy? Third, what stage in the purchase decision process have target organisations reached; are buyers in early or late stages and are they experienced or new? The marketing programme will need to consider, and attempt to answer, these questions in order to be successful.

SIC codes

Standard Industrial Classification (SIC) codes are often used to get an initial feel for the size of various markets. Although they are easily available and standardised, Walker's criticisms of SIC codes, namely that they suffer from being highly aggregated, often superficial and not based on customer need (cited by Mitchell and Wilson, 1998) has constrained their use. Indeed, SIC codes have limited application and are far from being a complete solution to business segmentation, although they do provide, as Naudé and Cheng (2003) suggest, 'some preliminary indication of the industrial segments in [a] market'. There is further information about SIC codes later in this chapter.

Segmenting by buyer characteristics

This set of criteria can be considered at two levels. The first level concerns the approach and requirements of the decision making unit (DMU). The second level focuses on the personal characteristics of key decision makers or members of the DMU.

Decision making unit

An organisation's decision making unit may have specific requirements that influence their purchase decisions in a particular market. There may be policy factors, purchasing strategies, a level of importance attached to these types of purchases, attitudes towards vendors and toward risk, all or some of which may help segregate groups of organisations for whom particular marketing programmes can be developed/refined and delivered.

Policy factors

Organisations may establish certain policies that govern purchasing decisions. A business may require specific delivery cycles to support manufacturing plans. Increasingly organisations require certain quality standards to be met by their suppliers, and membership of particular quality standards organisations (for example ISO 9002) is required as evidence of these thresholds having been reached. Policy may dictate that the reputation of all their suppliers is critical and that contracts can only be signed with organisations that meet certain internally determined criteria. For example, if a proposed supplier is currently contracted to a significant competitor it may be a sufficient signal to open negotiations.

Purchasing strategies

Cardozo (1980) determined that organisations tend towards one of two main purchasing strategies or profiles. These are referred to as optimisers and satisficers. **Optimisers** prefer to consider a wide range of potential suppliers and are prepared to evaluate a range of proposals before selecting a supplier. On the other hand, **satisficers** tend to prefer dealing with familiar suppliers and award contracts to the first supplying organisation to meet purchase requirements.

It is important for suppliers to appreciate the purchasing profile of buying organisations as it may help to allocate resources. A new entrant is likely to have more success becoming established by approaching optimisers rather than satisficers.

Level of importance

The importance of a purchase may be related to the value it represents to the purchasing organisation. However, the importance may also be perceived in terms of the opportunities it enables an organisation to exploit, such as its own new product development, entry to new markets or even the significance of the purchase in terms of the size and nature of the purchasing organisation. For example, buying a fork-lift truck may be fairly routine for an organisation such as Perkins Engines or Rolls Royce, but for a printer working on a small industrial estate, the fork-lift truck represents a major purchase, both financially and in terms of its work contribution.

SNAPSHOT 3.3

SEGMENTING BY TYPES OF BUYERS

A study, based on a manufacturer and distributor of steel strapping (for packaging), revealed four main segments. These were based on customer attitudes towards the price/service dimension.

Bargain hunters Sales $23m	Large volume buyers who are price sensitive. The product was very important to their operations.
Transaction buyers Sales $24m	Large and knowledgeable customers who consider the price/service trade but favour price. The product was very important to their operations.
Relationship buyers Sales $31m	Knowledgeable customers who valued the relationship. Did not push for concessions. The product was of moderate importance to their operations.
Programmed buyers Sales $6.6m	Neither price nor service sensitive and made purchases in a routinised way. The product was not of central importance to their operations.

As a result of these insights, the manufacturer was able to determine the costs of serving each segment and subsequently direct resources more efficiently and more effectively.

Source: Adapted from Rangan *et al.* (1992).

Relationships

The relationship between organisations is obviously a critical factor. While this is considered in greater depth elsewhere in the book, the attitudes and relationships between the people who represent organisations can be used as a means of segmentation. Segmentation might be based on the closeness and level of interdependence that may already exist between organisations. This could be measured in terms of a continuum from partners to unknowns. The attitude of DMUs may also be a determining factor, for example see Snapshot 3.3.

Attitude to risk

Organisational attitude towards risk and the degree to which an organisation is willing to experiment through the acquisition of new industrial products can vary a great deal. This variance is partly a reflection of the prevailing culture and philosophy, leadership and managerial style. The extent to which the buying organisation resists or embraces change is in turn reflected in the speed with which new product decisions are made, as well as the nature of the products selected and choice of suppliers.

Personal characteristics

Although individuals are normally considered to have a greater decision making impact in consumer rather than in business markets, the personal characteristics of some decision makers have been used in B2B segmentation.

Demographic variables such as age and education are often too simplistic to provide any significant bases for segmentation. However, personality, decision style, risk and lifestyle can provide interesting ways of segmenting B2B markets.

Some B2B market segments have been derived from an analysis of the decision making style and the preferred communication approach of B2B buyers. Using a grid, such as the one in Figure 3.2, can help determine the most empathetic approach for salespeople. By understanding the type of buyer and their key personality drivers, it is possible to frame and present sales messages for maximum effectiveness.

Figure 3.2 is based on two main behavioural dimensions, assertiveness and responsiveness. Assertiveness concerns the degree to which a person tries to control and direct the thoughts of others. Responsiveness is about the emotions and feelings a person displays to others. From this, four quadrants depicting different communication styles can be determined. The key characteristics associated with each of these communication styles are shown in Table 3.2.

The analysis proposes opportunities for sales people to adapt their own communications in order to complement the preferred or dominant style of each individual buyer. This level of segmentation is very individualistic and buyer-orientated, consequently it is difficult to plan and estimate in advance of meeting a buyer for the first time. However, this link between the level of segmentation and personal selling demonstrates how marketing plans can be extended right through to the detail of a salesperson's observations and introductory comments when meeting a buyer for the first time.

This brief synopsis of the communication styles approach does not detail the depth of information associated with this scheme. Readers interested in learning more should read Anderson and Dubinsky (2004), Alessandra et al. (1987) or Ingrascia (1981). The process is used by a large number of organisations as a sales training facility (for example, www.wilsonlearning.org) and is designed to encourage flexibility and adaptation skills in sales people (see also Chapter 12).

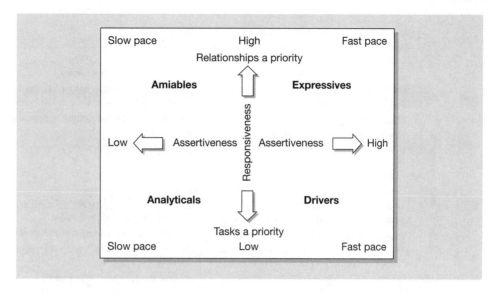

Figure 3.2 Key behavioural dimensions

Source: Adapted from Anderson, Rolph E. and Dubinsky, A.J. *Personal Selling*. Copyright © 2004 by Houghton Mifflin Company. Used with permission.

Table 3.2 Key characteristics of four communication styles

Style	Dimensions	Characteristics
Amiables	High responsiveness Low assertiveness	Open, warm and very people-orientated. These people work at a slow pace, listen attentively and place high emphasis on developing relationships with everyone as they are people- rather than task-orientated.
Expressives	High responsiveness High assertiveness	This group tend to be fast-paced workers who have strong extrovert dimensions to their personality. They prefer to be involved with people all the time and seek approval of their achievements. Although full of creative ideas they are prone to base their views on intuition rather than researched data.
Analyticals	Low responsiveness Low assertiveness	Analyticals work at a slow pace reflecting their deliberation, self-discipline and preference for logical reasoning and systematic approaches to problem solving. They need information and proof to support claims made by others.
Drivers	Low responsiveness High assertiveness	Very goal-orientated, these people work quickly, often impatiently and they tend to ignore facts and figures. They invariably attempt to control their environments because they believe only they can achieve success.

Source: Adapted from Anderson, Rolph, E. and Dubinsky, A.J., *Personal Selling*. Copyright © 2004 by Houghton Mifflin. Used with permission.

	Low	Level of assertiveness	High
High	**Amiables** Be friendly and agreeable Present products in an interactive and congenial way Use third-party testimonials and personal guarantees Be reassuring and not aggressive.		**Expressives** Be enthusiastic when asking questions Compliment them on their achievements Use stories and illustrations to present your products Be confident and positive.
Low	**Analyticals** Move from the greeting to the task quickly Provide detailed product performance information, present in a logical order and use lots of supporting facts and information Use detailed analysis and research to support your arguments Always summarise the advantages and disadvantages.		**Drivers** Be confident and businesslike Be prepared, organised and talk at pace Show how the product will help the buyer achieve their goals Involve them in any demonstration Always be straightforward and direct, taking time to emphasise the overall benefits.

(Left vertical axis: Level of responsiveness — High at top, Low at bottom.)

Figure 3.3 Key approaches to communicating with the four styles

Source: Adapted from Anderson, Rolph E. and Dubinsky, J., *Personal Selling*. Copyright © by Houghton Mifflin Company. Used with permission.

Databases

As mentioned in Chapter 2, relational databases and database management techniques have had a significant presence in business information systems since the late 1970s.

> The starting point of any business-to-business segmentation is a good database. A well-maintained database is high on the list in any audit of marketing excellence in a business-to-business company. The database should, as a minimum, contain the obvious details of correct address and telephone number together with a purchase history. Ideally it should also contain contact names of people involved in the decision-making unit, though this does present problems of keeping it up to date.
>
> B2B International, www.B2Binternational.com/whitepapers3p.html (Accessed 13 October 2002.)

Within such a database it is usual to include codes, such as the United Kingdom's Standard Industrial Classification (SIC), mentioned earlier, or internally defined codes for classifying/segmenting the entries. Queries or reports from the database can then be undertaken on the basis of these codes, or produced in sorted order.

SIC CODES

A Standard Industrial Classification (SIC) was first introduced into the United Kingdom in 1948 for use in classifying business establishments and other statistical units by the type of economic activity in which they are engaged. The classification provides a framework for the collection, tabulation, presentation and analysis of data and its use promotes uniformity. In addition, it can be used for administrative purposes and by non-government bodies as a convenient way of classifying industrial activities into a common structure.

Since 1948 the classification has been revised in 1958, 1968, 1980, 1992 and 1997. Revision is necessary because, over a period of time, new products and the new industries to produce them emerge and shifts of emphasis occur in existing industries. It is not always possible for the system to accommodate such developments and after a period of time updating the classification is the most sensible action. The 1997 changes were not a full-scale revision but a response to user demand for a limited number of additional subclasses together with some minor renumbering.

The need for change is equally true for all international classifications and they are revised from time to time to bring them up to date. Thus, a new International Standard Industrial Classification of All Economic Activities (ISIC Rev 3) was agreed in the Statistical Commission of the United Nations in February 1989, while on 9 October 1990 the European Communities' Internal Market Council (of Ministers) passed a regulation to introduce a new statistical classification of economic activities in the European Communities (NACE Rev 1).

Source: Introduction to UK standard industrial classification of economic activities UK SIC(92), http://www.statistics.gov.uk/methods_quality/sic/default.asp (Accessed October 2002.)

An example of a commercially maintained database using this sort of segmentation is 'prospect B2B' a service offered by UK company Prospect Swetenhams (www.prospectswetenhams.com). Their business-to-business mailing and telemarketing databases can be searched online by:

- job responsibility;
- business activity (UK SIC code);
- geographic region;
- turnover;
- number of employees.

The website shows 'breakdowns of the database to help you see just how many names you can select'. Snapshot 3.4 shows the breakdowns as listed in October 2002.

DATABASE INFORMATION AT PROSPECT SWETENHAMS

Job responsibility (function)	Total
Information technology	53,508
Human resources/personnel	51,286
Marketing	53,038
Finance	61,480
Sales	54,199
Purchasing	39,336
Production	27,750
Managing directors	68,205
Health and safety	15,088
Office products purchaser	14,920

Industry sector	Businesses
Agriculture, forestry and fishing	2,177
Construction and completion	20,248
Finance	11,184
Manufacturing	65,590
Mining and quarrying	1,250
Retail	18,723
Services	85,083
Transport and communications	11,943
Wholesale	41,534

No. of employees		Turnover (£)	
1–19	33,519	<1 million	37,605
20–99	81,519	1–5 million	70,735
100–499	52,464	5–10 million	33,781
500+	18,301	10 million +	72,518
Not disclosed	71,941	Not disclosed	43,105

Source: www.prospectswetenhams.com (Accessed October 2002.) Used with permission. (Formerly known as The Prospect Shop.)

Target market selection

The next step in the STP process is to select appropriate target segments that represent the best opportunities for the organisation, given their resources, strategy and the prevailing internal and external conditions. The selection of target segments should be based on a systematic analysis of the market. This involves first considering the **market characteristics** and then moving through to the **buyer characteristics**. The cost of this activity increases as buyer characteristics are considered. This is because the market characteristics can usually be drawn from secondary sources. Invariably the information necessary for the analysis of buyer characteristics has to be gained through primary research and this is where the required investment can rise substantially.

The role of market and marketing research in the segmentation process cannot be underestimated. Indeed, one of the reasons often cited for not analysing and identifying precise market segments is the research cost involved. Many organisations, particularly small and medium-sized organisations, do not have the time, expertise or financial resources to assign to this important foundation work. However, preliminary research need not be too expensive or time consuming, and can use third-party services/tools.

Commercially available databases and prospect-finding services, based on market characteristics, are becoming increasingly inexpensive. A free search in October 2002 of 'prospect B2B' for purchasing staff in the retail sector, in companies with 10–49 employees, produced 352 names. Renting 100 of those names on a single-use basis would cost £21.15 (see screen print, Snapshot 3.5). The question arises whether such information would be well-researched and up-to-date. The website claims that:

1 Prospect B2B sources the full set of data on UK limited companies compiled by Companies House, the legal repository for UK limited company information.

2 This data file is then analysed and enhanced by ProspectSwetenham's sister company ICC information.

3 Head office contact information is enhanced using telephone directory company Thomsons' tele-researched database.

4 Using a call centre, large companies in the database are called and details are checked and supplemented with vital contact information.

Each company called confirms which employee has ultimate responsibility for each key job function within the business.

The goal is to identify segments that in the medium to long term will provide suitable returns. This is not an easy task. Care needs to be taken to ensure that all the costs and benefits are understood. This entails considering the necessary changes to the products and services, pricing requirements, alterations and investments in distribution channels and the consequent knock-on impact on the promotional plans.

It is now generally accepted that use of the following criteria helps to identify valid and reliable segments:

■ All segments should be **measurable** – is the segment easy to identify and measure?

■ All segments should be **accessible** – can the buyers be reached effectively with marketing programmes?

- All segments should be **substantial** – is the segment sufficiently large to warrant a separate marketing programme and will it provide sufficient return on investment?

- All segments should be **actionable** – has the organisation the capability to reach the segment?

- All segments should be **compatible** – with current business strategy and expected market conditions.

These criteria, the basis for which was originally proposed by Kotler (1984), are only intended to be used as guidelines and are of greater use when segmenting consumer rather than B2B markets. Managerial discretion and judgement will determine which markets are selected and exploited and which are ignored. To that extent the segmentation process should not be regarded as a perfect marketing management activity. Much of what is passed off as segmentation is merely an *ad hoc* market adjustment to reflect product amendments and principal buyer requirements. Dibb and Wensley (2002) argue that the method of segmentation analysis is often inappropriate and the implementation is seriously blemished to the extent that the whole segmentation process is of 'limited practical value' (p. 1).

The STP process used earlier in this chapter looks at segmentation in a narrow way. Goller *et al.* (2002) present what they refer to as an integrative framework for business segmentation (see Figure 3.4).

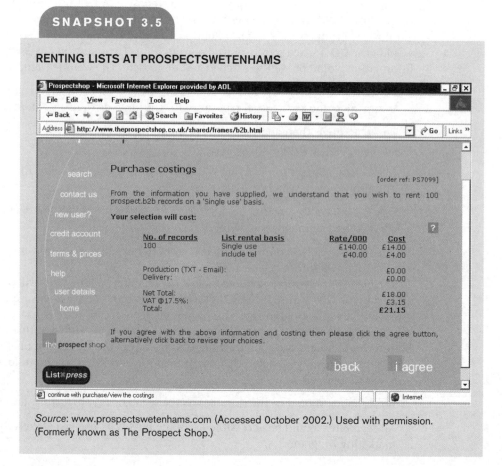

Source: www.prospectswetenhams.com (Accessed October 2002.) Used with permission. (Formerly known as The Prospect Shop.)

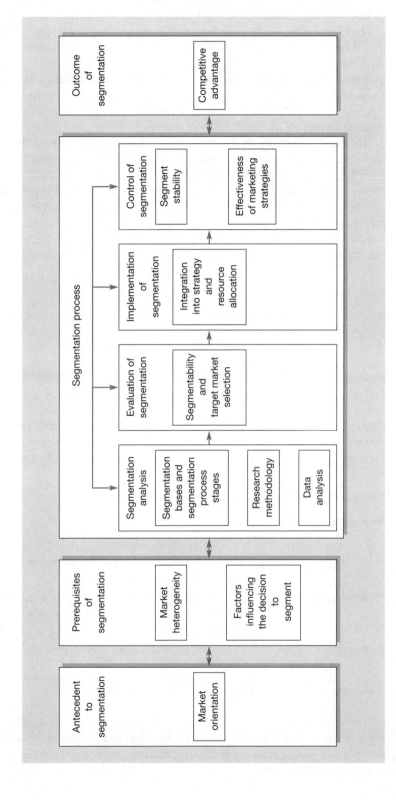

Figure 3.4 The process stages for segmenting business markets

Source: Goller, Hogg and Kalafatis (2002). Published with permission, Emerald Group Publishing Limited www.emeraldinsight.com

This framework is useful because it draws together the various factors that constitute business segmentation and provides an overview of the whole process.

The Goller framework assumes a more encompassing perspective and depicts four linked components. These are driven initially by the overall market orientation of the organisation. These authors argue that behaviour is manifest in the level of orientation that exists towards customers, competitors and interfunctional coordination. These impact on the subsequent components of the framework and the success of business segmentation is influenced largely by the degree to which the organisation is market-orientated.

One final comment regarding the Goller framework concerns the last component, the outcomes of the segmentation process. This aspect is often lost or neglected as attention can be focused on the nature of the segment bases and the size of the segments established. The purpose of business segmentation should be to develop a commercial advantage in order to improve efficiency and market effectiveness. Goller *et al.* suggest that the most advantageous outcome of business segmentation is gaining competitive advantage. This may be rather too broad, and difficult to measure easily, but the point that **segmentation for segmentation's sake** is worthless, is well made.

Barriers to segmentation

The processes involved in the evaluation and determination of suitable target markets is not as precise or clear cut as many authors suggest or imply. Dibb and Simkin (2001) point out that one of the major problems associated with segmentation in B2B markets is a failure of businesses to implement segmentation plans. They suggest that there are three main reasons for this failure. These are set out in Table 3.3.

Table 3.3 Barriers to segmentation

Segmentation barrier	Explanation
Infrastructure barriers	These concern the culture, structure and resources which can prevent the segmentation process starting or being completed successfully.
Process barriers	These barriers reflect a lack of experience, guidance and expertise concerning the way in which segmentation is undertaken and managed.
Implementation barriers	These are practical barriers concerning a move to a new segmentation model.

Source: After Dibb and Simkin (2001).

Dibb and Simkin argue that these three segmentation barriers serve to prevent businesses from either starting the segmentation process or from implementing their chosen course of action.

Infrastructure barriers are common and lie at the root of the problems facing many organisations. These concern the culture, structure and resources which prevent the segmentation process starting. For example, there may be a lack of financial resources to collect market data or a culture that is rigidly product-orientated. An organisation that has a strong product orientation will find it problematic to move to a new segmentation approach, especially one that follows the build-up method.

Process issues concern the lack of experience, guidance and expertise concerning the way in which segmentation is undertaken and managed. There is little information at both academic and practical levels to help managers with the processes involved with segmentation.

Increasingly, however, there are websites describing the processes and giving examples, which may help the less experienced with segmentation modelling, or offering consultancy or software tools; for example, www.marketsegmentation.co.uk and www.market-modelling.co.uk.

Many of the websites and consultants recommend using factor analysis when determining market segments. This is a statistical method for identifying a small number of variables or attributes that explain correlations in buyers' attitudes and behaviour. Examples might be age, gender or postcode. In consumer markets, factor analysis is performed on vast data sets collated from surveys, or point of sale systems. In B2B markets, the challenge is to acquire data in the first place and in sufficient numbers for the results to be statistically significant. It is quite easy to perform factor analysis using a statistical package such as SPSS, but care must be taken in deciding which factors to investigate and especially in interpreting the results. Interested readers are referred to en.wikipedia.org/wiki/Factor_analysis_(in_marketing).

Implementation barriers concern the way in which an organisation can move towards a new segmentation model. This may be due to a move away from a business model based on products (for example, engine sizes for fleet buyers), to one based on customer needs. Goller *et al.* (2002) suggest that there is insufficient information and practical guidance for managers in order that segmentation strategies be implemented successfully. It may be that the established ways of doing business become a barrier to moving over to a new approach. The practical issues involved in moving a business from one type of segmentation are often overlooked yet these invariably impede organisations from developing their segmentation policies. The JCB case in Snapshot 3.6 highlights some of these implementation barriers.

Segmentation in business markets should reflect the relationship needs of the parties involved and should not be based solely on the traditional consumer market approach, which is primarily the breakdown method. Through use of both the breakdown and the build-up approaches, a more accurate, in depth and potentially more profitable view of industrial markets can be achieved (Crittenden *et al.*, 2002). However, problems remain concerning the practical application and implementation of B2B segmentation. Managers report that the analysis processes are reasonably clear, but it is not clear how they should 'choose and evaluate between the market segments' which have been determined (Naudé and Cheng, 2003).

SNAPSHOT 3.6

JCB CONSTRUCTION

JCB is a UK company that is the European market leader in construction and earth-moving equipment. Following a period of systematic self-appraisal, the company realised that the prevailing organisational culture was essentially product-led. Even the well-established franchised dealership network was product-focused.

Their marketing department was based on product categories (for example, backhoe diggers) and customer sectors (road construction, public utilities). However, as more products and more customer groups became established so the business expanded and product lines and customer groups became complicated and confusing. However, customers seeking a variety of products had to liaise with different sales teams (and product groups) and, as a result, received multiple marketing communications messages and had to deal with an increasing number of internal departments.

Recognising the benefits that a market segmentation analysis might bring, the process began, only to become impeded by a number of variables. First, there was a lack of reliable data mainly because there was no JCB way of collecting or processing data. In addition, internal communication was poor at a number of levels. Product team managers failed to share information, production and R&D personnel did not consult with marketing and sales departments and the communication lines between head office and the branches was inadequate. It was not surprising therefore that the organisation did not have a formal process for carrying out the new segmentation work.

Solutions

One of the first requirements was to gather market intelligence. Questionnaires were sent out with warranty cards, telephone calls were made to customers, and exhibitions were used deliberately to collect information. A database was used to store and analyse data.

Workshops and meetings were used to structure the overall process and to disseminate information. Where previously there was a reluctance to share information, now team-work and regular meetings motivated increasing number of people from different areas to join in and contribute to the intelligence-gathering exercise. Even the dealers became involved once it was clear to them that their contributions and participation were welcome and valued.

The segmentation process enabled JCB to move towards the implementation of segments which were very customer-driven. As a result of the data collected JCB established three main divisions. These were the Heavyline, Midline and Compact Equipment divisions. Internal liaison facilities were established to assist customers whose requirements cut across machine groups. These enabled the business to serve customer groups with greater focus, which in turn facilitated the development and cultivation of selected relationships. Some of the dealerships became specialised and concentrated on particular types of customers, just as Toyota managed with the Lexus brand.

Source: Based on Dibb and Simkin (2001).

Positioning

Market segmentation and target marketing are prerequisites to successful positioning. Following the analysis, determination and final selection of market segments and target markets, the next task is to position the organisation, brand or product/service through the development and implementation of targeted marketing communication programmes. Positioning is the natural conclusion to the sequence of activities that constitute a core part of business marketing strategy.

Positioning takes place in the minds of the buyers in the target market. According to Ries and Trout (1972) it is not what you do to a product that matters, it is what you do to the mind of the prospect that is important. This is an important aspect of the positioning concept. Positioning is not about the product but what the buyer thinks about the product or organisation. It is not the physical nature of the product that is important for positioning, but how the product is perceived that matters.

Traditionally, and more commonly, this idea is applied to consumer markets but the principle is the same in business marketing. The difference between the two lies in the types of messages conveyed and the balance of the promotional mix used to deliver the positioning messages. Messages in B2B markets are traditionally rational and product-orientated, with the emphasis on personal selling and increasingly on direct marketing. This may be changing as marketing communications shows signs of conveying more emotional messages and ones which seek to develop business brands.

The aim of positioning, therefore, is to enable buyers and potential buyers to view a supplier or group of suppliers as different from other suppliers and as a source of added value. It is important that the supplier is regarded not only as different from other suppliers but also that they offer a set of values that will enable them to achieve their own goals more effectively and more efficiently.

All products and all organisations have a position. The position held by each organisation can be managed or it can be allowed to drift. Interest in business-to-business positioning has developed for two main reasons. The first is concerned with the increasingly competitive market conditions, where there is now little compositional, material or even structural difference between the products offered by many organisations. This has, in many cases, led to an increase in the provision of pre- and post-sales services, which have the potential to generate higher margins. Additionally, in markets where mobility barriers (ease of entry and exit to a market, for example plant and production costs) are relatively low, the need to position is also important.

The second reason is related to the seemingly incessant pressure to reduce costs and improve margins over the short term. By switching the emphasis of marketing communications from individual products (or categories) to development of the corporate brand, large savings in promotional activities can be achieved. The development and implementation of electronic-based marketing communications facilities has also helped to reduce costs. For example, the provision of product information through a corporate website has enabled salespeople to spend a greater proportion of their time in front of buyers and potential buyers, rather than servicing small, low-value and low-potential buyers. The switch to corporate branding and the development of web-based communications focuses marketing management attention on what the organisation stands for and how it should be presented to the target market.

Positioning strategies

As in consumer markets, there are two main approaches to positioning a brand, these are **functional** and **expressive** (or symbolic). Functionally positioned brands stress the features and benefits, while expressive positioning emphasises the ego, social and hedonic satisfactions that a brand can bring. Both approaches make a pledge, for example to deliver on time, every time (functional) or just to do business with nice people (symbolic). The first delivers a rational message, the second one is largely emotional.

As mentioned earlier, traditionally B2B marketers have used the former, rationally based approach which emphasises product features, attributes and benefit claims. A tried and trusted sales training aid is based around the concept of telling customers features and then drawing out the benefits. Some organisations have moved to a more expressive approach drawing on softer messages that attempt to develop associations.

The development of positions which buyers can relate to and understand is an important, even vital, part of the marketing communications plan. In essence, the position adopted is a statement about what the organisation (brand) is, what it stands for, and the values and beliefs that customers, hopefully, will come to associate with, and appreciate in, the particular brand.

Positioning approaches should also reflect the type of target market that has been selected. Positioning with regard to mainly transactional-based segments should be more rational and product-orientated, as the needs of buyers there are invariably purposeful and product-orientated. Positioning in target markets where relationship issues are significant and important should be more expressive, with a focus on support, participation, interaction between parties and a knowledge of and interest in the customer's business.

Developing a position

To develop a position it is recommended that a series of steps or process stages are followed. The following represents a composite from the literature (Boyd *et al.*, 1998; Fill, 2002).

1 Which positions are held by which competitors?

2 Identify the key or determinant attributes perceived by buyers as important. This will almost certainly require marketing research to determine attitudes and perceptions.

3 Sample the target segment and determine how they rate each product/service.

4 From the above, determine the current positions held by relevant products and organisations.

5 From the information gathered so far, is it possible to determine the desired position for the brand?

6 Is the strategy feasible in view of the competitors and any budgetary constraints? A long-term perspective is required, as the selected position has to be sustained.

7 Implement a programme to establish the desired position.

8 Monitor the perception held by customers and their changing tastes and requirements on a regular basis.

Positioning tactics

To implement the broad approaches a number of tactics have been developed. The list that follows is not intended to be comprehensive, nor to suggest that these approaches are discrete. They are outlined here to illustrate the tactical style. In reality, a number of hybrid approaches are often used.

Product features

Traditionally this is one of the easier concepts and one that is quite commonly adopted. The brand is set apart from the competition on the basis of key attributes or features that the brand has relative to the competition. For example, a product's superior durability, strength or design features are often used to provide customers with a means of differentiating various product offerings.

Price/quality

This strategy is more effectively managed than others because price itself can be a strong communicator of quality. This approach is particularly effective in segments where discrete exchanges predominate. A high price denotes high quality, just as a low price can deceive buyers into thinking a product to be of low quality and poor value.

User

Some organisations attempt to differentiate themselves and their products on the basis that they are of specific benefit to a particular type of user organisation or even individual buyer. IBM once claimed that no one ever got sacked for buying IBM, and Canon UK provides another example (see Snapshot 3.7).

SNAPSHOT 3.7

B2B POSITIONING AT CANON UK

Canon UK target the business market whose main customers include SoHos (Small office, Home office), small and medium-sized enterprises, large corporate players and government. For all of them Canon claims to be a world leading provider of innovative IT technologies.

Canon UK have developed a partnership with Solicitor's Own Software (SOS) to provide a total Legal/IT solution for the UK solicitors market. Therefore, Canon have positioned themselves specifically to meet the needs of a specific user group (solicitors).

In one particular example, Canon/SOS developed new IT solutions to enable sole practitioners and small practices to work from remote locations, for example at home. This helped them avoid the high costs of office accommodation but they still needed the back office support systems to operate successfully, which Canon/SOS provided.

This type of pioneering and leading-edge work helps establish both Canon and SOS as innovative organisations and as leading suppliers to this specific market segment.

Source: Adapted from material at www.canon.co.uk/Images/14_42170.pdf (Accessed 31 October 2003.) Used with permission.

Benefit

Positions can also be established by proclaiming the benefits that usage confers on the customer. This is an extension of the features position. By turning the feature into a benefit, the focus moves from the product to the customer and their needs. For example, many high technology companies and software vendors position themselves in terms of the benefits provided by their solutions to customer problems. These might be lower costs, quicker order processing, less wastage, more satisfied customers, higher levels of service or improved profitability.

Experience, depth of knowledge and corporate reputation

Many organisations attempt to position themselves on the grounds of their expertise, leading technical capabilities and, in some cases, the length of their corporate history. Hewlett Packard position themselves on their ability to be innovative and to bring their customers leading-edge technologies. These types of positions are used by organisations to convey quality, experience and depth of knowledge, to reduce risk and increase trust and credibility.

Whatever the position adopted by a brand or organisation, both the marketing and promotional mixes must endorse and support the position so that there is consistency throughout all communications. For example, if a leading high-technology position is taken, such as that of Cisco or Sun Microsystems, then product quality must be superior to the competition, price correspondingly high and distribution synonymous with quality and exclusivity. Sales promotion activity will be minimal, so as not to dilute these cues, and all other marketing communication messages should be visually affluent, rich in tone and copy, with complementary public relations and personal selling approaches.

The dimensions used to position brands must be relevant and important to the target audience and the image cues used must be believable and consistently credible. Positioning strategies should be developed over the long term if they are to prove effective, although minor adaptions can be made in order to reflect changing environmental conditions.

SNAPSHOT 3.8

COMPETITOR POSITIONS

Eatec operate in the oil and gas industry and provide organisations with a range of technical specific engineering-based services (for example, finite element analysis, data handling and fluid dynamics).

The company's competitors tend to position themselves on one of two main platforms. The first position is as an expert in one of the specific services that Eatec offers, such as fluid dynamics. The second position adopted by others is as an expert to the oil and gas industry segment or another such industry segment, for example the aerospace industry.

Source: Adapted from Naudé and Cheng (2003).

Summary

The principle associated with the use of segmentation techniques in B2B markets is undoubtedly sound. However, the established use of the breakdown method, whereby a mass market is divided into groups that share particular characteristics as a basis for developing target segment marketing programmes, is now being questioned.

The questions arise from the apparent incompatibility with the emerging relationship marketing paradigm, the recognition and acceptance that there are a number of major barriers that prevent the full implementation of B2B market segmentation. The response has been the emergence of approaches to segmentation that reflect the preferences of customers and their relationship needs. The build-up method recognises buyers' needs and should result in the determination of market segments that suit both buyer and seller. Whether this approach satisfies the relationship dimensions is still open to question.

Theoretical approaches to business segmentation have developed but the practical application of these various strategies is reported to be less than satisfactory. More research is required on the barriers to successful implementation of segmentation activities.

Organisations need to position themselves so that they are perceived by customers to differ from the competition and provide the potential for added value. Traditionally, the focus of positioning approaches has been on key attributes and features that seemingly add value. Increasingly, as corporate branding becomes a more central part of the marketing communications strategy, more emotional approaches to positioning are emerging.

Discussion questions

1 Make notes describing the principles that underpin the build-up and breakdown approaches to market segmentation. What are their main disadvantages?

2 Evaluate the bases used to segment B2B markets.

3 Identify five variables that might influence the nature of the decision making unit and its utility within the segmentation process.

4 Discuss the influence of interorganisational relationships on the development and maintenance of B2B segmentation strategies.

5 Describe the three main barriers to successful B2B segmentation. Consider ways in which these might be overcome.

6 Identify four organisations operating in the business market and determine their positioning strategies. Consider how these strategies differ and make proposals how each might be developed.

References

Abratt, R.R. (1993). 'Market segmentation practices of industrial marketers', *Industrial Marketing Management*, 22, pp. 79–84.

Acland, H. (2003). 'B2B data: the quest for quality', *Marketing Direct*, 25 July, www.brandrepublic.com/news/newsArticle.cfm?articleID=186500 (Accessed November 2003.)

Albert, T. (2003). 'Need based segmentation and customised communication strategies in a complex-commodity industry', *Industrial Marketing Management*, 32, 4, pp. 281–90.

Alessandra, A., Wexler, P. and Berrera, R. (1987). *Non-Manipulative Selling*, Englewood Cliffs, NJ: Prentice Hall.

Anderson, R.E. and Dubinsky, A.J. (2004). *Personal Selling*, New York, NY: Houghton Mifflin.

Beane, T.P. and Ennis, D.M. (1987). 'Market segmentation: A Review', *European Journal of Marketing*, 21, pp. 20–42.

Bonoma, T.V. and Shapiro, B.P. (1983). *Segmenting the Industrial Market*, Lexington, MA: Lexington Books.

Boyd, H.W., Walker, O.C. and Larreche, J.C. (1998). *Marketing management: a strategic approach with a global orientation*, 3rd international edn, New York: McGraw-Hill/Irwin.

Cardozo, R.N. (1980). 'Situational segmentation of industrial markets', *European Journal of Marketing*, 14, 5/6, pp. 264–76.

Crittenden, V.L., Crittenden, W.F. and Muzyka, D.F. (2002). 'Segmenting the business-to-business marketplace by product attributes and the decision process', *Journal of Strategic Marketing*, 10, pp. 3–20.

Dibb, S. and Simkin, L. (2001). 'Market segmentation: diagnosing and treating the barriers', *Industrial Marketing Management*, 30, 8 (November), pp. 609–25.

Dibb, S. and Wensley, R. (2002). 'Segmentation analysis for industrial markets', *European Journal of Marketing*, 36, 1/2, pp. 231–51.

Fill, C. (2002). *Marketing communications: contexts, strategies and applications*, 3rd edn Harlow: Pearson Education.

Freytag, P.V. and Clarke, A.H. (2001). 'Business to business segmentation', *Industrial Marketing Management*, 30, 6 (August), pp. 473–86.

Griffith R.L. and Pol, L.G. (1994). 'Segmenting industrial markets', *Industrial Marketing Management*, 23, pp. 39–46.

Goller, S., Hogg, A. and Kalafatis, S.P. (2002), 'A new research agenda for business segmentation', *European Journal of Marketing*, 36, 1/2, pp. 252–71.

Hooley, G.J. and Saunders, J.A. (1993). *Competitive Positioning: The Key to Market Success*, Englewood Cliffs, NJ: Prentice Hall.

Ingrascia, J. (1981). 'How to reach buyers in their comfort zones', *Industrial Marketing*, July, pp. 60–4.

Kotler, P. (1984). *Marketing Management*, International Edition, Englewood Cliffe, NJ: Prentice Hall.

Kotler, P. (2003). *Marketing Management*, 11th edn, Upper Saddle River,NJ: Pearson Education.

Kraemer, K.L. and Dedrick, J. (2002). 'Strategic use of the Internet and e-commerce: Cisco Systems', *Journal of Strategic Information Systems*, 11, pp. 5–29.

McKinsey, (2002). www.marketing.mckinsey.com/capabilities/research.htm (Accessed 13 October 2002.)

Mitchell, V.W. and Wilson, D.F. (1998). 'A reappraisal of business-to-business segmentation', *Industrial Marketing Management*, 27, 5 (September), pp. 429–45.

Naudé, P. and Cheng, L. (2003). 'Choosing between potential friends: market segmentation in a small company', Paper presented at the 19th IMP Conference, Lugano, Switzerland, www.impgroup.org/uploads/papers/4393.pdf (Accessed 26 January 2004.)

Plank, R.E. (1985). 'A critical review of industrial market segmentation', *Industrial Marketing Management*, 14, pp. 79–91.

Rangan, V.R., Moriarty, R.T. and Swartz, G.S. (1992). 'Segmenting customers in mature industrial markets', *Journal of Marketing*, 56 (October), pp. 72–82.

Ries, A. and Trout, J. (1972). ' The positioning era cometh', *Advertising Age*, 24 April, pp. 35–8.

Walker, O.C., Boyd, H.W. and Larreche, J.C. (1998) *Marketing Strategy*, OH: McGraw-Hill/Irwin.

Weinstein, A. (1994). *Market Segmentation*, Chicago, IL: Probus.

Whitely, D. (2000). *e-Commerce: Strategy, Technologies and Applications*, London: McGraw-Hill.

Wind, Y. (1978). 'Issues and advances in segmentation research', *Journal of Marketing Research*, 15, pp. 317–37.

Wind, Y. and Cardozo, R.N. (1974). 'Industrial market segmentation', *Industrial Marketing Management*, 3 (March), pp. 153–66.

Chapter 4

Business value – products, services and pricing

Chapter overview

This chapter begins by considering the various benefits a business product or service might confer and then describes how products might be classified according to the degree of standardisation and customisation that the organisation decides to offer. It is important to establish this background information before considering how organisations might develop strategies to manage their products, both established and new. Particular attention is given to portfolio management frameworks and the product life cycle before examining issues concerning the new product development process. This section concludes with a consideration of the technology adoption life cycle, appropriate in high technology markets.

The final part of the chapter is devoted to considering pricing issues and the value that the customers perceive in an organisation's product portfolio and its product and service policies.

Chapter aims

The aims of this chapter are to evaluate the nature of business products and to consider issues regarding pricing in these markets.

Objectives

The objectives of this chapter are to:

1 Examine the characteristics of business products and services.

2 Appreciate the nature and significance of product strategies.

3 Evaluate the usefulness of product portfolios.

4 Examine both the product and technology adoption life cycles and determine how these might impact on business.

5 Evaluate the new product development process.

6 Explore the role of pricing in business markets.

7 Examine some of the main influences on pricing in business markets.

8 Consider some of the main pricing methods and strategies.

Product attributes and benefits

The development of superior value is based on a number of elements. These may vary across sectors and markets but two of the main elements are discussed in this chapter: products, including services (see below), and prices.

Business products contribute significantly to customers' perception and evaluation of a supplier's competitive stance. However, products are more than just the pure physical form and utility they outwardly present. Products have two main types of attribute – tangible and intangible (see Table 4.1).

The **tangible** (or physical) attributes, consist of two elements, core and augmented. Core attributes represent the functional capability of a product, its primary features. For example, the core features of earth-moving equipment from JCB are strength, capability and reliability. In addition to core features there are also augmented or advanced properties providing various additional customer benefits and helping to differentiate products. Styling, performance capabilities, packaging, size or weight are features that help distinguish a product or enable it to perform better than competitive products. For example, JCB's wheeled excavators have stabilisers that can be operated independently.

The **intangible** attributes are all the other aspects that customers perceive to surround a product. These concern the psychological aspects associated with service and support, the warranties and guarantees, the financial services, the training and, very importantly, the reputation of the company and its perceived status. These intangible elements are increasingly recognised as important discriminators and can help customers understand the relative value of market offerings. As products can be copied faster and as basic levels of operational performance become standardised, so differentiation has to be achieved primarily through superior service and reputation. For example, JCB provide a 24-hour global support service helping to ensure that their clients are able to meet their customers' deadlines.

Table 4.1 Attributes and properties of business products

Attribute or property		Explanation
Tangible	Core	These are the basic features which describe the simple capabilities of the product. These are generic to all product offerings in the market.
	Augmented	These are features added to the core attributes, which either provide extra facilities and performance opportunities or provide marks to distinguish and differentiate the basic product from competitive offerings. For example, packaging, brand names and logos, quality achievements and fittings and attachments.
Intangible		Additional elements that are provided to improve the atmosphere that surrounds a product. Technical service and support, financial services, warranties and delivery serve to embellish products and assist differentiation.

INTANGIBLE ATTRIBUTES

The development of an extranet in 1997 enabled Harley-Davidson Inc. to provide improved service and support to its dealers by offering them an online facility to file warranty claims, check recall status and submit financial statements.

The percentage of claims filed electronically from dealers worldwide grew from 52 per cent in 1996 to 61 per cent in 1997. More than a third of that increase came from claims filed via the extranet, even though initially only US dealers could use it and only in the second half of the year.

Now dealers, of which there are well over 1,000 worldwide, can use the password protected extranet (www.h-dnet.com) to order parts and accessories, search for documents ranging from engine diagrams and servicing instructions to press releases, as well as handle their warranty claims electronically.

Source: Adapted from: www.cio.com/archive/webbusiness/040198_harley.html (Accessed 7 April 2003.) Reprinted through the courtesy of CIO. Copyright © 2003 CXO Media Inc. All rights reserved.

Product attributes also assume varying levels of importance for buyers at particular organisations and for those operating in a particular category or market sector. As a result, organisational buyers perceive business products as a bundle of attributes and therefore it is important to understand which bundle different buyers prefer. Hutt and Speh (2001) suggest that some attributes can be regarded as **determinant**, which means that they are perceived by buyers as both important and differentiating. Other attributes may be **non-determinant**, that is either important or differentiating but not both.

Determinant attributes   =   important and differentiating
Non-determinant attributes   =   either important or differentiating.

Consideration should be given to the perception buyers have of a firm's key attributes relative to that of the competition. What might be considered as a differentiating attribute may be perceived by buyers as a standard requirement in the market. In this situation a new form of differentiation would need to be developed such as a superior service support dimension.

Business services

The interrelationship between products and services has become more entwined and complex. This is because organisations are searching for new ways to add value and differentiate themselves in markets characterised by rapid growth and shortening life cycles.

Nearly all B2B organisations offer products which contain a level of service. Viewed as a continuum with completely 'tangible' products at one end and completely 'intangible' services at another, it becomes possible to see that two main groups can be identified: support services and pure services.

Support services are provided to augment product offerings. They are best characterised by high technology organisations such as IBM, Cisco or Sun Microsystems who
offer products such as servers, cabling and disk drives but support these with installation, downloadable updates, training and consultancy services. Distributors also offer
their channel partners a variety of added value services such as transportation, fulfilment and storage. The range and quality of services used to support the product offering
will inevitably vary but they provide organisations with a means of sustainable differentiation. In addition, the provision of support services can be very profitable, often with
margins higher than those generated through the sale of products alone.

Primary service providers do not have a tangible product and the service stands
alone. Business insurance, management consultancy, professional services such as
accountancy and financial audit services, security and advertising and marketing
research agencies reflect some of the core activities in this area. In these situations,
where there is an absence of a tangible product, the added value offered by service
providers has to be concentrated on the quality and consistency of the service alone,
as it cannot be bundled and dissipated across products.

Service characteristics

As Gronroos (2000) argues, above all else, services are essentially processes. These processes are made up of a number of activities which in turn use resources. Customers
interact directly with these activities so that at the point of production there is simultaneous consumption.

A large number of authors have turned their attention to issues concerning the
marketing of services and most agree that services can be distinguished by five main
characteristics (Kotler, 2003; Heskett *et al.*, 1997; Gronroos, 2000; Lovelock *et al.*,
1999). These are intangibility, perishability, lack of ownership, inseparability and het-
erogeneity (see Table 4.2).

The idea that services can be distinguished by their intangibility has been questioned (Gronroos, 2000; Zeithaml and Bitner, 2000). The argument is that products
are not always considered purely in terms of their tangible aspects and many services
are themselves sometimes augmented by the presence of a tangible element. For
example, consultancy services are perceived in terms of trust, feelings and overall confidence but part of the manifestation of a consultancy exercise is the tangible report
submitted as evidence at the end of the consultancy process.

Gronroos (2000) highlights two main classifications namely, high-touch/high-tech
services and discretely/continuously rendered services. High-touch services are those
which are very dependent on people for their delivery. In contrast high-tech services
are dependent upon physical resources such as IS&T for their delivery. Gronroos
recognises that there is often an overlap between these two, for example when people
need to recover from a high-tech systems failure, but in the main these two
approaches drive different approaches and service strategies.

Providers of continuously rendered services are typified by office cleaning, out-
sourced contract delivery companies, facilities management and financial services.
These represent a regularised flow of interaction through which it is possible to
develop relationships. By definition, providers of discretely rendered services, such as
brand or systems consultancy, printing, decoration or electrical testing services fail to
present sufficient opportunity for relationships to be developed.

Table 4.2 Key characteristics of services

Service characteristic	Explanation
Intangibility	Services are difficult to evaluate prior to purchase, they are perceived subjectively and are experienced at the point of consumption. Services deny people the opportunity to touch, feel, see or hear, prior to, during or after the consumption of a product, unlike products.
Perishability	Services are not capable of being stored, simply because they are created and consumed simultaneously.
Lack of ownership	Services are used but there is no transfer of ownership prior to consumption.
Inseparability	Services are produced and consumed simultaneously which means that the service providers and the customer are in contact with each other at the point of consumption.
Heterogeneity	Services involve the interaction of many people in their production and consumption. This means that each service encounter is likely to be different, making it difficult to deliver a consistent service experience for all customers.

Readers who would like a deeper understanding of the marketing of services and issues such as service measurement and quality are advised to refer to Gronroos, (2000), Heskett *et al.*, (1997), Parasuraman *et al.* (1985) and Lovelock *et al.* (1999).

Business product strategy

Normally, organisations offer a range of products (and services) to their target markets. These products vary in many ways but management must devise and implement strategies that enable the organisation to achieve its marketing and, ultimately, business objectives.

Product strategy should consider the organisation's portfolio of products. Within the portfolio, two elements should be examined. One concerns the individual products, and plans should be developed for them accordingly. The second element concerns the whole product range and how products contribute to the overall, strategic framework of goods and services that make up the portfolio. Strategically, the management of the product portfolio is crucial.

Portfolios are made up of individual product items, lines of products, product mixes and the depth within each line, as follows:

Product item:	each individual product.
Product line:	clusters of products and services that are offered, in combination, to a designated market segment(s).
Product mix:	the number of product lines.
Depth of line:	the number of products offered within each line.

Within the portfolio approach, the goal is to make decisions that enhance the long-term profitability of the total set of products. This involves trading off one product line against another. For example, one product line might not be as technologically advanced as that offered by some competitors, but because one particularly strategically important customer is satisfied with this line, it has to be continued.

Another issue might concern the development of new products. Innovation requires reallocating some resources away from current product lines. Decisions need to be made about the potential contribution of new products and the opportunity costs this involves.

Product lines

Organisations develop product strategies and policies. These concern the decisions that impact on the mix of products and product lines that an organisation chooses to offer its customers. Product lines are clusters of products and services that are offered together to a market segment(s). These lines should represent a coherent product mix so that when business customers move across segments, they perceive a consistency of value and hence competitive advantage. This has implications for positioning and marketing communications, which are considered in Part D of the book.

Therefore, it is through the company's line of products that superior value and competitive advantage can be developed. The policies and strategies adopted by a company should be designed to sustain any advantage that might have been gained or be part of the process that seeks out new advantages.

One way in which product lines can be classified is based on the degree to which the content of product lines is standardised and mass produced, or customised to meet the individual, personal needs of each business customer. Using this approach Shapiro (1977) suggested four main product line categories, each based on the level of customisation or the level of 'content specificity'.

Proprietary or catalogue products

These products are produced in anticipation of orders. Sellers speculate that there will be sufficient demand and stock is produced in a standard format. Although each type of proprietary good can have a number of different applications, the level of overall content specificity is limited and there is no opportunity to change the specification to meet the needs of different markets.

Product line decisions in this category concern levels of stock to be made and held, the type of stock to be carried (adding and deleting lines) and the repositioning of products within the line.

Custom-built products

Not to be confused with custom-designed, these are products which are assembled for customers using preformed parts, subassemblies and components. They are then configured in particular ways so that they meet a specific customer's needs. For example, a computer network is a system assembled by using, among other things, particular hardware, such as cables, servers and modulators and software applications to meet the requirements of a particular customer. Some of these same parts, perhaps in different quantities and using different software, could be used for a different customer.

The approach is similar to the Lego building block system, so apart from ensuring that the mix of 'blocks' is correct, product-line decisions revolve mainly around presenting different solutions to customer problems based upon a reconfiguration of the 'blocks'.

Custom-designed products

These products are custom-designed and built to meet the specific needs of a particular customer or very small group of customers. These products are often of high capital value. For example, a military tank or jet fighter, a power generation plant or a type of machine to be used by astronauts working on a space station.

Product-line decisions are based around identifying and understanding the very specific needs of customers and then being able to present proposals that provide a tight fit with those needs.

Business services

Almost all B2B organisations provide a service. The main offering may be a product but there are services attached such as order processing, invoicing, delivery and warranty-based support. Some organisations provide a specific service package to support their products (for example, computer support packages) while for some organisations service is their core business activity (for example, management consultants). Whatever the level of services provided they are, by definition, unique. As suggested earlier in this chapter, the very intangibility of a service means that each time it is delivered there will be a slight variance or difference in quality.

Product market strategies

The management of business products is tied closely with an organisation's business strategy. Business strategy is concerned with two main elements. The first element involves identifying the markets in which it chooses to compete, determining the products and/or services necessary to deliver superior value in those markets and deciding upon the resources and competences necessary for success. The second element of business strategy is about implementing these policies and decisions. It is about releasing and managing resources, building competences, driving change and stretching the organisation in order to achieve the objectives it has set for itself.

Core competences are the skills, capabilities and knowledge deemed necessary to compete in different markets. One of the key goals is to develop and maintain superior value in each market. To achieve this it is necessary to develop the core competences that will be required in the future, rather than at the moment. As the portfolio of products offered is an integral part of an organisation's core competences, analysis of it helps determine appropriate skills development.

SNAPSHOT 4.2

PRODUCT LINES AT AROPLUS

Aroplus are a manufacturer of specialist fluid management systems. Within their product range are two main lines of pumps and valves, designed for a range of industries. The first product line is for **fluid handling** and the second is for **fluid power**.

Note the depth of products and range of product items within the lines.

Fluid power	Fluid handling
Valves	**Piston pumps**
■ Solenoid actuated	■ Powder transfer systems
■ Pilot actuated	■ S-tran sanitary transfer
■ Manual actuated	■ De-watering pumps
■ Mechanical actuated	■ Aro-Tron accessories
■ Utility valves	■ Drum pumps
Cylinders	**Diaphragm pumps**
■ NFPA	■ Metallic: $\frac{1}{2}$"–3
■ Medium-duty round repairable	■ Non-metallic: $\frac{1}{4}$" through 2"
■ Disposable cylinders	
Air system components	**Speciality pumps**
■ F-R-Ls	■ Powder transfer systems
■ Blow guns	■ S-tran sanitary transfer
■ Balancers	■ De-watering pumps
■ Coil hose	■ Aro-Tron accessories
	■ Drum pumps
Air-logic and system communications	**Lubrication equipment**
■ Anti-tie down	■ Oil, grease and coolant pumps
■ Limit valves	■ Oil, grease and coolant packages
■ Controls	■ Drum pumps
■ Timers	**Mag-drive centrifugal pumps**
■ Elements	■ $\frac{1}{2}$" threaded through 80mm flange sizes
■ Liquid level sensors	
■ Systems communications	

Source: www.aroplus.co.uk/ (Accessed 29 October 2003.) Used with permission.

Portfolio models

To help analyse and understand the range and complexities of their products, organisations have used a number of portfolio management models. The Boston Consulting Group (BCG) Growth-Share, the General Electric and the Attractiveness-Strength Matrices are some of the better known models. These have been used for a number years, each has strengths and weaknesses, and none provides a complete solution.

The founding principle of these models is that business/products contribute to an organisation in different ways over the course of their life and according to the nature of the competition. A healthy portfolio is one which contains a balance of different products, all at different stages in their evolution. Readers wishing to know more about these particular portfolios and other management models are referred to www.valuebasedmanagement.net/methods_vbm.html.

These original grids offer useful insights and can help inform the strategic decisions necessary to maintain a competitive range of products. However, they are essentially historical constructs in that they reflect previous outcomes, namely sales. They fail to incorporate an indicative value of products for targeted, future customers. They represent a subjective interpretation of what relative market share actually means and there is an assumption that there is a direct relationship between market share and profitability, which may not be true or in line with an organisation's own measure of success. The other major shortcoming is that this is a snapshot of the position at a particular moment. What is really required is a form of time shift whereby this type of analysis can be projected into the future, then the question of core competencies can be re-evaluated.

One interesting new idea, based on the BCG matrix, is the Brand Leadership Matrix[RM] from Brandhub. Designed to assist strategy formulation in the consumer market, this matrix was developed specifically as a tool to analyse the strength of brands and the strategies used to support them. Using **market share** as an indicator of a brand's relative leadership position and **growth of market share** as an indicator of its relative market health, four brand types are distinguished. These are depicted at Figure 4.1.

Brands characterised as **underdogs** have low market visibility and low levels of customer awareness. They lack the investment necessary to enable them to compete successfully. The two most relevant strategies for underdogs are to exit the market or become a **challenger** brand through clear market segmentation and a strong differentiation strategy.

Challenger brands are growing and flexible as they meet the needs of clearly defined market segments. These brands often rely on a strong R&D and product development strategy and differentiate themselves clearly.

Leader brands dominate their market sector on a number of variables. In particular they are perceived to possess most of the determinant attributes or critical success factors necessary to be dominant. These brands have high levels of visibility and the majority of current and potential customers are aware of them. Continued investment in these brands is necessary, if only as a defence against aggressive challenger brands.

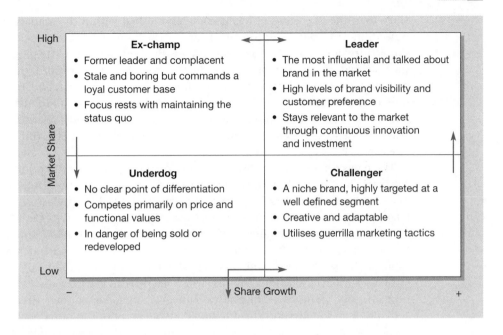

Figure 4.1 The Brand Leadership Matrix^{RM}. Copyright (2003) BrandHub Pte Ltd. All rights reserved.

Ex-champ brands have high market shares but experience negative or slowing market growth. These brands were once leader brands and are able to retain their established customers through strong levels of loyalty. However, ex-champ brands have difficulty attracting new customers because of low relevance and value to them. There are two main marketing strategies that can be followed. The first relies on milking the cash cow, as per the original BCG approach, and using the return to invest in other brands in the portfolio. The second strategy is based upon reversing the trend and returning the brand to leadership status. This might require heavy financial investment and suitable market opportunities.

Although developed for the consumer market, the Brand Leadership Matrix^{RM} could be used to interpret and analyse B2B product portfolios. While the detail of the marketing strategies might vary, for example there may be a different emphasis on the tools of the promotional mix used to communicate a product's positioning, this adaptation of the BCG grid approach is inherently intriguing and deserves a fuller B2B interpretation. More information about this approach can be found in Roolvink's paper (2002).

Product life cycle

The product life cycle (PLC) model follows the development of products in much the same way as the BCG suggests. Despite not using the term 'product life cycle', Dean (1950) is accredited with being the pioneer of the PLC model (Tibben-Lembke, 2002).

Since then the PLC concept has become established within the marketing literature. Indeed, most readers are probably aware of the basic dynamics associated with this simple interpretation of the way a market is thought to evolve. The product life cycle suggests that, like human beings, products have a life. They are born, they grow, they become mature and they eventually decline and die (Meenaghan and Turnbull, 1981; Rickard and Jackson, 2000). The theory describes the progress of products, in terms of sales volume, over time. In other words, it depicts the functional relationship between sales, the dependent variable and time, the independent variable (Brockhoff, 1967) (see Figure 4.2).

There has been some confusion about what the PLC represents and this has lead to a debate about how useful the concept really is. As a result of this, three main PLC formats have emerged. These are an industry or class interpretation (for example telephone communications), a product-based interpretation (for example wireless or mobile telephones) and a brand-based perspective (the Motorola V50). Each of these has particular characteristics, different shaped curves and different managerial implications. This book refers to the product category level of the product life cycle.

Many authors and commentators, when referring to the PLC, discuss the model in terms of four main stages or phases. However, this view ignores the development activities, investments and effort required by organisations to bring new products and services to the marketplace. In the light of this important phase, a five-stage model is considered more appropriate.

Development. In order to bring successful products to market a considerable amount of time and investment is devoted to comparing methods of construction, the efficacy of different materials, developing and field-testing prototypes and sample products and assessing their potential to deliver customer value. Depending upon the complexity and technical aspects of the product, time might be spent working with partner organisations. These may be collaborative suppliers or a buyer–seller partnership to exploit a market opportunity.

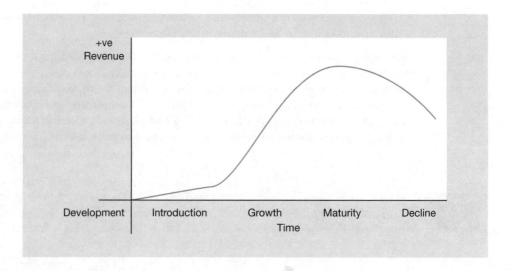

Figure 4.2 The product life cycle

Associated with this period is the training and personnel development necessary to launch products effectively. The level, intensity and scope of the training will reflect the nature of the product relative to the experience of the organisation. Those involved may typically be manufacturing, service delivery, customer support and sales personnel.

Introduction. This is the stage when the product enters the market for the first time. Not unsurprisingly, sales are low since most of the market are not aware of the new offering. With radically new products the supplier will have developed a new supply chain. During this period the supplier will experience a settling down period as organisations in the supply chain adapt to the new processes and procedures. Customers learn how to adapt their own systems and to incorporate or use the product within their own operations to their best advantage. It is a period in which marketing strategies are refined in the light of early feedback from initial customers.

Slowly sales build as more customers are attracted to and want to try the product. Profits remain low or even negative, reflecting the heavy development costs and initial promotional investment.

Growth. Also known as the 'take off stage', the period of growth signals market acceptance of the product. Increased demand boosts sales, which together with profits start to increase quickly and the overall market expands rapidly. Competitors who have been watching developments from the sidelines, in order to reduce their risk, now enter the market because demand is proven and their risk is lowered. However, the impact of this development is to increase supply and although sales volumes have increased rapidly, once competitive products enter the market the rate of growth will eventually subside. Therefore, organisations need to clearly differentiate their products. This normally involves developing particular attributes and offering a package of support facilities that provides greater value than that claimed by new (later) entrants. Growth results from the product being specified by B2B customers as an integral or significant part of their own product offerings. Care must be given to ensure that the new manufacturing volumes can be met and sustained.

Maturity. Demand continues to improve but at a decreasing rate. Most potential buyers have adopted the product and soon sales reach their highest point before starting to slow. Due to increased competition, an increasingly stagnant market and suppliers who have achieved high volumes of production, some even experiencing economies of scale, strategy becomes orientated to protecting the volume of production. Very often competitors resort to discounting and price-based strategies. The problem with this is that the focus is on market share rather than developing customer-perceived values, which would help to preserve margins.

One way to develop or refine value is to further segment the market and to find ways of differentiating the product more clearly. Levitt (1965) suggests that, in consumer markets, increased attention is given to packaging and advertising at this stage. In B2B markets increased attention should be given to service and customer support by leveraging the relationship. However, if these actions fail, or the product has been technologically superseded, the net result is that despite these investments, sales and profits start to fall.

Decline. The product eventually loses customer appeal as new products and new technologies enter the market. As a result the market consolidates as products (or organisations) are withdrawn. The focus of those that remain reverts to maintaining an efficient production capacity. Some companies will have major customers for whom maintaining supply of one product line is strategically important in order to sustain other orders from that customer. Those buyer and seller organisations with strong relationships will strive to support these declining products as part of the cooperative climate they have created. However, despite attempts to sustain these products, sales and profits decline.

In the light of the brief review above and the wealth of literature about the PLC, the following emerge as the main points of agreement:

- products have a limited life and their sales history follows an S-shaped path, at industry and product levels;
- products move through the different stages, within an overall cycle at different speeds (development, introduction, growth, maturity and decline);
- the life of the product can be extended by many ways, such as introducing new ways of using the product, finding new users, developing new attributes (for example, service enhancements);
- the average profitability per unit rises and then falls as products move through the later stages.

In the 1950s and 1960s, when markets focused on consumer goods, simple segmentation and unsophisticated communications, the product life cycle model was an acceptable interpretation of market dynamics (Wood, 1990). However, Dhalla and Yuspeh (1976) and then Wood began to cast doubt on the validity of the PLC concept. The former suggested that the sequential nature of the concept was the actual cause of its failure to be of any real assistance. They argued that the theory induces executives to neglect existing brands and place undue emphasis on new products. In this way, the company may not only lose an opportunity to prolong the life of a profitable offering, but also risk developing an ambitiously new product, one which requires a bigger budget than would be required to sustain an established product. Wood drew attention to the different levels of market stability that existed over the decades.

The PLC is a simple and intuitively appealing concept. Wood, Dhalla and Yuspeh and others have challenged its validity and practicality as a planning tool.

Technological applications and the PLC

Product lifecycle management solutions (PLM) are evolving to provide a way for all parties involved with different phases of the life cycle to collaborate with one another in order to reduce cycle costs and to reach their markets more quickly. Sometimes referred to as collaborative PLM, these systems seek to improve operational performance across the supply chain, from new product design through to decline and retirement.

SNAPSHOT 4.3

MATURE PUMPING MACHINERY

The pumping machinery industry provides some examples of the difficulties associated with managing products in the mature phase of the industry life cycle. Manufacturers in this industry deal largely with products which have been developed some time ago with heavy investment and which now represent an obstacle to change and development. As a result manufacturers must service, maintain and provide support, spare parts and associated maintenance data for product lines that are to a large extent obsolete.

Competition is intensive, especially as new players enter the market seeking to undercut established players. Price has become an important factor for those involved with market exchanges and catalogue items. However, many organisations are developing customised products, built on common engineering platforms. These are developed in what is referred to as an Engineered-to-Order (ETO) design environment and provide for increased differentiation and added value across a product range.

Source: Adapted from Dahl (2001), www.intellequip.com/publish/pdfs/FEDSM2001-18069.pdf (Accessed 1 December 2003.)

The material requirements, logistics and complex array of people, technologies and organisations involved with the cycle of product development and delivery mean that there has always been scope for inefficiency, communication breakdown and lengthy and expensive time delays. PLM applications are designed to foster collaboration among all those involved in managing the product life cycle, in particular the new product development process.

Modern PLM solutions use web-enabled technologies in order to blend all or some of the following applications: CAD/CAM (Computer Aided Design/Computer Aided Manufacturing), PDM, visualisation technologies, collaboration capabilities and integration with existing enterprise applications. PLM is considered to be an emerging market and although growth has to date been restricted, it is anticipated that these solutions will experience rapid growth. See, for example, offerings at www.applied-group.co.uk, the PLM pages on the IBM website www.ibm.com and articles at www.technologyevaluation.com.

It is expected that CAD/CAM, PDM, project management, sourcing and ERP and SCM integration capabilities will be the main constituents of leading PLM solutions over the next three years.

Strategic implications arising from the PLC

In order for a product to be successful, marketing activities need to be varied throughout its life. No one strategy is sufficient for a product to achieve its potential. Chattopadhyay (2001) believes that the way a product is managed, at each stage, is

Table 4.3 Features recommended for the different stages in the PLC

Authors	Introduction	Growth	Maturity	Decline
Fox and Rink (1977)	Low unit sales; losses or low profits; inexperience.	Sales increase more than 1% monthly; substantial profits.	Sales continue to increase but at a decreasing rate; profits levelling off and then declining.	Sales decline at an increasing rate 1% per month; declining profits.
Kotler (1991)	Low sales; negative profits; innovative costumers; few competitors.	Rapidly rising sales; increased profits; early adopters; increase in number of competitors.	Maximum sales; high profits level; all the potential consumers; stable competition starting to decrease.	Declining sales; low profits; laggard customers; low competition.
Parzinger (1997)	Slow sales growth; heavy expenses; no profits.	Rapid market acceptance; substantial profit increase.	Slow down in sales growth; profits stabilise.	Strong downward in sales; profits erode.

key to its survival. Each stage of the product life cycle requires different strategies. Each stage has particular characteristics and thus requires different strategies relating to promotion, pricing, distribution and competition, to achieve its objectives and to maximise profitability (Barksdale and Harris, 1982; Onkvisit and Shaw, 1983; Grantham, 1997).

Table 4.3 sets out some of the traditional tactics that some authors recommend should be employed for products at different stages. Although there are some semantic differences there is general agreement about the most appropriate tactics. However, these are normally proposed for consumer goods and avoid the strategic complications.

One strategy, referred to by Levitt (1965) is the 'used apple policy'. Here a company does not attempt to be first into a market, but chooses to wait while other companies do the pioneering and take the 'first bite of the apple'. If it is a 'juicy apple' these waiting organisations will then enter the market with a much reduced risk. The penalty for this approach is that they are unlikely to achieve market leadership and the best possible return on their investment. However, the second bite of a juicy apple is judged to be good enough. Shankar *et al.* (1999) support the 'used apple policy' as their research found that products which enter a market in the growth stage reach a high level of sales faster than the pioneer products. However, market strategies have already been shaped so there is reduced flexibility for radically changing elements of the marketing mix in order to improve their return.

Product differentiation is an important aspect of both the growth and maturity stages. Products that are able to find a strong position and which provide superior customer value are more likely to generate higher margins and help build relationships.

PLM AND CAR DEVELOPMENT

Product life cycle management (PLM) solutions help reduce product development costs and the time to market by implementing a pre-packaged set of capabilities specifically tailored for those in the supply chain. PLM applications provide a smooth flow of product information throughout an enterprise, a supply chain and across an entire product lifecycle.

For example, should a car manufacturer need to redesign a vehicle for markets with extremely cold environments, the entire (global) supply chain can be supplied digitally, with all necessary modification data. This enables suppliers to analyse and redesign each new component, thus ensuring the new design is engineered to perform to the new specifications.

Formula 1 racing car teams can make changes and experiment with new configurations much faster than before. Some major design changes are required between races, which may be just two weeks apart. These changes can result in quicker lap times, where even an improvement of just a fraction of a second can provide a team with a vital edge over its competitors. This would simply be impossible without digital, and in particular, PLM technology.

Source: Adapted from www.eds.be/html/newsroom/news_regional_jag.asp (Accessed 1 January 2004.); and www.ferret.com.au/articles/82/Oc01d582.asp (Accessed 18 August 2004.)

When a product reaches the latter end of its productive life, there are two main alternative ways to ending it. The first involves no managerial intervention and product sales decline steadily to the point where the product eventually dies. The second, which does require intervention, is referred to as 'euthanasia' and entails voluntary withdrawal of the product from the market. There is a possible third approach, which involves the rejuvenation of a product that was in decline, perhaps by proposing new uses or radically different target groups. This may require repositioning but, if physical changes are made, it is questionable whether it is the same product or a new one.

New product development (NPD)

An important part of the management of portfolios and product life cycles is to be able to control the development of new products. The reasons for this are many but the main ones include a need to balance the demise of older products, to provide new ways of providing superior customer value and to reduce the risks inherent when developing new products.

There are many approaches to new product development and the process and it would be wrong to suggest that there should be uniformity (Ozer, 2003). The procedures adopted by an organisation reflect its attitude to risk, its culture, strategy, the product and market and, above all else, its approach to customer relationships. This

Table 4.4 Four types of development project

Type of project	Explanation
Derivative projects	The incremental development of product and/or process improvements (e.g. new product features).
Platform projects	The creation of components that are shared by a mix of products and/or processes (e.g. a new battery to fit a range of products).
Breakthrough projects	The creation of genuine new products and/or processes (e.g. computer disks).
Research and development	The creation of new materials and technologies that lead to commercial development.

Source: Adapted from Wheelwright and Clark (1992).

ranges along a spectrum from an engineering approach at one end to a customer relationship perspective at the other. Those who exhibit an engineering approach tend to be product-orientated and prefer market or transactional exchanges. Some organisations try to generate new products either in response to gaps identified in markets or as a direct result of working with customers and developing products to meet their particular needs. These exhibit a preference for relational exchanges.

The term 'new products' can be misleading, because organisations do not just develop genuine new products. They also develop and extend products and services and they adapt and mould the processes associated with products. For example, in high-technology markets various project formats have been identified. Some projects centre on improving products but others focus on the associated manufacturing processes. Some projects look at both elements. Wheelwright and Clark (1992) suggest four types of development project (see Table 4.4).

Due to the complexity and risks associated with the development of new products, organisations usually adopt a procedural approach. These phases enable organisations to monitor progress, test-trial and consult before committing themselves to the market. The most common general new product development (NPD) process is set out at Figure 4.3. This sequence should be considered as a generalisation, and it should be appreciated that the various NPD episodes do not necessarily occur in the linear sequence that this depiction suggests. Furthermore, the process is essentially the same for both consumer and business markets. However, the one major difference concerns the level of end-user involvement. In consumer markets the level of customer involvement is restricted and distant. In business markets customer involvement, especially where collaborative relationship conditions exist, is actively encouraged and is an important driver in the overall process.

Idea generation

Ideas for new products should not be expected to emerge just from the marketing department. Responsibility for the generation of great ideas that lead to great new products should rest with everyone. That means a corporate culture which fosters creativity and supports people when they bring forward new ideas for product processes,

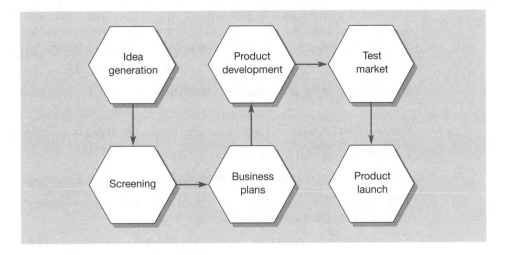

Figure 4.3 The new product development process

enhancements and other improvements. Ideally, new ideas should be driven by customers and so reflect a sharing and collaborative relationship. In many cases this happens but ideas can emerge from many other sources. The origin of these ideas can be classified as either internal or external sources.

Internal sources include R&D departments, customer service employees, the sales force, project development teams and secondary data sources such as sales records. This list should emphasise the breadth of the internal sources available to organisations when seeking to develop their portfolios.

External sources include market research data, competitors, website and sales literature analysis, and customers themselves who draw attention to specific problems or their own market opportunities.

In some business markets there are a few customers who dominate the volume of purchases made in that sector (for example, capital equipment markets). These small number of customers are referred to as **lead users** and are the equivalent to early adopters in consumer markets (von Hippel, 1982). Working with these lead users to identify opportunities can be beneficial, as it is probable that if their needs can be met then the rest of the market will subsequently follow on.

Screening

All ideas need to be evaluated in order that only those that meet predetermined criteria are taken forward. This screening process must be separate to the idea generation stage otherwise creativity might be hampered. Concept testing allows for a small representative sample of customers to review the product idea in order to gauge their attitudes before any substantial investment is made to develop the idea further.

Screening needs to ensure that the proposed new product meets strategic criteria and fits with organisational objectives. Following the earlier consideration of core competences, all new ideas should be evaluated in the light of the future competences that are determined as necessary to provide customer value. The other screening process involves considering the ideas in the light of how it is believed the market will react and the effort that the organisation will need to make to bring the product to the market.

Business plans and market analysis

Drucker (1985) determined that there were three main reasons why new products fail:

1 There is no market for the product.

2 There is a market need but the product does not meet customer requirements.

3 The product's ability to meet the market need, although satisfactory, is not adequately communicated to the target market.

It is crucial that, as well as a thorough analysis of the size, shape and dynamics of the market, a business plan is prepared. From this information the potential profitability can be established early on. Weak profit forecasts, problematic manufacturing requirements, market need already being met by stronger competitive products or the market simply not being strong enough, are all indicators that the product proposal may not be in the best interests of the organisation and should be dropped.

Product development and selection

Management must decide, in the light of all the information at their disposal, which of the ideas that have reached this stage in the process are selected for further development. Those ideas that are selected and progress from this point are now clearly deemed to have commercial potential.

It is at this stage that prototypes and test versions are developed and subjected to functional performance tests, design revisions, manufacturing requirements analysis, distribution investigations and a multitude of other testing procedures. The objective is to minimise risk and maximise potential. Consequently there is a trade-off between the need to test and reduce risk and the need to go to market and drive income.

SNAPSHOT 4.5

NPD AT IBM

In some situations organisations realise that their current new product development processes are insufficient or no longer appropriate. For example, IBM established a completely different NPD approach in order to design and launch their first PC. This was achieved by creating a team that was free of the rules and procedures that typified the then largely bureaucratic and hierarchically managed IBM.

Again when IBM developed their ThinkPad notebook computers in the 1990s, the organisation used new process and procedures to enable the collaboration of internal and external resources across three continents.

Source: Sakakibara (1995)

Test market

The urge to go to market is tempered by the penultimate stage of taking the product, in its finished format, to a test market. This piloting procedure is designed to launch and test the product under controlled, real market conditions. Using a particular geographical region or specific number of customer locations the intention is to evaluate the product and the whole marketing programme under real working conditions. Test marketing, or field trials, enable the product and marketing plan to be refined or adapted in the light of market reaction, before release to the whole market. Again the overriding goal is to reduce risk.

Test marketing in terms of regional or limited customer conditions does not apply to new products that have been developed through collaborative customer–seller relationships. Under these relational conditions the product is first tested by the customer, with the intention of fine tuning the final product.

Product launch

The launch of a final product into a target market represents the culmination of the preceding tests, analysis and development work. To launch a new product organisations normally prepare a **launch plan**. This considers the needs of distributors, end-user customers, marketing communication agencies and other relevant stakeholders, many of them internal. The objective is to schedule all those activities that are required to make the launch successful.

In addition to promotional work such as the preparation of articles and features to appear in trade and technical journals, customers and/or dealers need to be advised. First, they need to be informed and educated in terms of product capabilities; later, they need to be trained to use the product. In addition to the obvious need to train and instruct the sales force, internal customer support services, such as finance, distribution, order processing and the communications team should be included in the launch plan. The purpose is to enable them to provide product support based on appropriate knowledge and training so that they understand how customers are expected to use the product and what to do to enable them to derive its full benefits.

New product development issues

Cycle time

This development process will inevitably vary in length according to the type of project, market and the level of technical complexity. However, it is generally assumed that it is a good thing to reduce the amount of time given to new product development, the cycle time. In many sectors it can be vital to get new products to the market in the shortest possible time in order to gain competitive advantage. Indeed, some regard this

Table 4.5 Key factors that influence development cycle time

Factors associated with cycle time	Explanation
Project strategy	Product complexity, strategic intent, level of innovativeness and technical difficulty.
Development process characteristics	Formality, process structure, and number of steps.
Organisational characteristics	Level at which projects are assigned and the degree to which team work is required.
Firm characteristics	Type of leadership, firm size and level of innovation.

Source: Adapted from Griffin (1997). Copyright © 1997. With permission from Elsevier.

form of response to changing conditions in the environment as an imperative (Menon *et al.*, 2002). It is also assumed that shorter cycle time leads to successful new products. In addition, there is a strong argument that a shorter cycle time will reduce financial costs and thus enable employees to work on other projects (Griffin, 2002).

NPD processes are influenced by a four main factors (Griffin, 1997). These are the project strategy, development process characteristics, organisational characteristics and firm characteristics (see Table 4.5).

Research undertaken by Griffin (2002) into B2B cycle times did not find any statistically rigorous associations. However, she did determine that formalised product development procedures and processes have, on average, the shortest cycle times. These are best epitomised by new product development **committees** which operate with people assigned from functional departments and without formal power or resources. In stark contrast, new product development **departments** consisting of fully employed people, whose sole job it is to develop new products across the organisation, have the longest cycle times. This, she reflects, may be a function of the types of projects assigned to these respective groups, with the absence of any power, authority and resources (available to the committee format), provoking high levels of interpersonal skills in order to get things done.

Supplier involvement

A further significant issue concerns the degree to which suppliers should be involved in the new product development process. Good relationship management practice indicates that buyers and sellers should work in a collaborative manner. However, as levels of relationship vary, the degree to which suppliers should be involved in the NPD will also vary. Wynstra and Pierick, (2000) determined a supplier involvement portfolio in order that organisations assign suitable resources to the NPD process. Based on the level of responsibility assigned to the supplier and the level of risk, it is possible to determine four different types of supplier involvement (see Figure 4.4).

Each of these four types of supplier involvement leads to guidelines for managing the project-related relationship. These consider the levels of ambiguity and uncertainty felt by the supplier to determine the most appropriate communications in terms of type of media, frequency and the richness or quality of information conveyed.

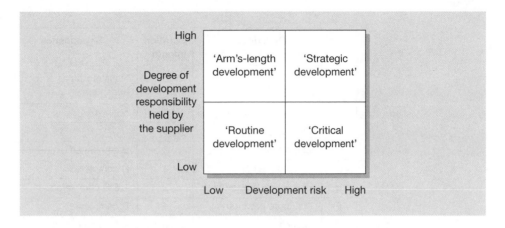

Figure 4.4 The supplier involvement portfolio

Source: Reprinted from Wynstra and Pierick, Copyright © (2000). With permission from Elsevier.

Use of technology in new product development

The launch of new products can be very complex so management need to be able to control and monitor the procedure, not least to ensure that key dates are met. Information systems and technology can play a significant role and provide a range of different benefits. Project management techniques, such as Gantt charts or critical path analysis (CPA) (see below), and the use of generic or bespoke software, such as PLM applications (see pp. 90–2) can be helpful. In terms of collecting information on potential markets and competitive products/services, the Internet can greatly facilitate

---

SNAPSHOT 4.6

COLLABORATIVE NPD AT PROFILE

Profile Respiratory Systems operate in the nebuliser and compressor technology business. Their new product development projects deliberately involve some of their customers and suppliers.

Collaboration is important to Profile because it is a means of reducing risk and acquiring the necessary skill sets. Approximately ten per cent of their suppliers are categorised as **Strategically Significant Suppliers** and these are actively involved with the development and refinement of the established product range.

In order to develop revolutionary new products their strategy is based on the involvement of either potential or established customers. They help in the design and specification of radically new products while Profile out-source (subcontract) the actual design and development work to appropriate companies who have the leading-edge skills in particular areas of design, engineering, electronics and related technologies.

Source: Personal interviews (April 2000). Used with permission.

Task	Description	Duration (months)	Dependency
S	Start	0	None (assumes proposal accepted)
A	Develop launch plan	2	S
B	Develop prototype	6	S
C	Test prototype	2	B completed
D	Test marketing	3	C completed
E	Train sales/support staff	2	A & D completed
F	Distribute product	1	D completed
Z	Launch	0	E & F completed

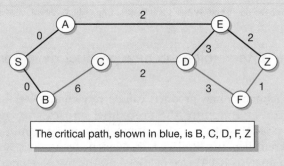

The critical path, shown in blue, is B, C, D, F, Z

Figure 4.5 An example of critical path analysis

the NPD process. The relevance of such research and usefulness of the findings will vary according to how innovative the product is, the level of collaboration with other partner organisations and, as Ozer (2003) postulates, will be greater for organisations operating in B2B rather than consumer markets.

Critical path analysis breaks down a project, such as new product development, into its constituent tasks and the relationship between them (see Figure 4.5). By estimating the time each task will take and analysing the inter-dependencies it is possible to see which tasks are crucial to completing the project on time. Less critical tasks can be delayed if necessary. As tasks are completed the CPA diagram is updated. Criticalities may change over time and should be monitored carefully. CPA software is available, for example within Microsoft Project, to facilitate the entry of tasks, experimentation with timescales and criticality and the output of charts and other project-planning devices.

Interested readers might like to try using the free CPA calculator available on-line at www.engin.umd.umich.edu/CIS/tinytools/cis375/f00/cpm/CPM(1).HTM to check, or change and recalculate, the critical path shown in Figure 4.5.

In addition to controlling the launch, it is important to measure and evaluate the impact and results of the launch process. Sales figures are often used but a more sophisticated approach would involve an appraisal of the extent to which various objectives were met in the process.

Stage gates

Cooper (1993) developed the idea of **stage gates** principally to eliminate weaker ideas very early in the overall process and to improve the success rate of new product launches. His research indicates that those organisations that use the approach experience superior new product success, although it should be added that the number appears to be limited.

Cooper claims that progression from one stage of the new product development process to another should be managed by the use of stage gates. These gates are predetermined milestones, or precise sets of goals, that must be reached before progress to the next stage is permitted. The goals consist of two main elements, one relating to the market/business and the other to the technical aspects of the product.

This process is based on a rigid managerial adherence to particular features of the process. In order for it to work, it is necessary to have quite extensive information which may explain why it is not widely used. An associated idea is the use of process owners (Griffin, 2002; McGrath *et al.* 1992). These individuals are responsible, across the organisation, for the enforcement of the new product development processes and procedures, regardless of the complexity, experience or level at which the process is taking place. Griffin reports that, in a large number of cases, process owners can reduce the cycle time.

The technology adoption life cycle

An interesting variant of the PLC is the technology adoption life cycle, proposed by Moore (1991). This model was developed to explain the way in which high-technology products are adopted by customers. Of particular interest are breakthrough or discontinuous innovations. These are new products/services that require users to break away from established behaviours, to behave differently and derive other benefits. Moore refers to dramatic changes in behaviour and spectacular benefits to be gained.

The idea builds on the innovation diffusion model, offered by Rogers (1983), but identifies different types of buyer (see Table 4.6).

From technophiles, through visionaries, pragmatists, conservatives to sceptics or laggards, these customer groups all use these discontinuous products but adopt them at different times, for different reasons. Business-to-business marketing should account for these different customer segments and develop appropriate strategies.

Sales of these high-technology products follow a cycle similar to that in Figure 4.6. Technophiles are influential in that they will provide credibility and endorsement for a new technical product. Visionaries on the other hand have the resources necessary to adopt these products. However, they will invariably demand changes and adaptions to the product which pose problems for the supplying organisation. Technophiles and visionaries provide early growth and visibility for these innovative products but, as Moore observed, sales often begin to fall after a bright start and a chasm develops between the visionaries and the pragmatists. Pragmatists are analytical and provide a route to the mass markets. The trick is to be able to cross the chasm

Table 4.6 Different types of buyer in high-technology markets

Type of customer		Key characteristics
Moore	**Rogers**	
Technophiles	Innovators	Customers who enjoy using and mastering new technological products. They like to be at the forefront of developments and to be seen to be involved in developing and shaping how products are perceived. They do not always have sufficient influence over resources to impact on organisation-wide adoption. However, they do have a big influence over visionaries.
Visionaries	Early adopters	Customers who can see the competitive advantage to be gained from being first to use new technology products in their industry. However, they often demand customised solutions which are often difficult to deliver. As in consumer markets, this group is characterised by their willingness to accept high levels of risk (for high reward).
Pragmatists	Early majority	Evolution rather than revolution characterises the views of this group. Rather than be passionately involved they see technology as a necessity. They will buy once the products have been tested by others and even then are dependent upon third-party recommendation. Despite their slightly cautious approach the majority of mainstream high-technology sales are made to this group.
Conservatives	Late majority	This group are reluctant to involve themselves with new technological solutions and doubt the value they bring to an organisation. Purchases are made because of a fear of being left behind the competition but even then price is a sensitive issue and they demand a great deal in negotiations.
Sceptics	Laggards	This is not a viable customer group as they are critical of technology and do not believe technology can improve productivity. They often strive to block new technological initiatives.

Source: Adapted from Moore (1991). Used with permission.

and sell into the high-volume purchasers and then sell on to the conservatives, who although reluctant to buy high-technology products do so because they do not want to be left behind in the market.

To get across the chasm the seller needs to find a niche market of pragmatists who are willing to risk purchase without the support of other pragmatists. A very customer-focused strategy is required to target buyers who have a real need for the innovation. Moore asserts that once the chasm is breached a tornado strategy often develops as sales rise rapidly. This is because these buyers prefer to buy from a market leader, which in turn leads to the development of new industry-wide standards and the rush of new peripheral products and software that support the product.

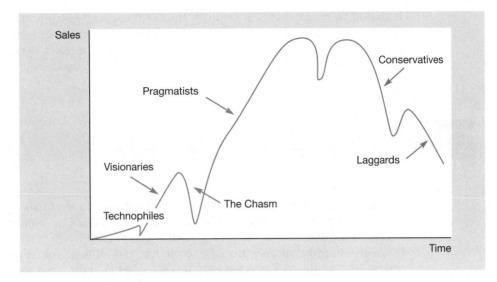

Figure 4.6 The technology adoption life cycle.

Source: Adapted from Moore, 1991. Copyright © 1991 by Geoffrey A. Moore Consulting Inc. Reprinted by permission of HarperCollins Publishers.

SNAPSHOT 4.7

TECHNOLOGY ADOPTION LIFE CYCLE

The development and relative success of online B2B market exchanges reflects many of the trends associated with the technology adoption life cycle.

The first generation exchanges were heralded as the future for all B2B exchange activity. A large number of exchanges were set up, by buyers, sellers and third parties. However, during this first phase sellers became increasingly wary of the process because they were generally having their prices cut and margins reduced. Sellers withdrew and as a result the industry retrenched as a period of shakeout took place.

The number of market exchanges in the car manufacturing industry have been severely reduced, but the Ford/General Motors-initiated exchange 'Covisint', formed out of the merger of their separate B2B operations, dominates. By way of contrast the UK Construction industry is relatively devoid of any significant exchanges, although it is reported that there are 80 independent yet small construction-related sites. The retail industry is populated with several sites, such as the Worldwide Retail Exchange (WWRE) and Transora, which is a sellers hub, but no standard appears to prevail.

So, after the initial growth there followed a period of consolidation in 2000 and 2001. Lately, however, there has been renewed interest in the development of privately owned exchanges, where membership is based on invitation, credentials are checked thoroughly and supported by non-disclosure contracts and agreements. Crossing the 'chasm' will be achieved through some of the very large players and the 'tornado' might be stimulated by the vast number of other suppliers and buyers who perceive the many cost and efficiency advantages of being involved where there is a standard platform and fair business model.

It should be noted that there is little empirical research to support Moore's ideas. However, there is a great deal of observational research that endorses this interpretation and the strategies that explain the initial break in sales development (the 'chasm') and the rush of sales (the 'tornado') that often occurs later.

Pricing

Product price is one of the more complex and critical decisions that managers must make. It is critical because price impacts not only on the volume of products sold, but also the contribution that the product makes to the organisation's overall profit performance. In addition, the price of one product can influence other products in the mix or line, while price is often used by customers as short-hand for quality, value and market position. Despite the importance and critical nature of pricing in B2B markets, according to Shipley and Jobber (2001) it is a poorly managed aspect of marketing management.

Price in business markets differs from consumer markets in many ways. Two of the more important differences concern the perception and flexibility of price. Although perceived value is a primary determinant of a product's worth to both consumers and business customers, consumers consider price in relation to similar, competitive products. Their evaluation of price can be strongly influenced by horizontal comparison. In business markets price can be evaluated in the context of the relative value the product represents within the customer's supply chain. For example, the more crucial a part or assembly is to the manufacturing process and the lower the opportunity for the customer to substitute one product with that of a rival, the higher the price (and margins) are likely to be.

Prices in retail markets are generally fixed (list prices) and these constitute a major part of a consumer's decision making process. In business markets price is subject to discounting, negotiation, tendering and competitive bidding approaches.

Prices can be set in two main ways. One is an **inside-out** approach and the other is **outside-in**.

Inside-out pricing

This approach to pricing assumes that price is a reflection of the costs incurred in developing, manufacturing and bringing the product to market. This **inside-out** approach, or cost-based pricing, is used a great deal in B2B marketing but it is problematic. One of the main problems concerns the identification and accurate allocation of the real costs involved in this process. Another problem is its lack of market orientation. By accumulating the costs and adding a margin, the resultant price may be higher than the market is willing or able to pay. As Christopher (2000) suggests, this approach assumes that customers are actually interested in the supplier's costs, whereas their principal concern rests with managing their own costs.

Outside-in pricing

This approach starts by considering the customer's perception of the price and the value they attribute to the product. This value is determined by the perceived benefits product ownership will bring. These benefits are assessed in terms of what the product will enable the customer to do, and/or how it will solve particular problems.

At the beginning of this chapter products were considered in terms of their tangible and intangible attributes. It is these intangible attributes, for example, the guarantees, support and servicing, that provide the enhanced value and the price that customers are willing to pay. Therefore, the pricing decision should be based on disaggregating the intangible attributes to determine the benefits customers perceive (value) in each of the individual elements that constitute the whole.

Inside-out approaches are intuitively more appealing and easier to determine through an organisation's financial management information systems. There are implementation difficulties associated with the outside-in approach, which impede its overall adoption. However, if pricing decisions are linked to segmentation strategy based on customers' perceived value, then it is easier to identify individual customer benefits. The use of customer questionnaires to isolate key attributes that deliver different value together with conjoint analysis to determine the trade-off customers are prepared to make between attributes at different price levels, enables suppliers to establish the perceived value of the different attributes. It is from this point that it becomes possible to build a price relative to customer value (see Christopher, 2000) for more information).

Strategic and tactical pricing

As with any management task the setting of objectives informs and frames the decisions that follow. Pricing objectives are no different and several overall goals should be considered when developing pricing strategy. The first concerns the level of desired profitability as price influences volume and margins. Second, price needs to be set in the context of the relationships the organisation has or hopes to develop. Setting what might be perceived as a maximum price within a category may be regarded as exploitative. This could lower trust and, in effect, raise barriers to a mutually beneficial long-term relationship. Therefore, price needs to be set such that the perceived value is deemed fair, relative to the benefits derived.

There are other strategic objectives which may have a direct impact on price. For example, an organisation may wish to maximise profits prior to selling a product (or an organisation). Price might be used to discourage competitors from entering a market, or to enter a new market and become established. There are a few pricing strategies and a number of methods.

Pricing strategies

Price skimming occurs when there are few competitors and customers are willing to pay higher prices in order be associated with the values and benefits of the new product. Skimming also occurs as a positioning tool, to convey prestige and high status.

Penetration pricing is the opposite to skimming. The goal is to sell at a low price during the introductory and growth stage of a new product. This approach, common in low-technology markets, can generate high relative market shares and can be effective in deterring competitors from entering the market.

Price leadership opportunities arise when an organisation has high market share and there are many ways in the category to develop customer value.

Follow the leader strategies are advisable when there few ways to reduce costs, relative to competitors, and the product category has few ways to increase value. This strategy can often be seen in commodity markets.

Pricing methods

Many of the methods used by organisations to price business products are based on the inside-out costing approach. These include:

Mark-up pricing involves applying a set percentage of the cost of production or purchase price.

Break-even pricing is similar to mark-up pricing except that both direct and variable costs are incorporated. The method requires the calculation of the number of units that need to be sold in order to cover all costs associated with the production of those units.

Peak-load pricing, unlike the previously mentioned methods, takes into account customer demand. By understanding levels of demand and system capacities it is possible to use price to smooth demand to manageable levels. Telephone companies will price off-peak calls at a lower rate, thereby encouraging some users to use the system at different times. The same principles apply to those supplying gas, electricity and water. The main advantage is that the overall system does not have to be built (capacity) to meet 100 per cent demand. This saves on investment, return and the overall cost base. Road-haulage and container-shipping companies use peak-load pricing concepts in order to smooth demand. For example, the Society of Glass and Ceramic Decorators reported that TSA shippers were planning to apply a $300 per container surcharge during the peak shipping season from 1 June to 30 November. (www.sgcd.org/update399_6.html) (Accessed 29 December 2003.)

Marginal cost pricing is often used by organisations such as airlines and hotels, who have high fixed costs. By trying to cover just the variable costs the organisation, especially in times of recession and economic downturn, is able to generate a contribution rather than no revenue at all.

Product line pricing moves away from an individual product, cost-based approach to one which takes into account the relationship between all the products in a particular line. The objective is to allow customers to choose lines according to their price (value) range and to allow the organisation to maximise their profits across the lines. Although this method is preferred more by retailers than by manufacturers, there are instances of manufacturers selling the same line to different markets, taking advantage of the different levels of price elasticity, to maximise profits.

Competitive bidding is undertaken by a significant number of organisations and forms the basis for a large number of transactions in both private and public sector organisations. For example, in the UK construction industry, the development and formulation of bids is thought to cost approximately 5 per cent of the total value of contracts awarded in any single year (Wykes, 2003). Therefore bidding not only consumes a large amount of resources but also represents an area in which significant efficiency gains can be made. Partly as a response to these issues online resources have been used to provide effective and more efficient solutions. For example, Freight Traders is an online intermediary, which uses web-based applications, many of them founded on game theory. (Game theory is a mathematical process used to determine the optimum decision in a situation in which two or more people, who share resources, have a similar decision to make. The key characteristic is that the various solutions represent various potential conflicts for all parties). Their aim is to bring shippers (with cargo to send) together with carriers (with transport capacity to fill). It uses tendering and quick quotes as the primary ways of broking parties' requirements (see Snapshot 4.8).

SNAPSHOT 4.8

TENDERING FOR KELLOGG'S DELIVERIES

The Kellogg Company approached Freight Traders with the task of improving the carrier base while holding costs and maintaining service. Freight Traders used the tendering process to negotiate contracts for the work of transporting Kellogg's breakfast cereal and snack foods from Manchester to over 100 UK destinations.

The competitive tenders, for both less than truckload (LTL) and full truck load (FTL), ran concurrently for ten days in the first quarter of 2002. The bidding process, which only took three months from start to the award of contracts, was based on partitioning the country into postcode regions and then inviting carriers to submit bids based on stem mileage and additional drops. There were three phases in the process: bid collection, scenario planning and finally a negotiation phase.

The 'stem mileage' is the cost to deliver between the source and the final destination postcode area, and 'additional drops' refers to the cost for each delivery en route. For example, a carrier offering a stem mileage of £250 with additional drops of £20 would charge £290 if there were two deliveries en route.

After analysing the bids, the lowest cost scenario had to be ruled out because it used more than one carrier per region (not desirable) and because it used 11 carriers there would have been expensive management costs. To achieve a regional solution, Freight Traders considered numerous scenarios. The eventual recommendation used eight carriers and was only slightly more than the lowest cost solution. Once the optimum solution was identified, Kellogg's approached the successful carriers, individually, to negotiate terms.

Source: Adapted from www.freight-traders.com/ (Accessed 30 December 2003). Used with permission.

Competitive bidding occurs when buyers ask suppliers to tender to supply particular goods or services. There are two main types of bidding, closed and open. In closed bids only the customer knows the value of all the bids and normally selects the lowest offer, although on occasions the best overall value bid is elected. In open bids suppliers are able to see each other's offers and make adjustments accordingly. The buyer uses this approach to drive up the value of the offers in order to maximise the potential of the work. The natural progression from closed and open bidding is an auction. New technology has given auctions a new dimension and enabled both buyers and suppliers to reduce their costs. Snapshot 4.9 shows an illustration of an online auction and more information about online auctions can be found in Chapter 5.

SNAPSHOT 4.9

Online Auction

Below is one example of an online auction posting taken from the DoveBid® Business Auctions & Valuations Worldwide site.

Automotive Exchange II (Europe)

Automotive Exchange II Europe including assets from **FORD**, **MESSIER BUGATTI**, **DELPHI DIESEL**, **ARVIN MERITOR**, **DANA AUTOMOTIVE**, **VALEO**

Automotive Equipment, Featuring CNC Machining Centres & Vertical Borers,

Gear, Tube, Toolroom, Finishing & Material Handling Equipment
Assets from France, Netherlands, Belgium, Germany & Italy

Auction Type	Location	Starts	Ends
Online*	DoveBid.com (Europe)	6/3/03 7:00 AM UTC+01	6/3/03 4:00 PM UTC+01

Main Asset Type(s):	Automotive Equipment, Featuring CNC Machining Centres & Vertical Borers, Gear, Tube, Toolroom, Finishing & Material Handling Equipment
	Commercial Transportation
	Metalworking & Machine Tools
	Plant Support, Material Handling & Facility Equipment

* To participate, bidders must create a DoveBid account and agree to any event-specific terms and conditions. Since bids are accepted and processed by a computer server, your results may differ from traditional auctioneer-led sales. No additional software is required.

Source: www.dovebid.com/default.asp
(Accessed 2 June 2003.) Used with permission.

The Internet allows for dynamic pricing, which can often be observed through reverse auctions (Smeltzer and Carr, 2002). This means that the market price for an item alters instantaneously when auctioned electronically. An assumption is made by sellers that as prices change in real time so prices will continue to decline until the market price is reached, a point at which demand is equal to supply. Sellers can see the actual price levels required to obtain the sell.

Leasing

An important variant to the outright purchase of products is leasing. The use of leasing in business markets has grown especially in markets where there are substantial fixed costs or where technology changes quickly. Three types of leases can be identified: sales/leaseback leases, operating leases and capital leases (Wengartner, 1987) (see Table 4.7).

Leasing enables organisations to reduce their exposure to debt and to concentrate their use of debt on areas where it is strategically more imperative. It frees up resources to enter markets or acquire the latest technology or capital equipment. Unfortunately, leasing can tie an organisation into particular equipment or a specific technology for a long period of time. This can prevent the organisation from making changes when the environment or internal conditions change.

In an attempt to improve the way in which organisations manage the pricing process, Shipley and Jobber (2001) suggest an integrative pricing technique. This multistage process, or 'wheel' seeks to incorporate a range of influences and issues into the pricing process. However, although this is admirable in terms of the process and range of issues covered, it perpetuates a costing orientation. Organisations need to develop a more relational approach to their pricing by understanding the value customers derive from the products and services and then work this information into their pricing procedures.

Finally, although the pricing of services is very similar to that of products, particular issues arise from the perishability characteristic. In an attempt to manage demand pricing must take into account the capacity of the service system and the likely or

Table 4.7 Types of leasing arrangements

Type of Lease	Explanation
Sales/leaseback	Assets are sold to a leasing company and then leased back to the original owners for a fee over a fixed period of time. The advantage of this approach is the cash receipt resulting from the initial sale.
Operating leases	Maintenance of the asset is often included in these financial arrangements. There is no transfer of ownership (of the asset) when the payment schedule is complete.
Capital leases	Having agreed a purchase price with the supplier, customers then arrange a capital lease with a leasing company. There is no maintenance facility within these leases nor can they be cancelled.

Source: After Wengartner (1987).

known patterns of demand that occur. Peak-load and off-peak pricing strategies can help smooth demand and in conjunction with a variety of price incentive programmes demand and capacity can be brought into a reasonable balance.

Readers who are interested in pricing issues and wish to know more about the pricing process, objectives and more detailed methodologies are referred to Brassington and Pettitt (2003) and Kotler (2003).

Summary

The value that organisations perceive within their relationships with suppliers, whether they be collaborative partners or price-orientated opportunists, is partly based on the business products and services transacted. Through the development of a consistent stream of new products, by developing appropriate core competences and by recognising the significance of both tangible and intangible attributes to particular customers, business organisations are able to develop market advantages based around the concept of superior value.

If superior value is competitively significant, organisations should ensure that they have suitable product and management strategies and processes. Although no one approach can be highlighted, best performances seem to emerge from the use of a wide range of techniques, some of which have been presented and reviewed in this chapter.

Realising product potential and managing an array of products through lines, mixes, portfolios and life cycles requires flexibility and a realistic understanding of market requirements some of which, especially in high-technology markets, are subject to sudden and rapid change.

Pricing is also a significant factor in the perception of superior value. As market value is determined by customers, it is important that supplying organisations understand the total contribution their offering provides their customers. This should be considered in terms of the life-time value to the customer and the associated total costs that a customer experiences. However, it should be recognised that in the majority of business-to-business markets and customer relationships, price alone does not create customer value.

Discussion questions

1 Identify and explain the four main product line categories which are based upon the level of customisation, as suggested by Shapiro (1977).

2 Prepare arguments for and against the use of product portfolios.

3 Identify the key characteristics and evaluate the different types of buyer said by Moore (1991) to typify high-technology markets.

4 Discuss some of the key issues associated with the new product development process.

5 Make a list of the various ways in which technology can be used to develop value through products and pricing.

6 Explain three pricing strategies and three pricing methods. Discuss the key characteristics associated with leasing and bidding.

References

Barksdale, H.C. and Harris, C.E. Jr (1982). 'Portfolio analysis and the product life cycle', *Long Range Planning*, 15, (December), pp. 74–83.

Brassington, F. and Pettitt, S. (2003). *Principles of Marketing*, 3rd edn, Harlow: Pearson Education.

Brockhoff, K. (1967). 'A test for the product life cycle', *Econometrica*, 35, 3–4, pp. 472–84.

Chattopadhyay, S.P. (2001). 'Relationship marketing in an enterprise resource planning environment', *Marketing Intelligence and Planning*, 19, 2, pp. 136–9.

Christopher, M. (2000). 'Pricing Strategy', in Cranfield School of Management (eds), *Marketing Management: A Relationship Marketing Perspective*, Basingstoke: Macmillan.

Cooper, R.G. (1993). *Winning at New Products*, Reading, MA: Addison Wesley.

Dahl, T. (2001). 'The evolution of the pump business in the information age', *Proceedings of ASME Fluids Engineering Division Summer Meeting*, New Orleans, LA, 29 May – 1 June, www.intellequip.com/publish/pdfs/FEDSM2001-18069.pdf (Accessed 1 December 2003).

Dean, J. (1950). 'Pricing policies for new products', *Harvard Business Review*, 28, 6, pp. 45–53.

Dhalla, N.K. and Yuspeth, S. (1976). 'Forget the product life cycle', *Harvard Business Review*, 54 (January/February), pp. 102–4.

Drucker, P. (1985). 'The discipline of innovation', *Harvard Business Review*, 63 (May–June), pp. 167–72.

Fox, H.W. and Rink, D.R. (1997). 'Coordination of purchasing with sales trends', *The Journal of Supply Chain Management*, 13, 4 (Winter), pp. 10–18.

Grantham, L.M. (1997). 'The validity of the product life cycle in the high-tech industry', *Marketing Intelligence and Planning*, 15, 1, pp. 4–10.

Griffin, A. (1997). 'The effect of project and process characteristics on product development cycle time', *Journal of Market Research*, 34, (February), pp. 24–35.

Griffin, A. (2002). 'Product development cycle time for business-to-business products', *Industrial Marketing Management*, 31, 4, pp. 291–304.

Gronroos, C. (2000). *Service Management and Marketing*, 2nd edn, Chichester: Wiley.

Heskett, J.L., Sasser, Jr., W.E. and Schlesinger, L.A. (1997). *The Service Profit Chain: How Leading Companies Link Profit and Growth to Loyalty, Satisfaction and Value*, New York, NY: The Free Press.

Hutt, M. and Speh, T. (2001). *Business Marketing Management*, 7th edn, Fort Worth, TX: Harcourt.

Kotler, P. (2003). *Marketing Management*, International Edition, 11th edn, Englewood Cliffs, NJ: Pearson Education.

Levitt, T. (1965). 'Exploit the product life cycle', *Harvard Business Review*, 43, (November/December), pp. 81–94.

Lovelock, C., Vandermerwe, S. and Lewis, B. (1999). *Services Marketing*, Hemel Hempstead: Financial Times/Prentice Hall.

McGrath, M.E., Anthony, M.T. and Shapiro, A.R. (1992). *Product Development: Success Through Product and Cycle-Time Excellence*, Stoneham, MA: Butterworth-Heinemann.

Meenaghan, A., and Turnbull, P.W. (1981). 'The application of product life cycle theory to popular record marketing', *European Journal of Marketing*, 15, 5, pp. 1–50.

Menon, A., Chowdhury, J. and Lukas, B.A. (2002) 'Antecedents and outcomes of new product development speed; an interdisciplinary conceptual framework', *Industrial Marketing Management*, 31, 4 (July) pp. 317–28.

Moore, G.A. (1991). *Crossing the Chasm: Marketing and Selling Technology Products to Mainstream Customers'*, New York, NY: HarperCollins.

Onkvist, S. and Shaw, J.F. (1983). 'Examination of the product life cycle and its applications within marketing', *Columbia Journal of Word Business*, 18 (Fall), pp. 73–99.

Ozer, M. (2003). 'Process implications of the use of the Internet in new product development: a conceptual analysis', *Industrial Marketing Management*, 32, 6 (August), pp. 517–30.

Parasuraman, A., Zeithamal, V.A. and Berry, L.L. (1985). 'A conceptual model of service quality and its implications for future research', *Journal of Marketing*, 49, pp. 41–50.

Parzinger, M. (1997). 'A stage-wise application of total quality management through the product life cycle', *Industrial Management and Data Systems*, 97, 3, pp. 125–30.

Rickard, L. and Jackson, K. (2000). *The Financial Times Marketing Casebook*, 2nd edn, London: Prentice Hall, pp. 52–9.

Rogers, E.M. (1983). *Diffusion of Innovations*, 3rd edn, New York, NY: Free Press.

Roolvink S. (2002) Brand Leadership Matrix[RM], www.brandchannel.com/images/papers/BrandLeadershipMatrix.pdf (Accessed 1 January 2004.)

Sakakibara, K. (1995). 'Global new product development: the case of IBM notebook computers', *Business Strategy Review*, 6, 2 (Summer) pp. 25–40.

Shankar, V., Carpenter, G.S., and Krishnamurthi, L. (1999). 'The advantages of entry in the growth stage of the product life cycle: an empirical analysis', *Journal of Marketing Research*, 36, 2, pp. 269–77.

Shapiro, B.P. (1977). *Industrial Product Policy: Managing the Existing Product Line*, Cambridge, MA: Marketing Science Institute, pp. 37–9.

Shipley, D. and Jobber, D. (2001). 'Integrative pricing via the pricing wheel', *Industrial Marketing Management*, 30, 3 (April), pp. 301–14.

Smeltzer, L.R. and Carr, A. (2002). 'Reverse auctions in industrial marketing and buying', *Business Horizons*, 45, 2 (March–April), pp. 47–52.

Tibben-Lembke, R.S. (2002). 'Life after death: reverse logistics and the product life cycle', *International Journal of Physical Distribution and Logistics Management*, 32, 3, pp. 223–44.

von Hippel, E. (1982) 'Get New Products from Customers', *Harvard Business Review*, 60, (March/April), pp. 117–122.

Wengartner, M.H. (1987). 'Leasing asset lives and uncertainty: guides to decision making', *Financial Management*, 16, 2 (Summer), pp. 5–13.

Wheelwright, S.C. and Clark, K.B. (1992). 'Creating product plans to focus product development', *Harvard Business Review*, 70 (March/April), pp. 70–82.

Wood, L. (1990). 'The end of the product life cycle? Education says goodbye to an old friend', *Journal of Marketing Management*, 6, 2, pp. 145–55.

Wykes, T. (2003). 'NCW News, The 4th Annual Construction Marketing Conference – 29 and 30 October'; www.ncw.org.uk/news/DisplayNews.cfm?EntryNum=92 (Accessed 30 January 2004.)

Wynstra, F. and ten, Pierick E. (2000). 'Managing supplier involvement in new product development: a portfolio approach', *European Journal of Purchasing and Supply Management*, 6, 1 (March), pp. 49–57.

Zeithaml, V.A. and Bitner, M.J. (2000). *Services Marketing*, New York, NY: McGraw-Hill.

Chapter 5
Organisational buying behaviour

Chapter overview

This chapter introduces traditional views about organisational buying behaviour, before progressing to consider the importance of relationships and the contribution that systems and technology have made to this aspect of business marketing.

The chapter starts with a comparison of the main characteristics associated with both consumer and organisational purchasing behaviour. Then, following an examination of the decision making unit and the decision making processes generally assumed to be adopted by organisations, the focus moves to reflect upon the different influences that can impact on an organisation's purchasing activities.

The last section of the chapter looks at the nature of risk and uncertainty and the way in which organisations attempt to reduce perceived risk. The final part examines the way in which relationships between buyers and sellers can evolve and affect the purchasing behaviour of organisations.

Chapter aims

The aim of the chapter is to examine the behaviour, characteristics and processes that organisations use to purchase products and services.

Objectives

The objectives of this chapter are to:

1   Compare the characteristics of organisational with consumer buying behaviour.
2   Explore the membership and main characteristics of the decision making unit.
3   Evaluate the different types of buying situations that organisations face.
4   Explain organisational decision making processes.
5   Consider the influences that impact on organisational buyer behaviour.
6   Examine the impact information technology and associated systems have on the way organisations buy products and services.
7   Determine and reflect upon the nature of risk in B2B markets and consider the impact that different relationships between buyers and sellers might have on purchasing behaviour.

Introduction

Organisational buying, according to Webster and Wind (1972), is 'the decision making process by which formal organisations establish the need for purchased products and services and identify, evaluate and choose among alternative brands and suppliers'. One of the important aspects of this definition is that organisational buying behaviour is a process rather than a static, one-off event. There are a number of stages, or phases, associated with product procurement, each one often requiring a key decision to be made. Organisations buy products and services on a regular basis and professional purchasing is a requirement in most businesses. Thus organisational buying behaviour is an integral part of the external relationships that an enterprise develops, either as a part of market-based exchanges or as fully developed relational exchanges.

The purchase of products and services by organisations presents a risk which varies according to many factors. For example, the complexity of the product or the frequency of purchase decisions may impact on the risk factor. The formalisation of buying behaviour in organisations symbolises the potential risk as well as being a means to reduce it. **Perceived risk** in this context will be examined later in the chapter.

Organisational buying behaviour is not just about the purchase of goods and services. In addition to this fundamental task, it is concerned with the development and management of interorganisational relationships. The placement of orders and contracts between organisations can confirm a current trading relationship, initiate a new set of relationships, or may even signal the demise of a relationship. Clearly this aspect of organisational buying behaviour is important where there are relational exchanges. However, even in market exchanges organisations should be alert to the relationship potential.

In order to explore organisational buying behaviour (OBB), attention will first be given to comparisons with consumer buying behaviour. This is followed by an exploration of the characteristics of the decision making unit, the different types of buying situations, the process stages that are often involved. In conclusion, the impact systems and communications have on organisational buying behaviour and the forces acting on organisational buying behaviour as a whole are considered.

A comparison of OBB with consumer buying

There is a natural inclination, when exploring organisational buyer behaviour, to refer to consumer buyer behaviour and to highlight the differences. However, this only serves to differentiate and fails to reveal areas of overlap and similarity. The intention here is to consider the main characteristics and evaluate both the differences and the similarities that exist between the two. The differences are presented in Table 5.1.

Table 5.1 A comparison of buying characteristics in organisational and consumer markets

	Consumer buying characteristics	Organisational buying characteristics
Number of buyers	Many	Few
Purchase initiation	Self	Others
Evaluative criteria	Social, ego and level of utility	Price, value and level of utility
Information search	Normally short	Normally long
Range of suppliers used	Small number of suppliers considered	Can be extensive
Importance of supplier choice	Normally limited	Can be critical
Size of orders	Small	Large
Frequency of orders	High	Low
Value of orders placed	Low	High
Complexity of decision making	Low to medium	Medium
Range of information inputs	Limited	Moderate to extensive

One of the main characteristics is that there are far fewer buyers in organisational markets than in consumer markets. Even though there may be several people associated with a buying decision in an organisation, the overall number of people involved in buying, say, packaging products or road construction equipment is very small compared with the millions of people who might potentially buy a chocolate bar. The financial value of organisational purchase orders is invariably larger and the frequency with which they are placed is much lower. It is quite common for agreements to be made between organisations for the supply of materials over a number of years. Similarly, depending upon the complexity of the product (for example, photocopying paper or a one-off satellite), the negotiation process may also take a long time.

Although there are differences, many of the characteristics associated with consumer decision making processes can still be observed in the organisational context. However, organisational buyers make decisions which ultimately contribute to the achievement of corporate objectives. To make the necessary decisions, a high volume of pertinent information is often required. This information needs to be relatively detailed and is normally presented in a rational and logical style. The needs of the buyers are many and complex and some may be personal. Goals, such as promotion and career advancement within the organisation, coupled with ego and employee satisfaction combine to make organisational buying an important task, one that requires professional training and the development of expertise if the role is to be performed optimally.

Similarities

It was mentioned earlier that, as well as the major differences between the two types of purchasing contexts, an increasing number of similarities are now being recognised. For example, the implied rationality of decision making in organisational contexts and the assumption that consumer decision making is more unstructured and emotionally driven is questionable. Many personal purchases are of such technical complexity (for example financial services) that consumers need to adopt a more rational, fact-based approach to their buying.

Wilson (2000) explores the issues related to rationality and the implied differences. For example, consumers make product-related purchase decisions based on a wide array of inputs from other people and not just those in the immediate family environment. This is akin to group buying dynamics associated with the DMU. He argues that the rationality normally associated with organisational decision making is misplaced, suggesting that in some circumstances the protracted nature of the process is more a reflection of organisational culture and the need to follow bureaucratic procedures and to show due diligence. In addition, issues concerning established behaviour patterns, difficulties and reluctance to break with traditional purchasing practices, intra- and interorganisational politics and relationships, and the costs associated with supplier switching all contribute to a more interpretive understanding of organisational decision making. Further support for this view is given by Mason and Gray (1999) who refer to the characteristics of decision making in the air travel market and note some strong similarities between consumers and business passengers.

It is interesting to observe the similarity between the extended problem solving, limited problem solving and routinised response behaviour phases of consumer buying and the new task, modified rebuy and rebuy states associated with organisational buying. There is a close match between the two sets in terms of the purpose, approach and content. Risk and involvement are relevant to both categories and, although the background to both may vary, the principles used to manage the various phases and conditions are essentially the same, just deployed in different ways.

It is important to recognise that many of the characteristics of both consumer and organisational decision making show a greater number of similarities than is normally assumed (or taught).

Decision making units – characteristics

Reference has been made on a number of occasions to organisational buyers, as if such people are the only representatives of an organisation to be involved with the purchase decision process. This is not the case, as very often a large number of people are involved in a purchase decision. This group is referred to as either the decision making unit (DMU) or the buying centre.

DMUs vary in size and composition in accordance with the nature of each individual task. Webster and Wind (1972) identified a number of roles within the buying centre (see Figure 5.1).

Initiators request the purchase of an item and propel the purchase decision process. They may be other members of the DMU or others in the organisation.

Users may not only initiate the purchase process but are sometimes involved in the specification process. They will use the product once it has been acquired and subsequently evaluate its performance. Their role is continuous, although it may vary from the peripheral to highly involved.

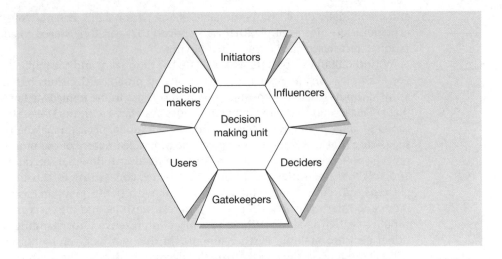

Figure 5.1 Membership of the decision making unit
Source: after Webster and Wind (1972).

Influencers very often help set the technical specifications for the proposed purchase and assist the evaluation of alternative offerings by potential suppliers. These may be consultants hired to complete a particular project. This is quite common in high-technology purchases where the customer has little relevant expertise.

Deciders are those who make purchasing decisions and they are the most difficult to identify. This is because they may not have formal authority to make a purchase decision yet are sufficiently influential internally that their decision carries most weight. In repeat buying activities the buyer may well also be the decider. However, it is normal practice to require that expenditure decisions involving sums over a certain financial limit be authorised by other, often senior, managers.

Buyers (purchasing managers) select suppliers and manage the process whereby the required products are procured. As suggested previously, buyers may not decide which product is to be purchased but they influence the framework within which the decision is made.

Gatekeepers have the potential to control the type and flow of information to the organisation and the members of the DMU. These gatekeepers may be assistants, technical personnel, secretaries or telephone switchboard operators.

The size and form of the buying centre is not static. It can vary according to the complexity of the product being considered and the degree of risk each decision is perceived to carry for the organisation. Different roles are required and adopted as the nature of the buying task changes with each new purchase situation (Bonoma, 1982). All of these roles might be subsumed within one individual for certain decisions. It is vital for seller organisations to identify members of the buying centre and to target and refine their messages to meet the needs of each member of the centre.

SNAPSHOT 5.1

USING TECHNOLOGY TO REACH GATEKEEPERS

In order to get face-to-face appointments with 1,000 of its prospects, the advertising department of a large trade publisher targeted administrative assistants through a combination of old and new technology. Each senior executive's office was called to request the name of the administrative assistant. The assistants received flowers, including cards saying the publisher valued their opinions and thanking them in advance for spending time determining whether advertising in the trade publication would meet the needs of their firms.

Follow-up phone calls found that the assistants were delighted with the flowers, were happy to accept calls and typically said 'I'll do what I can, send me something.' Most assistants agreed to accept an email outlining the offer and provided a specific time to call back. A summary of the key benefits, customised to the needs of the prospective firm, was prepared just for the administrative assistant.

These processes enabled the salespeople to have a two-way communication with the administrative assistant and this resulted in an appointment rate with executives that was twice the normal success rate.

Enrolling CEOs in a conference

In a different campaign targeted at similar gatekeepers, telemarketers explained the benefits of attending a particular conference. When the assistant suggested that the salesperson send them details the response was to offer to send an electronic file (pdf) of the brochure, via email, immediately. Asking for the assistant to agree to this effectively initiated two-way communication and the email attachment grabbed immediate attention.

These success stories have their roots in the recognition that the administrative assistants are an integral part of the campaign, and they were treated respectfully. Materials were planned and prepared in advance and through the use of simple email, a relationship based on the trust of the gatekeeper was developed.

Source: Gedney and Belbey (2002).

Ronchetto *et al.* (1989) provide some insight into how influential members of a DMU might be recognised. Their research suggests that there are several criteria that indicate those members who have above average influence. In addition to those members who occupy particularly significant hierarchical positions, they cite people who:

- work close to the organisational boundary;

- are near the centre in terms of work flow;

- play an active and positive role in communication across customer departments;

- are linked directly to senior managers.

It can be instructive to visit purchasing sections of organisational websites and try to determine both the emotional character and likely membership of a DMU. Readers are invited to consider the examples in Snapshot 5.2.

SNAPSHOT 5.2

EXAMPLES OF STATEMENTS ON PURCHASING DEPARTMENT WEBSITES

An American university

We are a team of professionals working to enhance the purchasing experience. We seek a partnership with all those in need of goods and services. We strive to provide a responsive and responsible service toward the collective support of the University – its educational, research and public service missions.

Further to our role is the consistent application of technology, policy, state and federal regulations, maintaining positive internal and external customer relationships, and developing skilled expertise. We do so with the highest legal and ethical standards accompanied with courtesy, professionalism, diplomacy, effective communication, vigilance, efficiency, teamwork and humor.

We deploy our resources toward safeguarding University assets and to insure appropriate stewardship of University funds. Our actions shall support and advance the University's objectives and protect it from unnecessary costs and legal and political challenges.

Source: ANON

A British food packaging company

Aluminium rolling is a global industry so we source our supplies around the world. Our buying strategy demands material produced to exacting press performance standards and only mills equipped with up-to-date process controls are qualified as suppliers.

Of course we invite potential new suppliers with the appropriate technology to contact our purchasing department.

Source: www.nichollfoodpackaging.co.uk/html/cosupp.htm
(Accessed 21 October 2003.) Used with permission.

An Australian health service provider

The ability to understand the ever-changing environment in which we work is a critical factor in the degree of success we have in achieving the aims and objectives of our Units, Hospitals, Area and State. In assisting our customers to achieve these objectives, the Area Purchasing Department is committed to providing a cost effective, timely and user friendly service.

An important objective for the Purchasing Department is to reduce, or contain, the ever-increasing cost of goods, services and equipment in the most effective manner.

Source: ANON. (All websites accessed 21 October 2003.)

Refer to the discussion questions at the end of this chapter.

Membership of the DMU is far from fixed, and this sheer fluidity poses problems for selling organisations simply because it is not always possible to identify key members or shifts in policy or requirements. As Spekman and Gronhaug (1986) point out, the DMU is a 'vague construct that can reach across a number of different functional roles with any number of individuals participating or exerting influence at any one time'. It is worth noting therefore, that within this context the behaviour of DMU members is also largely determined by the interpersonal relationships of the members of the centre.

The decision making process

Organisational buying decisions vary in terms of the nature of the product or service, the frequency and the relative value of purchases, their strategic impact (if any) and the type of relationship with suppliers. These, and many other factors, are potentially significant to individual buying organisations. However, there are some broad criteria that can be characterised within three main types of buying situations. Referred to by Robinson *et al.* (1967) as **buyclasses** these are: new task, modified rebuy and straight rebuy (see Table 5.2).

Table 5.2 Main characteristics of the buyclasses

Buyclass	Degree of familiarity with the problem	Information requirements	Alternative solutions
New buy	The problem is fresh to the decision makers.	A great deal of information is required.	Alternative solutions are unknown, all are considered new.
Modified rebuy	The requirement is not new but is different from previous situations.	More information is required but past experience is of use.	Buying decision needs new solutions.
Rebuy	The problem is identical to previous experience.	Little or no information is required.	Alternative solutions not sought or required.

Source: Based on Robinson *et al.* (1967).

Robinson *et al.* also determined that OBB consists of a series of sequential activities through which organisations proceed when making purchasing decisions. These they referred to as buying stages or **buyphases**. These are shown in Table 5.3 where the buyclasses are brought together with the buyphases.

This buygrid serves to illustrate the relationship between these two main elements and highlights the need to focus on buying situations rather than on products. At the time of its publication this was regarded as a major advance in our understanding of OBB. It is still an important foundation for this topic. The next few sections work first through the characteristics of the buyclasses and then proceed to examine the key aspects of each of the buyphases.

Table 5.3 The buygrid framework

Buyphases	New task	Buyclasses Modified rebuy	Straight rebuy
Problem recognition	Yes	Possibly	No
General need description	Yes	Possibly	No
Product specification	Yes	Yes	Yes
Supplier search	Yes	Possibly	No
Supplier selection	Yes	Possibly	No
Order process specification	Yes	Possibly	No
Performance review	Yes	Yes	Yes

Source: Based on Robinson *et al.* (1967).

Buyclasses

New task

As the name implies, the organisation is faced with a first-time buying situation. Risk is inevitably large at this point as there is little collective experience of the product/service or of the relevant suppliers. As a result of these factors there are normally a large number of decision participants. Each participant requires a lot of information and a relatively long period of time is needed for the information to be assimilated and a decision to be made.

In terms of decision making stages this is referred to as **extensive problem solving** (Howard and Sheth, 1969) and the main characteristic is the high risk that is derived from the uncertainty involved in the decision. The uncertainty might be containable because of the nature of the product or if the contribution it makes to the organisation's value system is negligible. However, the uncertainty might be high because of the potential to disrupt production or perhaps lead to customer dissatisfaction (for example, missed delivery dates).

Modified rebuy

Having purchased a product, uncertainty is reduced but not eliminated, so the organisation may request through their buyer(s) that certain modifications be made to future purchases. For example, adjustments to the specification of the product, further negotiation on price levels or perhaps the arrangement for alternative delivery patterns. Fewer people are involved in the decision process than in the new task situation.

In terms of decision making stages this is referred to as **limited problem solving** (Howard and Sheth, 1969) and the main characteristic is that buying organisations only perceive moderate risks involved in the decision, due to previous purchasing experience. While the decision criteria is understood there is uncertainty about which suppliers might be best suited to satisfy the revised specifications.

Straight rebuy

In this situation, the purchasing department reorders on a routine basis, very often working from an approved list of suppliers. These may be products that an organisation consumes in order to keep operating (for example, office stationery), or may be low-value materials used within the operational, value added part of the organisation (for example, manufacturing processes). No other people are involved with the exercise until different suppliers attempt to change the environment in which the decision is made. For example, a new supplier may interrupt the procedure with a potentially better offer. This may stimulate the emergence of a modified rebuy situation.

In terms of decision making stages, the straight rebuy situation is referred to as **routine problem solving**. Uncertainty is low and risk minimal because the buying criteria are established and there is little reason to find improved supplies and/or suppliers.

Straight rebuy presents classic conditions for the use of automatic reordering systems. Costs can be reduced, managerial time redirected to other projects and the relationship between buyer and seller embedded within a stronger framework. One possible difficulty is that both parties perceive the system to be a significant exit barrier should conditions change, and this may deter flexibility or restrict opportunities to develop the same or other relationships.

The use of electronic purchasing systems at the straight rebuy stage has enabled organisations to empower employees to make purchases although control still resides with purchasing managers. Employees can buy direct, through their PCs, from a catalogue list of authorised suppliers. The benefits are that employees are more involved, purchasing process is speeded up, costs are reduced and purchasing managers can spend more time with other higher priority activities.

Buyphases

Just as there are buyclasses so there are buyphases, or stages through which a buying decision moves before a conclusion is reached (Robinson *et al.*, 1967).

The following sequence of buyphases, developed from Robinson *et al.*'s (1967) original list, is peculiar to the new task situation. Many of these buyphases are often ignored or compressed according to the complexity of the product and when either a modified rebuy or a straight rebuy situation is encountered.

Need/problem recognition

Organisations buy products or services because of two main events (Cravens and Woodruff, 1986). Difficulties may be encountered, first as a result of a need to solve problems, such as a stock-out or new government regulations, and second, as a response to opportunities to improve performance or enter new markets. Essentially, the need/recognition phase is the identification of a gap. This is the gap between the benefits an organisation has now and the benefits it would like to have. For example, when a new product is to be produced there is an obvious gap between having the necessary materials and components and being out of stock and unable to build. The first decision therefore is about how to close this gap and there are two broad options: outsource the whole, or parts, of the production process or build/make the objects oneself. The need has been recognised and the gap identified. The rest of this section is based on a build decision being made.

SNAPSHOT 5.3

BUYING PUMPS

The procurement of pumping equipment and services is known as the inquiry/quotation process. The entire process is information intensive and costly, consisting of both technical and commercial information, involving all members of the supply chain.

To reduce costs, buyers seek ways of reducing the engineering resources required to process this information without compromising the quality of the competitive evaluation. Similarly, suppliers are developing methods for responding to inquiries with fewer resources and effort while striving to still provide high-quality quotations to their customers. Simplifying the inquiry/quotation process is an attractive proposition for both buyer and supplier.

Each of the interactions between buyer and supplier represents one or more information transactions. Savings are obtained by either eliminating a transaction, or substantially reducing the time or effort involved in performing that transaction. One approach is to structure the flow of information between companies to reduce information ambiguity and enhance common work practices.

'The basic activities involved in the selection and purchasing of pumps are substantially the same now as in the past, and will be in the future. However, the processes and technologies employed in performing these activities are changing rapidly as a consequence of the Information age. The motivations surrounding these changes are driven by the desire for shorter cycle times, higher quality, and lower costs in the selection and purchasing process. These objectives are driven by the availability of new and emerging information technologies that offer a more seamless and structured flow of information between the purchaser's and the supplier's sales, applications, engineering, and manufacturing functions. The availability of computer systems guarantees only that the infrastructure is in place to achieve the anticipated benefits. However, common work practices between buyers and suppliers must be adopted and adapted to these new technologies. These process changes, not the availability of new information technologies, will govern the speed in [*sic*] which the pump industry changes in the future.'

Source: Adapted from Dahl (2001), www.intellequip.com/publish/pdfs/FEDSM2001-18069.pdf (Accessed 1 December 2003.)

Product specification

As a result of identifying a problem and the size of the gap, influencers and users can determine the desired characteristics of the product needed to resolve the problem. This may take the form of a functional or general description or a much more detailed analysis and the creation of a detailed technical specification for a particular product. For example, what sort of photocopier is required? What is it expected to achieve? How many documents should it copy per minute? Is a collator or tray required? This is an important part of the process, because if it is executed properly it will narrow the supplier search and save on the costs associated with evaluation prior to a final decision. The results of the functional and detailed specifications are often combined within a purchase order specification which, according to van Weele (2002), consists of five main components. These are set out in Table 5.4.

Table 5.4 Dimensions of a purchase order specification

Dimension of a purchase order specification	Explanation
Quality specifications	Statement concerning the technical standards the product meets and whether there should be a quality certificate.
Logistics specifications	Statement concerning the quantity of products required and delivery details.
Maintenance specifications	Statement about how the supplier will service and maintain the product.
Legal and environmental requirements	Statement detailing how the product and associated processes should meet health, safety and environmental legislation.
Target budget	Statement about the financial constraints within which the product is to be produced, delivered and supported.

Source: Adapted from van Weele (2002).

Supplier and product search

At this stage the buyer actively seeks organisations which can supply the necessary product(s). There are two main issues at this point. First, will the product reach the required performance standards and match the specification? Second, will the potential supplier meet the other organisational requirements? In most circumstances organisations review the market and their internal sources of information and arrive at a decision that is based on rational criteria.

Organisations work, wherever possible, to reduce uncertainty and risk. By working with others who are known, of whom the organisation has direct experience and who can be trusted, risk and uncertainty can be substantially reduced. This highlights another reason why many organisations seek relational exchanges and operate within established networks and seek to support each other.

The quest for suppliers and products may be a short task for the buyer; however, if the established network cannot provide a solution, the buying organisation has to seek new suppliers, and hence new networks, to be able to identify and short-list appropriate supplier organisations.

Evaluation of proposals

Depending upon the complexity and value of the potential order(s), the proposal is a vital part of the process and should be prepared professionally. The proposals of the short-listed organisations are reviewed in the context of two main criteria: the purchase order specification and the evaluation of the supplying organisation. If the organisation is already a part of the network, little search and review time need be allocated. If the proposed supplier is new to the organisation, a review may be necessary to establish whether it will be appropriate (in terms of price, delivery and service) and whether there is the potential for a long-term relationship or whether this is a single purchase that is unlikely to be repeated.

Once again, therefore, is the relationship going to be based on a market exchange or a relational exchange? The actions of both organisations, and of some of the other organisations in the network to the new entrant, will be critical in determining the form and nature of future relationships.

Supplier selection

The DMU will undertake a supplier analysis and use a variety of criteria depending upon the particular type of item sought. This selection process takes place in the light of the comments made in the previous section. A further useful perspective is to view supplier organisations as a continuum, from reliance on a single source to the use of a wide variety of suppliers of the same product.

Jackson (1985) proposed that organisations might buy a product from a range of different suppliers, in other words maintaining a range of multiple sources (a practice of many government departments). She labelled this approach 'always a share', as several suppliers are given the opportunity to share the business available to the buying centre. The major disadvantage is that this approach fails to drive cost as low as possible, as the discounts derived from volume sales are not achieved. The advantage to the buying centre is that a relatively small investment is required and little risk is entailed in following such a strategy.

At the other end of the continuum are organisations which only use a single source supplier. All purchases are made from the single source until circumstances change to such a degree that the buyer's needs are no longer being satisfied. Jackson referred to these organisations as 'lost for good', because once a relationship with a new organisation has been developed they are lost for good to the original supplier. An increasing number of organisations are choosing to enter alliances with a limited number, or even a single source of suppliers. The objective is to build a long-term relationship, to work together to build quality and help each other achieve their goals. Out-sourcing manufacturing activities for non-core activities has increased, and this has moved the focus of communications from an internal to an external perspective.

Evaluation

The order is written against the selected supplier which is then monitored and evaluated against such diverse criteria as responsiveness to enquiries, modifications to the specification and timing of delivery. When the product is delivered it may reach the stated specification but fail to satisfy the original need. In this case, the specification needs to be rewritten before any future orders are placed.

Developments in the environment can impact on organisational buyers and change both the nature of decisions and the way they are made. For example, the decision to purchase new plant and machinery requires consideration of the future cash flows generated by the capital item. Many people will be involved in the decision, and the time necessary for consultation may mean that other parts of the decision making process are completed simultaneously.

SNAPSHOT 5.4

SELECTING SUPPLIERS AT ZION ELECTRONICS

Zion Electronics state that when selecting suppliers a key initial factor is the extent to which their costs will be minimised and, as a consequence, their profits enhanced. No orders are placed until this has been determined.

All products and services bought by Zion must meet the specifications requested as they wish to be sure that authorised suppliers have the necessary technical and production capabilities.

Zion also declare that selected suppliers should keep to agreed delivery schedules, no sooner or later than the agreed date shown on the purchase order. Suppliers must also be capable of increasing production volumes as Zion grows.

Interestingly, Zion also require that their suppliers' salespeople must have the authority to negotiate and finalise agreements and that all agreed prices are considered firm, subject to any contractual clause.

Influences shaping organisational buying behaviour

Not surprisingly, there are a number of forces that shape the way in which organisations purchase products. Organisational buying behaviour takes place in an environment which can change quickly and dynamically. Sellers need to understand the nature of the changes and either anticipate or react in appropriate ways. Four main areas of influence can be identified namely, internal, external, individual and relationship forces (see Figure 5.2).

Internal influences

One of the main issues internally is the way in which purchasing is structured. The policy may be that the organisation prefers to manage its buying from a central point. This enables tighter control and greater consistency. It allows for improved integration and costs can be reduced by buying on behalf of all operating units.

The alternative is to decentralise purchasing to divisions or geographically dispersed operating departments. This facilitates purchasing to meet local needs, enables flexibility and promotes a sense of empowerment. However, because management do not have as much control or influence, there tends to be a pressure to move towards a centralised approach and often this move is undertaken in the name of cost saving. Very often organisations will move towards a centralised structure when trading performance declines over several periods or when they are under attack from the stock market or competitors.

Other internal pressures emanate from purchasing policy (for example a move towards lean manufacturing), changes to the levels of authority and responsibility for

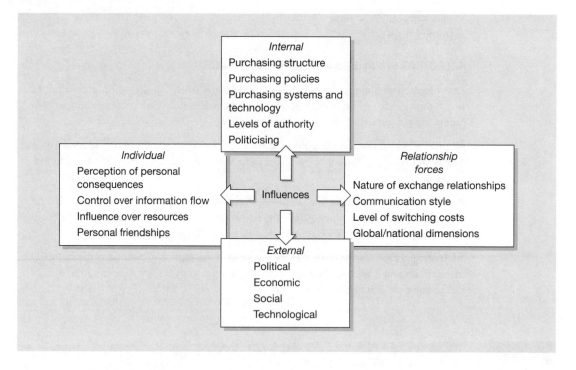

Figure 5.2 Major influences on organisational buying behaviour

purchasing activities, enhancements to purchasing systems and technology and, of course, organisational changes arising from restructuring, a change in ownership (or merger and acquisition activities) or any politicising.

External influences

The main source of external influence can be traced back through the political, economic, social and technological (PEST) framework.

Political and regulatory influence has the potential to radically change the nature of products and services that organisations purchase. Changes to packaging and labelling, adjustments to the safety requirements concerning the use of products and even changes to the taxation regulations can all influence the choice of supplier and the frequency of purchase.

Economy. Changes in the overall economy and confidence in the stock market can impact on the purchase behaviour. Because B2B markets are based primarily on derived demand, organisations need to be sensitive to expectations concerning the buoyancy of the end-user consumer market. Movements in interest rates can impact on particular sectors in the economy. For example, higher rates will tend to raise mortgages and suppress the housing market and all related activities, such as building materials, financial services and labour market employment, whereas printing, soft drinks and medicines will be unaffected. This suggests that changes in the economy are not necessarily always spread evenly.

Social changes can also affect organisational buying behaviour. Part of the aftermath of the 9/11 hostilities in the United States was the huge downturn in air travel. This lead to some airlines going out of business and aircraft manufacturers and associated supply chains having to retrench as airlines deferred or cancelled orders. Saturation in the mobile phone market caused cell phone manufacturers to reconfigure their production plans and make large numbers of staff redundant.

Technological changes have had a dramatic impact on organisational buying behaviour. The Internet has changed the ways organisations communicate, do business and interact with one another. Some of these systems, technology and communications facilities are exemplified throughout this book but the net effect has been to change the way organisations buy and sell to each other. Technical and engineering employees are enjoying greater participation in the DMU as the rate of technological change increases and the influence of the purchasing manager declines. Weiss and Hyde (1993) found that buyers tend to undertake more intense search efforts but spend less time on the overall search process when they detect that the pace of technological change is increasing. Technological changes have given rise to new types of intermediaries and suppliers in the marketing channels, both up and down stream. This means that the nature and form of the supply chain has also changed and required organisations to appraise and review their purchasing procedures.

Individual influences

Participation in the buying centre has been shown to be highly influenced by individuals' perceptions of the personal consequences of their contribution to each of the stages in the buying process. The more that individuals think they will be blamed for a bad decision or praised for a good one, the greater their participation, influence and visible DMU-related activity (McQuiston and Dickson, 1991). The nature and dispersal of power within the unit can influence the decisions that are made. Certain individuals are able to control the flow of information and/or the deployment of resources (Spekman and Gronhaug, 1986). This assertiveness can enable individuals to have undue influence within a DMU.

Individuals may develop personal friendships with suppliers and buyers. Such personal relationships overlie interorganisational relationships and work perfectly smoothly but they can also give rise to conflict, for example when interorganisational relationships change.

Relationship influences

Relationships develop between the focus organisation and other stakeholders in the network. The nature of the exchange relationship and the style of communications will influence buying decisions. If the relationship between organisations is trusting, mutually supportive and based upon a longer-term perspective (a relational structure) then the behaviour of the buying centre may be seen to be cooperative and constructive. If the relationship is formal, regular, unsupportive and based upon short-term convenience (a market structure-based relationship) then the purchase behaviour may be observed as courteous yet distant. It has been suggested that the major determinant of the organisational environment is the cost associated with switching from one supplier to another (Bowersox and Cooper, 1992).

When one organisation chooses to enter into a buying relationship with another, an investment is made in time, people, assets and systems. Should the relationship fail to work satisfactorily then a cost is incurred in switching to another supplier. These switching costs can heavily influence buying decisions. The higher the potential switching costs, the greater the loss in flexibility and the stronger the need to make the relationship appropriate at the outset.

Buyers and sellers that have a predominantly market exchange relationship can be hit hard by these forces, especially in comparison to those organisations that operate on a more relational exchange basis. Because they work together and anticipate changes that might disrupt their relationship, organisations within a relational exchange seek solutions to reduce the impact of some of these forces. The ability to be flexible, innovative and yet sufficiently enduring enables organisations to develop relationships and their purchasing systems in the face of the forces acting upon them. Organisational buying has shifted from a one-to-one dyadic encounter, salesperson to buyer, to a position where a buying team meets a selling team. The skills associated with this process are different and are becoming much more sophisticated while the demands on both buyers and sellers are more pronounced. The processes of buying and selling should not be underestimated as they are complex and interactive.

Suppliers that operate on a global basis face particular challenges as their customers themselves deal with a variety of local, international, complex and turbulent conditions. The development of global account management (GAM) is an attempt to enable organisations to provide effective supply management facilities through a network and open-minded managerial approach rather than the more traditional hierarchical control mechanisms used previously. GAM requires a more adaptive approach (Harvey *et al.*, 2003), one which enables greater independent thinking and use of initiative in order to supply global customers as they wish (see Figure 5.3, overleaf).

Through the development of linkages between a supplier and each customer's globally dispersed operating units, new forms of value can be created within the relationships.

eProcurement and the impact of IST on OBB

De Boer *et al.* (2002, p. 2) define eProcurement as 'using Internet technology in the purchasing process' and describe it as having six principal forms:

1 eMRO – to create and place purchase orders for maintenance, repair and operating supplies;

2 web-based ERP – to create and place purchase orders for product-related goods and services;

3 eSourcing – to identify/compare potential suppliers;

4 eTendering – to request/receive information and prices;

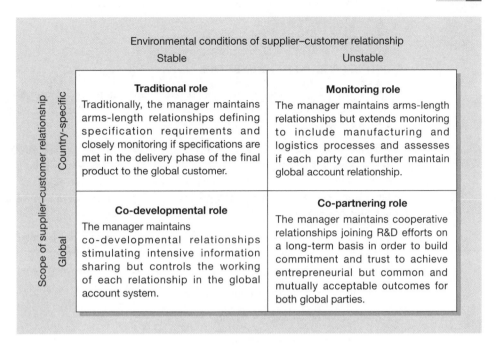

Figure 5.3 Managerial roles in global account supply management

Source: Harvey *et al.* (2003). Copyright © 2003. With permission from Elsevier.

5 eReverse auctioning – to buy goods and services (see more on eAuctions below);

6 eInforming – to exchange information internally and externally.

The benefits for suppliers that allow web-based access to their on-line catalogues include reduced printing and distribution costs and delays; the ability to market new products, or reduce prices on older ones, very quickly; fewer incoming telephone calls; more accurate ordering; and improved customer satisfaction. The benefits for buyers include access to up-to-date product and price data; fewer outgoing telephone calls; and, when online order processing is also available, faster ordering.

The disadvantages of eProcurement are largely felt by suppliers and include IST costs; downward pressure on prices; and the ease with which customers can compare and switch suppliers. Both suppliers and buyers may welcome or regret the decreased personal contact of sales visits, telephone calls and face-to-face competitive tendering.

eAuctions

Online auctions are becoming increasingly popular in two specific areas of B2B commerce: sourcing supplies and disposing of surplus stock or other assets. Unlike traditional auctions, online auctions tend to be longer and end at pre-set times. Buyers (or sellers) do not have to attend face-to-face, indeed participation is in real time, can be global and transaction costs drastically reduced (Sashi and O'Leary, 2002).

SNAPSHOT 5.5

ONLINE PROCUREMENT SYSTEMS

Alfa, a major Mexican industrial conglomerate with a turnover of over $4.56 billion, consists of five businesses and a series of alliances with more than 20 companies around the world.

The purchase of indirect goods and services was worth approximately $600 million per year, but each business managed their own purchases. As a result the process was highly fragmented and inefficient. To enhance its competitiveness across all businesses, Alfa explored the efficiencies and potential savings offered by a centralised on-line procurement system.

Part of the specification required that the system would connect seamlessly with the different SAP ERP implementations used throughout the corporation. By standardising and centralising the procurement process, Alfa achieved the following benefits:

- greater ability to fully leverage volume discounts

- better control of maverick buying

- improved spend management.

At the time the system was installed most domestic suppliers in Mexico were unfamiliar with this level of online procurement. BearingPoint, Alfa's consultants, undertook strategic sourcing and procurement methodology training, provided supplier on-boarding and jointly developed electronic catalogues.

Apart from radically changing the processes and procedures associated with the purchase of indirect goods, Alfa have made significant savings in terms of the time and costs associated with these purchases. The organisation is in a better position to control their spend and costs and have made savings of up to 50 per cent from the strategic sourcing effort of some indirect commodities.

This illustration demonstrates how IST can help organisations manage their purchases, make huge cost savings and advance an organisation by working with their suppliers. Although Alfa has continued to consolidate the supplier base and standardise the indirect procurement processes, installation of the online procurement tool has enabled the corporation to develop new competitive advantages and work with and benefit their preferred suppliers.

Source: Based on material retrieved and adapted from www.bearingpoint.com/ (Accessed 16 February 2003.) Permission to reproduce granted by Alfa.

A Google search in English for B2B and 'online auction' in May 2003, turned up 9,970 results. The listings obtained from following just one of those links is shown in Snapshot 5.6.

Chen and Wilson (2000) cited research suggesting that overall growth in B2B auctions would be from $8.7 billion in 1997 to $52.6 billion in 2002. eBay, which

SNAPSHOT 5.6

LISTINGS RESULTS FOR B2B MARKET FOR MACHINE TOOLS

1 **eBay: Machinery and tools B2B markets**
  Listing found in > **Machinery and tools B2B markets**
  Online marketplace for buying and selling machinery and tools.

2 **Machinery and tools B2B markets**
  Category found in > **Machinery and tools**
  Online business exchanges, marketplaces and auctions matching buyers and sellers
  of industrial machinery and tools.

3 **Machine net**
  Listing found in > **Machinery and tools B2B markets**
  Online trading system for machine tools and accessories.

4 **Machinetools.com**
  Listing found in > **Machinery and tools B2B markets**
  Business-to-business e-commerce site for the machine tool industry where the user
  can search new and used machinery, receive quotes from dealers around the world,
  and view online brochures for upcoming auctions.

Source: www.business.com/search/rslt_default.asp?query=b2b%20market%20for%20machine%20tools (Accessed 19 May 2003.)

increased its registered users, both personal and business, from just over 42 million at the end of 2001 to just under 62 million at the end of 2002, certainly welcomes the contribution of organisational buying and selling to its profitability and has a business-orientated **portal** (see p. 136) at business.ebay.com. Other examples, are 'Auction USA' (www.auction-usa.com/) which offers 'wholesale B2B and private party auctions' for all of the United States and Canada; and 'Indiamart' (auction.indiamart.com) 'Designed to enhance your business by bringing global B2B buyers and sellers together to make profitable deals online, day after day!'

Particularly of interest in B2B purchasing, is the 'reverse auction'. Instead of searching online auction sites for the supplies it needs and bidding for them, an organisation posts its requirements and invites potential suppliers to bid to fulfil them. The buying unit staff can do this themselves or use an intermediary such as FreeMarkets (see Snapshot 5.7).

For reverse auctions to operate effectively, Smeltzer and Carr (2003) identified four particular conditions that needed to exist. First, commodity specifications, such as ISO 9000 certification, order sizes, quantities and so forth, must be clearly stated. Second, purchase quantities or lots must be of sufficient size that suppliers want to bid. Size is important in order to generate transaction cost reductions and obtain production economies of scale. Third, the appropriate supply market conditions must exist, namely that there are a sufficient number of suppliers to make the market competitive and also sufficient incentives (for example excess supply capacity) to make it worthwhile for suppliers to become involved. Finally, these researchers identified that the correct organisational infrastructure must be in position for the buying organisation. This entails staff being trained, motivated and receptive to this form of

SNAPSHOT 5.7

REVERSE AUCTION SERVICE

FreeMarkets (www.freemarkets.com) offers a complete reverse auction service to B2B clients. The service includes working with the client to develop a 'Request for Quotation' (RFQ), seeking potential suppliers, helping to form bidding consortia, training suppliers to use FreeMarkets' own, free, bidding software, helping buyers evaluate bids and choose the best suppliers. FreeMarkets prides itself on carefully selecting suppliers to meet the buyers' needs.

Source: Adapted from Chen and Wilson (2000).

purchasing, plus having the necessary systems infrastructure in place to forecast accurately the amount required and communicate across a number of divisions when pooling occurs to increase the number of units being auctioned/bought.

eCollaboration

Interorganisational use of network technologies to share business information and coordinate supply chain activities has been termed **eCollaboration**. As noted by Karpinski (2001), 'Now comes the latest catchphrase, especially in B2B circles: collaboration. Suddenly, every supply chain and e-commerce vendor is rolling out collaborative commerce tools. Every e-marketplace is trumpeting its move from catalogues and auctions to collaborative design and forecasting.'

Despite the sceptical tone of that quote, there is an increasing number of well-documented cases of B2B eCollaboration. For example, Mirani *et al.* (2001) describe how a company in the energy management sector, Ion Systems, used a customised online Partner Relationship Management (PRM) application to improve collaboration with resellers. Before the system was implemented resellers of Ion's products and services could access general information from the company website or telephone for more specific requirements. Problems with these sources included outdated, unspecific information and unacceptable waiting times. Ion integrated an off-the-shelf PRM package with its current order management system to create a customised extranet for each reseller 'with product photos, selling strategies, purchasing and order verification capabilities – all tailored to the [reseller's] unique profile and needs' (Mirani *et al.*, 2001, p. 9). The improved access to targeted information, more efficient ordering and better service, were deemed to be responsible for a significant increase in online sales.

Hoffman *et al.* (2002) suggest that a substantial organisational IST budget will be spent in the next few years on setting up and operating these sorts of 'private exchanges: that is invitation-only networks that connect a single company to its customers, suppliers, or both'. While remarking on the similarities with EDI, they add that such networks enable the sharing of 'documents, drawings, spreadsheets and product designs in standard formats and in real time, thereby facilitating closer collaboration'.

Karpinski (2001) suggests that changing the B2B culture may be more of a barrier to successful eCollaboration than implementing the technological requirements. He quotes the chief executive officer of the World Wide Retail Exchange, an e-marketplace involving over 50 of the world's largest retailers, as saying 'collaborative planning, forecasting and replenishment (CPFR) has not taken hold in the past mainly because of the cultural issues around it ... Businesses have to get used to operating in a more transparent way and sharing information in ways not customary in the past.'

SNAPSHOT 5.8

MEET CHINA BECOMES MEET WORLD TRADE

MeetChina.com was founded by eCommerce specialist US Business Network (USBN), in association with six ministries of the Chinese government, to provide a window for buyers to source and buy products directly from Chinese companies. The name of the site was changed to reflect their expansion to five Asian countries.

Meet World Trade was an online network of Asian eMarketplaces that used a combination of online and offline resources to help purchasing professionals source vendors in developing economies. Meet World Trade was a strong local language Internet presence in China, Thailand, India and Korea and experienced support staff in these countries to assist companies to establish vendor networks in Asia in a compressed time frame.

The site supported an online catalogue of more than 70,000 suppliers and 150,000 products, and claimed to be the fastest-growing global trade exchange for sourcing products in Asia.

Source: Adapted from www.meetworldtrade.com/ (Accessed 31 December 2003.)

B2B web portals

The number of B2B portals has grown enormously and the value of US eCommerce transacted through portals was estimated by Forrester to reach approximately $1.4 trillion in 2004 (Clarke and Flaherty, 2003). This represents 53 per cent of all eCommerce transactions. A portal is an interface to other relevant content. There is no single type of portal or strategy for developing one. Figure 5.4 presents a categorisation of portal types which reflects the diversity, depth of content that can be accessed and the range of audiences that can be targeted.

In order to acquire and retain users with a B2B portal Clarke and Flaherty suggest there are three common themes:

- customisation – ease of use and adaptability;

- flexibility – to new technologies and information sources;

- relevance – of content and timing.

Internet-based trading communities can be either vertically or horizontally focused, bringing together buyers, suppliers and eBusiness service companies. Although there are issues about how seamlessly systems can meld these parties into true communities, there are notable benefits including cost savings, wider exposure within the marketplace, and virtually round-the-clock trading.

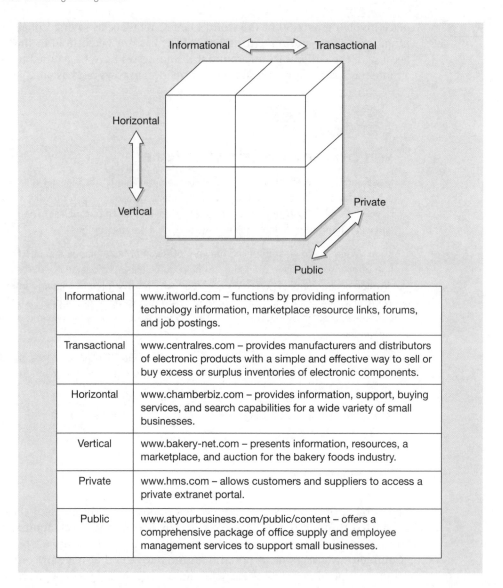

Informational	www.itworld.com – functions by providing information technology information, marketplace resource links, forums, and job postings.
Transactional	www.centralres.com – provides manufacturers and distributors of electronic products with a simple and effective way to sell or buy excess or surplus inventories of electronic components.
Horizontal	www.chamberbiz.com – provides information, support, buying services, and search capabilities for a wide variety of small businesses.
Vertical	www.bakery-net.com – presents information, resources, a marketplace, and auction for the bakery foods industry.
Private	www.hms.com – allows customers and suppliers to access a private extranet portal.
Public	www.atyourbusiness.com/public/content – offers a comprehensive package of office supply and employee management services to support small businesses.

Figure 5.4 A categorisation of web-based B2B portals

Source: Clarke and Flaherty (2003). Copyright © 2003. With permission from Elsevier.

Uncertainty, risk and relationships in OBB

As asserted previously, organisations encounter risk when purchasing products and services. The way organisations organise and manage purchasing activities is recognition of the existence of risk and a broad means by which they attempt to reduce their perceived risks.

The risk concept consists of three main elements, namely the potential loss, the significance of those losses and the uncertainty attached to the losses (Yates and

Table 5.5 Seven types of organisational decision-making risk

Risk type	Explanation
Technical risk	Will the parts, equipment or product/service perform as expected?
Financial risk	Does this represent value for money, could we have bought cheaper?
Delivery risk	Will delivery be on time, complete and in good order? Will our production schedule be disrupted?
Service risk	Will the equipment be supported properly and within agreed time parameters?
Personal risk	Am I comfortable dealing with this organisation, are my own social and ego needs threatened?
Relationship risk	To what extent is the long-term relationship with this organisation likely to be jeopardised by this decision?
Professional risk	How will this decision affect my professional standing in the eyes of others and how might my career and personal development be impacted?

Stone, 1992). Therefore perceived risk incorporates uncertainty but uncertainty itself is not the same as risk. Mitchell (1999) refers to Haakansson and Wootz (1979) who identified three types of uncertainty: need, transaction and market-related uncertainties. Valla (1982) suggested that there are five categories of organisational risk which must be addressed by buyers and suppliers. From these it is possible to identify seven types of risks that are relevant to organisational buyers (see Table 5.5).

A variety of factors might contribute to the level of perceived risk. Mitchell (1995) identifies 11 risk enhancing factors (see Figure 5.5). In order to reduce these risks organisations adopt a number of different approaches. By far the most common

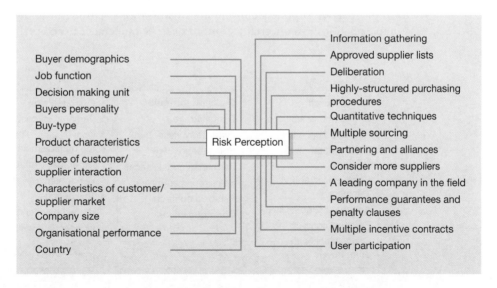

Figure 5.5 Factors that enhance organisational buyers' perceived risk

Source: Adapted from Mitchell (1995). Used with permission from Blackwell Publishing.

method is the search for information. This concerns both the nature of the information sought and also the amount of information (Newall, 1977). From a selling perspective organisations should seek to provide marketing communications messages that provide the information that buyers need and value. Traditionally the emphasis has been on use of the sales force, sales literature and direct marketing to provide both timely and appropriate information. Today, the use of websites, portals and extranets provides a fuller, more consistent and cost-effective way of fulfilling these risk reduction requirements. What is not quite so clear is how the information should be used by buying organisations to reduce their risks, nor is there much research on how cost-effective these information search activities are in reducing organisational perceived risk (Mitchell, 1995).

Research suggests that organisations configure their DMUs in the light of the level of perceived risk and the type of purchase under consideration (Wilson *et al.*, 1991). DMU size is likely to grow proportionally to the size of the risk and as modified rebuys and new task situations develop. Therefore, individual purchase actions give way to group DMUs as risk increases. Johnston and Lewin (1996) found that increases in risk are countered by:

■ an increase in the size of the DMU and populated with members with higher authority and status;

■ an intensifying information search;

■ DMU participants becoming more involved throughout the whole process;

■ organisations who are known to and preferred by the DMU becoming more likely to win the contract.

This last point suggests that the development of interorganisational relationships is important to both supplying and buying participants, particularly where new task situations are identified. Figure 5.6 sets out some of the more common approaches used by organisations to reduce risk. Organisational perceived risk should be reduced by both prospective suppliers and buying organisations. Through the development of suitable relationships uncertainty and risk can be moderated to acceptable levels.

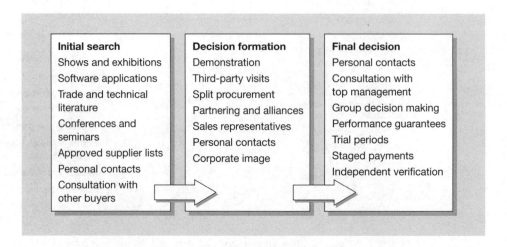

Figure 5.6 Risk reduction approaches for organisational purchase decisions

Purchasing risk is also observed in electronic trading formats. For example, in online reverse auctions Smeltzer and Carr (2003) identified different types of risk experienced by suppliers and buyers. One of the key risks experienced by buyers is that they might be destroying the trust that had developed with suppliers (in offline purchasing). A key risk for suppliers was that price becomes the only significant factor for the first and subsequent transactions. Therefore there is little motivation to invest in resources and support mechanisms because there is little incentive to develop a long-term relationship with the buyer.

SNAPSHOT 5.9

DECISION MAKERS' ATTITUDE TOWARDS RISK

B2B marketing consultants at Experian have found it useful to check the personal background of decision makers when trying to gauge their attitude to risk. For example, where a company has mainly male directors, who are broadsheet readers, nearing retirement, with no children at home, and low credit card use, the decision makers would be assumed to be risk averse. Within the same broad business sector, a business run by younger, male and female, directors with children, higher credit spending, and wider reading would probably have decision makers more likely to take risks.

Source: Adapted from McLuhan (2003).

Readers may recall the movement towards lean manufacturing and lean supply. This involves reducing the number of suppliers to a number that enables buyers to develop relationships with sellers that have a long(er)-term orientation and which may result in significant added value and competitive advantage. Knox (2000) suggests that there are three reasons why competitive advantage might be improved through stronger relationships.

1 Systems cost reduction – cost savings from improved working practices (e.g. improved order cycle times, reduced stock and working capital).

2 Increased effectiveness through innovation – as a relationship develops more information is exchanged and suppliers become more willing to invest in the relationship.

3 Enabling technologies – electronic systems and communications help suppliers to anticipate and understand the needs of their customers. Suppliers become better able to evaluate the cost-effectiveness of their customer portfolios and to determine where to invest.

Relationships, however, are far from similar and they add value in different ways. Knox offers the idea that supplier/buyer relationships should be regarded as a continuum.

Level 1. The relationship is based on market structure principles and the supplier provides specified products on the basis of price, service and quality.

Level 2. The supplier actively attempts to help the customer by reducing their costs and improving their competitiveness.

Level 3. The supplier takes responsibility for a major part of the customer's value adding capabilities and is in partnership with the customer. Outsourcing and subassembly arrangements typify this level of cooperation.

Level 4. Here there is a relational exchange and the supplier becomes a major source of strategic added value for the customer. For example, Norwich Union provide the financial expertise for Virgin's Financial Services. This co-branding arrangement enables the value within the technical expertise of the supplier to be partnered with the strong highly visible Virgin brand.

Knox suggests four levels but there could be more depending upon the required level of sophistication. Implicit within this approach is that DMU perceived purchase risk is associated with the actions of suppliers and that the relationship incorporates levels of trust. Gao *et al.* (2003) determine that a buyer's trust in a supplier is crucial to reducing their risk. Suppliers should therefore seek to build trust by allocating resources (for example, time, expertise, flexibility) to buyers in order to demonstrate commitment to the relationship and to be seen to be looking to the longer rather than the shorter term. Issues concerning trust and commitment are developed further in Chapter 9.

Summary

Organisational buying has a number of characteristics that reflect the importance and significance of this task. Organised and structured formally, groups of people coordinate their activities in order to make purchases for the organisation. Some of these purchases will be strategically critical and others will represent low-value consumables bought on a routine basis. Varying degrees of uncertainty are inherent, so organisations adopt processes and procedures in order to reduce risk as much as possible.

New technology has had a significant impact on organisational purchasing activities. It has introduced organisations to new suppliers, often based in different countries. It can reduce transaction costs and speed the process of negotiation and purchase. However, organisations need to ensure that their strategically important supplier relationships are protected and that technology is used to supplement, not destroy established, long-term, valued relationships. The notion that the relationship between suppliers and buyers develops from a purely transactional exchange through to one that is fully interconnected is intuitively interesting and is expanded in later chapters.

Discussion questions

1 Evaluate the key differences and similarities associated with both organisational and consumer buyer behaviour.

2 Write brief notes explaining the main characteristics and membership of the decision making unit.

3 With regard to the cases set out in Snapshot 5.2, discuss the key differences of the three approaches and suggest how they might each influence a potential supplier of photocopiers.

4 Name four different types of influences that impact on organisational decision making.

5 Find examples where IST has been used to help develop organisational buyer behaviour.

6 List Knox's different relationship levels and find examples to illustrate each level. Is this framework of value?

References

Bonoma, T.V. (1982). 'Major sales: who really does the buying?', *Harvard Business Review* (May/June), p. 113.

Bowersox, D. and Cooper, M. (1992). *Strategic Marketing Channel Management*, New York, NY: McGraw-Hill.

Chen, H.Y. and Wilson, D.T. (2000). 'Online auctions: are relationships doomed?', IMP Conference paper, www.bath.ac.uk/imp/pdf/xx_ChenWilson.pdf (Accessed 21 October 2003.)

Clarke III, I. and Flaherty, T.B. (2003). 'Web-based B2B portals', *Industrial Marketing Management*, 32, pp. 15–23.

Cravens, D.W. and Woodruff, R.B. (1986). *Marketing*, Reading, MA: Addison Wesley.

De Boer, L., Harink, J. and Heijboor, G. (2002). 'A conceptual model for assessing the impact of electronic procurement', *European Journal of Purchasing and Supply Management*, 8, 1, pp. 25–33.

Gao, T., Sirgy, M.J. and Bird, M.M. (2003). 'Reducing buyer decision making uncertainty in organisational purchasing: can supplier trust commitment and dependence help?', *Journal of Business Research*, www.sciencedirect.com/science (Accessed 11 September 2003.)

Gedney, K. and Belbey J. (2002), 'Embrace the gatekeeper', www.clickz.com/em_mkt/b2b_em_mkt/article.php/1476561 (Accessed 9 October 2002.)

Haakansson, H. and Wootz, B. (1979). 'A framework of industrial buying and selling', *Industrial Marketing Management*, 8, 1 (January), pp. 28–39.

Harvey, M.G, Novicevic, M.M., Hench, T. and Myers, M. (2003). 'Global account management: a supply side managerial view', *Industrial Marketing Management*, 32, 7 (October), pp. 563–71.

Hoffman, W., Keedy, J. and Roberts, K. (2002). 'The unexpected return of B2B', *The McKinsey Quarterly*, 3, www.mckinseyquarterly.com/article_print.asp?ar= 1210&L2=24&L3=47 (Accessed 12 May 2003.)

Howard, J. and Sheth, J.N. (1969). *The Theory of Buyer Behaviour*, New York: Wiley.

Jackson, B. (1985). 'Build customer relationships that last', *Harvard Business Review*, 63, 6, pp. 120–8.

Johnston, W.J. and Lewin, J.E. (1996). 'Organizational buyer behavior: towards an integrative framework', *Journal of Business Research*, 35, 1 (January), pp. 1–15.

Karpinski, R. (2001). 'E-Collaboration: hype or hope?', *Internet Week*, www.internetweek.com/transtoday01/ttoday030601.htm (Accessed 19 May 2003.)

Knox, S. (2000). 'Organisational buyer behaviour', in Cranfield School of Management (eds), *Marketing Management: A Relationship Marketing Perspective*, Basingstoke: Macmillan, pp. 62–76, .

Mason, K.J. and Gray, R. (1999). 'Stakeholders in a hybrid market: the example of air business passenger travel', *European Journal of Marketing*, 33, 9/10, pp. 844–58.

McLuhan, R. (2003). 'Add a little polish', *Database Marketing* (January), pp. 16–18.

McQuiston, D.H. and Dickson, P.R. (1991). 'The effect of perceived personal consequences on participation and influence in organisational buying', *Journal of Business*, 23, pp. 159–77.

Mirani, R., Moore, D. and Weber, J.A. (2001). 'Emerging technologies for enhancing supplier–reseller partnerships', *Industrial Marketing Management*, 30, 2, pp. 101–14.

Mitchell, V-M. (1995). 'Organisational risk perception and reduction: A literature review', *British Journal of Management*, 6, pp. 115–33.

Mitchell, V-M. (1999). 'Consumer perceived risk: conceptualisations and models', *European Journal of Marketing*, 33, 1/2, pp. 163–95.

Newall, J. (1977). 'Industrial buyer behaviour', *European Journal of Marketing*, 11, 3, pp. 166–211.

Robinson, P.J., Faris, C.W. and Wind, Y. (1967). *Industrial Buying and Creative Marketing*, Boston, MA: Allyn & Bacon.

Ronchetto, J.R., Hutt, M.D. and Reingen, P.H. (1989). 'Embedded patterns in organisational buying systems', *Journal of Marketing*, 53 (October), pp. 51–62.

Sashi, C.M. and O'Leary, B. (2002). 'The role of Internet auctions in the expansion of B2B markets', *Industrial Marketing Management*, 31, 2 (February), pp. 103–10.

Smeltzer, L.R. and Carr, A.S. (2003). 'Electronic reverse auctions: promises, risks and conditions for success', *Industrial Marketing Management*, 32, 6 (August), pp. 481–8.

Spekman, R.E. and Gronhaug, K. (1986). 'Conceptual and methodological issues in buying centre research', *European Journal of Marketing*, 20, 7, pp. 50–63.

Valla, J-P. (1982). 'The concept of risk in industrial buying behaviour', Workshop on Organisational Buying Behaviour, European Institute for Advanced Studies in Management, Brussels, December, pp. 9–10.

van Weele, A.J. (2002). *Purchasing and Supply Chain Management*, 3rd edn, London: Thomson Learning.

Webster, F.E. and Wind, Y. (1972). 'Organizational Buying Behaviour', Englewood Cliffs, NJ: Prentice Hall.

Weiss, A. M. and Hyde, J.B. (1993). 'The nature of organisational search in high technology markets', *Journal of Marketing Research*, 30 (May), pp. 220–33.

Wilson, D.F. (2000). 'Why divide consumer and organisational buyer behaviour?', *European Journal of Marketing*, 34, 7, pp. 780–96.

Wilson, E.J., Lilien, G.L. and Wilson, D.T. (1991). 'Developing and testing a contingency paradigm of group choice in organisational buying', *Journal of Marketing Research*, 28 (November), pp. 452–66.

Yates, J.F. and Stone, E.R. (1992). 'The risk construct', in J.F. Yates (ed.), *Risk Taking Behaviour*, Chichester: Wiley, pp. 3–25.

Chapter 6
Interorganisational relationships

Chapter overview

This chapter concludes Part B by introducing and examining relatively recent ideas associated with marketing management. The relationship marketing approach is offered as a counter to the prevailing wisdom of the 4Ps approach to marketing before issues concerning relationships with a wider array of stakeholders, especially others upstream in the supply chain, are introduced.

The deliberate development of collaborative and mutually rewarding relationships between suppliers and customers is considered to be fundamentally more appealing and an intuitively correct interpretation of business-to-business marketing. This view also sees the development of partnerships and alliances with other organisations as more appropriate than former adversarial ideas based on competition and where the sole focus is on customers.

Organisations are shown to have a portfolio of relationships with a range of stakeholders, most notably suppliers, employees, customers and shareholders. Primarily, this chapter considers the nature, development and characteristics of interorganisational relationships and, in addition, examines the potential of information systems for enhancing relationships with those customers and suppliers who choose to reciprocate and develop trust and commitment.

Chapter aims

The aims of this chapter are to consider the scope and nature of interorganisational relationships and to explore how this impacts on the contemporary view of business-to-business marketing.

Objectives

The objectives of this chapter are to:

1   Explore the development and evolution of relationship marketing.
2   Examine the conceptual underpinning associated with relationship marketing practices.
3   Introduce ideas concerning customer relationship life cycle.
4   Examine the nature and characteristics of partnerships and alliances with suppliers and other stakeholders.
5   Consider trust and commitment as key elements of business relationships.
6   Understand ways in which IST can influence interorganisational relationships.
7   Consider the nature of CRM and associated systems issues.

Introduction

In the mid-1990s, relationship marketing was proclaimed as a new marketing paradigm (Gronroos, 1994). A decade later, it is still regarded as somewhat novel, certainly different, and persistently challenges past interpretations of interorganisational marketing activity. While these may be sound observations and comments, relationship marketing does represent a totally new perspective. Marketing is, and always has been, about customers. The principles of looking after customers have not changed, although they might have been overlooked at times in the past. There has always been a relationship between buyers and sellers, even if the depth of understanding about the significance and character of different types is emergent. Ideas concerning the development of relationship marketing have evolved from extensive research based initially on exchange transactions and, in particular, buyer–seller interaction.

One of the broad characteristics of consumer marketing is that interaction and exchanges generally take place between anonymous individuals. By contrast, according to Easton and Araujo (1993), exchanges in interorganisational marketing contexts occur between individuals who are, in general, known to each other. The more frequent and intense these exchanges become, so the strength of the relationships between buyers and sellers improves. It is this that provided the infrastructure for a new perspective of marketing, one based on relationships between organisations (Spekman, 1988; Rowe and Barnes, 1998), rather than the objects of a transaction, namely products and services. It should be noted that the development of electronic trading formats may reduce the level and frequency of interpersonal contact for some types of transaction.

At the end of Chapter 1, following an introduction to value chain principles, reference was made to a range of different types of exchanges in which organisations engage. The continuum of value-orientated exchanges (Figure 1.4) expressed visually the diversity of exchanges with which organisations are involved; from one-off, short-term exchanges to those that are based upon collaboration and partnership.

Founding ideas about industrial marketing were based on market exchanges between organisations, where there was no prior history of exchange and no future exchanges expected. These paired organisations were considered to enter into transactions where products were the main focus and price was the key mechanism to exchange completion. Organisations were perceived to be adversarial and competition was paramount. These undertakings are referred to as market (or discrete) exchanges and often termed **transactional marketing**.

In contrast, relationship marketing is based on the principles that there is a history of exchanges and an expectation that there will be exchanges in the future. Furthermore, the perspective is on the long term, envisioning a form of loyalty or continued attachment by the buyer to the seller. Price as the key controlling mechanism is replaced by customer service and quality of interaction between the two organisations. The exchange is termed **relational** because the focus is on both organisations seeking to achieve their goals in a mutually rewarding way and not at the expense of one another (see Table 6.1 for a more comprehensive list of fundamental differences between transactional and relational exchange-based marketing).

SNAPSHOT 6.1

DISCRETE VERSUS RELATIONAL EXCHANGES

Car manufacturers do not normally sell cars direct to individual consumers. This is because consumers are relatively infrequent buyers of new cars and when they do buy from a dealer, it is normally a one-off or discrete exchange.

Car manufacturers normally develop relational exchanges with their fleet customers. These organisations tend to buy large quantities of cars on a regular basis. Communications and interaction between the parties tends to be continuous and designed to support the relationship over the longer term.

Car manufacturers sell batches of cars to their appointed dealers at pre-agreed dates. These exchanges cannot always be regarded as relational, as the goal of the manufacturer is stock turnover and their decisions are not always based on the financial or marketing situation facing each dealer. The element of collaboration and mutual self-help characteristic of relational exchanges is often missing within these relationships.

Table 6.1 Characteristics of market and relational exchanges

Attribute	Discrete exchange	Relational exchange
Chronological aspects of exchange	▨ Defined beginning	▨ Beginning can be traced back to earlier agreements
	▨ Short term	▨ Long term
	▨ Sudden end	▨ Reflects a continuous process
Expectations of the relationship	▨ Conflicts of interest/goals are expected	▨ Conflicts of interest expected
	▨ Immediate settlement ('cash payment')	▨ Future problems are overcome by trust and joint commitment
	▨ No problems expected in future	
Communication	▨ Minimal personal relations	▨ Both formal and informal communication used
	▨ Ritual-like communication predominates	
Transferability	▨ Totally transferable	▨ Limited transferability
	▨ It makes no difference who performs contractual obligations	▨ Exchanges are highly dependent on the identity of the parties
Cooperation	▨ No joint efforts	▨ Joint efforts at both planning and implementation stages
		▨ Modifications endemic over time
Division of burden and benefit	▨ Sharp distinction between parties	▨ Burden and benefits likely to be shared
	▨ Each party has its own, strictly defined obligations	▨ Division of benefits and burdens likely to vary over time

Source: Wagner and Boutellier (2002). Reprinted with permission from *Business Horizons*, 45, 6 (November–December 2002). Copyright © (2002) by The Trustees at Indiana University, Kelley School of Business.

The suggestion, implied in the terms **discrete** and **relational** exchanges, is that the former is devoid of a relationship component. However, although **discrete**, or **market**, exchanges focus on products and prices, there is not necessarily a complete absence of a relationship. Indeed, Cousins (2002) refers to the relationship marketing literature in terms of two broad perspectives. One of these is based on a behavioural dimension and the other is based on economic power. The former considers relationships as the prime determinant of interorganisational relations, while the latter considers market exchanges based on power and competition as the prevalent mechanism. Payne (2000) and Bruhn (2003) make the point that relationship marketing is not a new marketing paradigm, merely an extension of the marketing concept. The approach adopted in this book recognises the importance of both economic and behavioural dimensions and accepts that there is a relational dimension in all exchange activity. Rather, it is the case that the strength of focus varies between the two dimensions according to the contextual conditions facing organisations. Relationship marketing is therefore not necessarily a new marketing paradigm, but a fresh approach to marketing, one which puts relationships, not products, at the centre of marketing activities.

With this in mind Dwyer *et al.* (1987) refer to B2B relationship marketing as an approach which encompasses a wide range of relationships, not just with customers, but also those that organisations develop with suppliers, regulators, government, competitors, employees and others. From this, relationship marketing might be regarded as all marketing activities associated with the management of successful relational exchanges. Christopher *et al.* (2002) refer to a **six markets** model of relationship marketing, where, in addition to customer markets, relationships should be developed with recruitment, supplier, influence, internal and referral markets, on the grounds that these represent groups that contribute to an organisation's performance and marketplace contribution.

This chapter explores some of the characteristics associated with discrete and relational exchanges, it considers the development of relationship marketing, explores aspects of network interpretations and the impact on partnerships and alliances, not only with customers but suppliers and key stakeholders. In addition, it examines the role of IST in the management of interorganisational relationships, with particular emphasis on customer relationship management (CRM) systems.

Business relationships – background

In the commercial world, managers have long recognised the importance of relationships with their counterparts in other organisations. Both individual and interorganisational perspectives have been of interest. Academic research progressed in the 1990s with recognition of the varying, observable forms of relationships. Organisations were deemed to be capable of close collaborative relationships as well as remote, discrete relationships with other organisations. In addition, the dyadic approach, although still useful when considering market exchange-based relationships, appeared to provide a limited perspective on organisational conduct. Attention has moved on to consider triads and networks of interacting organisations. Presence and position in a network are considered to influence the actions of parties to a degree not previously considered.

Originally, marketing, especially B2B marketing theory, focused on the actions of individual organisations. This evolved into the recognition of interorganisational interaction with varying degrees of cooperation and dependency. Initially, attention concentrated on **dyads**, that is pairs of organisations interacting with market exchange principles guiding their relationship. At first consideration was given to pairings of individual people, but this changed to a group orientation with the 'introduction of buying centre and selling centre concepts' (Borders *et al.*, 2001, p. 201).

Business marketing in the 1960s, 1970s and early 1980s focused on the units of exchange, namely the products that were transacted between two organisations. The 4Ps approach to the marketing mix variables was used to guide and construct transaction behaviour. These transactions represented discrete exchanges between a single buying and a single selling organisation. The centre of attention was on the transaction between these two parties. Buyers were considered to be passive and sellers active in these short-term exchanges. According to Johanson and Mattsson (1994), cited by McLoughlin and Horan (2000), this early work was rooted in the stimulus-organism-response model, which assumes that passive buyers react to the offers of sellers in a more or less subservient and unquestioning manner. Consequently researchers, assuming a purchasing manager's perspective, sought to understand the processes that buyers used when making buying decisions. Work by Webster and Wind (1972) and Sheth (1973) typified this period. The goal was to develop marketing plans that made better use of resources and that targeted appropriate members of the buying centre. Business marketing was based on the premise that marketing and purchasing are separate activities and that the purchase activity involved just a single, one-off purchase event.

However, the assumption that buyers are passive was soon challenged by the notion that in reality business customers (organisations) are active problem solvers and seek

SNAPSHOT 6.2

COLLABORATION AT SAINSBURY'S

Sainsbury's has demonstrated a willingness to share sensitive information and develop relationships with members of its supply chain by entering into a collaborative scheme. Product and store information, based on sales and loyalty card (Nectar) data, is made available to suppliers, as the supermarket giant tries to align its product mix with customer demand.

The project allows suppliers to access information about repeat purchase rates, profiles of customers purchasing particular products and the most appropriate communication tools and methods to attract customers.

It is expected that the information will focus attention on key topics, namely product range, space, price and promotion. Through this approach Sainsbury's and its suppliers can be focused on customer needs and make better-informed decisions.

This collaborative scheme is one of several IST projects designed to add value. Others include a completely refreshed point-of-sale system and upgraded supply chain and logistics systems.

Source: Thomas (2003).

solutions that are both efficient and effective. It was then accepted that buyers actually practised cooperative behaviours in order to find suitable suppliers. For the first time the study of interorganisational behaviour became prevalent and focused on the relationship between the pair of organisations, rather than the products traded. Thus, research moved to encompass buying centre and selling centre characteristics, with one of the goals being to better align both parties to achieve greater efficiencies through improved cooperation. For example, the high profile given to just-in-time systems was a manifestation of the prevailing orientation. So, although research remained fixed on the buyer–seller dyad, interaction had now replaced reaction.

In essence, this was a move away from regarding purchasing as a single discrete event, to considering it as a stream of activities between two organisations. These activities are sometimes referred to as episodes. Typically these may be price negotiations, meetings at exhibitions or a buying decision but these all take place within the overall context of a relationship. Any one episode may be crucial to the relationship but analysing individual episodes is usually insufficient if the context, that is the overall relationship, is not understood. However, understanding the relationship alone does not produce a complete picture either, so as Ford (1980, p. 340) argues, 'it is important to analyse both individual episodes and the overall relationship, as well as to understand the interaction between the two'. Therefore, buyers and sellers were considered to behave (or interact) within the context of their own dyadic relationship. The unit of attention was no longer the product, or even the individual buying or selling unit, but the relationship, the stream of associated episodes and its attendant characteristics.

Around the same time, attention moved away from vertical integration as the preferred structural business model, to recognition of the significance and relevance of networks and loose alliances among organisations. In terms of understanding business interaction, this brought into consideration the potential influence of the indirect relationships that organisations have with one another. Relationship research (and marketing) needed to focus not just on buyers and sellers but on a wide range of other organisations each interacting with one another in a network of relationships. Understanding about the role and nature of relationships, within an interorganisational context, has therefore evolved over several decades.

Relationship marketing – theoretical foundations

The development and underpinning of relationship marketing can be traced through a variety of theoretical perspectives. These are reviewed extensively by others (Varey, 2002; Bruhn, 2003) and Table 6.2 sets out some of the more prominent conceptual interpretations. Of these concepts, three are considered here: social exchange theory, social penetration theory and interaction theory. These are considered in organisational terms but it should be remembered that many of these theories have their origins in individual relationships.

Table 6.2 The theoretical foundations of relationship marketing

	Theory	Authors	Focus
Neoclassic	Value theory	Implicit application based on a series of marketing publications	Significance of quality, customer satisfaction, perceived value, and relationship quality within relationship marketing
	Profit theory	Blattberg and Deighton (1996)	Evaluation of customer relationships from a corporate perspective
Neo-Institutional paradigm	Information economics	Klee (2000)	Explanation of interaction uncertainties and derivation of strategies to reduce uncertainty
		Ahlert, Kenning and Petermann (2001)	Trust as success factor for services-based corporations
	Transaction cost theory	Klee (2000)	Pre-conditions for an advantageous initiation of customer relationships
		Grönroos (1994)	Profitability of long-term business relationships
	Principal-agent theory	Jensen and Meckling (1976); Bergen *et al.* (1992)	Elucidation of customer and employee behaviour within customer relationships
Psychological theories			
Neo-behavioural paradigm	Learning theory	Sheth and Parvatiyar (1995)	Clarification and influencing factors for the emergence of customer relationships
	Risk theory	Sheth and Parvatiyar (1995)	Clarification and influencing factors for the emergence of customer relationships
		Fischer and Tewes (2001)	Trust and commitment as intermediary variables for service processes
	Cognitive dissonance theory	Sheth and Parvatiyar (1995)	Clarification and influencing factors for the emergence of customer relationships

Theory	Authors	Focus
Socio-psychological theories		
Interaction/Network approaches	IMP Group (1982); Grönroos (1994)	Structuring of interaction processes
Social exchange theory	Houston and Gassenheimer (1987)	Emergence and maintenance of customer relationships; evaluation, long-duration, and stability of customer relationships
Social penetration theory	Altman and Taylor (1973)	Emergence and development of customer relationships

Source: Bruhn (2003). Used with permission.

Social exchange theory

The central premise associated with social exchange theory (Blau, 1964) is that relationships are based upon the exchange of values between two or more parties. Whatever constitutes the nature of an exchange between the participants, equality or satisfaction must be felt as a result. An absence of equality means that an advantage might have been gained by one party and this will automatically result in negative consequences for another. Therefore, organisations seeking to maintain marketing channel relationships should not raise prices past threshold levels or allow levels of service output (see Chapter 7) to fall below those of competitors. If channel partners perceive a lack of added value from these exchanges they are more likely to compare performance with other potential suppliers and even withdraw from the relationship by establishing alternative sources of supply.

Exchanges can occur between two parties, three parties in sequence or between at least three parties within a wider network and not necessarily sequentially. Relationships evolve from exchange behaviour which serves to provide the rules of engagement. They are socially constructed and have been interpreted in terms of marriage and social relationships (Tynan, 1997). Social norms drive exchange reciprocity within relationships and serve to guide behaviour expectations.

Whether in personal or interorganisational relationships, exchanges are considered to consist of two main elements. First, there are value exchanges which are based on the exchange of resources (goods for money) and second, there are symbolic exchanges where, in an interorganisational context, goods are purchased for their utility plus the feelings and associations that are bestowed on the user.

Social exchange theory serves to explain customer retention on the basis that the rewards derived through exchanges exceed the associated costs. Should expectations about future satisfaction fall short of the levels established through past exchanges, or alternative possibilities with other organisations suggest potentially improved levels of satisfaction, then the current partner may be discarded and a new relationship encouraged.

Social penetration theory

This theory is based on the premise that as relationships develop individuals begin to reveal more about themselves. Every encounter between a buyer and seller will allow each party to discover more about the other and make judgements about assigning suitable levels of relationship confidence. Consequently, the behaviour and communications exhibited between organisations may well change from a very formal and awkward introduction to something more knowledgeable, relaxed and self-assured.

Altman and Taylor (1973) refer to personality depth and personality breadth as two key aspects of the social penetration approach. Personality breadth is concerned with the range of topics (or categories) discussed by the parties and the frequency with which organisations discuss each topic. Unsurprisingly, products and customer needs are two main categories that are discussed by organisations. The analogy of an onion is often used to describe the various layers that make up the depth of a personality. The outer layers are generally superficial, contain a number of elements (of personality) and are relatively easy to determine. However, the key personality characteristics, those which influence the structure of the outer levels, are embedded within the inner core. The term personality depth refers to the difficulties associated with penetrating these inner layers, often because of the risks associated with such revelations.

From an organisational perspective, personality depth can be interpreted in terms of the degree to which a seller understands each of its customers. This client knowledge will vary but may include the way they use the products, their strategies, resources, culture and ethos, difficulties, challenges, successes and other elements that characterise buying organisations. Through successive interactions each organisation develops more knowledge of the other, as more information is gradually exposed, revealed or made known. At the outset of relationships, organisations tend to restrict the amount of information they reveal about themselves, but as confidence and trust in the other party develops so the level of openness increases. Likewise, as relationships develop so the degree of formality between the parties decreases, becoming more informal. This relationship intensity impacts on the quality of the relationship between two, or more, organisations.

Deconstructing a relationship reveals that it is composed of a series, or layers, of interactions. Each interaction results in judgements about whether to terminate or proceed with the relationship. The judgement is based on the accumulation of interactions, the history of the relationship and the level of customer knowledge that has been revealed.

Interactional theory

The development of relationship marketing appears to coincide with the emergence of network approaches to interorganisational analysis. This is referred to as industrial network analysis, and has evolved from the original focus on dyadic relationships (Araujo and Easton, 1996). A significantly strong and influential body of research, focusing on the interaction between members of a network, has been developed by the International Marketing and Purchasing Group (IMP).

The IMP Group analyses relationships, rather than transactions between buyers and sellers but, unlike relationship marketing theorists, they believe that both parties are active participants. Relationships between buyers and sellers are regarded as long-term, close and complex and through episodes of exchange the links between organisations become institutionalised. Processes and roles become established, ingrained and expected of one another. It is particularly significant in this interactional approach that **other organisations** are considered to influence the relationship between a buyer and a seller. This incorporates ideas concerning network interpretations of business-to-business and channel configuration, considered in Chapter 8.

Table 6.3 Elements of exchange episodes

McLoughlin and Horan (2000)	IMP Group
Financial and economic exchange	Product/service exchange
Technological exchange	Information exchange
Information exchange	Financial exchange
Knowledge exchange	Social exchange
Legal exchange	

The interactional approach is based on relational exchanges with a variety of organisations within interlocking networks. An important aspect of network operation is the high degree of cooperation and reciprocity necessary between participants. This cooperation is manifest through the various exchanges that organisations undertake. McLoughlin and Horan (2000) identify five main exchange elements, while the IMP Group determine four, as set out in Table 6.3. These two lists are largely similar and both encompass formal and informal exchanges. These occur over time with varying levels of intensity between two or more organisations.

Relationships are developed through the different exchange episodes and are largely influenced by four main factors: technology, organisational determinants (size, structure and strategy), organisational experience and individuals. The result of this is an atmosphere in which a relationship exists and reflects issues of power-dependence, the degree of conflict or cooperation and the overall closeness or distance of the relationship.

The development of relationship marketing

In order that a buyer–seller dyad be established, both organisations need to be attracted to one another. Once they are paired, theory suggests that the strength and duration of a pairing was determined by the application of the marketing mix. However, Gronroos (1994) argued that the marketing mix concept, as postulated originally by McCarthy (1960) and then (mis)interpreted by Borden (1964) and by many since as a general theory of marketing, has its roots in microeconomic theory. It represents, essentially, a production-orientated approach to marketing whereby the ingredients are mixed, rather as a chef mixes ingredients in a recipe. The use of the marketing mix 4Ps concept encouraged a market exchange orientation. Sellers sought to attract buyers, negotiate and complete a transaction and then both parties left the pairing, suitably satisfied. However, with price as the market mechanism and little integration between the ingredients, the 4Ps approach began to be perceived as lacking substance and sufficient rigour to continue as the tacit general theory of marketing. The unit of analysis was the product embedded in the single transaction.

One of the next stages involved an understanding of transaction economics closely followed first by quality and then costs. From this emerged ideas about how customer relationships might be advantageous. Relationship cost theory identified benefits associated with stable and mutually rewarding relationships. Such customers avoided costly switching costs associated with finding new suppliers, while suppliers experienced reduced quality costs, incurred when adapting to the needs of new customers. Reichheld and Sasser (1990) identified an important association between a small (for example 5 per cent) increase in customer retention and a large (for example 60 per cent) improvement in profitability. So, a long-term relationship leads to lower relationship costs and higher profits. Since this early work there has been general acceptance that customers who are loyal not only improve an organisation's profits but also strengthen its competitive position (Day, 2000) because competitors have to work harder to dislodge or destabilise their loyalty. It should be noted that some authors suggest the link between loyalty and profitability is not that simple (Dowling and Uncles, 1997), while others argue that much more information and understanding is required about the association between profitability and loyalty, especially when there may be high costs associated with customer acquisition (Reinartz and Kumar, 2002). However, at this stage the new relationship marketing concept consisted of two main elements: customer attraction and customer retention.

The next step was to challenge the notion that all customers are good customers. Clearly, some customers are far less attractive than other customers, indeed some are barely profitable. Undertaking customer profitability analysis identifies those segments that are worth developing, and hence builds a portfolio of relationships, each of varying dimensions and potential. These relationships provide mutually rewarding benefits and provide a third dimension of the customer dynamic, namely customer development.

A more useful extension of this perspective is that the focus should not be the buyer–seller dyad but the interactions between organisations within a network of relationships. Consideration is given to the nature of networks later in this chapter.

Customer relationships life cycle

As already suggested, customer relationships move through a variety of phases and are therefore dynamic in nature and structure. By utilising the life cycle concept it is possible to chart these different phases over the natural course of a relationship. Just as different strategies can be applied to different phases of the product life cycle, it is possible to observe that customers have different requirements as a relationship evolves.

This particular life cycle tracks the evolution of relationships through time against the intensity of relationship at any one moment. The variables that constitute the intensity of relationship dimension are subject to various interpretations. Bruhn (2003) draws on psychological, behavioural and economic indicators, as depicted in Figure 6.1.

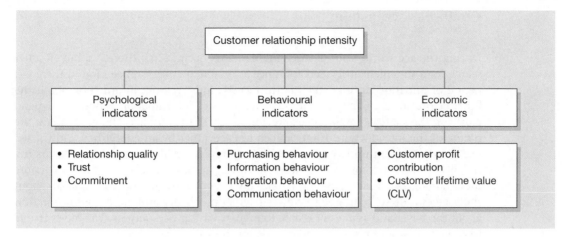

Figure 6.1 Indicators of customer relationship intensity
Source: Bruhn (2003). Used with permission.

Paramount to the psychological indicators are the concepts of trust and commitment. These are examined in greater detail later in this chapter but, for now, they should be regarded as foundations for establishing and maintaining ongoing, mutually rewarding two-way relationships. Behavioural indicators refer not just to purchasing but also to communication and information (search) behaviours.

It is possible to break down customer relationships into a number of different phases but at the aggregate level there are four, namely customer acquisition, development, retention and decline. The duration and intensity of each relationship phase will inevitably vary and it should be remembered that this representation is idealistic. A customer relationship cycle is represented at Figure 6.2.

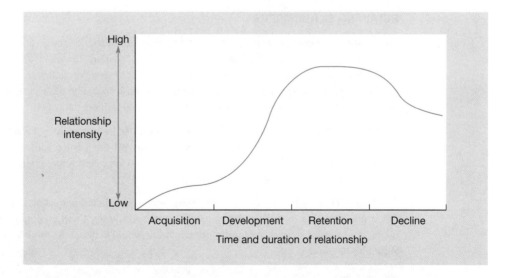

Figure 6.2 Customer relationship life cycle

Customer acquisition

During the acquisition phase three main events occur. First, there is a buyer–seller search for a suitable pairing. Second, once a suitable partner has been found there is a period of initiation during which both organisations seek out information about the other before any transaction occurs. The duration of this initiation period will depend partly on the strategic importance and complexity of the products and partly upon the nature of the introduction. If introduced to each other by an established and trusted organisation certain initiation rights will be shortened. Once a transaction occurs the socialisation period commences during which the buyer and seller start to become more familiar with each other and gradually begin to reveal more information about themselves. The seller is able to collect payment, delivery and handling information about the buyer and as a result is able to prepare customised outputs. The buyer is able to review the seller's products and experience the seller's service quality.

Customer development

During the development phase the seller encourages the buyer to try other products, to increase the volume of purchases, to engage with other added value services and to vary delivery times and quantities. The buyer will acquiesce according to specific needs and the level of drive to become more involved with the supplier. It is during this phase that the buyer is able to determine whether or not it is worth developing deeper relationships with the seller.

SNAPSHOT 6.3

RETAINING SUBSCRIBERS

The balance and costs of activities designed to stimulate customer acquisition and retention activities should always be considered. Magazine publishers, for example, often recruit new subscribers through two different channels – direct marketing activities and agents. The use of agents is attractive because there are few sunk costs and there is only a flat fee charge per recruit, which are invariably lower than those for direct marketing.

It became apparent to a particular publisher that after five years only 15 per cent of agent-recruited subscribers had been retained yet 30 per cent of direct-marketing recruits still subscribed. It was also known that agent-recruited subscribers were less responsive to renewal-based communications.

The publisher decided to move budget away from agent-based acquisition activities to direct marketing. Even though this decision increased the front end customer life cycle costs, the overall average profitability per customer would increase as more subscribers would be retained.

Source: Adapted from Grion (2003).

Customer retention

The retention phase will last as long as both the buyer and seller are able to meet their individual and joint goals. If the relationship has become more involved greater levels of trust and commitment between the partners will allow for increased cross-buying and product experimentation, joint projects and product development. However, the very essence of relationship marketing is for organisations to identify a portfolio of organisations with whom they wish to develop a range of relationships. This requires means to measure levels of retention and also determine when resources are moved from acquisition to retention and back to acquisition.

Customer decline

This period is concerned with the demise of the relationship. Termination may occur suddenly as a result of a serious problem or episode between the parties. The more likely process is that the buying organisation decides to reduce their reliance on the seller and either notifies them formally or begins to reduce the frequency and duration of contact and moves business to other, competitive organisations.

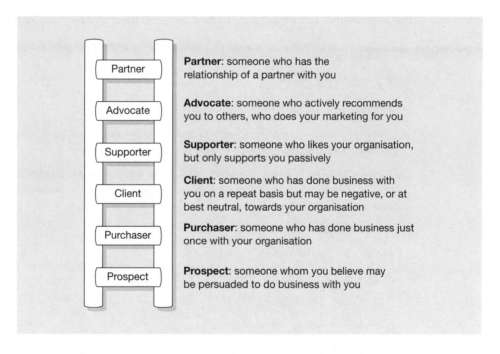

Figure 6.3 The relationship marketing ladder of loyalty

Source: Christopher *et al.* (2002). Copyright © 2002. With permission from Elsevier.

Customer loyalty

Implicit within this customer relationship cycle is the notion that retained customers are loyal. However, this may be deceptive as 'loyalty' may actually be camouflage for convenience or extended utility. Loyalty, however presented, takes different forms, just as there are customers who are more valued than others. Christopher *et al.* (2002) depict the various types of relationships as stages or steps on a ladder, the relationship marketing ladder of loyalty (see Figure 6.3).

A prospect becomes a purchaser, completed through a market or discrete exchange. Clients emerge from several completed transactions but remain ambivalent towards the seller organisation. Supporters, despite being passive about an organisation, are willing and able to enter into regular transactions. Advocates represent the next and penultimate step. They not only support an organisation and its products but actively recommend it to others by positive, word-of-mouth communications. Partners, who represent the top rung of the ladder, trust and support an organisation just as it trusts and supports them. Partnership status, discussed in greater detail later in this chapter, is the embodiment of relational exchanges and interorganisational collaboration.

This cycle of customer attraction (acquisition), customer retention and customer development represents a major difference to the 4Ps approach. It is, above all else, customer-focused and more appropriate to marketing values. However, even this approach is questionable as, although the focus of analysis is no longer the product but the relationship, the focus tends to be orientated towards the 'customer relationship'

SNAPSHOT 6.4

ASYMMETRIC RELATIONSHIP MARKETING

This is an extract from a CRM systems provider's website and reflects the asymmetric approach often adopted towards customer relationship marketing:

The idea of CRM is that it helps businesses use technology and human resources to gain insight into the behaviour of customers and the value of those customers. If it works as hoped, a business can:

- provide better customer service
- make call centres more efficient
- cross-sell products more effectively
- help sales staff close deals faster
- simplify marketing and sales processes
- discover new customers
- increase customer revenues.

Source: www.cio.com/research/crm/edit/crmabc.html (Accessed 16 February 2003.) Reprinted through the courtesy of CIO. Copyright © 2003 CXO Media Inc. All rights reserved.

rather than the relationship *per se*. In other words there is a degree of asymmetry inherent in the relationship marketing concept.

Differing types of relationships

The simplicity of the loyalty ladder concept illustrates the important point that customers represent different values to other organisations. That perceived value (or worth) may or may not be reciprocated, thus establishing the basis for a variety and complexity of different relationships.

The theoretical development of relationship marketing encompasses a number of different concepts. These involve a greater emphasis on cooperation rather than competition and the identification of different development phases within customer relationships, namely customer acquisition, development and retention.

According to Wagner and Boutellier (2002), the degree to which buyer–seller relationships are developed can depend on the configuration of internal and external factors. Internal factors involve the nature of the product, the degree of technological sophistication and the core competences of the organisation. The external factors involve the industry environment, the market, the competitive situation and the condition of the overall economy. Bringing these elements together and making relationship development decisions involves a level of management judgement but two guiding principles can be of assistance. These concern the strategic influence of the supplier's input goods and the degree to which supplying organisations can be substituted.

Organisations that supply goods and materials that are not strategic, that is, they do not provide added value or enable a degree of differentiation, do not warrant an investment in close relationship development. It is better that relationships should be remote, enabling buying flexibility and the exertion of downward pressures on price, quality and delivery. However, suppliers of goods and materials that are central to the buying organisation's strategic thrust, such as those that supply customised goods or critical systems architecture services are important. This is because they contribute to the development of customer value through differentiation. This requires the formation of close relationships, even partnerships and collaborative arrangements, to facilitate intensive negotiations and provide continuity of personal supply and continued customer value.

The second principle concerns the state of the market environment. In markets where the products are relatively standardised or simple, then a remote relationship is preferable due to the ease with which buyers can switch suppliers and substitute the source of their input goods. Where products are complex and or highly customised, then partnerships are preferable in order to provide continuity of supply. As a general rule therefore, when product supply is easy and there is active competition between suppliers for business, then a remote relationship may be advisable. When supply is tight, especially in growth markets, close collaboration and the development of partnerships with key suppliers is the best course of action.

Wagner and Boutellier (2002) cite DaimlerChrysler and their global procurement and supply strategy process as an example of an organisation that segments its suppliers and commodities based on the type of relationship it seeks. Using the following seven criteria, the organisation allocates commodities and input suppliers to one of four extended enterprise (EE) relationship types.

- share in value adding costs;
- dependency on suppliers' technical know-how;
- buyer's own knowledge about specifications and design;
- number of possible suppliers;
- switching costs and strength of exit barriers;
- supplier's negotiating power;
- importance to and contribution towards DC's own customers perceptions.

As Figure 6.4 demonstrates, DaimlerChrysler identify transaction, coordination, co-operation and alliance types of relationship. The first two are regarded as essentially operational and the second two as strategic types of relationship.

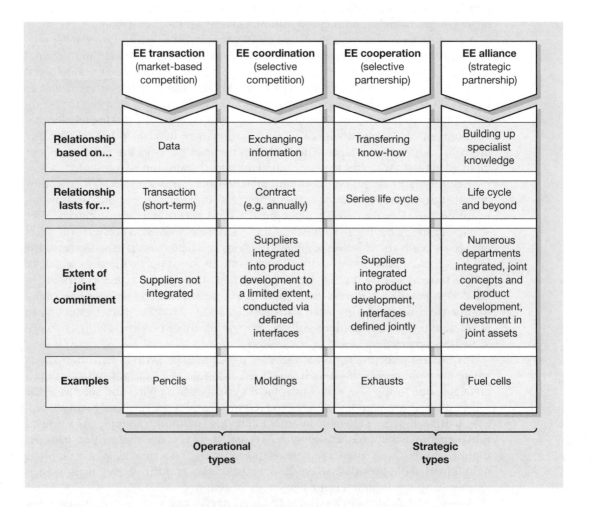

	EE transaction (market-based competition)	EE coordination (selective competition)	EE cooperation (selective partnership)	EE alliance (strategic partnership)
Relationship based on...	Data	Exchanging information	Transferring know-how	Building up specialist knowledge
Relationship lasts for...	Transaction (short-term)	Contract (e.g. annually)	Series life cycle	Life cycle and beyond
Extent of joint commitment	Suppliers not integrated	Suppliers integrated into product development to a limited extent, conducted via defined interfaces	Suppliers integrated into product development, interfaces defined jointly	Numerous departments integrated, joint concepts and product development, investment in joint assets
Examples	Pencils	Moldings	Exhausts	Fuel cells

Operational types	Strategic types

Figure 6.4 Types of relationship at DaimlerChrysler

Bensaou (1999) reported similar work with automobile manufacturers in Japan and the United States and identified four types of relationships, namely market exchange, captive supplier, captive buyer and strategic partnerships. Allocation to one of these categories is based on customer, supplier and product characteristics and each type of relationship requires particular strategies if the relationship is to be successful.

The development of suitable segmentation strategies is critical to understanding customers and their individual potential value to the seller, in order that they develop appropriate relationships (Tinsley, 2002). Decisions concerning segmentation require that database management and associated systems generate appropriate information. However, as Tinsley also points out, reliance on simplistic information systems to determine the potential of a customer who is currently of low value status is problematic and insufficiently strategic.

The development and implementation of a relationship marketing strategy can impact on a wide range of organisational activities. One of these concerns implementation and the range of resources required to be successful (Tinsley, 2002). Not all relationships are the same, indeed each may require different approaches and resources. An organisation has finite resources so must decide, among its portfolio of buyers, which warrant developing relationships and the type of relationships to nurture. Resources can then be allocated accordingly.

Partnerships and alliances

The development of strategic alliances is a step that some organisations undertake, very often with organisations with whom they already work closely, in order to gain competitive advantage through their complementary resources or core competences. An alliance in this sense implies a commitment to another organisation(s) in which partners invest resources to achieve particular goals. It is strategic because the relationship is long-term, all partners are committed and the relationship is mutually supportive.

The term **alliance** is just one of many used to describe the way some organisations have tried to gain advantage and reduce uncertainty through the development of committed working partnerships. According to Teece (1992), such organisations can obtain complementary resources in a fast, flexible and cost-efficient way. Terms such as channel partners, distribution partners and partnerships are also used in this context. Unlike vertical integration, where ownership dominance and control are the prime structural factors, strategic distribution-based alliances rely on trust and commitment to achieve the agreed outcomes.

The main advantages of forming such alliances is that they enable organisations to reduce the uncertainties associated with developing channel operations and relationships and, through cooperation, the partners are able to strengthen their market positions. Lerner and Merges (1997) refer to small biotechnology firms who partner large and established pharmaceutical firms in order to gain access to large markets and distribution and marketing resources while the pharmaceutical firm develops knowledge in new products and leading-edge research. Airlines such as British Airways and Quantas form alliances so that their flights can be connected to each

BRITANNIA AND BESPAK MAKE AN ALLIANCE

In October 2003 Britannia Pharmaceuticals and Bespak announced that they had signed an agreement to accelerate the development of AdSurf®, a novel clinical approach to the prevention of surgical adhesions that has been under development by Britannia.

Britannia were to be responsible for AdSurf's clinical development, as well as its manufacturing, while Bespak assumed responsibility for the development of a commercially viable delivery device (for the product). Britannia and Bespak agreed to share the intellectual property resulting from the alliance.

It was said that the companies would be seeking a licensing partner to assist them in bringing AdSurf to market and to manage worldwide sales of the product.

Source: Adapted from a press release, www.click2newsites.com/pressrelease15102003-18.htm (Accessed 13 November 2003.)

other. Passengers prefer the continuity, and the airlines generate increased traffic flows (Bamberger, *et al.*, 2001).

For manufacturers, long lead times and high extended costs, associated with building both distributor relationships and the core skills necessary to operate in a variety of markets, can be reduced through a single partner. The ideal partner organisation, possessing the experience and core competences required by the manufacturer, can implement market solutions more or less immediately.

Distribution alliances require all parties to work together and be flexible in their approach to the inevitable problems that arise through such activities. Kanter (1994) suggests that there are five levels of integration necessary if strategic alliances are to be successful (see Table 6.4).

Table 6.4 Five levels of alliance integration

Type of integration	Explanation
Strategic	Post-contract dialogue between senior managers to maintain and enhance the relationship.
Tactical	Middle managers to develop systems to facilitate the transfer of knowledge and to cement interorganisational infrastructures.
Operational	The information necessary to complete the day-to-day activities associated with the alliance.
Interpersonal	The development of personal knowledge of other people in the partnership.
Cultural	All managers to develop awareness and communication skills to bridge the cultural gaps that arise between the organisations.

Source: Adapted from Kanter (1994).

The reasons for forming alliances vary according to the position occupied in the marketing channel. Distributors and retailers seek alliances upstream in order to ensure a flow of desirable products and in doing so differentiate themselves from other distributors and retailers. Although manufacturers look for better market coverage and lower costs, some of the increasingly important reasons for alliances with downstream channel members concern the logistical advantages of lower order cycle times, lower stock-related costs and higher service output levels.

In order for a supplier to achieve partnership status Lemke *et al.* (2003) determined five key constructs:

- that the business relationship is developed at a personal rather than organisational level;

- that the supplier is capable of supplying bespoke products;

- that the supplier contributes to the new product development process of the manufacturer;

- that there is regular, active relationship management;

- that the supplier is located near to the manufacturer for both interaction and delivery purposes.

Contemporary supplier–manufacturer partnerships are therefore less orientated, than around 10 years ago, to product quality, on-time delivery and competitive pricing as these are now commonly expected factors and are no longer critical discriminators.

There are numerous examples of distribution alliances such as those between Pepsi Cola and Cadbury Schweppes, Yahoo with Compaq Europe, Gateway, Hewlett-Packard, IBM, Micron Electronics, and alliances between Hitachi Data Systems and Network Appliances and Sun Microsystems.

The success factors associated with external collaboration and partnerships are goal congruence, trust at all levels of interaction and intensive positive communication. Additionally, for partnerships to be successful, attention must be given to internal factors. As with a change management project, senior management must provide their support and the use of cross-functional teams appears to be an integral aspect of successful alliances (Wagner and Boutellier, 2002).

B2B eCommerce alliances have been categorised by Dai and Kauffman (2002) into four functional types, which are set out in Table 6.5.

SNAPSHOT 6.6

LASTMINUTE/TESCO ALLIANCE

Lastminute.com, said to be Europe's leading online travel agent, joined with Tesco.com, the United Kingdoms's largest online grocer, to create a new travel website. By providing complementary services the goal was to reach affluent families who shop online at Tesco and who take at least one major holiday a year plus regular weekend breaks.

Source: Adapted from Porter (2003).

Table 6.5 Functional types of alliances

Type of eMarket Alliance	Explanation
Marketing alliances	To facilitate improved promotion and distribution of online services.
Participation alliances	To improve levels of cooperation and involvement in online exchanges.
Functionality alliances	To improve the utility offered by a marketplace so that it works more efficiently and more effectively.
Connection alliances	To encourage linkages into an electronic marketplace.

Source: Adapted from Dai and Kauffman (2002).

The first two types, marketing and participation alliances, seek to develop the number of organisations involved in the exchange. In doing so they are essentially relationally orientated. The other two try to improve the technical services offered to participants of the marketplace.

Trust, commitment and customer satisfaction

Many writers contend that one of the crucial factors associated with the development and maintenance of interorganisational relationships is trust (Morgan and Hunt, 1994; Doney and Cannon, 1997). However, Cousins and Stanwix (2001) believe that the concepts, although important, are difficult to define and suggest that many authors fail to specify clearly what they mean when using them. A review of the literature indicates that trust is an element of personal, intraorganisational and interorganisational relationships, being both necessary for and resulting from their perpetuation. As Gambetta (1988) argues, trust is a means of reducing uncertainty in order that effective relationships can develop.

Cousins and Stanwix also suggest that, although trust is a term used to explain how B2B relationships work, often it actually refers to ideas concerning risk, power and dependency and these propositions are used interchangeably. From their research of vehicle manufacturers, it emerges that B2B relationships are about the creation of mutual business advantage and the degree of confidence that one organisation has in another.

Interorganisational trust is based on two main dimensions; credibility and benevolence. Credibility concerns the extent to which one organisation believes (is confident) that another organisation will undertake and complete its agreed roles and tasks. Benevolence is concerned with goodwill, that the other organisation will not act opportunistically, even if the conditions for exploitation should arise (Pavlou, 2002). In other words, interorganisational trust involves judgements about another organisation's reliability and integrity.

It has been suggested that interorganisational trust consists of three main elements (Zucker, 1986; Luo, 2002). **Characteristic** trust, based on the similarities between parties, **process** trust, developed through familiarity and typically fostered by successive

Table 6.6 Elements of institutional trust

Element of institutional trust	Key aspect
Perceived monitoring	Refers to the supervision of transactions by, for example, regulatory authorities or owners of B2B market exchanges. This can mitigate uncertainty through a perception that sellers or buyers who fail to conform with established rules and regulations will be penalised.
Perceived accreditation	Refers to badges or symbols that denote membership of externally recognised bodies that bestow credibility, authority, security and privacy on a selling organisation.
Perceived legal bonds	Refers to contracts between buyers, sellers and independent third parties, so that the costs of breaking a contract are perceived to be greater than the benefits of such an action. Trust in the selling organisation is therefore enhanced when bonds are present.
Perceived feedback	Refers to signals about the quality of an organisation's reputation and such feedback from other buyers about sellers, perhaps through word-of-mouth communication can deter sellers from undertaking opportunistic behaviour.
Perceived cooperative norms	Refers to the values, standards and principles adopted by those party to a series of exchanges. Cooperative norms and values signal good faith and behavioural intent, through which trust is developed.

Source: Adapted from Pavlou (2002).

exchange transactions and **institutional** trust, see below. This third category might be considered to be the most important, especially at the outset of a relationship when familiarity and similarity factors are non-existent or hard to discern respectively.

Pavlou (2002) argues that there are five means by which institutional trust can be encouraged (see Table 6.6). Institutional trust is clearly vital in B2C markets where online perceived risk is present and known to prevent many people from purchasing online. In the B2B market, institutional trust is also important but more in terms of the overall reputation of the organisation. The development and establishment of trust is valuable because of the outcomes that can be anticipated. Three major outcomes from the development of trust have been identified by Pavlou (2002) namely satisfaction, perceived risk and continuity.

Trust reduces conflict and the threat of opportunism and that in turn enhances the probability of buyer satisfaction, an important positive outcome of institutional trust. Perceived risk is concerned with the expectation of loss and is therefore tied closely with organisational performance. Trust that a seller will not take advantage of the imbalance of information between buyer and seller effectively reduces risk. Continuity is related to business volumes, necessary in online B2B marketplaces, and the development of both on- and offline enduring relationships. Trust is associated with continuity and when present is therefore indicative of long-term relationships.

According to Young and Wilkinson (1989) the presence of trust within a relationship is influenced by four main factors. These are the duration of the relationship, the

relative power of the participants, the presence of cooperation and various environmental factors that may be present at any one moment. Extending these ideas into
what is now regarded by many as a seminal paper in the relationship marketing literature, Morgan and Hunt (1994) argued, and supported with empirical evidence, that
the presence of both commitment and trust leads to cooperative behaviour and this
in turn is conducive to successful relationship marketing.

Morgan and Hunt regard commitment as the desire that a relationship continue
(endure) in order that a valued relationship be maintained or strengthened. They postulated that commitment and trust are key mediating variables (KMV) between five
antecedents and five outcomes (see Figure 6.5).

According to the KMV model the greater the losses anticipated through the termination of a relationship the greater the commitment will be expressed by the
exchange partners. Likewise, when these partners share the same values commitment
increases. Trust is enhanced when communication is perceived to be of high quality
but decreases when one organisation knowingly takes action that will be to the detriment of the other to seek to benefit from the relationship.

Kumar *et al.* (1994) distinguish between **affective** and **calculative** commitment.
The former is rooted in positive feelings towards the other party and a desire to
maintain the relationship. The latter is negatively orientated and is determined by the
extent to which one party perceives it is (not) possible to replace the other party,
advantageously.

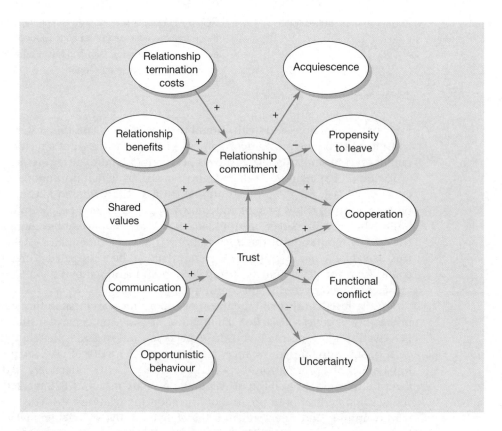

Figure 6.5 The KMV model of commitment and trust

Source: Morgan and Hunt (1994). Used with permission of the American Marketing Association.

The centrality of the trust and commitment concepts to relationship marketing has thus been established and they are as central to marketing channel relationships as to other B2B relationships (Achrol, 1991; Goodman and Dion, 2001).

Systems impact on interorganisational relationships

From the early days of electronic data interchange (EDI) through to advanced eBusiness systems and solutions, organisations have sought to use IST to improve their internal and external transactions. As described in Chapter 2, databases, communications networks, office and business applications have all contributed to increasing sophistication in this area. Such systems have had a significant impact not only on transactional efficiency but also on interorganisational relationships. For example, as Borders *et al.* (2001) observe, systems such as enterprise resource planning (ERP) and customer relationship management (CRM) bolt onto the upstream and downstream sides of the value chain.

In order to develop and maintain viable and credible customer relationships it is crucial to acquire and manage appropriate customer information. IST has provided organisations with improved opportunities to gather, process and analyse such information. However, the application and implementation of technology to improve the quality of customer relationships has proved problematic for a number of reasons. As will be examined shortly, two concerns are a failure to retain a customer orientation (Fournier *et al.*, 1998) and the implementation of information systems that are incompatible with the prevailing organisational culture and established technology (Piercy, 1998).

Organisations have been categorised as technically mature or immature (Feeny *et al.*, 1997) and this influences the way new technologies are implemented. When technically mature organisations seek to adopt a new systems-based approach, such as CRM, they focus on implementing the new application in the most efficient way. They seek to enhance established processes and improve the overall management of information. In organisations that are less technically experienced the focus appears to be on determining the potential value of individual technological applications and the way in which current processes will be affected, rather than on an organisation-wide, developmental perspective. This, the authors speculate, is simply due to lack of experience in managing or integrating electronic-based information systems.

The use of interorganisational telecommunication networks has for a long time been regarded as a means of improving efficiency and effectiveness. Efficiency is improved due to lower costs, faster (order) processing, increased accuracy of information and operations being not time-restricted. Interorganisational relationships based on the specialised information generated within such networks may even effectively lock in trading partners and create opportunities to provide greater customisation (of products and services).

Electronic networks can be considered in terms of their location of production (Williamson, 1975) and as a form of control. In this sense, **hierarchies** refer to in-house production with management making economic decisions and controlling the selection of suppliers. The term **market** is used here to refer to outsourcing where purchasing activity is subject to the rules of demand and supply, with control focused on the price mechanism. Originally, electronic data exchange networks were developed on the hierarchical principle. A dominant organisation would install a network for use with selected suppliers. Operating over a private network, the primary goal was to improve purchasing activities by reducing the number of suppliers and locking the chosen few suppliers into the dominant organisation through the creation of exit barriers and then forcing prices down (Steinfield *et al.*, 1995).

As telecommunications costs fell and the availability of public networks improved considerably, so the restrictions associated with the hierarchical approaches gave way to more open electronic marketplaces. The close-coupled arrangements of trading partner hierarchies were challenged by open-coupling arrangements, which enable access by a large number of active and non-active buyers and sellers. Whereas technology was once a trading barrier, it has become a trading format or one of the rules of business engagement.

Various trading models have been developed but according to Weill and Vitale (2001), cited by Chen (2003), four major formats can be distinguished from nearly 30 separate Internet business models:

- the supply chain model – consisting of direct sales, intermediary and/or portal applications;

- the revenue model – income is generated by customer transactions or through free-sites where income is driven by sponsorship and advertising;

- the B2C versus. B2B model – a perspective based upon markets served;

- the clicks-and-mortar versus pure-play model – income generation is assisted through offline assets or is dedicated online.

This demarcation is very broad but useful because it sets out the range of applications and business models. Within each model there are several levels of sophistication and complexity, reflecting in part the nature of particular customers and markets and in part the level of risk and opportunity that individual organisations perceive.

CRM systems

The development of CRM systems has been an important aspect of the expansion of eCommerce in recent years. Regarded as a front-end application, early CRM applications were designed for supplier organisations to enable them to manage their end-user customers. CRM applications were originally developed as sales force support systems (mainly sales force automation) and have subsequently evolved as a more sophisticated means of managing direct customers.

The aim of CRM systems is to provide all employees who interact with customers, either directly or indirectly, access to real-time customer information. To avoid fragmentation, a complete history of each customer needs to be available to all staff who interact with customers. This is necessary in order to answer two types of questions. First, there are questions prompted by customers about orders, quotations or products, and second, questions prompted by internal managers concerning, for example, strategy, segmentation, relationship potential, sales forecasts and sales force management. CRM applications typically consist of call management, lead management, customer record, sales support and payment systems. They are representative of a common per-

SNAPSHOT 6.7

CRM AT ADAMS HEALTHCARE ECOLAB

Adams Healthcare Ecolab operates in three main areas, pharmaceuticals, contamination control and dermatological retail. Its core competence rests with infection control and many of its products are used in the clean rooms of pharmaceutical companies and hospitals.

Formed in 1997, one of the organisation's early goals was to integrate sales into the business management system in order that the market drive the business. Part of the specification for their CRM system was that territory managers could view customer data, for example, current and back orders, stock levels, customer pricing structures and items awaiting dispatch. This enabled the sales team to provide improved levels of customer service through improved management information, improved targeting and improved opportunities for faster product development.

Adams Healthcare has embarked on a policy of acquisition in order to penetrate current and enter new markets. The policy is that the CRM system be rolled out and distributed to all new companies that join the group.

Source: Adapted from www.ascent.scala.ro/ascent/download/casestudies/ asc_adamshealthcare.pdf (Accessed 28 November 2003.) Used with permission.

ception of customer relationships which, although multi-faceted, has the potential to achieve only a limited impact. Whether concentrating on loyalty schemes, cleansing the content of relational databases or even improving performance in customer contact centres, the perspective is anything but the overall **management** of customers.

Ideally, CRM systems should be incorporated as part of an overall strategic approach (Wightman, 2000). However, such systems are invariably treated as add-on applications that are expected to resolve customer interface difficulties. Unsurprisingly, many clients have voiced their dissatisfaction with CRM as many of the promises and expectations have not been fulfilled. Sood (2002) suggests that problems have arisen with CRM implementation in B2B marketing because the technology vendors have not properly understood the need 'to manage all relationships with all major partners, customers, suppliers ... across all points of interaction, including Web, email and voice'. In presenting a useful table of 'touch points' by industry, Sood highlights the 'two subsets of a CRM solution', that is supplier relationship management (SRM) and dealer relationship management (DRM), and points out that B2B CRM applications 'are extending into functional areas originally covered by SCM and e-procurement applications'.

Disappointment with CRM systems can be regarded as a failure to understand the central tenets of a customer-focused philosophy and the need to adopt a strategic business approach to managing customer relationships. If the centrality of concepts such as trust and commitment is not understood, nor a willingness displayed to share information and achieve relationship symmetry, the installation of databases and data warehouses will not, and to date has not, changed the quality of an organisation's relationships with its customers.

O'Malley and Mitussis (2002) also refer to the failure of CRM systems in terms of internal political squabbling and associated issues about who owns particular systems and data. Where an organisation has not established a customer-orientated culture nor begun to implement enterprise-wide systems and procedures, it is probable that access to certain data might be impeded or at least made problematic. From this, they claim, it is not surprising that conflict may arise between functional managers and information systems managers. Contributors to the keynote session on the future of CRM at the Technology for Marketing exhibition and conference in London in February 2003, acknowledged the need for staff who could broker communications between the IT specialists and marketers in an organisation, if the real promise of CRM – better relationships, rather than 'whizzier' systems – was to be achieved.

Stone (2002), when referring to customer management systems in the public sector, draws on experience of CRM in the private sector. He argues that good customer management is never achieved just by changing the interface, for example introducing a call centre or developing a web site or portal. Good customer management requires attention to an organisation's culture, training, strategy, propositions and processes. Regretfully, too many organisations focus on the interface or fail to understand the broader picture (see Snapshot 6.8).

As if in response to these criticisms of CRM, Payne (2003) has developed what he refers to as a strategic framework for customer relationship marketing. This is depicted at Figure 6.6.

SNAPSHOT 6.8

SOME PROBLEMS EXPERIENCED WITH CRM

Action Instruments, a $20-million firm that makes electronic devices for manufacturers, installed a small call centre and an order and technical services package so that they could capture a greater amount of customer information. Difficulties concerning customisation of the standard package and the types of reporting led to delays in the successful implementation. However, the biggest problem occurred when the company was taken over by Invensys and they insisted that Action use their CRM system. Integrating diverse systems, designed to achieve different goals can be problematic.

BMC Software used three generations of technology for their sales organisation before learning how to use it effectively. They realised there were changes in selling methodology that needed to take place. There was too much emphasis on technology and not enough on people.

Source: Ericson (2001).

Some companies maintain multiple call centers to perform similar business processes across sales, service, and marketing departments. A company may also have centers within those same departments performing similar business processes. For example, brand-specific service contact centers are common, as are sales or marketing centers set up to sell or promote specific products. Marketing groups may outsource certain promotions even though they could handle these programs internally.

Corporate leaders frequently discover that no one understands the complete contact center capability of the organization across functional areas. To make matters worse, functional areas within the same organization perform similar work differently, which leads to the unhappy phenomenon of customers being treated differently by different groups within the same company.

Source: Morgan (2001).

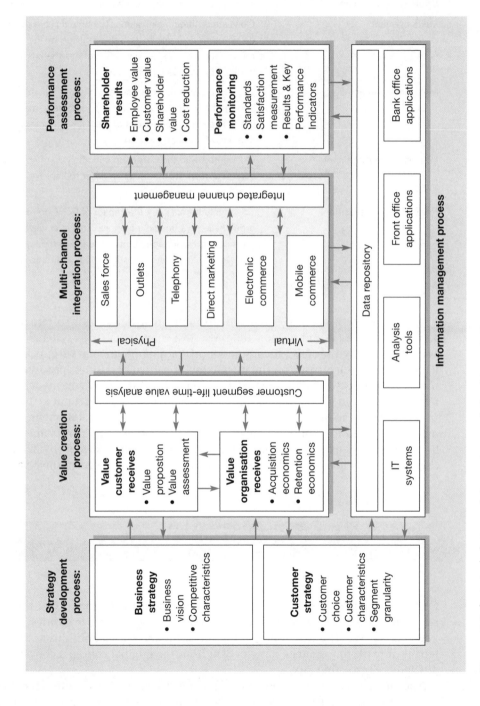

Figure 6.6 A strategic framework for customer relationship marketing

Source: Payne (2003). Used with permission.

Table 6.7 Key business processes for effective CRM

Business process	Key elements
Strategy development	Concerned with both business and customer strategies.
Value creation	Consists of three main values. The actual value that is delivered to customers, the value realised by the organisation and the maximisation of the life-time value of particular customers (segments).
Multichannel integration	Concerned with the integration and management of appropriate channels in order that customers' maximise their experience, regardless of their varying points of contact with the organisation.
Information management	Concerned with the collection and analysis of appropriate customer-related information in order to improve the customer experience.
Performance assessment	This element considers the impact of CRM on the organisation's strategic intentions. This is achieved by considering the linkages between each of the following: employee value, customer value and shareholder value.

Source: Adapted from Payne (2000).

This framework may be enhanced through incorporation of softer, personnel aspects to encourage and support the process of change that such systems stimulate. Most importantly the active incorporation of training programmes seems important. Payne's framework is based on the interaction of particular business processes, which, if managed collectively and repeatedly, should avoid the problems associated with fragmentation and CRM underperformance. These processes are set out in Table 6.7.

It is important to understand that even the most sophisticated CRM systems are based on data about an organisation's contacts and the transactions with them. While these can be processed to supply one-touch, real-time multi-dimensional views of any B2B relationship, they do not manage it. That, as ever, is the challenge for the people involved.

Summary

One of the primary characteristics of B2B marketing is the importance of the various relationships that organisations develop in order to achieve their business and marketing objectives. The development of interorganisational relationships as the central tenant of marketing strategy has emerged from the original concepts concerning the 4Ps and the marketing mix.

The initial focus on the product as the unit of exchange shifted to one which centred on the buyer–seller relationship, where the customer was dominant. Customer relationship marketing has developed in many ways but now both parties are seen to be in a relationship. A further extension is that these buyer–seller relationships are a part of a wider array of relationships, namely a network of interacting organisations, and the actions and behaviour of organisations need to be seen in this broader context.

However, it would be mistaken to expect an organisation to embrace deep meaningful relationships with every other organisation with which it enters into an exchange. Some exchanges need to be brief and based on products and low prices. Others require deeper collaboration and partnerships to create exchanges that are symmetrical and represent competitive advantage and added value. If interorganisational relationships are to be the foundation of contemporary B2B marketing practice then the supply chain and associated networks become a central aspect of marketing, and exchange value is vested within the chain.

Finally, new technology has revolutionised B2B marketing and has enabled organisations to undertake exchanges faster, more efficiently and has drastically reduced the cost base for many supply chains. Above all else, technology has given organisations the opportunity to reassess the value of their interactions with customers and suppliers and to forge a portfolio of interorganisational relationships.

Discussion questions

1 Find examples of three distribution alliances and consider the benefits the new arrangement might have brought to the constituent organisations.

2 Write brief notes outlining the differences between market exchanges and relational exchanges.

3 Prepare notes for a presentation to be given to colleagues in which you seek to explain the differences between social, exchange, penetration and interaction theories.

4 Discuss the extent to which customer-driven relationship marketing concepts can be applied to suppliers and members of an organisation's supply chain.

5 Identify the main elements that are used to characterise interorganisational trust.

6 How might the future development of CRM systems, overcome some of the problems incurred to date?

References

Achrol, R.S. (1991). 'Evolution of the marketing organisation: new forms for turbulent environments', *Journal of Marketing*, 55, 4, pp. 77–93.

Altman, I. and Taylor, D.A. (1973). *Social Penetration: The Development of Interpersonal Relationships*, New York, NY: Holt, Reinhart and Winston.

Araujo, L. and Easton, G. (1996). 'Networks in socioeconomic systems: a critical review', in D. Iacobucci, (ed.), *Networks in Marketing*, Thousand Oaks, CA: Sage.

Ahlert, D., Kenning P. von and Petermann, F. (2001) 'Die Bedeutung von Vertrauen fur die Interaktionsbeziehungen zwischen Dienstleistungsanbietern und Nachfragern', in Bruhn, M. and Strauss, B. (eds) *Dienstleistungsmanagement, Jahrbuch 2001. Interaktionen im Dienstleistungsbereich*, Wiesbaden:Gaber, pp. 239–318

Bamberger, G.E., Carlton, D.W. and Neumann, L.R. (2001). 'An Empirical investigation of the competitive effects of domestic airline alliances', Working paper, Graduate School of Business, University of Chicago, Chicago, IL.

Bensaou, B.M. (1999). 'Portfolios of buyer–seller relationships', *Sloan Management Review*, 40, 4, (Summer), pp. 35–44.

Bergen, U., Dutta, S. and Walker, Jr. O.C. (1992). 'Agency Relationships in Marketing. A Review of Implications and Applications of Agency and Related Theories', *Journal of Marketing*, 56, 2, pp. 1–24.

Blattberg, R.C. and Deighton, A.R. (1996). 'Manage marketing by the Customer Equity Test', *Harvard Business Review*, 74, 4, pp. 136–44.

Blau, P. (1964). *Exchange and Power in Social Life*, New York, NY: John Wiley & Sons.

Borden, N.H. (1964) 'The concept of the marketing mix', *Journal of Advertising Research*, 4 (June), pp. 2–7.

Borders, A.L., Johnston, W.J. and Rigdon, E.E. (2001). 'Electronic commerce and network perspectives in industrial marketing management', *Industrial Marketing Management*, 30, 2 (February), pp. 199–205.

Bruhn, M. (2003). *Relationship Marketing: Management of Customer Relationships*, Harlow: Financial Times/Prentice Hall.

Chen, S. (2003). 'The real value of "e-business models"', *Business Horizons*, (November–December), pp. 27–33.

Christopher, M., Payne, A. and Ballantyne, D. (2002). *Relationship Marketing: Creating Stakeholder Value*, Oxford: Butterworth-Heinemann.

Cousins, P.D. (2002). 'A conceptual model for managing long term inter-organisational relationships', *European Journal of Purchasing and Supply Management*, 8, 2 (June) pp. 71–82.

Cousins, P. and Stanwix, E. (2001). 'It's only a matter of confidence! A comparison of relationship management between Japanese and UK non-owned vehicle manufacturers', *International Journal of Operations and Production Management*, 21, 9 (October) pp. 1160–80.

Dai, Q. and Kauffman, R.J. (2002). 'Understanding B2B e-Market alliance strategies', presented at the 2002 Workshop on Information Systems and Economics, Barcelona, Spain, December 2002. Current working paper version available at the MIS Research Center website, www.misrc.csom.umn.edu

Day, G. (2000). 'Managing market relationships', *Journal of the Academy of Marketing Science*, 28, 1 (Winter) pp. 24–30.

Doney, P.M. and Cannon, J.P. (1997). 'An examination of the nature of trust in buyer–seller relationships', *Journal of Marketing*, 62, 2, pp. 1–13.

Dowling, G.R. and Uncles, M. (1997). 'Do customer loyalty programs work?', *Sloan Management Review*, eLibrary.com, 22 June 1997, www.static.elibrary.com/s/sloanmanagementreview/june221997/docustomerloyaltyprogramsreallywork.

Dwyer, R.F., Schurr, P.H. and Oh, S. (1987). 'Developing buyer–seller relationships', *Journal of Marketing*, 51 (April), pp. 11–27.

Easton, G. and Araujo, L. (1993). 'A resource-based view of industrial networks', in *Proceedings of the Ninth IMP International Conference on International Marketing* (Bath: University of Bath, School of Management).

Ericson, J. (2001). 'The "Failure" of CRM', *Line 56*, Thursday August 2001, www.line56.com/articles/default.asp?News10 = 2802 (Accessed 1 January 2004.)

Feeny, D.F., Earl, M.J. and Edwards, B. (1997). 'Information systems organisation: the roles of users and specialists', in L. Willcocks, D. Feeny and G. Islei (eds), *Managing IT as a Strategic Resource*. London: McGraw-Hill, pp. 151–68.

Fischer, T. and Tewes, M. (2001). 'Vertrauen und Commitment in der Dienstleistungsinteraktion', in Bruhn, M. and Strauss, B. (eds), *Dienstleistungsmanagement, Jahrbuch 2001. Interaktionen in Dienstleistungsbereich*, Weisbaden: Gaber, pp. 299–318.

Ford, D. (1980). 'The development of buyer–seller relationships in industrial markets', *European Journal of Marketing*, 14, 5/6, pp. 339–54.

Fournier, S., Dobscha, S. and Mick, D.G. (1998). 'Preventing the premature death of relationship marketing', *Harvard Business Review*, 76, 1 (January/February) pp. 42–51.

Gambetta, D. (1988). *Trust: Making and breaking Co-operative Relations*, New York, NY: Blackwell.

Goodman, L.E. and Dion, P.A. (2001). 'The determinants of commitment in the distributor–manufacturer relationship', *Industrial Marketing Management*, 30, 3 (April) pp. 287–300.

Grion, R.S. (2003). 'Rethinking customer acquisition before talking retention', *Journal of Integrated Communications*, 2002–03 issue, pp. 29–33, www.medill.northwestern.edu/imc/studentwork/pubs/jic/journal/2002/grion.pdf (Accessed 5 December 2003.)

Gronroos, C. (1994). 'From marketing mix to relationship marketing', *Management Decision*, 32, 2, pp. 4–20.

Houston, F.S. and Gassenheimer, J.B. (1987). 'Market and exchange', *Journal of Marketing*, 51, 4, pp. 3–18.

IMP Group (1982). *International Marketing and Purchasing of Industrial Goods*, Hakansoon, H. (ed.), Chichester: Wiley.

Jensen, M.C. and Meckling, W. (1976). 'The theory of the firm: managerial behavior–agency costs and capital structure', *Journal of Financial Economics*, 3, pp. 305–60.

Johanson, J. and Mattsson, L-G. (1994). 'The markets as networks tradition in Sweden', in G. Laurent, G.L. Lilien, and Pras, B. (eds), *Research traditions in marketing*, Boston MA: Kluwer Academic Publishing, pp. 321–42.

Kanter, R.M. (1994). 'Collaborative advantage: the art of alliances', *Harvard Business Review*, July–August, pp. 96–108.

Klee, A. (2000). *Strategisches Berziehungsmanagement: ein integrativer Ansatz zur strategischen Planning und Implementierung des Beziehungsmanagement*, Aachen: Shaker.

Kumar, N., Hibbard, J.D. and Stern, L.W. (1994). *The Nature and Consequences of Marketing Channel Intermediary Commitment, Marketing Science Institute Report No. 94–115*, Cambridge, MA: Marketing Science Institute.

Lemke, F., Goffin, K. and Szwejczewski, M. (2003). 'Investigating the meaning of supplier–manufacturer partnerships', *International Journal of Physical Distribution and Logistics Management*, 33, 1, pp. 12–35.

Lerner, J. and Merges, R.P. (1997). 'The control of strategic alliances: an empirical analysis of biotechnology collaborations', Working Paper 6014, National Bureau of Economic Research, Cambridge, MA.

Luo., X. (2002). 'A framework based on relationship marketing and social exchange theory', Industrial Marketing Management, 31, 2 (February) pp. 111–18.

McCarthy, E.J. (1960). *Basic Marketing: A Managerial Approach*. Homewood, IL: Irwin.

McLoughlin, D. and Horan, C. (2000). 'Perspectives from the Markets-as-Networks Approach', *Industrial Marketing Management*, 29, 4, pp. 285–92.

Morgan, B. (2001). 'How does your call centre grow?', *Operations and Fulfillment*, 1 July 2001, www.opsandfulfillment.com/ar/fulfillment_call_center_grow/ (Accessed 1 January 2004.)

Morgan, R.M. and Hunt, S.D. (1994). 'The commitment-trust theory of relationship marketing', *Journal of Marketing*, 58 (July), pp. 20–38.

O'Malley, L. and Mitussis, D. (2002). 'Relationships and technology: strategic implications', *Journal of Strategic Marketing*, 10, 3 (September), pp. 225–38.

Pavlou, P.A. (2002). 'Institution-based trust in interorganisational exchange relationships: the role of online B2B marketplaces on trust formation', *Journal of Strategic Information Systems*, 11, 3–4, (December), pp. 215–43.

Payne, A. (2000). 'Relationship Marketing: Managing Multiple Markets', in Cranfield School of Management (eds), *Marketing Management. A Relationship Marketing Perspective*, Basingstoke: MacMillan, pp. 16–30.

Payne, A.F.T. (2003). 'A strategic framework for CRM', draft working document, Cranfield School of Management, Cranfield University.

Piercy, N.F. (1998). 'Barriers to implementing relationship marketing: analysing the internal marketplace', *Journal of Strategic Marketing*, 6, 3 (September), pp. 209–22.

Porter, A. (2003). 'Lastminute clicks with Tesco', *Sunday Times Business Section*, 10 August 2003, p. 2.

Reichheld, F.F. and Sasser, E.W. (1990). 'Zero defections: quality comes to services', *Harvard Business Review* (September), pp. 105–11.

Reinartz, W.J. and Kumar, V. (2002). 'The mismanagement of customer loyalty', *Harvard Business Review* (July), pp. 86–94.

Rowe, W.G. and Barnes, J.G. (1998). 'Relationship marketing and sustained competitive advantage', *Journal of Market-Focused Management*, 2, 3, pp. 281–97.

Sheth, J. (1973), 'A model of industrial buyer behaviour', *Journal of Marketing*, 37 (October), pp. 50–6.

Sheth, J.N. and Parvatiyar, A. (1995). 'Relationship marketing in consumer markets: antecedents and consequences', *Journal of the Academy of Marketing Science*, 23, 4, pp. 255–71.

Sood, B. (2002). 'CRM in B2B: developing customer-centric practices for partner and supplier relationships', www.intelligentcrm.com/020509/508feat2_2.shtml (Accessed 28 April 2003.)

Spekman, R. (1988). 'Perceptions of strategic vulnerability among industrial buyers and its effect on information search and supplier evaluation', *Journal of Business Research*, 17, pp. 313–326.

Steinfield, C., Kraut, R. and Plummer, A. (1995). 'The impact of interorganizational networks, on buyer–seller relationships', *Journal of Computer Mediated Communication*, 1, 3, www.ascusc.org/jcmc/vol1/issue3/steinfld.html

Stone, M. (2002). 'Managing public sector customers', *What's New in Marketing* (October); www.wnim.com/ (Accessed October 2002.)

Teece, D.J. (1992). 'Competition, cooperation and innovation: arrangements for regimes of rapid technological progress', *Journal of Economic Behaviour and Organization*, 18, pp. 1–25.

Thomas, D. (2003). 'Sainsbury's boosts supplier collaboration', *Computer Weekly*, 12 October; www.computerweekly.com/articles/ (Accessed 29 November 2003.)

Tinsley, D.B. (2002). 'Relationship marketing's strategic array', *Business Horizons*, 45, 1 (January/February), pp. 70–6.

Tynan, C. (1997). 'A review of the marriage analogy in relationship marketing', *Journal of Marketing Management*, 13, pp. 695–703.

Varey, R.J. (2002). *Relationship Marketing: Dialogue and Networks in the e-Commerce Era*, Chichester: Wiley.

Wagner, S. and Boutellier, R. (2002). 'Capabilities for managing a portfolio of supplier relationships', *Business Horizons* (November–December), **46**, 6, pp. 79–8.

Webster, F.E. and Wind, Y. (1972). 'A general model for understanding organisational buying behaviour', *Journal of Marketing*, 36 (April), pp. 12–14.

Weill, P. and Vitale, M.R. (2001). *Place to Space: Migrating to eBusiness Models*, Boston, MA: Harvard Business School Press.

Wightman, T. (2000). 'e-CRM: the critical dot.com discipline', *Admap* (April) pp. 46–8.

Williamson, O.E. (1975). *Markets and Hierarchies*, New York, NY: The Free Press.

Young, L.C. and Wilkinson, I.F. (1989). 'The role of trust and co-operation in marketing channels: a preliminary study', *European Journal of Marketing*, 23, 2, pp. 109–22.

Zucker, L. (1986). 'Production of trust: institutional sources of economic structure 1840–1920,' *Research in Organisation Behaviour*, 8, 1, pp. 53–111.

Part C
Marketing channels and networks

The focus of this part of the book is upon marketing channels, supply chains, and networks. It examines their roles, purposes and structures, and explores the issues and challenges of managing interorganisational relationships. This section builds on and develops theories about relationships considered previously.

Chapter 7 examines the different types and purposes of marketing channels and considers related concepts about service output theory, channel flows and the main roles that channel participants assume.

Chapter 8 builds on the previous chapter by considering the variety of structures that exist in marketing channels. The characteristics of supply chains and marketing channels are explored but the main goal of this chapter is to review different channel structures and contemporary multi-channel approaches.

Chapter 9 explores the behaviour and management of the interorganisational relationships that are developed between channel members and network partners. Some of the key managerial issues such as power and conflict, trust, commitment and satisfaction are examined.

Throughout these chapters, readers are encouraged to consider the application and impact of IST. The use of digital technologies and the development of new electronic trading formats have important implications for the structure and management of marketing channels and supply chains.

Chapter 7

Marketing channels

Chapter overview

This chapter is the first of three that examine issues concerning marketing channels and the intermediaries that populate them. In this chapter, attention is focused on understanding the principles and core concepts associated with marketing channels. In particular, there is an examination of their purpose, basic structure and key intermediaries – their characteristics and contribution to the way in which channels work.

This chapter provides foundation material in order to explore some of the more advanced ideas about channel structure, design, interaction and networks that follow in Chapter 8. The final chapter in this third section, Chapter 9, examines the way in which behaviour within marketing channels can be managed.

Chapter aims

The aims of this chapter are to introduce and explore core concepts associated with marketing channels.

Objectives

The objectives of this chapter are to:

1 Define the nature and concept of marketing channels.

2 Examine the purpose of, and tasks associated with, marketing channels.

3 Introduce some basic principles concerning the types and structure of marketing channels.

4 Appreciate the importance of uncertainty and risk within channel management.

5 Appraise the significance of service output theory and explain how it can be used to reduce channel member uncertainty.

6 Consider ideas concerning channel flows.

7 Explore the roles and main characteristics of key members of marketing channels.

8 Consider the impact information systems and technology can have on marketing channels.

An introduction to marketing channels

In Chapter 1 the notion of value chains was introduced as an important foundation for understanding business-to-business marketing. In that chapter, it was suggested that organisations choose to work together in order to provide added value for end-user customers. The notion that organisations interact with each other underpins the concept of channel marketing. Marketing channels consist of a chain of organisations that collectively develop products and services, each adding something of value before passing it to the next, in order that the product or service be presented in the most convenient and valued format for end-user purchase and consumption.

Marketing channels, also called distribution channels, are concerned with the interorganisational management of the processes and activities involved in moving products from manufacturers to end-user customers. The term interorganisational is important because marketing channel activities are concerned with the coordination of activities that are necessary to make products readily available to end users. Coordination between channel members is necessary to convert subassemblies and raw materials into final products and services that represent superior value to the end users of each channel. Each of the various organisations electing to coordinate activities performs a different role in the chain of activities. Some act as manufacturers, some as agents and others may be distributors, dealers, value added resellers, wholesalers or retailers. Whatever the role, it is normally specific and geared to refining and moving the product closer to the end user.

Each organisation is a customer to the previous organisation in an industry's value chain. As discussed in Chapter 1, some organisations work closely together, coordinating and integrating their activities, while others cooperate on a looser, often temporary, basis. In both cases however, these organisations can be observed to be operating as members of a partnership, of differing strength and dimensions, with the express intention of achieving their objectives with their partners' assistance and cooperation. So, in addition to the end user, a further set of customers (partners) can be determined: all those who make up the marketing channel.

The distribution of products involves two main elements. The first is the management of the tangible or physical aspects of moving a product from the producer to the end user. This must be undertaken in such a way that the customer can freely access an offering and that the final act of the buying process is as easy as possible. This is part of supply chain management and entails the logistics associated with moving products closer to end users. The second element concerns the management of the intangible aspects or issues of ownership, control and flows of communication between the parties responsible for making the offering accessible to the customer. The focus of this chapter is on the second of these elements, commonly referred to as channel management.

Function and purpose of marketing channels

The range of skills necessary to source and assemble appropriate parts, to manufacture and distribute products to a diversity of customers, perhaps regionally, nationally or even globally and then provide suitable levels of service and support is too wide and too complex for most organisations to provide entirely by themselves. There are some specific uncertainties associated with buying and selling. For example, the risks associated with producing too much or too little for the target market, those to do with customers' buying behaviours and motivations, and those of storage, the incumbent finance and working capital costs. The uncertainty of the outcomes associated with these and other market-related activities, is usually too large for a single organisation to carry.

Marketing channels exist because they provide a means by which these uncertainties can be reduced or shared. By combining with other organisations who have different specialised skills (for example customer access, finance, transportation, storage) these uncertainties can be diminished. The added value provided by each of these organisations contributes to the superior value perceived by end users and contributes to competitive advantage. To achieve this level of competitive advantage, organisations need to enter interorganisational exchanges to share their specialised services and the uncertainties.

SNAPSHOT 7.1

CHANNEL UNCERTAINTY

Although Cisco Systems had great experience of using indirect channels outside of North America, the majority of its home market had been served through a direct channel. When it entered the small and medium-sized business markets in North America, it was decided that the organisation had to change the channel structure. A central part of the organisation's business strategy is the provision of high levels of customer support. As it felt unable to provide and sustain suitable levels internally, the company created a level of distributors and resellers and helped train them to provide the necessary support and, in doing so, reduce risk.

Part of the training was carried out at the Cisco Networking Academy. Here customers, distributors and college students could train to manage Cisco's networks. By creating a swathe of Cisco-trained and certificated technicians and engineers, they developed a free market source of support for customers to employ at a time when there was a particular network engineering skills shortage.

Source: Adapted from Kraemer and Dedrick (2002).

Exchanges

The primary purpose of marketing channels is to enable organisations to enter into a series of exchanges that allow each party to move towards satisfying their individual, and in some circumstances collective, goals. The exchange of products and/or services is of course the most obvious element of activity. In addition, organisations must exchange information, either technical, corporate or market-orientated, so that a transaction can be completed and the relationship between the parties extended. Further, in commercial transactions, there needs to be a financial exchange so that the transaction can be concluded. Finally, there is a social exchange attached to the behaviour of marketing channel members. In order for there to be either a single market exchange or long-term series of exchanges, there must be a level of trust and commitment between all parties.

Therefore, organisations combine together to reduce uncertainty by exchanging products and services which are of value to others in the channel. The degree of uncertainty, or business risk, is associated with the complexity of the various tasks to be completed in the channel. By reducing the uncertainty experienced by all members in a channel they are better positioned to concentrate on other tasks.

Reducing complexity

The first aspects of complexity to be considered concern the number of transactions, and frequency of contact, with which a producer interacts with each individual end-user customer. As noted above, producers need to complete a number of tasks in order to reach and service their markets. These include pricing, transportation, negotiations, delivery, stock holding and payment. For convenience, the term **exchange** will

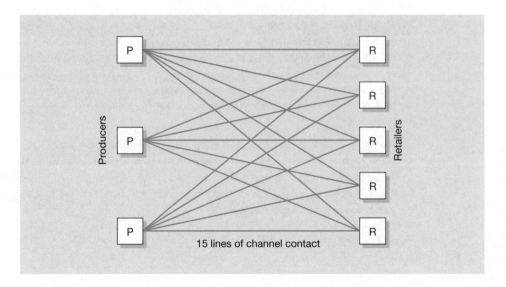

Figure 7.1 The complexity of channel exchanges without Intermediaries

be used to embrace all of these activities. For a producer to meet the needs of a market, without intermediaries, there needs to be a complete exchange with **each** end-user customer. This level of exchange activity, which ignores the search and processing time involved in selling to each customer, is so intense and potentially inefficient that it can become disproportionately expensive.

From Figure 7.1 it should be clear that without the use of an intermediary there are a myriad of exchanges that producers are required to undertake. However, if an intermediary is introduced between the producer and its end-user customers, the number of direct exchanges is drastically reduced (see Figure 7.2).

It is clear that the use of intermediaries redistributes and reduces the number of exchanges that producers undertake. Their contact with the market is directed to the needs of intermediaries, enabling them to focus on their core activities, production or manufacturing. In the meantime, end-user customers are better able to obtain improved individual support and service levels from channel members, than they would have received just from producers. The cost of this new level in the marketing channel is the margin that intermediaries earn for their part in the value adding process. From the end-user customers' perspective, this cost should be outweighed by the superior benefits that they derive.

This notion that the use of intermediaries reduces the number of contacts producers have with end users, and is therefore a good thing, is not universally agreed. Mudambi and Aggarwal (2003) suggest that increasing the number of contacts that producers make with end users can lead to greater choice. Through greater use of direct marketing and incorporating new technology using online selling, Internet-based market exchanges and B2B auction sites, breadth of market coverage can be achieved. For end users, however, risks concerning stock availability, servicing and support increase as the number of intermediaries falls.

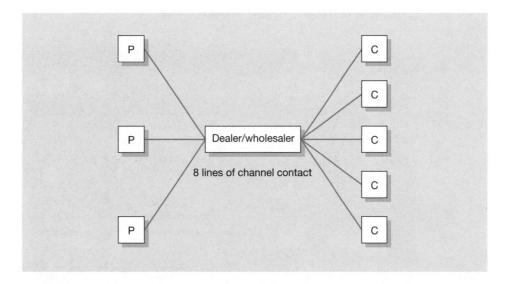

Figure 7.2 The impact of intermediaries on channel exchanges

SNAPSHOT 7.2

TEXYARD.COM – A B2B MARKET EXCHANGE

B2B exchanges, online marketplaces for buyers and sellers to meet and agree deals, have had varying levels of success. Many have failed and the expectation is that only private exchanges will be sufficiently attractive to sellers in the future, and that means that the market exchange industry is likely to consolidate. (See Chapter 5 above for more details.)

TexYard.com is the European exchange for the apparel industry. Designed to improve the efficiency associated with sourcing and buying, one of the objectives for users is to reduce the time taken to bring new products to market.

Buyers are able to put their entire sourcing process online, use a major database to find new global suppliers and gain access to new European retailers.

Source: Adapted from Kenjale and Phatak (2003).

For producers, costs rise as more intermediaries enter the channel. However, more intermediaries enables producers, indirectly, to reach a wider array of end-user customers. Therefore, the risk is represented by the trade-off between the number of intermediaries and the breadth of the end-user market that is reached (see Figure 7.3).

In an attempt to reduce channel costs many suppliers have been cutting the number of intermediaries they use in their supply chains. Often this means moving from national warehousing systems to just a single, pan-European warehousing facility that feeds regional distribution centres. This can endanger customer service levels because end-user customers desire shorter and quicker response times and an increase in the level of service provided (Roe *et al.*, 1998).

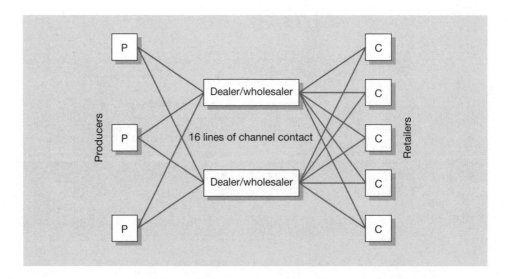

Figure 7.3 The impact of multiple intermediaries on the number of channel exchanges

There is an assumption here that all intermediary costs are the same. This is clearly untrue and different intermediaries provide value adding services at different costs. As a result, there are many types of intermediary and there are many routes into markets. It is not surprising, therefore, that channel design and strategy decisions are further complicated by the complexity and dynamic nature of end-user customer needs. Although this is discussed in greater depth at the end of this chapter and in Chapter 8, it is worth mentioning the impact technology has had on shaping channel structures. One area of impact has been the development, in certain markets, of direct selling and the removal of intermediaries from the channel. This process is known as **disintermediation**. However, Internet technologies have also helped develop new types of online intermediaries, a process known as **reintermediation**.

Increasing value and competitive advantage

The other major reason why producers utilise intermediaries is to reduce the risk that customers will reject the product or service. This is achieved by improving the overall value that customers perceive in an offering. By generating a level of superior value, relative to competing products and customer experience, producers are able to reduce the risk of purchase uncertainty. Producers acting alone do not normally have the skills and core competences necessary to meet end-user requirements. Their skills lie with the production or manufacturing of goods and services. Intermediaries are better placed to understand, interact and deliver the value that end-user customers desire. The better the service provided by an intermediary, the greater the competitive advantage over rival intermediaries and producers. Note that competitive advantage can be considered from a channel perspective, as well as from that of an individual organisation or product. Competitive advantage can be characterised in terms of the efficiency with which the transactions are completed and the quality and value of the services provided.

Routinisation

By improving transaction efficiency, costs can be lowered and business performance improved. This is achieved by encouraging routinisation, that is, the standardisation of the transaction process. Instead of negotiating each transaction and incurring all the attendant costs, routinisation promotes cost efficiencies and the production of goods and services that are most highly valued by target markets. Distribution costs can be reduced and processes automated to regularise operations. Standardisation is encouraged by regulating order size, delivery cycles and payment frequency. This in turn promotes relationships which may evolve into relational-based transactions.

This routinisation process can be facilitated by computer-based technology such as electronic data interchange (EDI) and continuous replenishment programmes (CRP) designed to smooth out stock levels to meet customer demand yet achieve efficiency (see Chapter 8).

EDI AT PHARMACIA BIOTECH

DHL Sweden and Pharmacia Biotech used EDI as one of the tools for creating a joint distribution process for delivering Pharmacia Biotech's pharmaceutical products to its clients across Europe. In the past, Pharmacia's market companies in Europe maintained their own inventories of products and delivered them to local customers. Intense competition in the industry led Pharmacia to a rationalisation and cost-cutting programme which led to the closing of the local inventory facilities and the creation of a central European inventory at Uppsala in Sweden. A new distribution process was required to deliver products directly to customers throughout Europe from the central inventory.

Pharmacia Biotech were primarily driven by the need to cut stock and distribution costs but also by customer demands for next day delivery. They also wished to set a late deadline for last-minute orders. From DHL's point of view it could not have handled the volumes without EDI and break bulk shipments and they also saw the opportunity to form long-term partnerships with clients to secure its position in the marketplace. Pharmacia and DHL have worked together to create a fast and reliable distribution process spanning the entire order cycle from the moment when the client order is transferred by EDI to the central inventory to the moment when that order has been successfully delivered.

The distribution process replaces paper airway bills with barcode readable labels which combine Pharmacia's order information with DHL's consignment note. Pharmacia undertook responsibility for developing the equipment necessary to print the labels. Details about the airway bill numbers assigned to particular orders are transferred by EDI from the central inventory to the local marketing companies. This enables the local companies to take advantage of DHL's track-and-trace services as they need to be able to link their own order numbers to DHL's airway bill numbers.

One of the key factors ensuring the success of the Pharmacia project has been the strong partnership forged between Pharmacia and DHL Sweden. The project spanned almost five years since beginning with pilot deliveries and expanded, enabled by the new EDI/break bulk distribution process to cover six European countries. The project highlights the project management, process analysis, technical and long-term planning skills required as well as the need to develop and maintain close relations with business partners.

Source: Adapted from Roberts and Flight (1995).

Specialisation

Value is also improved for customers by helping them to search for and identify sources of products that they want. Here, intermediaries can provide resources and skills that producers do not have, nor wish to develop. This specialisation adds value for end-user customers. For example, the provision of training services, frequent but small load deliveries and credit facilities can represent significant value to some retailers or OEMs.

One major dilemma concerning distribution is that manufacturers tend to want to produce large quantities of a limited variety of goods, while end-user customers, consumers, only want a limited quantity of a wide variety of goods. Therefore, intermediaries sort out all the goods produced by different manufacturers and present them in quantities and formats that enable consumers to buy easily and as frequently as they wish. This is referred to as **sorting and smoothing** (see Table 7.1).

Table 7.1 Aspects of sorting and smoothing

Aspect	Explanation
Sorting out	Grading products into different sizes, qualities or grades. For example potatoes, eggs or fruit.
Accumulation	The bringing together of different products from different producers to provide a wider category choice.
Allocation	Often referred to as breaking bulk (by wholesalers), this involves disaggregating bulk deliveries into smaller lot sizes that customers are able (and prefer) to buy.
Assorting	Assembling different collections of goods/services thought to be of value to the customer (retailers and consumers).

Service outputs

Channels should be designed to meet end-user customer needs, otherwise the marketing focus is lost and a producer orientation is introduced. According to Bucklin (1966) customers seek utility from marketing channels. This utility can be observed in many forms but is essentially concerned with levels of service provided by a channel. Customers are more likely to be attracted to channels that offer higher levels of service. Bucklin argued that this channel service consists of four main elements: unit size, spatial convenience, waiting time and product variety.

Unit or lot size refers to the number of product units end-user customers are required to buy. Producers make large quantities based on mass production but marketing channels break up the production into smaller units to enable customers to consume more quickly and hold lower stocks. This process is known as **breaking bulk**. The more a channel breaks up the units of production into smaller and smaller unit sizes the less stock has to be held in the system, particularly by end users, and the higher the level of service, as perceived by end-user customers. However, the higher the level of service the higher the price paid per unit.

Spatial convenience is concerned with the transportation and search costs end-user customers experience. The easier it is for customers to access products the higher the level of service output. Classic examples are shopping centres which not only provide a range of shops under a single roofed area, free of motor vehicles, they also provide parking facilities. Local convenience stores and even vending machines also provide spatial convenience and improved service output. Home shopping facilities, either by telephone or increasingly the Internet, provide new ways of furnishing 'time-poor' customers with spatial convenience. Tesco and Sainsbury's reduce the search and transportation costs for their shoppers by providing home delivery services. Customers pay for the higher utility as a trade-off against the costs associated with visiting the store.

Waiting or delivery time. The time a customer waits between ordering and receiving products represents a period of inconvenience. In most circumstances customers prefer to receive their products immediately they are ordered. The shorter the waiting time the higher the level of service. Price is used to compensate customers for having to wait for delivery. Furniture manufacturers have traditionally presented long wait times, as they prefer to operate batch production systems. The development of self-assembly furniture (for example MFI and Ikea) has helped companies develop shorter waiting times but very often at the expense of quality.

Product variety. Customers experience a higher level of utility when they are able to select from a broader or wider range of products. The greater the assortment of products available for customers to choose from, the higher the service output. Again price is the control mechanism and customers pay for shorter waiting times through higher prices.

By understanding the level of service outputs desired by customers, it becomes easier to segment markets, profile consumer groups and to design channels that are better able to meet customer needs. If end-user customers wish to purchase in small quantities it is necessary to build a longer channel and involve a large number of intermediaries. If breaking bulk is not important then a small number of intermediaries will suffice and price can be lowered.

Bucklin argues, as a general principle, that the more a channel has to provide in order to satisfy the level of service output expectations, the higher will be the cost and hence price that customers must pay for that level of utility. However, it is useful to consider the value of service output theory within the context of out-sourcing and electronic trading formats. Bucklin developed his theory within a radically different trading environment to that which exists today. Price may still be important within market exchanges but may not be the coordinating mechanism it was once considered to be within relational exchanges, and may now be surpassed by concepts of relative value and competitive advantage. This aspect will be discussed further later in this chapter.

Channel flows

So far reference has been made to channel activities. The term activities suggests that these events are discrete and unconnected. Nothing could be further from the truth. Interorganisational coordination requires that there is flow of processes that sweep up and down the channel in order that all participants are able to undertake their roles effectively and efficiently.

Channel flows engage participants according to their roles and the nature of the flow. The most obvious type of flow is information, which moves between channel members in formal and informal ways. Rosenbloom (1999) identifies five flows and Coughlan *et al.* (2001) identify eight different types of flow. Whatever the number, the principle holds that these flows provide a linkage, helping to bind together organ-isations in marketing (see Figure 7.4).

Physical flow refers to the transportation and storage of products between channel members. There are costs associated with this flow such as warehousing, and perhaps specialised protection such as refrigeration, plus the transportation costs associated with moving products to new locations. However, it is important to note that these costs are not the costs of ownership. When the **legal title** to products changes there are different costs associated with owning stock – for example, market value, which is treated as an asset (working capital) – which in turn impacts on profitability.

Negotiation flows concern the dialogue associated with a (possible) change in ownership or how service or maintenance arrangements are to be developed. With regard to Figure 7.4, note how the dialogue is represented by a two-way arrow. The key element associated with negotiation flows is the cost of the time that the parties devote to the discussions. Any legal advice and documentation costs are also attributed to this type of flow.

Finance flows refer to the credit extended to intermediaries. Most commonly this is seen in terms of the 30-, 60-, 90-day period in which customers are required, or have agreed, as part of the negotiation flow, to pay for the goods and services that they have taken into their possession. Title of ownership passes once the payment flow is completed. This 30-day period represents the time the seller agrees to finance the purchase costs of the buyer and represents a lost opportunity to use the money elsewhere.

Promotion flows reflect the need to complete particular marketing communications tasks. This may be the development of awareness levels, educating current customers or persuading potential customers. The tools used for the promotion flow are primarily personal selling and direct marketing but advertising, public relations and sales promotion can also play significant roles. When considered as a whole, the promotion flow is instrumental in building and maintaining strong relationships with customers.

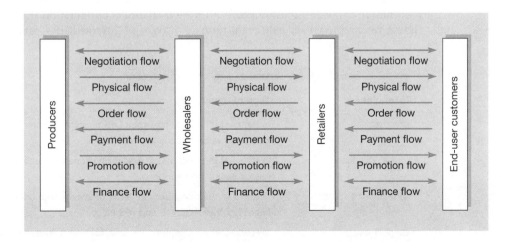

Figure 7.4 Channel flows in marketing channels

There are also *order flows* and the subsequent *payment flows*, both of which move from customers towards successive intermediaries back towards the producers. These one-way flows have been subject to electronic improvements. Many purchases of rebuy items and their subsequent payments have been automated to reduce costs and improve turnaround times.

Channel flows help identify legitimate members of the marketing channel. Those organisations who participate in the negotiation and ownership flows (the buying, selling and transfer of title) are fully constitutional members of the marketing channel. Channel flows also reflect the complexity associated with channel activities and the huge number of opportunities that are emerging to use new technologies, systems and communications to improve some of these flows, to make them faster, to make them more accurate and efficient and to reduce the costs associated with these aspects of marketing channel management.

Types of distribution channel

Producers are faced with a basic decision. Should they sell direct to consumers or should they sell to another organisation that will in turn market the product to end users? These two extremes represent the **direct channel** and the **indirect channel** respectively. Issues surrounding the nature and benefits of using an indirect channel are the focus of this chapter and Chapters 8 and 9, but the decision to adopt one or the other is really a function of the uncertainty surrounding the performance of the customers, products and services, intermediaries, competitors and suppliers (see Table 7.2).

Indirect channels are selected when the degree of uncertainty concerning the delivery of end-user value exceeds acceptable levels. All organisations experience uncertainty and they use a variety of strategies, methods and techniques to contain and reduce specific risks to an acceptable level. Cooperating with organisations which have particular skills and competences is a strategic approach to reducing and sharing such uncertainty.

The structure of distribution channels varies according to whether end users are consumers or business customers. Within each channel configuration there are several levels, each representing a different number or types of intermediaries, each of whom is

Table 7.2 Stakeholder uncertainties and channel selection

Stakeholder	Type of uncertainty
Customers	In terms of their location, types and buying characteristics, their perceived value and desirable satisfaction levels.
Products/Services	In terms of their attributes, availability, speed of perishability, customisation and support.
Intermediaries	In terms of their capability in terms of selling, distribution and financing, their ability to add real value.
Competitors	In terms of their channel decisions, skills and level of interaction.
Suppliers	In terms of their size, resources, level of openness and reliability.

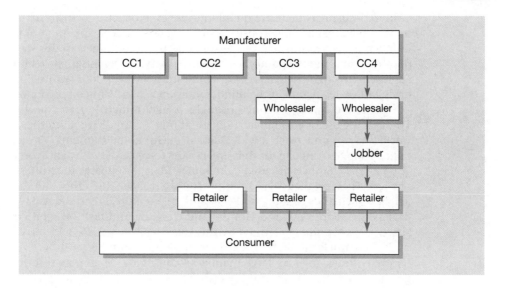

Figure 7.5 Levels of marketing channels for consumer markets

involved in bringing products closer to end users. The length of a channel, therefore, is a function of the number of intermediaries involved in moving products from producers to end users. These various configurations are presented in Figures 7.5 and 7.6. Readers should note the variety of channel members and the number of channel opportunities available. Consumer channels of type 1 (CC1) are direct-marketing channels and contain no intermediaries. All other channel types are regarded as indirect channels and contain a varying number of channel members.

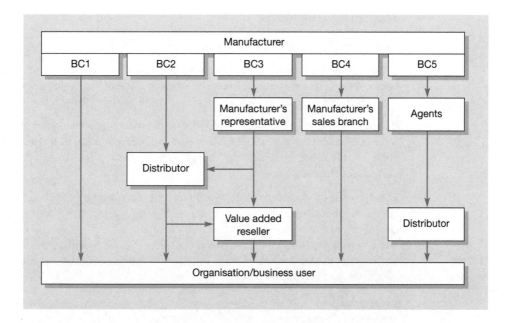

Figure 7.6 Levels of marketing channels for business customer markets

In CC1 channels there are no intermediaries, products move directly from producer to consumer; for example, consumers visiting farms to collect eggs or to pick their own fruit. For many years insurance was sold directly to consumers in this way, for example the 'Man from the Pru', and many financial services organisations still use this direct approach. Recently there has been significant home- (or door-step) selling activity following the deregulation of the utilities industries in the United Kingdom.

Internet technologies have brought a new dimension to the direct channel. Through the use of eCommerce, organisations that once relied on the distribution of catalogues can now reach a wider audience with home shopping. Avon now have an online shop to complement their direct sales force activities (www.avon.co.uk/).

CC2-type channels are used by manufacturers to sell large quantities of product to retailers. These retailers have multiple stores through which they can distribute stock. Retailers such as large supermarket chains (Tesco, Sainsbury's and Asda Wal-Mart), car dealerships (Ford, VW and Honda) and clothing and fashion retailers (Marks and Spencer, H&M and Matalan) typify this approach.

CC3 channels are used when there are a huge number of different retail outlets necessary to reach a very large number of consumers. Shampoo, soft drinks, chewing gum and newspapers are typically distributed via wholesalers to a plethora of retailers.

CC4 channels include the use of agents. Jobbers, agents or brokers as they are sometimes called, are used by producers or even wholesalers, in order that the product sells into a variety of retail outlets. Fish, meat, fruit and other food that is to be processed is often managed in this way.

In channels where the end user is a business or organisation, level BC1 represents the same characteristics as level CC1. It is quite common for expensive industrial products to be distributed through a direct channel, if only because the negotiation flow involves a high level of interaction in order to agree the specification and order requirements and to provide the appropriate level of post-purchase technical support and service. For example, most military and high engineering contracts, such as the

SNAPSHOT 7.4

DANISH DISTRIBUTION CHANNELS

In the Danish electronics business two main distribution channels are used. First, manufacturers use their own subsidiary organisations to distribute to customers and second, they use agents, wholesalers and distributors in order to reach their customers.

A report into the structure and nature of these channels found that direct channels can be expected to play a more significant part in the distribution of these products in Europe in the future. However, distribution to other parts of the world will continue to use indirect channels.

This movement towards direct channels has an impact on the transportation arrangements. A greater reliance on direct channels means a reduction in the number of distributors or distribution nodes. This leads to an increase in warehouse centralisation and a consequent reduction in the overall volume of trips made and a possible change in the nature of the transportation used. The overall logistics cost structure can fall by anything up to 82 per cent.

Source: Adapted from Lemoine, Dagnas, and Jorgenson (2002), www.transportstudier.dk/udgivelser/pdf/ Re-engineering the Danish supply chains.pdf (Accessed November 2003.) Used with permission.

Italian-designed, Pendolinos-styled tilting trains bought by Virgin, were negotiated thorough direct channels (www.railway-technology.com/projects/virgin/; accessed 23 November 2003).

Direct channel marketing in the business-to-business sector has grown as new technology enables organisations to build relationships directly with each of their customers. Electronic channels represent opportunities for manufacturers to reach end-user customers but also to provide intermediaries with higher levels of service and support.

SNAPSHOT 7.5

DIRECT CHANNEL MARKETING AT BOC GASES

For more than 10 years, BOC Gases have developed innovative products and processes designed to reduce the total cost of ownership for compressed gas products and services. For example, the recent expansion of the BOC Arrowhead's cylinder tracking system, a networked customer application, enables customized cylinder tracking, buy-site access and exchange connectivity, for compressed gases and equipment users. This has now been equipped to provide wireless communications access. BOC customers are equipped with handheld devices that provide real-time connectivity to the Arrowhead system or other BOC services such as its on-line catalogue and configurator, which allows customers to customize their gas mixtures.

Customers can now use the handheld device to place orders or conduct stock transactions while walking around their facilities. In addition this device can be used to connect to other on-line services offered by BOC such as on-line product specifications, certificates of analysis, shelf-life expiration tracking and other technologies.

Companies in industries such as chemicals, petroleum, pulp and paper, pharmaceutical and power generation use a variety of compressed and special gases to control processes, perform testing and track emissions. For organizations with multiple locations that may have numerous purchasers ordering a wide range of compressed gases and equipment, this technology offers easy access to the most up-to-date data and transactions.

BOC's wide range of service offerings – from Vendor Managed Inventory (VMI) systems that manage customers' gas and equipment requirements, to BOC's *Sentry* Site Services™ for on-site staffing, to eBusiness systems that allow customers to track their cylinders and transactions – are tailored to meet each customer's specific needs and to achieve reductions in the total cost of ownership for compressed gases.

Wireless technology represents the next logical step and by enabling wireless access to BOC's web-based tools, customers benefit from improved supply chain management and overall convenience.

Source: Reproduced with kind permission of the BOC Group, Inc., from www.boc.com/news/copyfriendly–article–detail.cfn (Accessed March 2003.) © The BOC Group, Inc., 2004. All rights reserved.

The use of an industrial distributor enables producers to reach a variety of business buyers. Business channel 2 (BC2) is a commonly used route to reach organisational buyers, especially when a producer has many geographically dispersed customers. For example, building materials suppliers and photocopier suppliers use distributors. Similarly, when a product has a broad market appeal and is sold in small quantities, such as office stationery, furniture and equipment, distributors provide business customers a level of support that the producer could not provide for all end-user businesses. Distributors hold stock and assist the ownership, negotiation, finance, payment and promotion flows. Their role in these markets can be pivotal in providing the level of service that business customers require and the breadth of market coverage that producers need to be successful.

BC3 shows that when manufacturers' representatives are used they coordinate with distributors or resellers in order to access end-user customers. Representatives are used to provide market information, business advice and selling skills. These are especially useful for smaller organisations that do not have the resources necessary to reach new markets or launch new products. Some organisations prefer to use their own sales branches in order to reach particular geographically spread clusters of customers, as shown at BC4.

The final business-to-business channel, BC5, incorporates agents and distributors. This route is frequently used by manufacturers that do not have a sales force but wish to operate in international markets. Agents are used to service and support overseas agents and provide specialist support in terms of ownership (importing), promotion and negotiation flows.

This explanation of different marketing channels is not intended to suggest that manufacturers choose a single channel for business activities. In reality, organisations employ a multichannel strategy. This is because different segments prefer to use (value) different channels. A multichannel strategy is necessary in order that production efficiencies are achieved and all customer types have access to the product.

Channel roles and membership

Membership of an organisation, or in this case a marketing channel, involves an obligation to fulfil a designated and agreed role, or roles. Within roles there are specific tasks that need to be undertaken and completed. It is important that members carry out their assigned roles, in order that all members achieve their objectives. Should a member fail to fulfil its role, either completely or partially, pressure is placed upon others to make good the shortfall. The whole channel then becomes less efficient and the added value perceived by end-user customers is threatened.

There are a number of tasks to be completed in a marketing channel. Some of the traditional ones are subject to change and evolution as technology, in particular, becomes more significant (see for example the BOC case, Snapshot 7.5). However, the key roles are those occupied by manufacturers, wholesalers, retailers and end-user customers. The sections that follow examine the tasks that these core members undertake. Each of the main channel members is considered in the context of a traditional, uncomplicated channel. This serves as a basis for understanding fundamental tasks and roles before exploring some of the wider, structural and more strategic issues in Chapter 8.

Manufacturers

Manufacturers, or producers, are the source of products and services that are distributed through marketing channels. Their number and variety is immense, ranging from manufacturers of nails, milk and clothing to gas turbines, computers and space rockets. The size of these organisations also varies from sole traders to multinationals operating in many different countries and regions across the world. Despite these disparities, they have a common thread in that they must all produce goods and services that are valued by end-user customers and distributed in such a way that they are available and accessible in their target markets.

The overall role of manufacturers is to assemble parts and materials from various suppliers and to distribute these, often through intermediaries, to different market segments. To do this, manufacturers need to undertake specific roles within particular channel flows. Their participation in the physical, ownership, negotiation, finance, payment and promotion flows delineates their significance in the marketing channel. Their role is instrumental in stimulating the channel to respond to end-user customer needs.

Intermediaries

The term intermediary refers to all those organisations that link together manufacturers and end users. The overall role is acting as a go-between to ensure that end users are able to access the products and services they require in quantities and locations that provide greatest utility. In Bucklin's terms, intermediaries seek to provide optimum levels of service outputs.

There are many types of intermediary but the most common are wholesalers, merchants, brokers, manufacturers representatives, dealers, distributors, agents, retailers and value added resellers. Many of these perform similar functions but the terminology reflects market needs and historical precedent. Essentially there are two main types of intermediary, wholesalers and retailers.

Wholesalers

The term wholesalers embraces merchants, brokers, manufacturers representatives, agents, distributors and dealers. They are (normally) independently owned and buy products from producers and resell them to retailers, other wholesalers and end-user business customers. They perform tasks that assist producers (upstream) and they also perform tasks that assist their customers (downstream). These tasks are set out in Table 7.3.

There is a small technical difference between a wholesaler and a distributor. A wholesaler distributes products to other intermediaries but distributors sell directly to end-user customers, invariably business customers. This difference is to be noted but this text focuses on wholesalers as if they encompass distributors.

Table 7.3 Wholesaler tasks – upstream and downstream

Upstream tasks	Activities
Market uncertainty	Market coverage
	Collecting and analysing market information
	Making sales contacts
	Relationship maintenance
Transaction uncertainty	Holding stock
	Processing orders
	Providing customer support

Downstream tasks	Activities
Product uncertainty	Stock availability and delivery
	Breaking bulk
	Product quality and reliability
	Assortment
Service and support uncertainty	Extended credit
	Technical support and advice
	General service
	Customer relationship development

The role of wholesalers is linked to the tasks they perform in order that the channel operates efficiently. Their **upstream tasks** are to reduce the uncertainty producers experience. This uncertainty concerns the market for the producer's goods and the transaction activities associated with buying and selling. Of these, the provision of suitable and adequate market coverage is one of the more important tasks undertaken for producers. Jackson and d'Amico (1989) point out that the probability that wholesalers will be used increases as the geographic dispersion of customers widens, the number of industries served broadens, order frequency increases and lead times decline.

Associated with market coverage is the role and significance of the sales force. The uncertainty associated with maintaining a large sales force prohibits many manufacturing and producer organisations from employing their own dedicated sales forces. Experience and research show that it is more effective to leave this skilled and expensive operation to those with local knowledge and who are also better placed to develop and maintain relationships. Through good relationships it is possible to generate quality market information which can be fed back to manufacturers to influence marketing strategy and help product/service development.

Wholesalers hold stock on behalf of producers. In a sense they can be regarded as an extension to a manufacturer's production capacity in that they share the uncertainty associated with production by reducing the quantities of stock manufacturers might otherwise have to retain. This has an impact on finance through the amount of working capital each stakeholder holds.

In addition to these benefits, wholesalers contribute to the risks associated with order processing. Wholesalers buy large quantities of stock and break bulk in order to provide retailers and end-user customers with the smaller quantities they prefer to buy. Manufacturers dislike the inefficiencies associated with servicing a large number of small orders.

Wholesalers also undertake a range of **downstream tasks** to reduce the uncertainty experienced by retailers and end-user business customers. This uncertainty concerns both product-related issues and the mechanisms necessary to support and service each exchange. Retailers and end-user customers prefer that products are easily and quickly available. Wholesalers are better able than manufacturers to provide this function. Stock can be stored, delivered and even collected for repair and servicing quickly and regularly by wholesalers, improving the service outputs for end-user customers.

Financial uncertainty can be reduced through the use of extended credit. By allowing retailers to resell products and end-user business buyers to use the products before having to pay for them, so wholesalers help those downstream. In addition to this wholesalers hold stock which can be called off by retailers as and when it is convenient to them. This represents a further reduction in financial risk because retailers do not have to pay for holding stock until it is actually required.

Wholesalers break bulk for those lower down the channel and provide an assortment of products from an array of manufacturers that retailers and end users prefer. By providing technical and general support the operational risks experienced by retailers can be reduced, while the perceived performance and physical risks associated with some business product purchases can be minimised.

Not all wholesalers perform all of these tasks as they vary according to industry. However, wholesalers perform a series of important roles for both upstream manufacturers and downstream retailers and end-user customers. They facilitate the movement of goods through the channel and smooth the buying processes by raising

---

SNAPSHOT 7.6

ROYAL LEMKES – A DUTCH PLANT WHOLESALER

The Plantania marketing channel consists of three main organisations: OBI (a German home-improvement chain), Royal Lemkes (a plant wholesaler) and Decorum Plants (a plant retailer). The channel deals with all aspects of floriculture from plant production to retail sales. It is a closed channel in that the three main constituent companies work together to compete against rival channels.

The wholesale role that Royal Lemkes undertakes has changed. Originally the role was to buy plants from growers at auction and then sell these to retailers. Part of the problem concerned excessive wastage as the system was product-orientated and consumers did not always like the products offered them so wastage levels of 20 per cent were not uncommon. The role changed when the wholesaler became part of Plantania and is now based on coordination and allocation.

Plantania is a market-orientated channel so the retailer's demands now influence the role of the wholesaler. Now the key tasks are to bring together particular assortments of plants and allocate them at times and configurations that the retailer (hence consumer) demands. Therefore, the upstream task is to manage the growers such that they produce the right combinations and quantities of plants and the downstream task is to provide OBI, the retailer, particular plant combinations that have been predetermined by the market.

Source: adapted from Engelbart and Rijswijk (2001), www.isnar.cgiar.org/shiip/plantania.htm (Accessed November 2003.)

service output levels and in doing so reducing perceived risks. Wholesalers are involved with the negotiation, ownership, finance, promotion, physical, order and payment flows.

Retailers

Retailing is concerned with the identification of consumer demands, finding the right mix of stock and making it available to them at times and in formats that they prefer. This means that retailers enter into exchanges with consumers, unlike wholesalers who exchange with resellers and end-user business organisations. Coughlan *et al.* (2001) state that this demarcation is important because it highlights the different buying motivations and processes that both wholesalers and retailers must address in their marketing strategies and, in particular, their segmentation policies.

Retailers undertake a number of tasks for their upstream partners, namely wholesalers, manufacturers and other intermediaries. The uncertainty experienced by these upstream partners revolves around their need to have stock moved and broken down into smaller allotments. This helps their finance flows and assists the order processing flow. While wholesalers break bulk for producers, so retailers perform the same exercise for wholesalers, although the scale of each individual operation is smaller. Retailers provide wholesalers with sales contacts and sales outlets through which stock is transferred to individual consumers for consumption. It is more efficient for retailers to undertake this operation than for wholesalers.

Table 7.4 Retailer tasks – upstream and downstream

Upstream tasks	Activities
Product uncertainty	Breaking bulk
	Sales contacts
	Storage
Market uncertainty	Collecting and analysing market information
	Promotion
	Collecting and processing orders

Downstream tasks	Activities
Demand uncertainty	Turnover/margin model
	Spatial convenience
	Waiting time
	Lot size
	Product variety
Service and support uncertainty	Stock availability and delivery
	Extended credit
	Technical support and advice
	Customer relationship development

In a similar way retailers reduce wholesalers' storage risks by taking small amounts of stock on a regular basis. This enables wholesalers to plan their own stock-holding operations more accurately. Uncertainty is shared by spreading stock, in different amounts, throughout the entire channel. Stock levels constitute a major area of uncertainty for retailers. For example, a great deal could depend on a manufacturer's or wholesaler's policy on accepting returned products. Should the policy accommodate returns then it is likely that retailers will over-order and hence over-stock (Tsay, 2002). This sharing of risk might improve downstream service levels but can result in stock being returned and the wholesaler's performance reduced.

Retailers provide a point of contact with consumers that not only stimulates the order and payment flows but also offers other upstream parties a means by which they can collect market information. Indeed this market research function has become a source of influence for many retailers who have become 'data rich'. The use of new technology, in particular databases, has enabled retailers (and manufacturers) to overcome the complexity associated with getting to know customers' preferences and needs (O'Malley and Mitussis, 2002). Through understanding these aspects of their customers, it becomes possible to develop meaningful and mutually rewarding relationships. Uncertainty about consumer demand can be reduced by a retailer's choice of level of service outputs and their positioning decision regarding the turnover/margin model that they adopt.

According to Coughlan *et al.* (2001) there are two main retail models. The established retail model works on the basis of high margins and low stock turnover. Retailers offer consumers products in small quantities but charge a higher price and hence earn a higher margin as compensation. The second, more contemporary, model has evolved on the basis that it is more efficient to generate lower margins on a high stock turnover. Under this model, retailers offer consumers the opportunity to buy large amounts of stock and they are compensated with a lower unit price. There are a large number of variants based on these two simple constructs but what emerges is the impact on the level of service output offered to customers.

As a generalisation, the first model provides a high level of service output and is consumer-centric. The second model presents a lower level of service output and is channel-centric. There is, of course, a mixture of both models in existence, reflecting the needs of different segments. Indeed, it is not really about just higher or lower levels of service output, but about the different value that consumers and channel members now attribute to various types and combinations of service output. For example, Sweeny and Soutar (2001) propose that consumers now use four primary dimensions with which to assess the value of a consumer durable good: emotional, social, quality/performance and price/value for money. This should be reflected in the retailer proposition communicated through promotion, store location and ambience, stocking levels and levels of personal service.

It is worth noting that, although the channel-centric model reflects a concentration on the efficiencies of production and distribution, consumer preferences and shopping habits have changed. Consumers are more time-poor, more affluent and better educated. As a result they value different service outputs in diverse ways. Retailers have moved to reflect this, literally, by moving out-of-town and creating huge retail stores in order to provide a wide range of stock at lower services but with a higher level of personal service and support. Consumers therefore still value spatial convenience, but that convenience is reflected in easy parking, collection of goods and, in some categories, even self-assembly. New technology allows retailers and manufacturers to offer home shopping facilities to increase the perceived value of their services by emphasising convenience.

SNAPSHOT 7.7

TESCO HOME SHOPPING

As well as groceries, on 4 March 2003 the Tesco website (www.tesco.com) was offering the following 'warehouses':

- Baby and toddler
- Books
- DVDs
- Electrical
- Flowers
- Games

- Healthy living
- Music
- Personal finance
- Travelcare
- Videos
- Wine

Waiting times can be reduced by retailers through over-stocking, a strategy supported by favourable manufacturer's return policies, mentioned earlier. Hand-held scanners allowing consumers to self-scan purchases have yet to achieve widespread use but will help time-poor consumers by reducing checkout time.

The decisions retailers make about product variety also have strategic importance. A seller stocking a narrow variety but deep range of products will often be perceived by consumers as a specialist or expert retailer. In these circumstances there should be high levels of service output and customer support. For example, Jessops for photographic equipment or Clarks shoe shops. Retailers who provide a broad variety of products but little depth within each line, for example Asda Wal-Mart, will be perceived as convenient and price-orientated stores. Here low margin and high stock turnover combined with good customer service is the preferred model.

Top-performing supermarket retailers were found to excel because they offered broader assortments of stock and have high performing own label brands, charge significantly lower everyday prices, process and feature advertising, the promotion flow, that drives store traffic (Dhar *et al.* 2001).

In addition to dealing with demand uncertainty, retailers also deal with the uncertainties, associated with consumer service and support. By providing credit facilities, consumer uncertainty with respect to financial risks can be overcome. The level of in-store personal service needs to reflect the overall positioning of the store and complement the balance of service outputs provided. Although more staff can lead to higher levels of service output, it also means that there is a higher cost base and this drives a need to earn higher margins. Out-of-store support can also be important in some categories such as domestic appliances, computers and financial services sectors. Here guaranteed call-out times, extended warranties and use of authorised out-sourced providers all serve to reduce the pre-purchase uncertainties experienced by consumers.

The range and different forms of uncertainty experienced by retailers, the variety of combinations of service output levels and the expectations of different consumer segments lead to an array of retail types. Table 7.5 reflects this diversity.

Table 7.5 Categories of retailers

Type of retailer	Focus on margin or turnover	Breaking bulk	Spatial C	Waiting and delivery time	Variety (breadth of stock)	Assortment (depth of range)
Department store (e.g. Debenhams)	M	Y	M	Low	Broad	Shallow
Speciality store (e.g. Gap)	M	Y	M	Low	Narrow	Deep
Mail order (e.g. Hawkshead)	M	Y	V V High	Moderate	Narrow	Moderate
Convenience store (e.g. Tesco Express)	Both	Y	V High	Low	Broad	Shallow
Category killer (e.g. Toys-Я-Us)	T	Y	Low	Low	Narrow	Deep
Mass merchandiser (e.g. Wal-Mart)	T	Y	Low	Moderate	Broad	Shallow
Hypermarket (e.g. Carrefour)	T	Y	Low	Moderate	Broad	Moderate
Warehouse Club (e.g. Costco)	T	N	Low	Moderate	Broad	Shallow

Source: Adapted from Coughlan *et al.* (2001). Coughlan, Anderson, Stem, El-Ansary, *Marketing Channels*, 6th edn. © 2001. Adapted by permission of Pearson Education, Inc., Upper Saddle River, NJ.

Retailers perform a number of important tasks and undertake significant roles in the marketing channel. This section has presented some of the uncertainties and models and methods used to resolve them. All policies undertaken by retailers have implications right the way through a marketing channel and this highlights the importance of coordinated channel strategies and clear segmentation policies.

End users

End users are as much a part of marketing channels as the intermediaries referred to above. There are two types of end user – individual consumers and business customers – constituting an integral part of the processes and flows that a marketing channel supports. For example, end users buy products from retailers or purchase direct from manufacturers or wholesalers and in doing so generate payment, order processing, stock holding and ownership flows. They enable the channel to function and the various flows to be actioned. End users stimulate the payment flow by prompting customer orders. From these orders there is a reason for stock to be made, moved, stored or presented.

Impact of technology on marketing channels

The impact of technology can be seen from a number of perspectives. Here, two are taken, service outputs and channel flows.

Service outputs

One of the reasons manufacturers use intermediaries is to break bulk. However, the development of electronically driven direct channels means that the manufacturer has, invariably, to take over this role. The task now becomes one of shipping a few units to a large number of addresses and this is not usually a skill manufacturers' have. The usual result is that this task is out-sourced but then greater uncertainty arises with respect to fulfilment.

There is of course a high level of spatial convenience associated with direct purchasing. The speed and time utility is a major advantage for customers buying but problems can occur, especially within B2C markets, when there can be a high number of returns. The inconvenience associated with repackaging and returning items can be partially overcome with house collections but even then customers need to be there and wait for collection.

The attractiveness of Internet technology as a direct channel is hampered by the waiting and delivery time service outputs. Accepting that many service-based products can be delivered immediately online, for example music, software, insurance and other financial transactions, it is the time taken to deliver physical products that can vary enormously. Many organisations offer graduated delivery pricing, where it is possible to receive goods the following day in return for a price premium. Some companies seek an advantage by guaranteeing delivery times, if ordered before a certain time the previous day. For example, Electrocomponents plc offer 'Market-leading delivery times and options – guaranteed, free next-day in the UK, with options for delivery by 9am, 10am and noon' (www.electrocomponents.com/about_us/service.htm, accessed 4 March 2003).

The potential associated with the assortment and variety of products is huge through the direct channel. Two main opportunities exist. First, single-site online resellers are not restrained by the stock-holding capability of a bricks and mortar store. Vast arrays of stock can be stored and presented to website visitors. Online shopping malls increase further the range and variety of stock available.

Second, some manufacturers, such as several car manufacturers, have joined together to provide a parts buying marketsite; for example the Covisint site formed by Ford, General Motors and Volvo. This enables them to provide lower prices through greater buying power, while customers also benefit from the huge assortment and variety of products.

Manufacturers who decide to utilise the direct channel have the potential to offer higher levels of service output than those provide offline. However, there is much evidence to suggest that the variety of products made available and the speed of both purchase and payment flows is not always counterbalanced by the physical product flow, as seen through waiting and delivery times.

Channel flows

One of the great advantages of technology is that it has increased many of the dimensions of communication. For example, it can increase the speed of information delivery and transactions, the quantities of information conveyed, the efficiency of information exchange and transactions and the accuracy of information, thus improving clarity and reducing ambiguity. It has also reduced dependency on specific location for communication, since it is possible to access, send and receive information from almost anywhere. Thus, with regard to the various flows within marketing channels, digital technology has had a considerable impact.

In terms of the physical flows, new technology can enable the transportation and storage of products between channel members to be undertaken more quickly and more efficiently. The storage and distribution of products can now be scientifically determined to reduce waste and inefficiency. As a result, costs associated with the physical flow such as warehousing and transportation can be controlled more efficiently while customer service and convenience improves.

The order processing flow, especially for routine B2B transactions, can now be undertaken electronically. Not only does this reduce the order delivery cycle but improvements, in terms of accuracy of order specifications plus improved production scheduling and stock control, all help to enhance efficiency and reduce costs.

Negotiation flows can be speeded up by reducing the amount of physical travel executives are required to undertake and through various online systems buyers can interrogate suppliers' stock levels. The speed of information flow, the accuracy of contractual documentation and the variety of people who can be involved, regardless of geographic location, has improved immeasurably through the use of new technology.

Financial flows have changed as payment can be instantaneous and monies transferred throughout the world, with the only delay caused by banks holding onto overnight interest funds.

The final flow is the promotion flow. The Internet enables organisations to provide depth and range of information about products, services and the organisation, 24/7, 365 days a year. As will be seen in Chapter 12, one of the consequences of this facility is that customers are no longer dependent upon paper brochures or technical information sheets, and selling organisations can divert marketing resources into more efficient and productive areas.

Summary

Marketing channels are a necessary structural format in order that organisations can provide end-user customers with the products and services they require. Through cooperation and collaboration organisations can develop and deliver products and services that represent value to each other and to end-user customers in the most convenient and timely manner possible. Marketing channels help reduce the level of uncertainty that organisations experience.

Within marketing channels it is possible to determine a variety of flows between organisations. These flows, for example the product, order processing and communication flows, are essential for channel members to coordinate their activities. Through such coordination and optimisation appropriate levels of service output become possible. Service outputs reflect the different utilities that customers expect when engaging with marketing channels and buying products and services.

The most common types of organisation that make up a marketing channel are manufacturers, wholesalers and distributors, retailers and value added resellers. They all have different core competences and skills which the other organisations in the channel do not have. This complementary approach enables marketing channels both to function and to differentiate one channel from another.

The nature and complexity of market channels has increased due to many environmental developments, most notably the rapid advances in technology. New electronic trading formats have driven the emergence of new types of intermediary and the demise of others.

Discussion questions

1 Discuss the extent to which the use of channel intermediaries reduces organisational uncertainty and complexity.

2 Explore the potential contribution of EDI to the performance and development of marketing channels.

3 Identify the four elements that Bucklin argued determined the level of service outputs experienced by customers in a marketing channel.

4 Explain four types of channel flow and evaluate the extent to which IS&T might improve the efficiency of flow and performance.

5 Compare and contrast two marketing channels and evaluate the different levels and functions of the various participants.

6 Discuss the extent to which the general tasks of wholesalers in marketing channels differ from those of retailers.

References

Bucklin, L. (1966). *A Theory of Distribution Channel Structure*, Berkeley, CA: IBER Special Publications.

Coughlan, A.T., Anderson, S.L. and El-Ansary, A. (2001). *Marketing Channels*, 6th edn, Englewood Cliffs, NJ: Prentice Hall.

Dhar, S. K., Hoch, S.J. and Kumar, N. (2001), 'Effective category management depends on the role of the category', *Journal of Retailing*, 77, pp. 165–84.

Engelbart, F.W.G.A. and Rijswijk, L.W. (2001) *Plantania: A Business Case Description*, The Hague: Agri-Chain Competence Center (ACC), www.isnar.cgiar.org/shiip/plantania.htm (Accessed 20 November 2003.)

Jackson, D.M. and d'Amico, M.F. (1989). 'Products and markets served by distributors and agents', *Industrial Marketing Management*, 18, 1 (February), pp. 27–33.

Kenjale, K. and Phatak, A. (2003). 'B2B Exchanges: now that we know better, how to move forward from here', Syntel – White Paper, www.syntelinc.com/syntel/english/0000026A/Syntel_B2B.pdf (Accessed 9 January 2004.)

Kraemer, K.L. and Dedrick, J. (2002). 'Strategic use of the Internet and e-commerce: Cisco Systems', *Journal of Strategic Information Systems*, 11, pp. 5–29.

Lemoine, W., Dagnas, L. and Jorgenson, N. (2002). 'Re-engineering the Danish supply chains: consequences for transport', Euro Environment Conference, October 2002; www.transportstudier.dk/udgivelser/pdf/Re-engineering the Danish supply chains.pdf (Accessed 16 January 2004.)

Mudambi, S. and Aggarwal, R. (2003). 'Industrial distributors: can they survive in the new economy?', *Industrial Marketing Management*, 32, 4, pp. 317–25.

O'Malley, L. and Mitussis, D. (2002). 'Relationships and technology: strategic implications', *Journal of Strategic Marketing*, 10, pp. 225–38.

Roberts, B. and Flight, G. (1995). 'The enabling role of EDI in business process re-engineering', www.infosys.kingston.ac.uk/isschool/Staff/Papers/Roberts/EDI_BPR.html (Accessed 25 October 2002.)

Roe, M., Weinstein, M., Bumstead, J. and Charron, H. (1998), 'Forging a strong European chain', *Transportation and Distribution*, 39, 6 (June), pp. 100–1.

Rosenbloom, B. (1999). *Marketing Channels: a Management View*, 6th edn, Orlando, FL: Harcourt Brace.

Sweeny, J.C. and Soutar, G.N. (2001). 'Consumer perceived value: the development of a multiple item scale', *Journal of Retailing*, 77, pp. 203–20.

Tsay, A.A. (2002). 'Risk sensitivity in distribution channel partnerships: implications for manufacturer return policies', *Journal of Retailing*, 78, pp. 147–60.

Chapter 8

Channel organisation, structures and networks

Chapter overview

In the last chapter a number of fundamental ideas concerning the nature and characteristics of marketing channels were considered. In this chapter time is spent developing and exploring some of these issues and ideas, with a particular emphasis on how organisations should design and structure the channels they need to reach their target markets. Readers may wish to refer to Chapter 6 where many important and related concepts concerning interorganisational relationships are explored.

This chapter opens with a consideration of supply chains and logistics before examining some of the ways organisations choose to organise and structure their channels, including channel design and the use of supporting software and systems. The chapter deals with the nature and structure of interorganisational relationships and explores the variety of structural configurations used by organisations. Attention is given to conventional marketing channel structures, vertical marketing systems and network approaches to interorganisational channel structures. The chapter concludes with an exploration of the electronic channel structures and new trading formats.

Chapter aims

The aims of this chapter are to examine different marketing channel formats and structures and to explore ways in which organisations cooperate with one another in order to make their products and services available to end-user customers.

Objectives

The objectives of this chapter are to:

1   Introduce notions of organisational interdependence and independence.

2   Examine the issues associated with the physical distribution of finished goods and to understand the meaning of supply chain management.

3   Examine the design and structure of different marketing channels.

4   Consider the nature and form of alliances and partnerships.

5   Consider contemporary forms of organisational networks.

6   Introduce ideas concerning electronic channels and new B2B trading formats.

Introduction

Two important concepts underpin ideas relating to marketing channels. The first of these is the dichotomy between the freedom organisations seek to operate autonomously and the necessity to cooperate and combine their resources in order to work with other organisations. The need to balance the drive for independence and the need to be interdependent can often be a point of tension for organisations. Decisions regarding the selection and de-selection of channel partners, the degree to which organisations can or should use direct marketing and decisions to enter into alliances, undertake new roles in established channels or to develop new channels all require judgement about the appropriate balance of interdependence.

Following a decision to be interdependent and to work with other organisations, the second underpinning concept concerns the degree to which an organisation should cooperate and coordinate activities with other organisations. At one end of a spectrum of coordination, cooperation may be casual, cursory and perfunctory. At the other end, cooperation may be intense, involved and fully supportive of the other channel participants. In other words, the level of cooperation is partly a function of the type of relationship that exists in the channel. At one end there are market exchanges and at the other purely relational exchanges. Most organisations adopt a position between these two extremes.

Supply chains

The majority of organisations have little choice but to cooperate with other organisations. Through cooperation organisations link themselves to other organisations that have the necessary specialist skills, resources and core competences. These linkages are an external representation of the (internal) value chains that organisations use to enhance the products and services with which they are involved. These chains are referred to as marketing channels.

Organisations that choose to cooperate with one another, in order to deliver superior value for end-user customers, join their individual value chains together and form what are termed marketing channels. In addition to the added value concept associated with marketing channels, there are activities associated with the management of the physical flow, namely the movement of parts, supplies and finished products, from the very first supplier in the chain to the end-user customer. These linkages are referred to as supply chains and current terminology refers to this concept as supply chain management (SCM).

Although there are many subtle differences in terminology, SCM is a more contemporary term for **logistics** and before that **physical distribution**. Definitions and interpretations vary widely, with some arguing that the supply chain starts with the suppliers of raw materials (New and Payne, 1995) and others arguing that it only deals with finished goods (Christopher *et al.*, 1998). The approach adopted here is that SCM is concerned with the whole value creation chain of physical distribution activities.

These start with the suppliers of the basic raw materials and parts of a product, continue through the assembly and manufacturing stages, and distribution to the eventual consumption by the end-user customer.

Key elements in supply chain management

Integrated SCM is concerned with the business processes associated with the efficient movement of parts, raw materials, work in progress and finished goods. The goal of SCM is to improve efficiency and effectiveness with regard to the physical movement of products. In contrast to marketing channels, which are concerned with the management of customer behaviour, finished goods and the added value that interorganisational relationships can bring, SCM is essentially about the management of all the business activities necessary to get the right product, in the right place, for the right customer to access in a timely and convenient way.

To achieve this integration, all participants in a supply chain need to reconstruct their internal functional activities so that they can coordinate events and share information with their partner organisations. The detailed nature of these events will be examined shortly, but it is worth establishing the overall tasks that SCM needs to accomplish.

Brewer and Speh (2000) argue that SCM seeks to achieve four main goals. These are waste reduction, time compression, flexible response and unit cost reduction (see Table 8.1).

Table 8.1 SCM goals

Goal	Explanation
Waste reduction	By reducing the level of duplicated and excess stock in the chain, it becomes possible to harmonise operations between organisations to achieve new levels of uniformity and standardisation.
Time compression	Reducing the order-to-delivery cycle time improves efficiency and customer service outputs. A faster cycle indicates a smoother and more efficient operation and associated processes. Faster times mean less stock, faster cash flow and higher levels of service output.
Flexible response	By managing the order processing elements (size, time, configuration, handling) specific customer requirements can be met without causing them inconvenience and contributes to efficiency and service delivery.
Unit cost reduction	By understanding the level of service output that is required by the end-user customers it then becomes possible to minimise the costs involved in delivering to that required standard.

Source: Adapted from Brewer and Speh (2000).

RE-ENGINEERING THE HP SUPPLY CHAIN

In the late 1990s Hewlett Packard (HP) were market leaders in the compact disc rewritable (CD-RW) industry. Having developed products for the business market they moved into the consumer market where sales started to double annually. Sales rose from 100k in 1997 to 5m in 2001. However, this spectacular growth was accompanied by many new entrants which led to falling prices and the erosion of HP's profitability.

HP manufactured the product at two supplier locations in Asia which then shipped, independently of each other, to a number of regional distribution centres in North America, Europe and Asia Pacific. This resulted in the product being 30 days at sea, in stock for 91 days and an order/delivery cycle time of 126 days. The supply chain costs resulting from this excessive stock handling reduced profitability to a minimum.

The solution was to redesign the supply chain in such a way that it cut the order/delivery cycle time and with it, the attendant costs. Fourteen HP organisations and five external partner organisations were involved in reconfiguring the supply chain. Eight new scenarios were modelled and project teams worked on the project for over a year.

The configuration that emerged required the development of a single worldwide distribution centre, located in Asia. This undertook all the conversion, localisation and distribution work, using air freight to ship direct to all HP customers (resellers). One of the suppliers was appointed preferred supplier and promised 80 per cent of the business, while other suppliers were designated second tier to supply as demand required.

The impact of this was to reduce order/delivery cycle time from 126 to just 8 days. Even the cash-to-cash cycle time became negative as the preferred supplier accepted a 45-day settlement period. Stock turn increased from 3 to 45 and saved $50m each year for HP. The savings recouped the investment made by HP in just a single month.

This case demonstrates the importance of SCM and the need to reduce waste, compress time and to be flexible when responding to market needs.

Source: Adapted from Hammel *et al.* (2002). Published with permission, Emerald Publishing Group Limited.

By achieving these four goals the efficiency of a supply chain is improved and, as a result, end-user customers experience increased levels of service output.

For the purposes of this text, the primary element of SCM is regarded as logistics. The foundation stones of logistics are the activities necessary to move products through to end users and to do so in such a way that the four efficiency goals are met. By concentrating on particular supply chain activities, organisations are better placed to achieve the efficiency goals. These activities are: stock management, warehousing, fulfilment and transportation (see Figure 8.1).

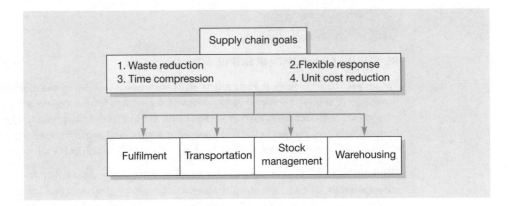

Figure 8.1 Key supply chain activity areas

Stock management

Stock management is crucial to all organisations involved in the production and distribution of finished and unfinished products. The management of stock embraces storage and warehousing issues and this includes related matters of stock quality, security, insurance and value. This last item has important implications for the channel members. The value of finished stock represents on the one hand an opportunity to provide higher levels of service output but on the other a high financial inventory or working capital cost which is reflected in the profit and loss account. One important question, therefore, is how much stock should an intermediary hold?

Finished goods cost more than unfinished goods to hold in stock. If demand allows, manufacturers prefer to withhold production until the very last moment or pass finished goods to intermediaries. This could be seen as simply a matter of transferring costs to other parts of the supply chain, but this would not reflect a strong relationship in which members seek to support each other.

Two interesting theories associated with the transfer of stock and associated service outputs are **postponement** and **speculation**. Postponement is about delaying the point at which products become finished goods. So, the greater the period of time that products can remain undifferentiated and postponed within the marketing channel, the lower will be the associated costs.

Speculation is concerned with the anticipation of desired service outputs, that customers want products now and are not prepared to wait. This means creating finished goods at the earliest opportunity. Through this approach costs can be reduced through long production runs. By reducing the number of stock outs, the costs associated with customer dissatisfaction can be reduced together with the frequency with which orders are placed by intermediaries. Postponement is about having more work in progress and speculation is about more finished goods in the channel.

SNAPSHOT 8.2

POSTPONEMENT AT SENDO

The manufacturing market for mobile phones has been dominated by a few major organisations, namely Nokia and Motorola. Sendo, a British organisation, entered the international market when the market reached maturity and supply began to seriously outstrip demand. However, Sendo's strategy has been based on providing modular handsets that can be customised to meet the needs of its clients, the network providers.

Blank radio receivers are made in the Czech Republic and then shipped to Holland where client specific software is installed and customised covers snapped on. This allows Sendo to tailor-make phones with the features, logos, games and colours requested by customers.

Source: Adapted from Durman (2003).

Paint manufacturers are happy to supply end-user customers with the popular colours of paint in huge quantities and in a variety of sized containers. But, because it is not economic to produce and to shelf-stock paint that has limited appeal, retailers will make up cans of these tones and shades, on-site and on-demand in front of the end-user customer. This is achieved using bulk quantities of specific base paints mixed to manufacturers specifications. In this way it is possible to meet the specific requirements of customers, in-store and in this case with limited waiting time. Therefore, paint manufacturers practice both speculation, with regard to the popular colours, and postponement, with regard to the less popular tints and shades.

The Wine Society uses software to record orders before some wines become available and, if demand exceeds supply, to allocate stock fairly (Maginus, 2003). The data from this allocation system is passed to the software described below, in the fulfilment section.

Warehousing

Finished and unfinished products should spend as little time waiting to be used or consumed as is possible. This waiting time is referred to as storage and in many cases storage is undertaken in warehouses.

The location of warehouses is an important strategic aspect of logistics. Indeed, the location, size, design and operating systems used in warehouses can have a considerable impact on the level of service outputs experienced by subsequent members of the supply chain. The number and location of warehouses is a function of many variables but one of these concerns the structure of the marketing channel. In channels where producers use distributors, a lower number of warehouses will be necessary as distributors take ownership and physical possession of stock. In channels where agents and manufacturers' representatives are preferred, a higher number of warehouses are required because these intermediaries do not take ownership or physical possession.

Some companies outsource their storage and warehousing activities with the benefit of lower fixed costs and improved flexibility with regard to transportation and associated activities. For example, in February 2003 the International Warehouse Logistics Association website listed 486 members worldwide, who offer 'nearly 400,000,000 square feet of public and contract warehouse space and provide the most timely and cost-effective global logistics solutions for their customers'. (For more information see www.warehouselogistics.org.)

Distribution centres have developed as a complement to warehouses. The main difference between the two is that warehouses are used to store goods on a long-term basis while distribution centres hold minimal quantities for a short period of time. Distribution centres are often located near to customers (retail outlets) in order that they are better positioned to deliver low numbers of units at a high frequency.

Fulfilment

Once orders are received and flow upstream, it becomes necessary to pick and pack stock to make up orders. The contemporary terminology is **fulfilment** or **materials handling** and it is about locating and picking stock, packing and securing it before shipping the selected items or bundle to the next channel member.

This part of the logistics system can be critical to the overall efficiency of a supply chain. Very often specialist equipment and software systems are required to ensure that intra-warehouse stock movement is minimised while inter-warehouse movement is optimised.

For example, the Wine Society uses Maginus software to control warehousing and picking of over 1,000 products, which are sold in full or mixed cases or by the bottle. This is part of an integrated eCommerce system. (For more information see www.maginus.com)

The ability to fulfil an order quickly and accurately, can provide a point of differentiation for a marketing channel. Cross-docking represents an attempt at minimising fulfilment costs and time. Under this approach, instead of receiving, storing, picking, packing and despatching items for an order, supplies are received already packaged so that they are received at one door of a warehouse and are then sent out immediately from another despatch bay. For example, supply chain management and system integration specialists Microlise describe their solution to cross-docking for GlaxoSmithKline (see Snapshot 8.3).

Transportation

Transportation is about routing and delivering selected items which are bundled as an order. Transportation is expensive so pick up and delivery points become an important part of analysis within the management of logistics. Location is important because of the need to reduce costs and yet provide members with a high frequency of low-unit-size deliveries.

Transportation involves documentation and, when goods are shipped, freight forwarders provide services such as the preparation of all necessary documentation for import/export or for meeting other transportation requirements such as safety, when moving hazardous materials.

CROSS-DOCKING AT GLAXOSMITHKLINE

The GlaxoSmithKline distribution centre at Welwyn Garden City receives pharmaceutical and promotional support stock items, from GlaxoSmithKline production sites in the United Kingdom and various European suppliers. It despatches products to major UK retailers, distributors, hospitals, GPs, the Ministry of Defence and to customers abroad.

The warehousing operation spans three separate buildings on the site. Incoming palletised stock is stored in the four aisles of VNA [Very Narrow Aisle] racking at the bulk warehouse, from which products for export are picked. These are then transferred to the separate export building for checking, packing and despatch. In the other buildings, the UK pharmaceutical and promotional picking areas are fed with pallet stock from the bulk warehouse on a demand-led basis.

Source: Adapted from www.microlise.com/case/glaxo.htm (Accessed 4 March 2003.) Used with permission.

Transportation becomes an important factor in redirecting materials and part finished goods. Through alliances and what is known as third-party logistics providers (3PL) organisations join together to provide new forms of service outputs for producers. These new members of the supply chain are referred to as contract logistics providers. They represent combinations of members from within the logistics system, such as the pairing of freight forwarders and transportation agencies, or fulfilment and transportation specialists.

Principles of supply chain management

Having considered the foundation stones associated with logistics management it should be apparent that a primary goal within the supply chain is to move products towards end-user customers as quickly and efficiently as possible. An adequate supply of products in marketing channels is the basis for delivering acceptable service output levels. The faster and more cost effectively a supply chain can move materials and products, the greater the potential competitive advantage.

With ever-shortening life cycles, much reduced manufacturing costs, increases in competition and better educated, more aware and demanding customers, many organisations have been forced to move from physical logistics management towards the more integrated and software-based solutions offered by supply chain management providers. Through the use of information and communications technologies such as databases, communication systems and advanced computer software, it is possible to develop cost-effective supply chain management.

SNAPSHOT 8.4

EXEL PROVIDE THIRD PARTY LOGISTICS FOR BAYER

The testing equipment provided by Bayer Diagnostics is used in a wide variety of medical disciplines throughout the globe from hospitals through to nursing homes and medical offices. A significant proportion of its products are temperature sensitive which require fast and timely transportation solutions. For Exel, the challenge was to develop a supply chain solution that ensured Bayer's products reached their destinations within 48–72 hours of leaving their manufacturing origin in the UK and that internal packaging maintained the prescribed temperature during transit.

Exel studied the supply chain and identified that in order to satisfy the needs of one of the world's largest and fastest growing medical diagnostics businesses it would need to develop an effective account management programme. The solution was a time-defined airfreight export service, from the UK to destinations worldwide. Shipments which are temperature controlled are all shipped on direct IATA flights due to their nature, whilst nonrestrictive products are moved on Exel's airfreight consolidation service. Exel collects all restricted cargo on its day of readiness and, depending on the destination and transit time involved, delivers between 24 and 48 hours later. Exel ships in excess of 1,500 shipments per annum for Bayer Diagnostics, with consignments varying from 1 kg up to 2000 kg.

David Norbury, Exel's Freight Management UK Corporate Account Manager – Healthcare, comments: 'Exel's relationship with Bayer Diagnostics has grown from strength to strength and we are continuously looking for ways in which Exel can create new value in Bayer's supply chain across a wider geography, as its business develops. One of the key success factors in our partnership with Bayer Diagnostics has been the strong relationship that has built up between the two companies over the years enabling Exel to fully understand Bayer's business and the nature of its products to ensure the most effective transportation solutions are provided.'

Source: www.exel.com/mediacentre/casestudies/ (Accessed 1 February 2004.) Used with permission.

Electronic data interchange (EDI) provides an important facility for sharing information between partnering organisations. EDI is the electronic transfer, using agreed standards, of structured data from one organisation's computers to another. Through EDI, organisations can integrate much of their logistics and improve efficiency and customer service. However, Borders *et al.* (2001, p. 4) suggest that the high costs and rigidity of EDI systems 'makes them ill suited to a rapidly changing competitive landscape'.

As stated earlier, SCM is about being faster and more efficient in providing end-user customers with the products they need. There are many ways of achieving these goals but two are very important: quick response and efficient customer response systems. Both of these approaches are founded on the same pull-based, that is to say customer driven, principles. The customers inform the supply chain about what assortment to make, what to despatch and where and when it should arrive.

Quick response (QR) systems are designed to enable manufacturers to adapt to unpredictable and volatile demand, such as that experienced in the fashion clothing industry. When consumers shop for clothes they do not know in advance what they want, what they will like and whether the size and cut will be appropriate. Their

SNAPSHOT 8.5

INTEGRATED SUPPLY CHAIN PROCESSING

UK commerce software provider (Maginus) offer a suite of programmes for managing supply chain processes. These include:

Forecasting	Purchasing
Replenishment	Warehouse management
Picking/packing and fulfilment	Proof of delivery
Customs and excise	Returns
Production scheduling	

The business benefits claimed are:

- reduced stock holding costs;

- improved order fulfilment, accuracy and customer satisfaction;

- more efficient warehousing, order processing and fulfilment;

- tighter control on supplier relationships.

Source: Adapted from Maginus Data Sheet 'Supply Chain: Delivering the e-promise' distributed at 'Technology for Marketing' event, at Olympia, London, February 2003.

decisions are usually made at the point of purchase, that is, in the store. Benetton, an early pioneer of QR systems, were often faced with large stocks of unsold (and hence unfashionable) stock. They developed a system that enabled retailers to feed back early customer preferences based on limited amounts of demonstration stock. Only once this feedback was received did Benetton dye its wool and then produce, often through an out-sourced production team, the large quantities of clothing ranges that retailers and customers preferred. This process was accomplished in a very short period and stock was delivered within a few weeks to their retail partners, at any location in the world. Benetton now use POS (Point of Sale) technology to inform about preferred colours and sizes but the principle to develop flexible and responsive manufacturing facilities is the hallmark of QR approaches.

Efficient consumer response (ECR) systems are based on the same ideas. The concept emerged within the FMCG sector and seeks to reduce waste by predicting demand accurately, based on the premise that consumers know what they want to buy, ahead of the purchase occasion. Therefore, the decision is not about what to make, it is about how many to make and when to make them available. Storage of these items is possible, subject to perishability issues, as, unlike fashion items, they do not have a limited life or very brief fad cycles. The emphasis with ECR therefore, is not on manufacturing but on distribution and marketing communications, especially sales promotions to stimulate demand in the short term.

One particular form of ECR is continuous replenishment programmes (CRP). These operate on the basis that when a sale is made to a consumer, the stock is automatically replaced. Through use of POS equipment and scanners retail stock is maintained at pre-determined optimum levels. The principle is that CRP reduces the opportunity for stock outs which can lead to lengthy waiting times, a fall in service output levels and consumer inconvenience. Indeed, Zhao, Xie and Zhang (2002) report work by Lee *et al.* (1997) which found that both producers and retailers can benefit through sharing information with CRP. Retailers also benefit as CRP systems are run and maintained by other intermediaries. There is little to suggest that manufacturers who operate CRP earn any more from the system than they might normally. However, as Vergin and Barr (1999) suggest, CRP might lock retailers into particular manufacturers and in doing so act as an exit barrier.

In B2B markets, just-in-time systems seek to achieve the same type of goals as CRP. Here suppliers dovetail their deliveries to the manufacturer's production schedule, and in doing so eliminate waste and reduce storage costs. As a result, the number of deliveries increases, the number of units delivered decreases and the pressure on logistics increases to maintain the cycle. Trust, commitment and an integration of software systems, or EDI, becomes necessary to enable the system to operate smoothly.

Both ECR and QR offer advantages and disadvantages. They impact on relationships and channel structures. For example, the pressure on members in QR situations can be intense and discourage the development of trust, while the variability in demand might reflect on commitment. In these situations, some manufacturers prefer to use vertical integration as a means of controlling the retail function in markets where QR predominates. By owning the retailing part of the operation it is possible to generate fast feedback about changing demand. In addition, vertical integration to control the design function is critical to manufacturing and associated activities. Benetton never lost control over the design process and for a long time was managed directly by one of the Benetton family. Although the retail operation is largely a franchise arrangement, Benetton own a few outlets in most countries, simply to be close to the market and be able to feed back quickly any changes in consumer preferences.

In comparison, ECR approaches focus on the need for all channel participants to work and trust each other. There should be a high propensity to share information among the members and the channel structure can be more flexible and open, as long as the logistics are operated tightly.

Logistics can influence marketing decisions and reduce channel costs. The challenge for supply chain managers is to make decisions that are primarily founded on end-user demand, rather than cost reduction.

Channel design

Channel design and structure decisions are made either when a new product or organisation starts up, or, more commonly, when an existing channel structure is modified in order to adapt to changing market conditions. Assuming a decision has been made previously to use an indirect channel, the channel design decision process requires consideration of three main factors.

1 The level of purchase convenience required by the different end-user customer segments to be served, the distribution intensity decision.

2 The number and types of intermediaries necessary to deliver products to the sales outlets, the channel configuration decision.

3 The number of different types of channels to be used, the multi-channel decision.

Distribution intensity

Sometimes termed coverage, distribution intensity refers to the number of outlets from which an end-user customer can buy a particular product. This decision, therefore, is concerned with the degree of convenience customers expect and suppliers need to provide to be competitive. One of the major implications of this is that the wider the coverage the greater the number of intermediaries and this impacts on cost, management control of the intermediaries and the consequent perceived level of service outputs. There are three levels of distribution intensity: intense, selective and exclusive.

Intense distribution

Consumers expect some products to be available from a variety of different outlets. These products often carry little perceived risk, are capable of easy and quick substitution and require little thought or time to purchase. For example, products such as chewing gum, newspapers, breakfast cereals and chocolate bars are readily available from a variety of stores. These may be supermarkets, CTNs (Confectioners, Tobacconists and Newsagents), vending machines and convenience stores. By offering the product through a large number of outlets, so the wide availability promotes the opportunity for high-volume sales.

Selective distribution

By placing the offering in a limited number of outlets a more favourable image can be generated and the producer can determine which intermediaries would be best suited to deliver the required service outputs. Customers are more involved with the purchase, and the level of perceived risk is correspondingly higher. As a result, buyers are prepared to seek out appropriate suppliers, and those that best match the overall requirements of the customer will be successful. Televisions, hi-fi equipment and clothing are suitable examples of this form of distribution.

Exclusive distribution

Some customers may perceive a product to be of such high prestige or to be positioned so far away from the competition that just a single outlet in a particular trading area would be sufficient to meet the needs of the channel.

There is little need to make these products available from a number of different stores. Products such as cars are bought infrequently and are expected to be the subject of considerable search and consideration. For example, Mazda cars are normally only available from a single outlet in any one area. If the offering requires complex servicing arrangements or tight control then the exclusive form of distribution may be best, as it fosters closer relationships. A further reason not to make a product widely available would be the threat of price competition, which would be inconsistent with the positioning strategy these products would normally adopt.

Channel configuration

Arising from the decision about the number and types of outlets that end-user customers require to access products is the next question about the number and types of intermediaries necessary to maintain adequate stock and levels of service in the channel. Resolving this concerns both the length and breadth of the channel, essentially the number and types of intermediaries to be involved.

Length is about the number of channel levels necessary to optimise the overall service outputs. In many industries this is determined by custom and practice, where there is an established approach to using particular types of intermediary. In other industries there is scope for flexibility and development. The more challenging decision concerns not the type (and hence length) of the channel but the numbers of each type of intermediary to be used. This horizontal or breadth dimension reflects the desired intensity at each level.

The issues of intensive, selective and exclusive distribution, mentioned earlier with regard to sales outlets, apply equally to each of the other levels in a marketing channel. However, there are certain other matters concerning the intensity of channel members at different levels.

Multiple channels

Today it is quite common for manufacturers to use a number of marketing channels in order to reach different target markets. This is referred to as dual distribution. This can of course be the cause of some tension between channel partners but recognition

SNAPSHOT 8.6

MULTIPLE CHANNELS

The financial services sector has experienced major changes over the last few years. As a result of changing demographics, social values, legislation, new technology and major stock market fluctuations there has been a need to develop new marketing channels. Established routes through high street brokers, point-of-sale materials and direct sales channels are now complemented by the use of tied agents, independent financial advisers (IFAs), direct marketing in the form of telemarketing and direct mail plus new technology channels such as IFA portals, extranets and websites. Much of this is channelled through customer call centres using software to integrate all customer contact.

of the different levels of service output required by different segments leads to the creation of multiple channels. Many FMCG brands use supermarkets, convenience stores, vending machines and distress purchase[1] outlets to distribute their products in order to maximise their distribution and optimise their sales and profits opportunities.

Decisions about channel structure and design involve all three of these elements, namely, what level of intensity is appropriate, how long channels should be and how many channels should be used in order to provide the right level of service outputs expected by end-user customers.

Generally speaking the greater the intensity of distribution desired by manufacturers (of retailers and distributors) the greater the number of intermediaries required to service them. The greater the number of intermediaries the lower influence a manufacturer has over them. This then poses an interesting problem for manufacturers. On the one hand, greater channel intensity leads to higher rewards but on the other hand, it reduces the level of influence that they have over their channel partners and it raises costs.

Retailers and distributors also face a dilemma because they want, or prefer to have, exclusivity. They want to distribute the leading brands but on the basis that they are the only stockists in a particular geographical area. This gives customers a reason to shop, or be drawn into a store. However, as the number of outlets that a brand is available from increases, so the exclusivity and reasons to shop at a particular store decreases. As markets become saturated or shop sales decrease, pressure is applied upstream in terms of lower wholesale prices in order to drive higher margins. Stores (and distributors) then drive end-user customers to products and brands where there is a higher margin.

This signals an important issue for manufacturers when selecting new members or when reconfiguring marketing channels. First and foremost, channel decisions should be based on a channel's perspective and what is in the best interests of channel partners. Adopting this principle helps avoid dysfunctional conflict (see Chapter 9) and sub-optimal channel performance.

Channel structure

So far marketing channels have been considered in terms of different types of intermediaries who are brought together because of a shared need to cooperate and combine resources. However, the assumption that these organisations remain independent is not necessarily correct. The structure of marketing channels reflects other factors, of which the desire to control or influence other organisations is particularly strong.

While the design of a channel should be based on end-user customer requirements, the structural pattern that any channel assumes is partly a result of the relationships between the individual organisations that compose the channel. Channels are dynamic, so the structure should be flexible in order that it can respond to a changing environment.

---

1 A 'distress purchase' is made by people when they have little choice in the decision about where and when to make the purchase. Many pharmacy products are distress purchases because of pain or sickness – and the immediate need to get relief. Further examples are funerals, petrol and, often, corner shops for immediate food supplies such as a loaf of bread or pint of milk.

CISCO RESTRUCTURES EUROPEAN DISTRIBUTION

In March 2002, Cisco implemented a strategy to reduce the number of European dealers from seventeen to seven. The larger distributors became Cisco Distribution Partners (CDPs), and smaller distributors became Cisco Accredited Distributors (CADs) and have to purchase from the CDPs.

The goal was to improve the supply chain to its resellers and increase the speed with which its products reached the market. Cisco are better able to manage stock availability more effectively and make it easier to have the right inventory mix. The logistics experts were given a key role in the process and in doing so increased their level of involvement and helped improve the availability of products.

Source: Adapted from Flinders (2001).

There is, of course, no single optimal channel structure and the design varies according to the manufacturers' perception of the needs of the markets they serve. However, it is useful to look at some of the more common approaches ranging from those where there is little overt influence over the performance of others by a single channel member to those where there is total control and direction of channel activities.

A spectrum of influence in channel structures

Traditionally, organisations group together to reduce uncertainty. Through cooperation each is in a better position to achieve its objectives. By working together members can concentrate upon those activities that they do best. This may be retailing or manufacturing, but, whatever it is, the objectives of each organisation are best served by allowing others to perform alternative, specialist functions for them. This principle underpins the growth in out-sourcing experienced in recent years. The degree of influence that one organisation has over another varies considerably. In Figure 8.2 the spectrum of influence is represented in terms of the different channel structures that have emerged.

Opportunity networks

At one end of the spectrum are **opportunity networks** (Achrol, 1997). These are loose alliances of independent organisations that often come together to provide a one-off solution for a customer. Once the task is completed, the alliance might disband. The network is based on interorganisational relationships that promote close cooperation and win–win situations for all involved. They work together as a response to fast-

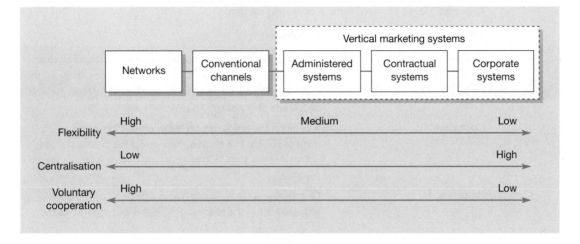

Figure 8.2 A spectrum of marketing channel structures

changing market conditions. No one organisation is dominant or able to assert undue influence on others. Opportunity networks are a recent development and are a response to turbulent and unpredictable market conditions. Network configuration is discussed in greater depth later in this chapter.

Conventional channels

These channels are characterised by the temporary, often loosely aligned, partnerships with a range of organisations. Organisations in this alignment retain their independence and autonomy. Bipolar relationships typify these structures, as decisions are often self-orientated and reflect the needs of just the two members.

As a consequence of this self-interest, the level of influence that any member has over the others in the channel is minimal, except where access to an important raw material or product can be affected. This framework allows offerings to move through the entire system or through parts of it. There is no single controlling organisation and the framework is viewed as a set of independent organisations working in free association with one another. Market coverage is free of any overt influence.

Attempts to secure coverage usually result in a loss of control in the marketing channel. Furthermore, the level of loyalty is low, which is indicative of the instability that exists in these configurations as organisations are able to enter and exit with relative freedom.

Vertical marketing systems

The following three types of channel structure are characterised by the influence that one organisation is able to exert over other organisations in the channel. These structures are known as vertical marketing systems (VMS) and the three forms are administered, contractual and corporate (see Table 8.2).

Table 8.2 Three forms of vertical marketing system

Form of VMS	Explanation
Administered	A loose alignment of organisations who voluntarily choose to work together. One organisation assumes responsibility for the channel activities, the channel leader or captain. High risk and high levels of flexibility.
Contractual	A contract is used to specify roles, expectations and responsibilities. The organisation issuing the contract largely determines the trading strategies and formats. Medium risk and flexibility.
Corporate	One organisation owns and hence influences all the other organisations in the channel. Risk is low and so is flexibility.

VMSs attempt to trade off distribution intensity against the lack of influence or control – more control means less coverage. They have evolved since the mid-1970s and consist of vertically aligned and coordinated sets of marketing partners. They function as a system, centrally driven by an organisation that is able to assert itself through a collaborative partnership in an attempt to satisfy end-user customer needs.

The tighter cooperation and interdependence of members is formally recognised and a planned approach ensures that a greater degree of stability is achieved. The entry and exit of partners to the system is controlled to meet the needs of the channel and not any one member. The coupling between members is tight and the level of connectedness is similarly strong.

Administered systems

Administered systems are similar to conventional channels in that members work together and are tied by the attraction of potential rewards. The main difference between the two is that with administered systems one organisation is able to exert influence over others. These organisations have influence due to their size and power which might, for example, be developed through their access to particular resources, size of market share, breadth and depth of product range, research and development skills or corporate reputation. These organisations are sometimes referred to as the **channel leader** or **channel captain**.

Organisations work together to fulfil strategies developed by a limited number of channel partners. These strategies are administered through informal 'voluntary' collaborative agreements, led by the channel leader. It is important to recognise that members of this system retain their own authority and that each member's commitment to the system is largely motivated by self-interest.

Contractual systems

When voluntary agreements fail to produce the required level of channel performance, channel members develop a more formal arrangement. This is rooted within a contract, which brings legally binding terms and conditions to the roles and expectations of all involved in the channel system. These contractual partnerships consist of a written agreement between a dominant member and the other members of the channel, setting out members' rights and obligations. There are three kinds of contractual arrangement.

Wholesaler-sponsored chains. These consist of independent retailers who, under the organisation of a wholesaler, agree to work together to obtain discounts and other advantages in purchasing, distribution and promotion, in order to compete against large chain organisations, for example Mace.

Retailer-sponsored chains. Similar to the wholesaler chains, independent retailers join together to jointly own the wholesale operation. The sponsored chain approach allows small and medium-sized organisations to compete against the purchasing power of many retail and wholesale multiples. Spar and VG are examples of retailer cooperatives.

Franchise. There are three forms of franchise:

1 Manufacturer-sponsored retailer systems, for example Ford.

2 Manufacturer-sponsored wholesaler systems, for example Coca-Cola.

3 Service-sponsored retailer systems, for example McDonald's.

Franchise arrangements are a fast growing form of retailing. Under franchise arrangements the right to distribute a particular product or service is agreed between two parties. There are two main approaches to franchising. The first is a **product franchise**, where the channel's dominant organisation authorises particular organisations to distribute their offering. In other words, organisations are selected into a channel and each is permitted to use the trade name and promotional materials (which are deemed to be of value to the customer) of the dominant organisation. Various German kitchen appliance and furniture manufacturers use this form of authorisation to allow particular UK retailers (independent kitchen design-and-fit organisations) to distribute their offerings. The second form of franchise can be referred to as a **business franchise**. Under this format not only is the product permitted to be used by the franchisee but the whole trading approach must be utilised. McDonald's restaurants are an example of the latter, with franchisees having to adopt the entire established trading style.

Corporate systems

A corporate vertical marketing system (CVMS) is a discrete grouping of organisations that are owned, and hence controlled, by one dominant member. This structural arrangement provides for the greatest influence in comparison to the previous two forms of VMS. These structures often emerge when there are few alternatives. Uncertainty is reduced to a minimum and the influence of the dominant organisation is maximised, often in an attempt to achieve economies of scale.

Corporate systems are achieved through either backward or forward vertical integration. Organisations can choose to integrate upstream (backward) to control their sources of supply (their inputs), or they can move downstream (forward) and seek to control the distribution of their offerings, or both. However, the inherent lack of flexibility associated with corporate systems has led many organisations to move away from this structure.

Traditionally, breweries owned not only the brewing and production facilities, but also the public houses and restaurants and hotels through which beer was distributed.

SNAPSHOT 8.8

TUI – A VERTICAL MARKETING SYSTEM

TUI Northern Europe is part of TUI AG, the largest tourism and services group in the world. It is a market leader in Europe and includes:

- Specialist Holidays Group;

- TUI Ireland;

- TUI Nordic;

- TUI UK.

TUI UK, the largest holiday company in the United Kingdom, in turn includes Thomson Holidays (a holiday and tour operator) and Lunn Poly (a branded chain of high street travel retailers) plus smaller agencies. Therefore, TUI UK own a substantial share of holiday capacity and the travel agencies, to enable customers to buy holidays. The company claims to have about a third of the UK market. It offers a wide range of holiday types and resorts, but attempts to be consistent with best value-for-money brand messages. The Glasgow call centre deals with around 1 million holidays a year, including direct bookings for Thomson, Lunn Poly and Portland.

Source: Adapted from www.thomsontravelgroup.com/companyback/index.htm (Accessed 4 March 2003). Used with permission.

Networks

Much of this chapter depicts marketing channel structures as a vertical alignment of organisations, one which is linear and essentially bipolar. That is, interorganisational relationships are regarded as one-to-one or dyadic in nature, as if to exclude the impact and influence that other organisations bring to a relationship. One of the difficulties of this approach is that organisations are viewed out of the true context in which they operate. It is better to consider the whole system of affiliations, because that of any two organisations is contingent upon the direct and indirect relationships of all the organisations (Andersson, 1992). A network of relationships therefore provides the context within which exchange behaviour occurs.

Organisations are embedded not just in a set of exclusive buyer–seller relationships, but in a variety of associations with different organisations. These can be intertwined, resulting in various networks of relationships. Each organisation (and individual) is a member of a rich mosaic of networks, embedded in them to different degrees depending upon levels of dependence and of access to the resources of other members (Halinen and Törnroos, 1998). There appears to be growing recognition that networks of interacting organisations are a more satisfactory interpretation of management practice than the relatively rigid distribution channels approach so widely accepted in the 1970s and 1980s.

Networks hold together partly through 'an elaborate pattern of interdependence and reciprocity' (Achrol, 1997, p. 59). The position an organisation occupies in a network is important. It is determined by the functions performed, their importance, the strength of relationships with other organisations and the identity of the organisations with which there are direct and indirect relationships (Mattsson, 1989). The position of an organisation, and the degree to which it is connected to others, partly determines the extent to which it can mobilise resources and achieve designated goals. As Achrol states, the strength and duration of a relationship is partly dependent upon 'the network of relationships that collectively define and administer the norms by which dyadic relationships are conducted'. He goes on to quote Macneil (1978, p. 57) who suggested that the more relational an exchange becomes the more it takes on the properties of 'a minisociety with a vast array of norms beyond those centered on the exchange and its immediate processes'. Network approaches provide a dynamic interpretation of the relationships that organisations have with one another.

The ability of an organisation to manage the networks in which it operates has been termed 'network competence' (Ritter and Gemünden, 2003). They distinguish between the skills and competences necessary to manage single dyadic relationships and those that are necessary to manage a portfolio or network of relationships. Although their research is embryonic (at the time of writing) they conclude that there appears to be a strong link between an organisation's network competence and the degree to which its technology and systems are involved (interwoven) with other interdependent organisations. They go further to claim that there is a significant link between this type of competence and new product development and innovation success.

Value networks

Particular forms of marketing channels and business strategies are emerging based on the principles of voluntary, flexible, cooperative relationships in which members share specific core competences. Businesses are shedding their involvement in activities that are no longer regarded as core. So, activities such as order processing, finance, IT, manufacturing and logistics are being out-sourced to trading partners with those core competences. These activities are processed by many different organisations as if they were one organisation. Thus, **value networks** can be regarded as virtual organisations, comprising constellations of networked companies.

Value networks are characterised by the collaborative, and often relatively temporary, structures that are assembled by organisations, each with specialist skills. The extent to which a network is capable of creating superior value is largely determined by the core capabilities and competences of the members (Kothandaraman and Wilson, 2001). The nature of the organisational relationships in a network shapes its value. The network forms in response to a customer's problem or market opportunity. Once the solution to the problem is identified and implemented the network might, but not necessarily, disband. Some members remain within these networks because they have a common and consistent role to play. However, some members might have only a temporary role, dependent upon the nature of their core capability. It is the flexibility and close relationships between members that separate networks from all other channel structures.

Based largely on Porter's (1985) value chain ideas, all previous channel structures consist of individual organisations who are each regarded as individual value creators.

In the network interpretation, value is vested in the collaborative group of organisations, the network itself. Reference has already been made to this idea in terms of an industry value chain. However, one of the major differences concerns the nature and duration of the structure. In industry value chains the participants are invariably the same and work together over the long term. In value networks (VNs) membership can vary according to the task, and membership requires deep levels of integration, co-ordination and connectedness. A distinguishing characteristic of value networks is the level of electronic integration between partners. Just as individual value chains can be linked up so can value networks, into what IBM refer to as **ecosystems**. Whereas value networks deliver component solutions for end-user customers, ecosystems consist of networks of collaborating, system-to-system connected organisations, all geared to deliver total solutions for end-user customers.

To enable the flow of information within value networks and to provide superior value, IBM argue that four technology enablers, or tools, need to be in place:

Enterprise resource planning tools seek to provide an electronic platform that connects all VN members so that there is system-to-system connection. An enterprise resource planning system is a packaged business software system that allows a company to automate and integrate the majority of its business processes, to share common data and practices across the entire enterprise, and to produce and access information in a real-time environment (*source*: www.sap.info, February 2003). Suppliers include Oracle and SAP.

Supply chain management tools manage the information flows, forecast demand, and facilitate timely, collaborative planning. Suppliers include Ariba, i2 Technologies, Manugistics, Oracle and SAP. Between 1999 and 2002, vendors sold more than $15 billion of SCM software licences, on top of which buyers would still have installation, training and maintenance costs (Kanakamedala *et al.*, 2003). A good source of information and articles, both academic and commercial, can be found at ITtoolbox.com (supplychain.ittoolbox.com/rd.asp).

SNAPSHOT 8.9

SUPPLY CHAIN MANAGEMENT SOFTWARE

Kanakamedala *et al.* (2003) studied the use of SCM software in 63 high-tech companies in the Fortune 1000 from 1995 to 2001, using stock turn as 'a suitable indicator of the health of a supply chain'. They found that by improving the processes and using correctly designated and installed software the best advances in supply chain management were generated.

They determined that supply-chain-management software should assist stock level reductions and improve delivery schedule. In doing this, customers should experience higher levels of satisfaction. However, their research found that these improvements were not always achieved. Some companies, such as Dell Computer and Wal-Mart, have utilised these applications and improved their supply chains. Other organisations have experienced huge problems and have invested vast sums in this area without generating commensurate returns.

Source: Kanakamedala *et al.* (2003).

Customer relationship management tools attempt to help organisations improve their understanding of customers' characteristics, values and behaviour in order to better meet their needs and retain their loyalty. Suppliers include Maginus, Microsoft and Siebel.

CRM systems have been the focus of hot debate in the United Kingdom recently. For example, the keynote panel at the 'Technology for Marketing' event at Olympia, London in February 2003, felt that a period of rapid change from technology-driven to marketing, or preferably customer-driven approaches was long overdue. It was stated that 70 per cent of call-centre staff stress was attributable to the shortcomings of hardware and software. A fuller exploration of CRM systems can be found in Chapter 6.

Exchanges, which have evolved from simple online transactions between two parties, via third-party market creation tools, to consortiums which 'seek to exchange huge virtual markets, attempt to smooth out demand and lead to fewer inventories'. (Lichtenthal and Eliaz, 2003, p. 8).

A further structural approach is based on the notion of business **ecologies**. These consist of much larger communities of organisations (than virtual networks) all supporting a particular standard or system but not necessarily contracted in a formal way to the core or focus organisation. The key feature in ecologies is that they all support a dominant platform or leading technology (Kraemer and Dedrick, 2002). For example, ecologies have developed around the IBM mainframe, Cisco's Internet networking systems, and the Microsoft Windows operating system. Organisations such as Dell, IBM, Microsoft and Cisco have adopted the ecology approach, partly because it enables them to achieve and sustain leadership status in their respective markets (see Table 8.3).

There is room for ideas about traditional marketing channels, value networks and ecologies. Conventional thoughts about marketing channels delivering added value may be appropriate for stable market conditions, such as those experienced in FMCG markets. Contemporary thoughts about flexible, nimble and responsive networks are more appropriate for fast changing, dynamic market conditions, such as those experienced in high technology and fashion clothing markets. Competitive advantage in value networks lies in managing the complexity of relationships that make up the network where organisations compete through the alliances and partnerships that

Table 8.3 Virtual organisations and business ecologies

Structure	Explanation
Value networks	Independent organisations who work for a central or focus company to whom they are formally connected. Very often they are designated subcontractors or out-sourced business partners. The have a generally fixed role to play in providing a part of the focus organisation's activities. Value is vested in the collaboration of all network partners.
Business ecologies	Independent organisations, only some of whom, a minority, have any formal relationship with the focus organisation. The essential aspect is that these organisations all support a central and dominant technological standard.

focal organisations create around themselves (Christopher *et al.*, 2002) and by shedding non-core work and concentrating on core competences.

Electronic channels

In the previous chapter particular attention was given to the contribution that Internet-based technologies have made to the development and enhancement of service outputs. Similarly, any consideration of marketing channel structures would not be complete without examining the opportunities available through these channels.

The Internet offers producers and manufacturers the opportunity to communicate and enter into exchanges with end-user customers, without the use of intermediaries. In comparison to conventional channels, Internet channels offer B2B enterprises the opportunity to reach new market segments, to cut costs and to not only conduct business transactions more quickly and efficiently but also to undertake business in new and innovative ways.

Direct systems integration is costly and has to be customised for each trading partner or application. Only the largest companies have been willing to invest in such connections, and then only for a small percentage of their biggest, highest-volume trading partners. These barriers, however, are coming down fast. As the Internet, packaged software and data and messaging standards mature, integration options are becoming cheaper and less complex (Murphy, 2003).

Structural impact

For some organisations the Internet is the only channel open to them, but these were invariably set up expressly to deal with particular markets on a direct basis. The most obvious impact of a strategy that introduces Internet-based channels into an established organisation is to remove some or all of the established distribution intermediaries. However, this need not always be the case as current channel members may have their role enhanced or it may be left unchanged. Very rarely will an established organisation abandon all of its established marketing channel partners and move all their business activities online. The safer and more obvious route is gradually to adopt a mixed channel structure.

The introduction of an Internet channel enables established organisations to adapt their segmentation policies, to develop incrementally their eCommerce offerings or to use the direct channel to reach particular segments. Established intermediaries are then used to service other segments which cannot be reached effectively through the Internet or they are forced to adopt new roles. The use of extranets enables organisations to pursue multi-channel strategies, especially when there are low levels of competition (Dou and Chou, 2002). End-user customers may interact directly with the producer but extranets, for example, enable intermediaries to be kept informed of the direct business in their domain and be in a better position to service and support the client once the initial exchange is completed.

The decision to retain intermediaries is primarily a function of the value that they bring to particular markets, customers and producers. Should a channel member or horizontal level of intermediaries fail to add sufficient value to the marketing and supply chain processes then they will be bypassed. This process is referred to as **disintermediation** and there is much evidence of this process in both B2C and B2B markets.

Just as existing intermediaries may be removed through the introduction of direct Internet channels, so might new ones emerge as innovative roles and facilities are identified to add fresh forms of value. The process whereby new online channel members evolve is referred to as **reintermediation** and the members themselves are referred to as **cybermediaries**. These organisations seek to supply downstream services by providing search information for end-user buyers and upstream services in terms of market coverage and wider accessibility for producers.

There are many types of cybermediaries including those that provide cross-market evaluation or comparator services, online communities, portals and emarketplaces plus directories and financial services. In the B2B market, one of the more significant types of cybermediary brings buyers and sellers together. These organisations are known as **infomediaries** and they add value by becoming a single point of contact, often in fragmented and diverse markets.

Internet trading formats

The development of Internet-based technologies has enabled new electronic trading formats and services to emerge. Dou and Chou (2002) report that eCommerce business models have been classified into three main categories. These are the cybermediary model, introduced earlier, the manufacturer model and the auction model.

The cybermediary model is similar to the offline linear interpretation. An intermediary provides services that add value, and typically this is based on comparison shopping and information provision. The cybermediary collects a large range of products in a particular category and then provides customers with facilities to browse, collect information and to then make a decision and complete the exchange.

SNAPSHOT 8.10

INFOMEDIARIES

The National Transportation Exchange (NTE) in the United States provides an online market solution to generate greater efficiency and profitability to the industry. By bringing together buyers and sellers in the freight industry the number of lorries running empty is reduced. The system works by matching the needs of the market to deliver freight (loads) with lorries returning empty (spare capacity). In essence this is a spot market for loads with the NTE receiving a commission on the value of each deal completed.

Chemdex is a well-known exchange which caters for research chemists. The exchange supersedes the use of catalogues by bringing together several hundred suppliers offering 500,000 laboratory products.

The manufacturer model represents the direct channel route represented by organisations such as Dell and Cisco Systems. There are no intermediaries although aspects of shipment and delivery are out-sourced to trading partners.

The auction model allows for sellers and buyers to trade. In a **forward auction** buyers bid for stock in the traditional manner. Sellers place a reserve price on stock and when bidding finishes on or beyond that price, an exchange is undertaken. The highest price wins. In B2B markets, these auctions are often used to offload excess or slow-moving stock.

In **reverse auctions**, buyers ask suppliers to bid against a tender, specification and/or guide price. Suppliers then compete with one another for the contract, and very often the lowest price wins. B2B enterprises use reverse auctions to source scarce materials and products, to reconfigure the list of regular suppliers.

The recent rapid development of digital facilities has enabled organisations to reshape their markets and the way in which they conduct business. As a result of this reshaping the relationships they hold have also changed.

In non-digital or conventional marketplaces, business exchanges take place at a location where there is a physical presence. In digital markets there is no physical or tangible dimension, and exchanges occur in a virtual environment or what Rayport and Sviokla (1996) refer to as an **electronic marketspace**. These marketspaces have been used in different ways to create a variety of new trading environments and facilities, known as **marketsites**.

According to Barratt and Rosdahl (2002) the main motive for buyers entering marketsites is to drive down costs and to improve processes. For suppliers, they argue, the main reason is to expand their markets. However, Kaplan and Sawhney (2000) consider marketsites in terms of the buying behaviour exhibited by participants. They consider behaviour in terms of the nature of how businesses buy and what they buy and from this a matrix emerges, consisting of four different types of marketplaces (see Figure 8.3).

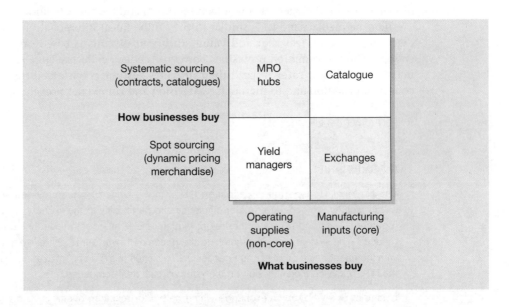

Figure 8.3 How and what businesses buy

The 'how' dimension is based upon whether businesses buy products from pre-vetted suppliers and where there may be an established relationship (systematic sourcing) or whether the purchase is made in response to an immediate need, often commodities such as energy and oil (spot sourcing). The 'what' dimension is based simply on whether the products are for production (raw materials) or non-production use (office stationery, repairs and maintenance).

From this Kaplan and Sawhney identify that **MRO hubs** are established when it is necessary to improve the efficiency of regularly purchased non-core items. **Yield managers** seek to stabilise the volatility experienced when there is price fluctuation in a market. **Exchanges** are created to deal with the purchase of commodity items used in the production process. **Catalogue marketsites** deal with products that have a high level of specialisation and are created to improve supply chain management through streamlined sourcing by process automation.

Marketsites (marketplaces or hubs) can also be considered in terms of their industry alignment, namely whether they serve buyers and sellers within an industry (vertical alignment) or whether their primary task is to serve those across industries (horizontal alignment). Vertical marketsites, created by buyers or a cybermediary, are designed to serve an industry (for example PaperExchange is the hub for the paper industry), often concentrating on procurement with a view to making the whole industry more efficient. They enable buyers to locate products and materials quickly and help sellers maintain appropriate levels of stock, find new buyers and drive more positive cash flows. The flow of information is more equitable as the procurement process becomes more transparent.

Horizontal (or functional) marketsites offer buyers products that are available across industry sectors. For instance, logistics monitoring and measurement services (for example Celarix), project management (for example Bidcom), energy management (for example YOUtilities), credit checking and electronic payment facilities are just some examples of these marketplaces (Dou and Chou, 2002). One of the key characteristics of these markets is that the products and services be capable of process standardisation and automation to complement business activities.

One of the first industries to become involved with vertical marketsites was the energy industry. Characterised by fragmentation and dispersed buyers and sellers, organisations in the oil, natural gas and power supplies industries sought to use vertical marketsites to cut costs and improve the overall speed with which transactions were completed. Chevron, Ariba and later Texaco formed Petrocosm, a vertical marketsite designed to provide an electronic marketplace for equipment and services used in the oil and gas supply chains. However, like many early marketsites this one collapsed in 2003 due to a lack of liquidity arising from insufficient activity.

This brief insight into digital marketsites and electronic channels clearly indicates that technology is helping to change the structure of marketing channels by encouraging the formation of new trading formats. The principle of intermediaries adding value by helping suppliers and buyers to reach more customers, to manage stock more efficiently and to reduce process costs is as pertinent in digital online channels as it is offline. However, the added dimension of electronic channels is that the number of intermediaries is often lower and the manner, speed and costs of trading are changed dramatically. Nevertheless, Kanakamedala *et al.* (2003) remind us that 'Software on its own can't fix basic shortcomings in supply chain management ... companies that figure out how to make the software and improved processes work together to create a more efficient supply chain, will see a better return on their investment.'

Summary

The essence of this chapter has been to consider the structural configurations used by organisations to manage their marketing channels. Care has been taken to segregate supply chain management from marketing channels. SCM is commonly referred to as logistics management and is concerned with the physical movement of goods through the channel in order to present the end-user customer with products and services at times and places that afford end users maximum utility and convenience. A variety of software systems have been developed to improve efficiency as well as effectiveness. Indeed, the emphasis of discrete or market exchanges is often placed on the marketing mix where price is an important differentiator. However, where collaborative relationships are in position, price is less important and the maintenance of the relationship predominates. Therefore, the efficiency aspect may be superseded by the need to be more effective.

Conventional channels, vertical marketing systems and, more recently, value networks and business ecologies all reflect varying degrees of cooperation, interdependence, independence and autonomy. The development of electronic channels has presented new opportunities for organisations to interact in new and different ways with channel partners. New trading formats and a partial disintegration and reconfiguration of the established marketing channels and the arrival of new infomediaries have been responsible for the use of multichannel approaches to markets.

Discussion questions

1 Explain why some organisations decide to retain a large degree of autonomy while others willingly become interdependent with some other organisations.

2 Briefly discuss the purpose and role of supply chains and identify how they differ from marketing channels.

3 Describe the main functions associated with logistics management and, using the Internet, identify an example of each listing and their stated core activities.

4 Vertical marketing systems are no longer suitable marketing channels for organisations in the twenty-first century. Critically appraise this statement.

5 Consider the contribution of network theory to our understanding of marketing channels.

6 Explain some of the advantages offered by electronic marketing channels, and consider the nature and variety of new trading formats that have emerged.

References

Achrol, R.S. (1997). 'Changes in the theory of interorganisational relations in marketing: toward a network paradigm', *Journal of the Academy of Marketing Science*, 25, 1, pp. 56–71.

Andersson, P. (1992). 'Analysing distribution channel dynamics: loose and tight coupling in distribution networks', *European Journal of Marketing*, 26, 2, pp. 47–68.

Barratt, M. and Rosdahl, K. (2002). 'Exploring business-to-business marketsites', *European Journal of Purchasing and Supply Management*, 8, 2 (June), pp. 111–22.

Borders, A.L., Johnston, W.J. and Rigdon, E.E. (2001). 'Beyond the dyad: electronic commerce and network perspectives in industrial marketing management', *Industrial Marketing Management*, 30, 2 (February) pp. 199–205.

Brewer, P.C. and Speh, T.W. (2000). 'Using the balanced scorecard to measure supply chain performance', *Journal of Business Logistics*, 21, 1 (Spring), pp. 75–95.

Christopher, M., Magrill, L. and Wills, G. (1998). 'Educational development for marketing logistics', *International Journal of Physical Distribution and Logistics Management*, 28, 4, pp. 234–41.

Christopher, M., Payne, A. and Ballantyne, D. (2002). *Relationship Marketing: Creating Stakeholder Value*, Oxford: Butterworth-Heinemann.

Dou, W. and Chou, D.C. (2002). 'A structural analysis of business digital markets', *Industrial Marketing Management*, 31, 2 (February), pp. 165–76.

Durman, P. (2003). 'Mobile phone minnow snaps up trade from the giants', *The Sunday Times Online*, 10 August, www.timesonline.co.uk/article/ø,,2095-772094,øø.html (Accessed 21 May 2004.)

Flinders, K. (2001). 'Cisco gets its channels sorted out', *Computer Reseller News*, 29 October 2001; www.vnunet.com/News/1126509 (Accessed 16 March 2003.)

Halinen, A. and Törnroos J.Å. (1998). 'The role of embeddedness in the evolution of business networks', *Scandinavian Journal of Management*, 14, 3, pp. 187–205.

Hammel, T., Phelps, T. and Kuettner, D. (2002). 'The re-engineering of Hewlett Packard's CD-RW supply chain', *Supply Chain Management: An International Journal*, 7, 3, pp. 113–18.

Kaplan, S. and Sawhney, M. (2000). 'E-hubs: the new B2B marketplaces', *Harvard Business Review*, 78, 3, pp. 97–103.

Kanakamedala, K., Ramsdell, G. and Srivatsan, V. (2003). 'Getting supply chain software right', *McKinsey Quarterly*, www.mckinseyquarterly.com/ar_g.asp?ar=1272&pagenum=1&L2=13&L3=13&srid=27&gp=0 (Accessed February 2003.)

Kothandaraman, P. and Wilson, D. (2001). 'The future of competition: value creating networks', *Industrial Marketing Management*, 30, 4 (May), pp. 379–89.

Kraemer, K.L. and Dedrick, J. (2002). 'Strategic use of the Internet and e-commerce: Cisco Systems', *Journal of Strategic Information Systems*, 11, pp. 5–29.

Lee, H., Padmanabhan, V. and Whang, S. (1997) 'Information distortion in a supply chain: the bullwhip effect', *Management Science*, 43, pp. 546–58.

Lichtenthal, J.D. and Eliaz, S. (2003). 'Internet integration in business marketing tactics', *Industrial Marketing Management*, 32, 1, pp. 3–13.

Macneil, I.R. (1978). 'Contracts: adjustment of long-term economic relations under classical, neoclassical and relational contract law', *Northwestern University Law Review*, 72 (January–February), pp. 854–905.

Maginus (2003). *The Wine Society*, case study issued at the Marketing Technologies Exhibition, Olympia, 11 February 2003.

Mattsson, L.-G. (1989). 'Development of firms in networks: positions and investments'. *Advances in International Marketing*, 3, pp. 121–39.

Murphy, J. (2003). 'Supply-chain integration poised to accelerate as barriers fall', www.glscs.com/archives/02.03.integration.htm?adcode=25 (Accessed 16 February 2003.)

New, S.J. and Payne, P. (1995). 'Research frameworks in logistics: three models, seven dinners and a survey', *International Journal of Physical Distribution and Logistics Management*, 25, 10, pp. 60–77.

Porter, M.E. (1985). 'The generic value chain' in M.E. Porter, *Competitive Advantage: Creating and Sustaining Superior Performance*, New York, NY: The Free Press.

Rayport, J. and Sviokla, J. (1996). 'Exploiting the virtual chain', *The McKinsey Quarterly*, 1, pp. 121–36.

Ritter, T. and Gemünden, H.G. (2003). 'Network competence: its impact on innovation success and its antecedents', *Journal of Business Research*, 56, 9 (September) pp. 745–55.

Vergin, R.C. and Barr, K. (1999). 'Building competitiveness in grocery supply through continuous replenishment planning: insights from the field', *Industrial Marketing Management*, 28, 2, pp. 145–53.

Zhao, X., Xie, J. and Zhang, W.J. (2002). 'The impact of sharing and ordering co-ordination on supply chain performance', *Supply Chain Management: An International Journal*, 17, 1, pp. 24–40.

Chapter 9
B2B management issues

Chapter overview

To conclude this part of the book this chapter focuses on some of the managerial issues, processes and systems associated with the management of interorganisational relationships. First, the nature, dispersion and use of power in relationships is examined, then time is spent looking at channel conflict and ways in which it can be minimised, even though some conflict can be constructive.

The chapter concludes with a consideration of two important concepts, trust and commitment. These form the foundation of successful B2B relationships and are now considered by many to supersede power as the means of managing interorganisational relationships.

Chapter aims

The aims of this chapter are to consider some of the behavioural concepts associated with the management of interorganisational relationships, especially those in marketing channels.

Objectives

The objectives of this chapter are to:

1 Explore the concept of power and to appreciate its significance in B2B relationships.

2 Examine the various sources of channel power and consider the different influence strategies that organisations can use.

3 Introduce basic principles concerning channel conflict and examine ways in which tensions between organisations can be managed.

4 Appreciate the dimensions and significance of trust and commitment in relationships as a means for building cooperation and channel collaboration.

5 Consider how communication and information systems can assist the management of power, conflict, trust and commitment with a view to enhancing the quality of B2B relationships.

Introduction

The management of interorganisational relationships is complicated by a number of different issues. These involve the nature and distribution of power and the degree of conflict that exists between organisations and especially those in marketing channels. These two topics are interrelated because the use or misuse of power can be a source of conflict (Welch and Wilkinson, 2002). In order to manage these interrelated concepts and help ensure all participating organisations achieve their performance objectives, it is important to develop suitable forms of cooperation.

Cooperation can be achieved in two main ways. One way is to exercise authority through the use of the power that one organisation may have over others. Another way is to establish trust and a spirit of collaboration between organisations. Through trust it is possible to develop a sense of commitment so that all organisations attempt to support one another.

This chapter first explores ideas concerned with power, then examines the nature and causes of interorganisational conflict and concludes with an examination of trust and commitment as a foundation for the development of superior B2B marketing relationships.

The concept of power

As already established, organisations seek to achieve their objectives by working with other organisations in an interdependent manner. To work effectively and efficiently the interdependence, specialisation and expertise of individual organisations should be encouraged (Rosenbloom, 1978). However, interdependence is rarely distributed in a uniform and equitable way. Therefore, the inequality of organisational interdependence becomes a major source of power. This asymmetric distribution means that no single organisation can have absolute power (Stern and Gorman, 1969) but does provide some organisations the opportunity to exploit others.

Power concerns the ability to get another (individual or organisation) to do what they/it would not normally have done. In a channel context, power is obtained through the possession and control of resources that are valued by another member. Channel and interorganisational relationships can be regarded as a reflection of the balance of power that exists between organisations. Emerson (1962) referred to power as a function of dependency. The more dependent X is on Y, the greater power Y has over X. As all members of a channel are interdependent then all members have a degree of power. It is therefore imperative that the power wielded by constituent members is utilised to further the development of the collective membership of a marketing channel (or network) and the achievement of its objectives and goals. If used otherwise, power may lead to negative consequences for the member and in turn for the channel.

Dependency is concerned with two main elements, the value that one organisation derives from interacting with another and the number of alternative sources of equivalent value that an organisation has. Such dependency is encapsulated in social exchange theory (see Chapter 6). According to Stern and El-Ansary (1992), there are two main constructs associated with this theory: comparison level (CL) and comparison level of alternatives (CLalt). The former concerns the expected performance levels of channel members based on experience. The latter is based on the expected performance of the best alternative organisation to a current channel member. As this is true for all channel members, there is a certain level of dependence upon each other. This means that each channel member can affect, by its own actions, the performance of others. It is this ability to influence the performance of others that is seen by advocates of social exchange theory as a source of power.

Sources of power

In a classic study French and Raven (1959), determined five bases for power: rewards, coercion, expertise, legitimate and reference bases.

Rewards are one of the more common sources of power. They are based on the belief that one organisation intends, and is able, to reward another with a resource (source of value) that the other desires if agreed actions are accomplished. For example, a manufacturer might grant a wholesaler particular discounts dependent upon the volume of products bought during an agreed period. A value added reseller might be included on a high-profile manufacturer's list of preferred distributors, should it achieve the necessary standards of performance.

Coercion is the other side of the 'reward-based' coin, where negative measures, or punishments may be administered. These sanctions may take the form of reduced margins, changes to delivery cycles, withdrawal of product range privileges or perhaps alterations to geographic or territorial areas the organisation is entitled to serve. One of the difficulties associated with the use of coercive power is that it is perceived as an attack, which often provokes self-defence and a counterattack. For example, should a retailer feel threatened by a manufacturer then a range of responses might include, delisting, reduced stocking, moving orders to a competitor or even competing directly by developing their own manufacturing facilities or developing competitive eCommerce facilities to enter new markets.

Expert power is based on the perception that one organisation considers another to possess particular knowledge and expertise that they do not possess but require if they are to fulfil their obligations. This makes them dependent upon the flow of (expert) information from the source organisation. Interestingly, the expert power exercised by leading pharmaceutical manufacturers is derived from the dependency of the pharmacies and general practitioners (GPs) on them and not so much on the dependency of the wholesalers. Franchise systems are based on the expertise owned by the franchisor. Problems can arise through the transfer of expertise, over time, which, if not controlled through government licensing arrangements, may enable other recipient organisations to operate independently of the expert organisation.

Legitimate power exists when one party recognises the authority of another to manage a relationship. This is similar to a manager recognising the authority of an executive director. Legitimacy is provided either through the judicial system (for example trademarks and contracts) or through the norms and social values established within particular markets and industries. At the heart of this source of

RESOURCE POWER AT YAOHAN STORES

Yaohan is a Japanese department store located at home and in China and Hong Kong. Part of its development has been built on a substantial shop-in-shop (or concessionaire) operation. Other retailers entered partnership arrangements to operate small shops within the department store. They were attracted initially by the very favourable sub-rental leases offered by Yaohan, a form of resource power.

However, many partners are reported to be pulling out of these partnerships because Yaohan have lost their bargaining power with their landlords, and hence the source of their power, resulting in the rental costs becoming too onerous.

Source: Adapted from Wong (1998).

power is the notion of consent, that one organisation acknowledges the right of another to assert themselves in a particular way. However, the use of legitimate power is relatively uncommon in conventional channels and it is only in contractual and corporate vertical marketing systems (for example franchisors) where legitimate power can be exercised.

Referent power works on the basis of association and identification – 'being in the same boat' as Rosenbloom refers to it. If members of a network are able to share and empathise with the problems of their 'channel partners' then a channel-wide solution to a common problem may well result in increased understanding, collaboration and trust. Referent power is about public acknowledgement in order to gain increased value. Therefore, a retailer may find it beneficial, that is of increased value, to be able to carry particular prestigious brands as the association will enhance the perception end-user customers will have of them. Similarly, some manufacturers may benefit from distribution through association with particular retailers. Chu and Chu (1994) refer to this as 'renting a reputation'.

These power bases need to be considered as a collective group, not as separate sources. This means that there is a level of reinforcement between different types of power. Thus, reward power may be used to support expert power or legitimate power may be used in combination with referent power. Equally, it is likely that there may be conflict between certain types of power, especially when coercion is used. This may negate any expertise or referent power that might have been established.

Power is not distributed symmetrically and no one organisation is totally dependent upon another. Therefore, power needs to be understood as an imbalance between organisations who are, to varying extents, dependent upon each other.

Using power for influence

By recognising and understanding the bases of power, the levels of cooperation and the form of the relationships between members, the nature of communication, its pattern, its frequency and its style can be adjusted to complement the prevailing conditions. Furthermore, such an understanding can be useful to help shape the power relationships of the future and to enhance corporate/marketing strategies. Once the current and anticipated power bases are determined, influence strategies can assist the shaping process. Of the power propositions provided by French and Raven, reward and coercion seem more apt for use within channels where market exchange-based transactions predominate. Legitimate and expert power might be better applied in channels with a high level of relational exchanges.

Organisations seek to influence interorganisational relationships through a variety of communication strategies. Coughlan *et al.* (2001) claim the most common ones are those as set out in Table 9.1.

Southam (2002) reports a survey of 9,000 consumers who claim to have made online purchases. In the course of an online purchase 80% agreed they had visited a manufacturer's site during the buying cycle. They also agreed that they do not really distinguish between retailers and manufacturers, they just find the information they need and this may mean that they avoid visiting or using retailers' sites. Typically this segment of buyers seek:

- Product information – only manufacturers can provide the necessary product information/specification sought by the segment.

- Transaction information/capabilities – consumers prefer to use manufacturer's sites for information about pricing and retail availability. They do not believe retailers hold sufficient knowledge to answer these questions.

- Product help/support – citing an example about how 60 per cent of shoppers bought a Clinique product in-store only after getting a sample from clinique.com, it is claimed that a large proportion of shoppers visit manufacturer sites for help with product use, preparation and installation tips, cross-sells and other support.

Table 9.1 Influence strategies

Strategy	Message	Power source
Promise strategy	If you do what we wish we will reward you.	Reward
Threat strategy	If you do not do what we wish we will punish you.	Coercion
Legalistic strategy	You agreed, so you should do what we wish.	Legitimacy
Request strategy	Please do what we wish.	Referent, reward, coercion
Information exchange strategy	We will not mention what we wish.	Expertise, reward
Recommendation strategy	If you do what we wish you will be rewarded (e.g. more profitable).	Expertise, reward

Source: Adapted from Coughlan *et al.* (2001). Coughlan, Anderson, Stem, El-Ansary, *Marketing Channel*, 6th edn. © 2001. Adapted by permission of Pearson Education, Inc., Upper Saddle River, NJ.

What this suggests is that, for some segments, where consumers use online communications as an integral part of the buying process, there has been a swing in the balance of power, away from retailers to manufacturers, from down- to upstream sites. Therefore, manufacturers need to be aware of this source of influence over their end-user groups and develop information channels accordingly.

The use of power within marketing channels can be effective in helping to achieve a number of outcomes. Among these are activities associated with the provision of information, operations and channel developmental linkages and channel development through training and the selection of new members. Some of these are set out in Table 9.2.

Table 9.2 Power-enabled channel outcomes

■ Information services
    customer/channel information
    trade promotions/joint sales activities

■ Channel operations
    standards
    operational linkages

■ Channel development
    new channel partners
    training
    reward and compensation systems

Channel conflict

It is inevitable that there will be some level of conflict between channel members, if only because channels are open social systems (Katz and Kahn, 1978). The degree of conflict will also vary from channel to channel and from organisation to organisation but, despite this, conflict has always been considered to be widely prevalent in dyadic relationships (Hunt and Nevin, 1974). In B2B markets, interorganisational conflict can be observed between vertically aligned channel members and also between organisations that operate across (channels) horizontally. Conflict occurs in established offline channels, in new online channels and in multichannel situations. In many cases, the development of multichannel distribution systems has given rise to increased levels of conflict, not only between organisations but also between channels within a single organisation (Webb and Hogan, 2002).

As mentioned earlier, interorganisational cooperation is important because of the varying degrees to which members are interdependent. Enabling the continuity of the interdependent conditions is crucial if channel and organisational goals are to be achieved. It is assumed that conflict impairs channel performance but some research, cited by Duarte and Davies (2003) suggests that the reverse is true and that conflict can improve channel performance (Rosson and Ford, 1980; Assael, 1969). This supports the view that conflict can be functional as well as dysfunctional in its impact on channel members.

SNAPSHOT 9.2

CHANGING CHANNELS

Vidal Sassoon used to sell their hair-care products only through professional hair salons, as not only did this extract a higher margin but it was also consistent with its desired positioning, namely upmarket, elite and desirable.

This positioning was damaged when Vidal Sassoon products became available through Target, a US-based retail store whose trading format is based on high-quality merchandise at low prices in what they describe as 'surroundings that make shopping fun'.

The Sassoon brand was diluted and salons soon lost interest and ceased stocking the brand. Selling prices tumbled from $10 for a bottle of shampoo to under $4.

Source: Adapted from www.reshare.com/managingcc.htm. (Accessed 5 February 2003.) Used with permission.

Duarte and Davies also argue that performance effectiveness, such as meeting sales targets, is not affected by conflict. They contend that conflict is triggered by a failure (of a dependent channel member) to reach performance threshold levels. In other words, managers should be concerned more with efficiency rather than performance effectiveness when managing conflict. This research exercise was only concerned with UK car dealership channels and may therefore only be relevant to business-to-business relationships where there is a high level of dependency.

So, if conflict is a result of a breakdown in the levels of cooperation between channel partners (Shipley and Egan, 1992) and may well affect channel performance, management has a prime responsibility to manage conflict. Invariably, managers attend to conflict when it breaks out but management should also seek to prevent conflict occurring and hence be proactive in reducing tension and creating cooperation and dialogue. Therefore, the task of conflict management is to manage relationships such that the frequency, intensity and duration of interorganisational conflict is minimised.

The nature of conflict

Technically, the word conflict has its roots in the word collision and the idea of two moving parts colliding and causing conflict is well founded. A more relevant interpretation is that conflict concerns an incompatibility of ideas, purpose, understanding and aims. By finding new, shared solutions to an incompatibility of ideas or purpose, improved levels of understanding may arise which in turn can lead to improved cooperation and enhanced performance. There are a number of definitions of channel-based conflict but perhaps one of the more typical and straightforward comes from Gaski who states that it is 'the perception on the part of a channel member that its goal attainment is being impeded by another, with stress or tension the result' (Gaski, 1984, p. 11).

Negative, or dysfunctional, conflict is normally associated with hostility, disagreement, friction and contention. As mentioned earlier, dysfunctional conflict is often assumed to have a negative impact on channel performance, although there is little empirical evidence to support this. Indeed, this negative view is countered by those who regard conflict as capable of having positive outcomes (Anderson and Narus, 1990; Morgan and Hunt, 1994). They suggest that positive or functional conflict can be healthy as it may encourage change and development, often by generating a new, more efficient allocation of resources. Rosenbloom (1978) argues that conflict is more likely to be constructive, or functional, when there are moderate levels of conflict present and dysfunctional when there are either very high or very low levels of conflict.

Rose and Shoham (2002) identify a further means of categorising conflict, namely task and emotional conflict. Using the work of Amason (1996), Jehn (1994) and Menon *et al.*, (1996) they identify task conflict to be incompatibilities and disagreements between organisations about respective responsibilities. It is based on judgements about the most appropriate way to achieve shared goals. On the other hand, emotional conflict is concerned with interpersonal incompatibilities and friction between members of each participating group.

Competition or conflict

Conflict should not be confused with competition and competitive behaviour. Conflict is behaviour that is opponent-centred, it is personal and direct. In a channel or B2B context this means that upstream or downstream members attempt to block, or are perceived to be blocking or impeding another member from achieving their goals.

On the other hand, competition is behaviour that is object-centred, it is impersonal and indirect. In a channel or B2B context, this means that members of different channels attempt to attain goals controlled by others such as customers or those who control or regulate performance. Channel competition is about members striving, with others, to overcome their environment, whereas channel conflict is about members struggling with one another (Coughlan *et al.*, 2001).

Dimensions of conflict

Conflict is far from being a one-dimensional concept. Organisations do not experience either uniform levels of conflict or no conflict at all. In reality, conflict is a complex, dynamic (Rosenberg and Stern, 1970) and multi-dimensional concept. Conflict is complex because it is thought to occur at a number of levels, ranging from the latent, through perceived, affective, manifest and aftermath states (Pondy, 1967).

It should be understood that movement through these stages is not necessarily sequential and does not have to incorporate all stages all of the time. In addition to these different levels of conflict there are major variations in the intensity and frequency of conflict and there are varying degrees of importance attached to different conflict issues, hence the multi-dimensional aspect. These levels or states have been accepted and used by many authors, partly because they have a general validity (Duarte and Davies, 2003) based upon our understanding of the attitude construct. However, they have never been proved empirically and to that extent remain a useful but hypothetical construct.

The introduction of eCommerce has made many manufacturers concerned about channel conflict as development and implementation can bring them into direct competition with existing channels. Difficulties lie not just externally but also internally. Internal conflicts arising from the development of multi-channels can be observed, involving competition either for finite internal resources, or for the same customers (Webb, 2002). Inevitably intermediaries become confused and frustrated in their own attempts to secure their own goals, and conflict emerges.

As with conflict which originates offline, the intensity, frequency and duration will depend on many factors, including the nature of each organisation and the industry in which it operates. Manufacturers who introduce online facilities yet do not closely control their offline distribution channels risk damaging channel relationships and revenue streams. However, organisations that do control their own channels and introduce online facilities are at risk of cannibalising their revenues by taking customers out of existing channels and decreasing the profitability of those older channels.

Southam (2002) explains how eCommerce conflict can arise. Established distribution channels can be challenged because new media channels provide the same service but much quicker and at lower cost. Indeed the information provided is also more comprehensive and a potential rival for the development of customer relationships (see Figure 9.1).

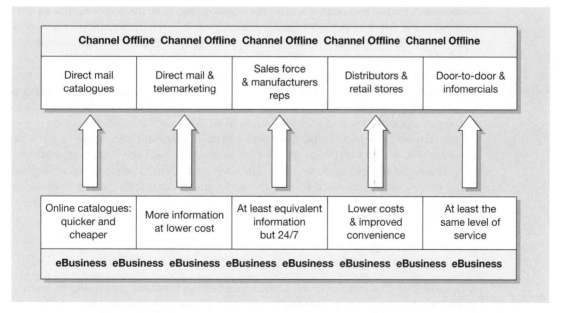

Figure 9.1 eBusiness and channel conflict

Source: Adapted from Southam (2002). Used with permission.

Reasons for conflict

The reasons why conflict emerges clearly need to be appreciated, as identification of the appropriate cause can lead to marketing management strategies that prevent, remedy or at least seek to repair any damage. Tension can arise between organisations for any number of reasons but some of the more common reasons are: deviance from agreed roles and responsibilities, disagreements about resources or the decisions other members make, differences in the way organisations perceive the actions of others and poor interorganisational communications.

All of these reasons can be distilled into three main factors (Stern and Heskett, 1969). These concern differences relating to:

- competing or incompatible goals;
- domains;
- perceptions of reality.

Underpinning all of them is inadequate communication.

Competing goals

This is a common form of conflict and typically occurs when one upstream member changes strategy so that its goals become difficult for other downstream members to support. For example, a manufacturer may decide that it wants to reach new market sectors but current dealers might resist this strategy as it is not in their interest to supply other (new) channels with the same products. Indeed, if actioned it might give rise to increased channel competition and then impact on dealer revenues and profits.

Another example of competing goals can be seen when retailers try to increase performance by lowering their stock levels. Conflict is likely as the manufacturer's goal is to increase the level of stock in the channel, while intermediaries prefer to be able to pull down stock on demand and, hence, avoid working capital costs.

Alternatively, a departmental manager in a retail organisation may not be too concerned which product offerings in a particular category help the department achieve its volume and margin contributions. However, the manufacturer of an individual brand will be most concerned if its brand is not included in the retailer's portfolio of category brands. The two have different goals, yet the same product focus.

Domain differences

A channel domain refers to an area, field or sphere of function. According to Stern *et al.* (1996) it has four main elements: population, territory, member roles and issues concerning technology and marketing. So, disputes can arise because one channel member perceives another member operating outside of the previously designated (agreed) area, perhaps geographically, or in terms of its role. For example, a wholesaler and a manufacturer may disagree about margins, training, marketing policies or, more

SNAPSHOT 9.3

MILLER ELECTRIC AND DOMAIN-BASED CONFLICT

Miller Electric, a manufacturer of welding equipment, and Linweld, a key distributor of industrial and medical gases and welding supplies experienced domain-based conflict concerning a change in channel strategy.

Miller Electric's website receives 60,000 visitors every month and over half result in sales. Miller Electric wanted to move to a direct channel strategy with distributors responsible for delivering the goods. However, ownership of the sales transaction meant that Miller Electric would be able to set prices and eventually cut the channel out completely. The intermediaries rejected the strategy.

Miller Electric compromised and sales leads generated by Miller Electric's website were given to distributors. Once customers designate items they want to buy on Miller Electric's site, they must choose from a list of nearby distributors. The customers and their shopping lists are then whisked off to the selected distributor's website, where they receive pricing and availability information prior to completing the order.

However, another problem arose concerning which distributor gets the lead. Miller Electric's process for listing distributors works on the basis that when a customer inputs a zip code, the three closest distributors pop up. Moreover, only the distributor's name, address, and contact information are provided. Such a simple process does not reflect Linweld's power, importance and size of investment compared to many smaller and more provincial distributors. In reaching a solution, Miller had to recognise Linweld's powerful position based on the volume and value of business placed through Miller Electric.

Source: Adapted from Kaneshige (2001).

commonly, territorial issues. McGrath and Hardy (1986) see conflict emanating from manufacturers' policies, such as sales order policies. The tighter and more constricting they are, the greater the likelihood that conflict will erupt than if the policies are flexible and can be adjusted to meet the needs of both parties.

So, wholesalers who start to sell direct to end-user consumers, or retailers who begin to sell to other retailers, are blatantly adopting a new role and this may infringe upon another member's role and prevent or impede them from achieving their objectives.

A more common example exists when a manufacturer decides to sell through a dealer's competitors, to the extent of even breaking an exclusivity arrangement. The reverse of this intra-channel type of conflict can also cause conflict, when a manufacturer perceives an intermediary selling another (competing) manufacturer's products at the expense of its own range of products.

Another cause of domain-based conflict concerns the emergence of multiple channels. An intermediary might feel threatened by increased competition and reduced financial performance opportunities.

Disagreements about pricing, sales areas or sales order processing, for example, are sensitive issues that can also lead to channel conflict. Once agreement has been made about policy terms or operational formats, any changes should be negotiated and managed in a cooperative and considered way. Indeed, some channels often stipulate the way in which changes to key domain-based issues should be managed.

Perceptions of reality

Through the process of selective perception any number of members may react to the same stimulus in completely different and conflicting ways. The objectives of each of the channel members are different, however well bonded they are to the objectives of the distribution system. It is also likely that each member perceives different ways of achieving the overall goals, all of which are recipes for conflict. As each member organisation perceives the world differently, their perception of others and their actions may lead to tensions and disagreements. So, an action taken by member X with one intention might be perceived differently by member Y. Any action that Y takes as a result of this perception may result in conflict. Perceptions about a product attribute, its applications and appropriate segments can all give rise to perceptually based conflict.

Apart from poor or incomplete communication, the main reason for this tendency to have differing perspectives on information or actions may arise because, in the absence of a strong cooperative relationship, different channel members are focused on different business elements (Coughlan *et al.*, 2001). A manufacturer might be focused on products and processes, whereas a dealer may be concentrating on customers and how to meet their needs. Cultural differences in perception and focus may arise amongst channel members. What may be an appropriate behaviour in one culture may simply be different from that in another, or may not be understood. This can obviously be a problem for internationally based organisations.

Managing interorganisational conflict

Conflict cannot be eradicated but it can be managed. Through the provision of adequate pro-active strategies, the frequency, intensity and duration of conflict can be reduced even if it cannot be totally prevented. Although the management of interorganisational conflict is a continuous activity, it can be considered in two contexts. The first context concerns the management of conflict at the early stages of development, from latent through to felt stages. Here the management goal is to diffuse levels of incompatibility, in terms of its intensity and frequency, with a view to preventing any escalation. The task is to manage or contain any disagreement. The second context concerns the management of conflict when it breaks out or reaches the manifest stage. The task now is to resolve or bring to an end the conflict or cause of disagreement, so that relationships between all parties can be restored to a point of equilibrium that enables exchanges to continue and relationships to develop constructively. These two aspects of containment and resolution are considered and depicted at Figure 9.2.

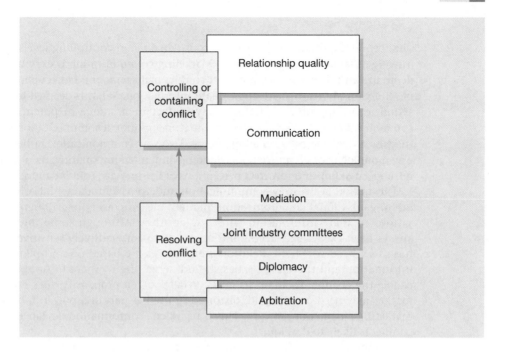

Figure 9.2 Approaches to managing conflict

Context one – controlling or containing conflict

There are a number of methods that can be used, but at the root of them all are two overriding factors, the quality of the relationship between organisations and the quality of the (marketing) communications used to bind participating organisations together.

Relationship quality

It is clear that one of the founding principles for successful performance in the business-to-business sector is the development of flourishing interorganisational relationships. These relationships concern not only buyers and sellers in and across marketing channels but also all other organisations that participate or contribute to active networks and supply chains.

As outlined in Chapter 6, the key to the formation and maintenance of interorganisational relationships is the development of trust and commitment (Morgan and Hunt, 1994). These important concepts are explored in more depth later in this chapter. One of the ways trust between organisations can be developed is an awareness by all parties of the need to consider how others in the network of relationships will react to a particular strategy, policy change or initiative – by gauging the reaction and needs of others in advance so that areas of incompatibility can be minimised and opportunities for conflict to emerge, reduced.

The importance and significance of the roles played by boundary spanning staff in the development of interorganisational relationships cannot be underestimated. Larson (1992) reports that conflict and uncertainty is reduced through the use of suitable personal relationship management staff. As a result, interorganisational trust improves.

Communication

The second important element to be considered when controlling levels of conflict is interorganisational communications. Marketing communication is examined in greater depth in Part D but, for now, note that conflict management is based upon a willingness of all organisations to share appropriate information. What is deemed by one organisation as an appropriate strategy may in fact be a source of potential conflict if communication is ineffective. Effective interorganisational communication requires that there be a dialogue between all members. Two-way communication rather than a one-way monologue can improve understanding and, more importantly, reduce or minimise misunderstanding and incorrect perceptions of the message content and source.

This notion of two-way communication underpins a fundamental construct within interorganisational communication, namely the propensity or willingness of organisations to share information with one another. Although some information has always been exchanged, access and openness to competitively sensitive information has often been withheld. Relational exchanges are based on an open exchange of information and therefore parties should be willing to share information that will enable the channel to attain its goals. Where such a propensity does not exist information may become withheld, distorted or used as part of a power imbalance in the marketing channel or network. This is regarded as information deviance, from which conflict is likely to develop.

Communication between organisations can be formal or informal. Formal communication is characterised by the use of technology such as EDI. Interorganisational cooperation might improve because of the impact of EDI on channel formalisation and because it can reduce task uncertainty (Nakayama, 2003). On the other hand, sharing sensitive information may affect the distribution of power and influence negotiations between suppliers and retailers. For example, suppliers might be in a better bargaining position regarding the amount of promotional support retailers will receive, if EDI supplies them with point of sale and stock information. What Nakayama points out is that risks and benefits associated with the use of EDI are not always shared equally between all members of a marketing channel.

Communication between organisations can be improved and the incidence of conflict reduced by an exchange of people. This may involve a single senior manager or a number of managerial staff being deployed to either a similar position or to the operational level at their customers' sites. Through direct experience of the other party's environment and a constant flow of information, conflict can be managed and contained without causing widespread damage.

Informal communications consist of a variety of soft methods and techniques. Some of these are conferences, seminars, memos, emails, telephone conversations and corridor meetings and are used in parallel with more formal communication methods. By improving the quality and frequency of communication, by regularising activities and even establishing ways of behaving or institutionalising, conflict containment can become a matter for all parties in a network, with relationships conditioned by the communication and interaction.

Context two – resolving conflict

In order to resolve conflict that has broken out between organisations, a number of approaches have been proposed. Many of these approaches have the potential to contain conflict as well as resolve conflict that has reached damaging proportions.

Rosenberg and Stern (1970) suggested the use of a joint industry committee or group, composed of elected members from the industry. The group would be able to provide a forum for the views of the organisations in conflict to be heard. Larger industry forums can establish various subcommittees entrusted with responsibility for particular aspects of the industry's affairs. Trade associations such as the Engineering Employers' Federation, the Freight Transport Association and the Cementitious Slag Makers Association provide this mechanism and by forming voluntary rules and procedures, enable constituent organisations to work to agreed behaviour patterns. Therefore, trade associations provide a means by which conflict can be contained and also resolved.

The same principle of cooperation enables manufacturers to meet groups of industry-wide dealers to discuss problems and complaints; to review proposed pricing strategies; to consider advertising and marketing communications campaigns; to hear ways in which dealers perceive the actions of manufacturers; as well as providing a means for putting forward new ideas and advancing channel-wide performance.

The use of diplomacy can also be used to resolve and contain conflict. By appointing an individual or a customer centre that has responsibility for a particular dealer or set of retailers, and empowering them with decision making capability, it becomes possible to resolve conflict before it becomes a potent force. Although diplomacy might have a defensive orientation, it can be localised and prevent conflict from spreading to other intermediaries.

An alternative approach to these internally driven mechanisms is the introduction of an external agent. These can provide objectivity and a fresh perspective to any disagreement. Arbitration is an externally based facility that is capable of providing a fast and confidential means of resolving conflict. It is less expensive than legal action and

SNAPSHOT 9.4

ONLINE ARBITRATION

The American Arbitration Association (AAA), a non-profit conflict management and dispute resolution provider, offers an online facility for preventing, minimising and resolving B2B online disagreements. Referred to as the 'Dispute Risk Management' portal, the site recognises that an increasing number of companies are going online and the number of disputes that need to be resolved is also climbing.

The site features several tools for online resolution, such as an online process for submission of B2B disputes and for management of B2B cases. The case management tools and services can resolve disputes through on-call mediation or online 'documents-only' arbitration.

By allowing users to share documents, search directories, and access the AAA's Alternative Dispute Resolution (ADR) library it is hoped that many disputes can be prevented from escalating unduly.

The site also provides information on current events and other news related to B2B dispute risk management, as well as education advisory services.

Source: Adapted from Chimino (2001) and www.adr.org/index2.1.jsp?JSPssid=15765 (Accessed November 2003.)

can be officiated by people who understand the industry or context within which the conflict has occurred. With arbitration, the third party makes the final decision, and the organisations in conflict are bound by that decision.

In contrast to arbitration, mediation requires a third party to be involved but their role is to encourage dialogue to enable the parties to reach their own agreement. Encouragement can be in the form of floating possible solutions, suggesting solutions, establishing the facts and once a solution is agreed ensuring that it is implemented correctly.

Finally, to conclude this section on conflict management there are a number of overall strategies that can be employed to deal with conflict and interorganisational disagreements; these are set out in Table 9.3.

The strategies depicted range from selfishness (and to some degree stubbornness) and refusal to work with other organisations, through compromise and cooperativeness to seeking entirely to accommodate the views of other parties, to the extent that one's own position may be jeopardised. The selection and deployment of these strategies is a function of the prevailing corporate culture, attitude towards risk and the sense of power that exists within coalitions.

Table 9.3 Conflict resolution strategies

Strategy	Explanation
Accommodation	Modify expectations to incorporate requirements of others.
Argument	A considered attempt to convince others of the correctness of your position.
Avoidance	Removal from the point of conflict.
Compromise	Meet the requirements of others half way.
Cooperation	Mutual reconciliation through cooperation.
Instrumentality	Agree minimal requirements to secure short-term agreement.
Self-seeking	Seek agreement on own terms or refuse further cooperation.

eCommerce and conflict

Many of the current disputes between organisations concern the introduction of an online sales channel. These online channels may be designed by a manufacturer (upstream) to complement current offline distributor arrangements. Alternatively they may be used to augment their direct sales force (external and internal conflict possibilities). Alternatively, a distributor (downstream), against the wishes of the upstream partner, may decide to offer a manufacturer's brand through their own online channels.

In order to build a successful online channel care should be taken not to enrage current intermediaries, indeed every effort should be made to find an online channel solution that will help build trust and commitment. Of the many channel strategies open to manufacturers, some are incompatible with established offline channel approaches and openly invite tension and conflict. There are a number of strategies that manufacturers can employ when developing eCommerce facilities, although not all of them are appropriate as they often generate mistrust and conflict.

An **independent strategy** refers to manufacturers who develop an online channel and either bypass their established offline intermediaries or enter into direct online competition with them. This invariably leads to conflict and if the product has no significant or unique features dealers will substitute the manufacturer's brand and take their business elsewhere. The **inertia strategy** concerns those manufacturers who either do not provide a website or fail to provide suitable content, referral sites or online purchasing facilities. Retailers perceive this as a failure to provide competitive parity so inevitably retailer frustration and subsequent conflict results in retailers delisting these manufacturers. The **lead generator strategy** provides customers with information about the location of its retailers. If the information is unbiased and covers all authorised outlets this model can be perceived positively by retailers. However, this positive view arises because the manufacturer site merely becomes a traffic generator. Retailers are free to cross-sell different brands to these leads as the manufacturer loses control over their own brand and those who expressed interest. The **participatory strategy** requires that once customers have selected their products at the manufacturer's site they then select a retailer and, through a co-branded site with the retailer, complete the purchase. This can be successful as all parties are involved and rewarded when transactions are completed. The **win–win strategy** enables manufacturers to retain brand control and avoid conflict with channel partners. Selling directly to end-user customers online, the manufacturer helps the end-user customer to select the brand they want and choose the channel partner they prefer for post-purchase service and support. Through this arrangement, channel partners are involved, not excluded, and are rewarded through profit and volume for their contribution to the customer experience.

SNAPSHOT 9.5

THE LUGGAGE INDUSTRY

The luggage industry consists primarily of manufacturers and retailers with 70 per cent of all products sold through specialty stores and 30 per cent through department stores.

Luggage is an infrequently purchased item and consumers are all too often more loyal to a luggage brand rather than a store. However, they want to physically touch and see the product before purchasing and these retail purchases are made based upon attributes such as features, colour, available selection and store location. Few retailers can afford to stock all the ranges offered by manufacturers.

Despite these factors some luggage manufacturers such as Tumi have created an online branded shopping experience. Consumers can specify the size, features and colour, buy the product at www.tumi.com, entering their name, address and payment information. Based on postcode, the consumer must select a retailer from a localised list. If the retailer is not listed, or the consumer is from out of town, a search engine is available to locate the appropriate retailer.

The chosen retailer receives financial credit for their portion of the profit and is expected to handle support, services and any returns. Everyone in the channel is notified of the sale. This gives the retailer the opportunity to provide additional products and services. It also gives the manufacturer invaluable geo-demographic and marketing information.

Source: Adapted from Southam (2002), www.reshare.com (Accessed 5 February 2003.) Used with permission.

At a tactical level there are a number of other reasons that can generate conflict within a B2B eCommerce context. Standifer and Wall (2003) found that there are two main issues which give rise to conflict. These are technical and socially induced causes of conflict. Technical problems concern difficulties with incompatible systems interfaces, system crashes for example when placing orders or problems concerning product identification codes not being read and matched by the 'other' system. Social problems tended to centre on either internal interpersonal conflicts, such as the unwillingness of one person to assist another with the system, or socio-technical interactions demonstrated by a reluctance or refusal to change codes or processes to be compatible with the design of the system.

These authors found that such disagreements did not always escalate into conflict. However, when it did become difficult, high costs, problem reoccurrence, uncertainty and a lack of cooperation appeared to be the most frequent catalysts, as they termed them.

Building relationships

There are a number of factors that contribute to the development of strong relationships and reduced levels of conflict but linking them all are ideas concerning trust and commitment. At one time, power was regarded as the best means to manage a marketing channel and avoid conflict. As the relationship marketing approach has gathered momentum, so trust and commitment have become the focus for conflict resolution and avoidance.

Trust

The interdependence of organisations and indeed of most strong and longer running buyer–seller relationships, is founded on a degree of trust between parties. Trust is the confidence that one party has in the other's reliability and integrity. In a B2B context, trust is the confidence that one organisation has interacting with another organisation with respect to their reliability, integrity and predictability regarding desirable outcomes. A lack of trust can lead to uncertainty and from that position, conflict and dissatisfaction.

Trust brings feelings of security, it can reduce uncertainty and create a supportive climate. It follows that honesty and benevolence are an integral part of the trust concept and an important part of the relationships that evolve between organisations. Honesty is concerned with the belief that a partner stands by their word, fulfils their role, meets their obligations and is sincere. Benevolence is about the belief that one partner is interested in the welfare of the other and will not take unexpected actions (opportunistic behaviour) that might be to the detriment of the partner (Geyskens and Steenkamp, 1995). Interestingly, Svensson (2001) refers to the establishment of a trust chain running through a marketing channel.

A further perspective on trust concerns the demarcation made by Shankar *et al.* (2002) and others regarding offline and online trust. Although it is recognised that there are many similarities, online trust is different because the focus is not so much about people, such as sales representatives and customer support staff, as about trust with respect to technology, whether it be a website, eCommerce channel, email or a kiosk. The linkage between offline and online trust is also important and the interaction between the two, especially in multi-channel systems must not be overlooked.

Commitment

Commitment is associated with a partner's consistency, competence, honesty, fairness and willingness to make sacrifices, take responsibility, be helpful and benevolent. The level of commitment determines acquiescence and hence the partner's propensity to exit the relationship.

Commitment can be interpreted as the desire to continue and maintain a valued relationship. Therefore, a strong relationship requires that trust be established between channel members. Once trust is formed the opportunity arises for relationship commitment and it is through this cooperation that a major outcome might be end user satisfaction.

In Chapter 6 relationship marketing was discussed, with the work of Morgan and Hunt (1994) being given particular prominence. However, in terms of interorganisational conflict the development of trust is important in limiting the development of conflict in the first place. If conflict should emerge, the presence of trust should determine that any conflict will be functional and should go some way towards reducing the intensity and duration of any incompatibility or tension. If there is a high degree of commitment then the fact that both parties value the relationship will go a long way to preventing the issue giving rise to conflict emerging in the first place.

Cooperation

There is general agreement that effective supply (and marketing) chain management requires trust and communication (Tan, 2001; Grieco, 1989). As already identified, Morgan and Hunt proposed that building a relationship based on trust and commitment can give rise to a number of benefits. Some of these include developing a set of shared values, reducing costs when the relationship finishes and increasing profitability as a greater number of end-user customers are retained because of the inherent value and satisfaction they experience. Cooperation arises from a relationship driven by high levels of both trust and commitment (Morgan and Hunt, 1994).

Mohr et al. (1999) refer to cooperation as the extent to which organisations voluntarily undertake similar or complementary actions to achieve mutual or singular outcomes with expected reciprocation over time. Therefore, in view of prevailing uncertainties before collaborative relationships are reached, organisations need to calculate the appropriate level of cooperation they judge to be necessary. Harris and Dibben (1999) suggest that the criteria necessary for cooperation between parties is a reflection of the factors set out in Table 9.4.

Table 9.4 Factors influencing level of cooperation

Factor	Cooperative element
Utility	A perception of the potential economic value associated with remaining in the relationship.
Importance	A perception of the non-economic value associated with remaining in the relationship.
Competence	A perception of the potential social/economic loss of remaining in the relationship.
Self-competence	An individual's perception of their own ability within the relationship.
Risk	A perception of the professional ability of another (organisation).

These are useful because they focus attention on the importance of perception in the maintenance and management of interorganisational relationships. However, they do not provide sufficient managerial precision to direct these important decisions. Southam (2002) suggests that in an eCommerce channel, margins, brand strength, customer involvement, intensity of competition and whether customer value is added through the Internet or at the retailers' location shapes decisions about between whom, where and when cooperation should occur. In addition there are certain intra-organisational factors that will shape a channel strategy, namely a range of resources such as finance, technological and human factors, let alone the organisational structure, culture, fulfilment and marketing capabilities amongst others.

Forms of channel cooperation

One of the principles of relationship marketing is that all channel members cooperate, collaborate and share information in order to achieve agreed goals. Part of this collaborative approach requires varying levels of prominence and effort on behalf of manufacturers/producers and retailers not only to acquire and satisfy consumers but also to share the support and performance-related rewards. Through improved channel relationships and associated collaborative activity, the intensity, frequency and duration of channel conflict can be significantly reduced.

The development and maintenance of trust and commitment must be actively considered when developing eCommerce strategies. Webb (2002) suggests that the following guiding principles might enable manufacturers or producer organisations to introduce online facilities without endangering the relationships with established intermediaries. Webb proposes that supplier organisations can reduce conflict in the following ways:

> ### SNAPSHOT 9.6
>
> **MATTEL**
>
> The world's largest toy manufacturer, Mattel, normally works through major toy retailers. However, it began selling direct to consumers through its www.barbie.com site and through catalogues sent direct to 4 million US homes. The aim was to raise brand awareness, not to compete with their channel partners.
>
> Prices were set 15 per cent higher than the retailers' prices and best-selling items were not included. Arrangements are in place for retailers to provide fulfilment tasks and be rewarded accordingly. Following this strategy, retailers have remained comfortable with their relationship with Mattel and overt conflict has remained dormant.
>
> *Source*: Adapted from Webb (2002).

1 Always pricing website products higher than those available for resale by channel partners.

2 Providing product information without taking orders.

3 Passing fulfilment tasks to channel partners.

4 Promoting their channel partners on their website.

5 Encouraging channel partners to advertise on their website.

6 Not offering their entire range on their website.

7 Using different (unique) brand names for products offered on their website.

8 Using their own websites to promote products that are in the earlier stages of the life cycle.

Manufacturer/retailer relationships can take several forms and four are highlighted in Table 9.5. These reflect whether the manufacturer or retailer is the main marketing influence or whether the parties cooperate or act as partners.

These different approaches reflect differing levels of customer ownership. Where **retailers** have primary influence the manufacturer provides information, technical support and advice. The retailer has prime responsibility for all customer interaction and all marketing focuses on the retailer's store or website. Where **manufacturers** have the primary marketing influence over the end-user customer, the retailer plays the supporting role, often enacting previously agreed contractual obligations. For example a producer such as McDonald's has franchise agreements with most of their retail outlets. Here the maintenance of the brand is the responsibility of the producer and retailers contribute to the producer's marketing costs through royalty payments.

A **cooperative** arrangement still allows manufacturers to get close to the end-user customer and to exercise control over their brand and capture a greater share of the sales revenue.

The most intimate form of interorganisational collaboration emerges when both upstream and downstream parties develop a partnership. **Partners** will share responsibility for their end-user customers, pursue similar objectives and share custody of the brand. As a result of the superior value experienced by customers both partners will be rewarded with a premium price and higher margin.

Table 9.5 Types of interorganisational collaboration

Lead marketing influencer	Customer ownership	Support	Financials
Retailer	Retailer owns the customer relationship.	Retailer provides assortment and service; promotes the brand. Manufacturer provides support for retailer.	Retailer keeps the margin and reduces costs with manufacturer merchandising and marketing help.
Producer or Manufacturer	Manufacturer owns the customer relationship managed by strong consumer branding campaigns.	Producer promotes the brand. Retailer supports the brand often through agreement (e.g. franchise).	Retailer pays manufacturer a percentage of their revenue/profit as contribution to marketing effort driven by manufacturer.
Cooperative	Manufacturer and retailer share customer base and related data.	Manufacturer and retailer cooperate over marketing strategy and plans.	Manufacturer and retailer share performance-based revenue.
Partnership	Manufacturer and retailer jointly manage marketing strategy.	Manufacturer and retailer build a single brand experience through partnership.	Manufacturer and retailer split revenues.

Impact of technology on channel relationships

The development of electronic and Internet technologies has helped to transform the nature of channel management and related issues. eCommerce has evolved and developed so much that through automation, standardisation and improved communications greater efficiencies and increased quantities of targeted information have helped all members of marketing channels. Webb (2002) claims that electronic direct marketing is beginning to take over, or at least substitute for the established marketing channels. This may be true in particular markets but there is no doubt that established channels have benefited from new technology.

The impact of electronic trading facilities and formats on the structural dimensions of channels has already been noted. However, new technology has also had a major impact on the relationships between organisations. One view of web-based auctions (Chapter 5) is that they have the potential to destroy previously established buyer–seller relationships. It is thought that they can lead suppliers to distrust buyers who move to reverse auction formats because price is perceived as the dominant issue and there is little apparent scope to develop relationships.

The counterview is that web-based auctions present an opportunity to develop new relationships with channel members. However, web auctions might reduce channel length and width (Sashi and O'Leary, 2002). These researchers postulate that where auction intermediaries are formed by groups of suppliers or buyers there are occasions where competition may be weakened because certain organisations are excluded. The dominant exchange therefore might succeed to a more powerful position than in offline situations and price collusion and market manipulation becomes a threat.

With supply chain actions still required regardless of the method of buying, organisations need to be sure that their portfolio of relationships takes account of the buying opportunities afforded by the Internet and that these are offset against situations where strategic purchase items are held within a collaborative relationship. This view was developed by Skjott-Larsen *et al.* (2003). They formulated a procurement portfolio based on a firm's different forms of supplier relationships and various types of Internet-driven electronic marketplaces (IEMPs) (see Figure 9.3).

The outcome is that the Internet should be used in certain purchasing situations according to the significance of different types of purchase items so that some strategically orientated purchases may be maintained through strong relationships between partnerships and alliances. For further information readers should see Skjott-Larsen, Kotazab and Grieger (2003).

Business ethics

The management of interorganisational relationships involves trust, commitment, conflict prevention or resolution and, inevitably, issues relating to the exercise of

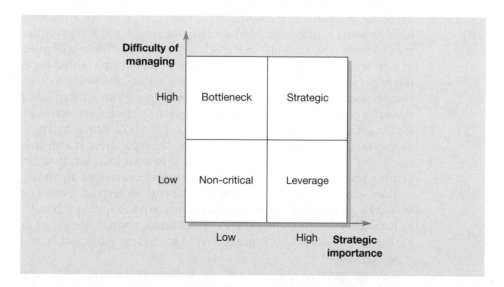

Figure 9.3 The Olsen and Ellram portfolio model for purchases over IEMPs.

Source: Skjott-Larsen *et al.* (2003). Copyright © 2003. With permission from Elsevier.

power. This is the sphere of business ethics and related themes of corporate and social responsibility (CSR).

Organisations, regardless of whether they operate in consumer or business markets, have a responsibility to a wide range of stakeholders, not just their customers. Ideally, planned marketing activities should encompass a range of social, ethical and community considerations, with both corporate and individual decision makers properly aware of, and sensitive to, the issues, rather than addressing them as an afterthought. For example, the Co-op Bank's ethical positioning strategy is supported by its decision to reject £4m of business because the companies which were seeking loans or banking services were involved in arms dealing, animal testing, exploitative labour practices and nuclear power (Treanor, 2003).

Business ethics encompass notions of right and wrong and what is morally acceptable business behaviour. Christy (2002) suggests that these can be considered from a perspective of **duty**, where some actions are always bad and others always good, or **consequences**, where the results of an action are a key factor.

The consequences approach can be developed to consider the rewards that are derived from business decision making. These may, for example, be rewards for shareholders who have funded the organisation and accepted the associated risks. Alternatively the rewards may fall to the managers of an organisation who have used the funding to drive above average rewards for themselves, possibly at the expense of shareholders' dividends and their return on investment. Recent hostile annual general meetings (AGMs) (for example GlaxoSmithKline) where shareholders have openly revolted against the chief executive officer (CEO) and their remuneration and or termination packages offered by the board of directors, have served to bring these issues into public focus.

Ethical awareness should pervade an organisation at both an individual and organisational performance level. While both these categories may be considered independently, they are also intertwined. For example, the decisions an individual makes can impact on the long-term interests of the organisation while an organisation (represented by the board of directors) may make a decision that impacts on particular individuals. Examples at the individual level are a salesperson offering a bribe to win a contract, or refraining from doing so and accepting that the contract may go elsewhere. Examples at the organisational level include decisions not to trade in certain countries if it means condoning a brutal regime, initiating pay cuts across the board in order not to make staff redundant or, conversely, out-sourcing jobs to cheaper locations regardless of redundancies among current staff and the impact on the wider community. Managerial awareness of the issues, respect and reciprocity can lead to greater understanding and consistent levels of ethical behaviour throughout an organisation, as well as enhanced corporate reputation. However, the collapse of the Italian company Parmalat, appears to have been founded on active policies concerning CSR. The desire 'to keep money-losing operations afloat, to pay wages to workers who might otherwise have been laid off, to keep companies in business that should have been shut down, to fund community and social programs' lay at the root of Parmalat's demise, rather than any deliberate corrupt scheme to defraud the tax authorities or to act dishonourably towards any particular stakeholder group (Corcoran, 2004).

A survey reported and discussed online (Industrial Focus, 2003) claimed that, globally, 65 per cent of CEOs accept personal responsibility for managing corporate reputation, contrasting with a figure of only 14 per cent for boards. In a European sub-set, 44 per cent of CEOs took individual responsibility, and boards 38 per cent. A total of 257 completed surveys were analysed from executives at 199 public and 54 private companies in North America, Europe and Asia. Respondents also placed unethical behaviour as one of the top two threats to corporate reputation.

In terms of B2B marketing and associated activities there are numerous decision areas where ethical considerations arise. For example, decisions concerning product announcements and performance claims, sales force activities, claims made in trade and customer advertising plus adhering to contractual obligations, non-exploitative pricing and providing appropriate training and support. One critical area concerns the ethical and moral behaviour within the relationships that organisations develop. Immediate relationships between organisations and their professional advisers, for example advertising and public relations agencies, auditors, financial and management consultants, depend upon trust and a strong ethical code of conduct. Some of the high-profile B2B relationships which have broken down recently have involved financial advisers such as those between Enron and Arthur Anderson.

Other key relationships involve buyers and sellers and players in the marketing channel. These relationships might be individually underpinned by friendship and mutual respect, or perhaps induced by hospitality or bribery. Alternatively, they may be organisationally driven in terms of supplier selection or channel design and management. Exclusive distribution practices were mentioned earlier, whereby only one reseller is permitted to sell an organisation's products within a specified geographical area. In addition these distributors may not be permitted to sell competitors' products, a practice used extensively in the UK car market, although now challenged by the European Commission. Some dealers may be coerced into stocking the producer's full product line which may not be in their own best interests. These and similar practices may be challenged on both legal and moral grounds, because, among other things, they might fail to serve the wider interests of the community and be restrictive in terms of target market access.

Business ethics should be an important and priority issue for organisations. Readers wishing to learn more about this subject are advised to read Christy (2002), or for a fuller account, Sternberg (1994) or de George (1999).

Summary

The management of interorganisational and marketing channel relationships is critical for the achievement of B2B marketing goals. Conflict is to be expected when organisations seek to cooperate with one another, but the use of relative power positions based on access to and control of resources is no longer regarded as the preferred and pervasive marketing management tool. With the focus turning to the development and maintenance of buyer–seller relationships, trust and commitment have emerged as significant contemporary managerial concepts.

The development of electronic trading formats has threatened established channel relationships but these new facilities should be regarded as supplementary tools. By understanding the various types of purchases an organisation makes, particularly with regard to their strategic significance, electronic purchase instruments can be deployed to improve the overall efficiency of an organisation as well as to also preserve and enhance marketing channel relationships.

Conflict can be generated by a member of the marketing channel introducing an ill-conceived strategic eCommerce model. Alternatively, conflict can emerge at an operational level through both social and technically induced disputes. Whatever the source, solutions need to be determined quickly if only to re-establish trust and prevent a reoccurrence of the problem and hence the conflict.

Discussion questions

1 Evaluate social exchange theory as a means of explaining dependency and power.

2 Identify the five bases of power cited by French and Raven and then write brief notes explaining how three of them work.

3 What are the main reasons for interorganisational conflict within marketing channels? How can the impact of these different types of conflict be reduced?

4 Find three examples of channel conflict and using theoretical concepts explain why the conflict developed in each case.

5 Explain how an understanding of relationships and communication might help resolve conflict.

6 Determine the extent to which IS&T has the potential to influence channel relationships, paying particular attention to interorganisational trust, conflict and satisfaction.

References

Amason, A.C. (1996). 'Distinguishing the effects of functional and dysfunctional conflict on strategic decision making: resolving a paradox for top management teams', *Academy of Management Journal*, 39, 1, pp. 123–48.

Anderson, J.C. and Narus, J.A. (1990). 'A model of distributor firm and manufacturer firm working partnerships', *Journal of Marketing*, 54 (January), pp. 42–58.

Assael, H. (1969). 'Constructive role of interorganisational conflict', *Administrative Science Quarterly*, 14 (December), pp. 573–82.

Chimino, K. (2001). 'Site launched to settle b2b disputes online', *eCommerce Times*, 13 July, www.ecommercetimes.com/perl/story/11971.html (Accessed November 2003.)

Christy, R. (2002) 'Ethics in marketing communications', in C. Fill, *Marketing Communications; Contexts, Strategies and Applications*, 3rd edn, Harlow: Pearson Education, pp. 145–71.

Chu, W. and Chu. W. (1994). 'Signaling quality by selling through a reputable retailer: an example of renting the reputation of another agent', *Marketing Science*, 13 (Spring), pp. 177–89.

Corcoran, T. (2004). 'Practising corporate social responsibility is a sure recipe for corporate disaster', www.wbcsd.org/. (Accessed 12 March 2004.)

Coughlan, A.T., Anderson, Stern, L. and El-Ansary, A. (2001). *Marketing Channels*, 6th edn, Englewood Cliffs, NJ: Prentice Hall.

de George, R.T. (1999). *Business Ethics*, 5th edn, Englewood Cliffs, NJ: Prentice Hall.

Duarte, M. and Davies, G. (2003). 'Testing the conflict-performance assumption in business-to-business relationships', *Industrial Marketing Management*, 32, 2 (February), pp. 91–93.

Emerson, R. (1962). 'Power-dependence relations', *American Sociological Review*, 27 (February), pp. 32–3.

French, J.R. and Raven, B. (1959). 'The bases of social power', in D. Cartwright (ed.), *Studies in Social Power*, Ann Arbor: University of Michigan.

Gaski, J.F. (1984). 'The theory of power and conflict in channels of distribution', *Journal of Marketing*, 48 (Summer), pp. 9–29.

Geyskens, I. and Steenkamp. J.-B. (1995). *An Investigation into the Joint Effects of Trust and Interdependence on Relationship Commitment*, Proceedings of the European Marketing Academy Conference, 1995.

Grieco, Jr, P.L. (1989). 'Why supplier certification? And will it work?', *Production and Inventory Management Review and APIC News*, 9, 5, pp. 38–42.

Harris, S. and Dibben, M.R. (1999). 'Trust and co-operation in business relationship development: exploring the influence of national values', *Journal of Marketing Management*, 15 (July), pp. 463–83.

Hunt, S.B. and Nevin, J.R. (1974). 'Power in channel of distribution: sources and consequences', *Journal of Marketing Research*, 11, pp. 186–93.

Industrial Focus (2003). 'CEOs give corporate governance mixed reviews', www.industrialfocus.co.uk/cgi-bin/article.cgi?ID=2493&SECTION=News (Accessed March 2004.)

Jehn, K.A. (1994) 'Enhancing effectiveness: an investigation of advantages and disadvantages of value based intra group conflict', *International Journal of Conflict Management*, 5,3, pp. 223–38.

Kaneshige, T. (2001). 'Avoiding channel conflict', *Line56 Magazine*, March, www.line56.com/articles/default.asp?NewsID=2382 (Accessed 3 December 2003.)

Katz, D. and Kahn, R.L. (1978). *The Social Psychology of Organisation*, 2nd edn, New York, NY: John Wiley.

Larson, A. (1992). 'Network dyads in entrepreneurial settings: a study of governance of exchange relationships', *Administrative Science Quarterly*, 37, pp. 76–104.

McGrath, A. and Hardy, K. (1986). 'A strategic paradigm for predicting manufacturer–reseller conflict', *European Journal of Marketing*, 23, 2, pp. 94–108.

Menon, A., Bharadwaj, S.G. and Howell, R. (1996). 'The quality and effectiveness of marketing strategy: effects of functional and dysfunctional conflict in interorganisational relationships', *Journal of Academy of Marketing Science*, 24, 4, pp. 299–313.

Mohr, J., Fisher, R., Nevin, J. (1999). 'Communicating for better channel relationships', *Journal of Marketing Management*, 8, 2 (Summer), pp. 39–45.

Morgan, R.M. and Hunt, S.D. (1994). 'The commitment-trust theory of relationship marketing', *Journal of Marketing*, 58 (July), pp. 20–38.

Nakayama, M. (2003). 'An assessment of EDI use and other channel communications on trading behaviour and trading partner knowledge', *Information and Management*, 40, 6 (July), pp. 563–81.

Pondy, L.R. (1967). 'Organisational conflict: conflict and models', *Administrative Science Quarterly*, 12 (September), pp. 296–320.

Rose, G.M. and Shoham, A. (2002). 'Interorganisational task and emotional conflict with international channels of distrubution', *Journal of Business Research*, 57, 9 (September), pp. 942–50.

Rosenbloom, B. (1978). 'Motivating independent distribution channel members' *Industrial Marketing Management*, 7 (November), pp. 275-81.

Rosenberg, L.J. and Stern, L.W. (1970). 'Toward the analysis of conflict in distribution channels: a descriptive model', *Journal of Marketing*, 34, 4 (October), pp. 40–6.

Rosson, P. and Ford, D. (1980). 'Stake, conflict and performance in export marketing channels', *Management International Review*, 20, 4, pp. 31–7.

Sashi, C.M. and O'Leary, B. (2002). 'The role of Internet auctions in the expansion of B2B markets', *Industrial Marketing Management*, 31, 2 (February), pp. 103–10.

Shankar, V., Urban, G.L. and Sultan, F. (2002). 'Online trust: a stakeholder perspective, concepts, implications and future directions', *Journal of Strategic Information Systems*, 11, 3–4, (December), pp. 325–44.

Shipley, D. and Egan, C. (1992). 'Power, conflict and co-operation in brewer–tenant distribution channels'. *International Journal of Service Industry Management*, 3, 4, pp. 44–62.

Skjott-Larsen, T., Kotazab, H. and Grieger, M. (2003). 'Electronic marketplaces and supply chain relationships', *Industrial Marketing Management*, 32, 3 (April), pp. 199–210.

Southam, A.G. (2002). 'Understanding channel conflict'; www.reshare.com. (Accessed 5 February 2003.)

Standifer, R.L. and Wall, Jnr., J.A. (2003). 'Managing conflict in B2B e-commerce', *Business Horizons*, March–April, pp. 65–70.

Stern, L.W. and El-Ansary, A. (1992). *Marketing Channels*, 4th edn, Englewood Cliffs, NJ: Prentice Hall.

Stern, L.W., El-Ansary, A.I. and Coughlan, A.T. (1996). *Marketing Channels*, 5th edn, Englewood Cliffs, NJ: Prentice Hall.

Stern, L.W. and Gorman, R.H. (1969). 'Conflict in distribution channels: an exploration in distribution channels', in L.W. Stern (ed.), *Distribution Channels: Behavioural Dimensions*, Boston, MA: Houghton Mifflin, pp. 156–75.

Stern, L.W. and Heskett, J.L. (1969). 'Conflict management in interorganisational relations: a conceptual framework', in L.W. Stern (ed.) *Distribution Channels: Behavioural Dimensions*, Boston, MA: Houghton Mifflin, pp. 288–305.

Sternberg, E. (1994) *Just Business*, London: Warner.

Svensson, G. (2001). 'Extending trust and mutual trust in business relationships towards a synchronized trust chain in marketing channels', *Management Decision*, 39, 6, pp. 431–40.

Tan, K.C. (2000). 'A framework of supply chain management literature', *European Journal of Purchasing and Supply Management*, 7, 1 (March), pp. 39–48.

Treanor, J. (2003). 'Co-op passes up £4m to maintain ethics'; www.guardian.co.uk/ (12 March 2004).

Webb, K.L. and Hogan, J.E. (2002). 'Hybrid channel conflict: causes and effects on channel performance', *Journal of Business and Industrial Marketing*, 17, 5, pp. 338–56.

Webb, K.L. (2002). 'Marketing channels of distribution in the age of electronic commerce', *Industrial Marketing Management*, 31, 2, (February), pp. 95–102.

Welch, C. and Wilkinson, I. (2002). 'Network perspectives on interfirm conflict; reassessing a critical case in international business', *Journal of Business Research*, available online.

Wong, Y.H. (1998). 'Key to key account management: relationship (guanxi) model', *International Marketing Review*, 15, 3, pp. 215–31.

Part D
B2B marketing communications

This final part of the book considers interorganisational marketing communications. It draws on the technological aspects, relationship marketing characteristics and behavioural concepts developed earlier in the book.

Chapter 10 examines some of the roles and strategic issues associated with interorganisational marketing communications. The core characteristics and roles of marketing communications are examined before considering the key marketing communication strategies that can be pursued by organisations.

Chapter 11 examines the nature and characteristics of the individual communication tools and media used within B2B promotional mixes. Attention is given to exhibitions, sponsorships and the role of the Internet within B2B marketing communications. Reference is also made to the different ways in which the promotional mix can be configured, based on the key strengths of the particular tools.

Chapter 12 focuses on the role and characteristics of personal selling. The chapter considers the key characteristics of personal selling and reflects upon a number of different ways in which the sales force can be organised and supported, including key account management.

Throughout this final part of the book significant attention is given to the importance of using marketing communications to develop and maintain interorganisational relationships. The contribution of IST is highlighted.

Chapter 10

B2B marketing communications strategy

Chapter overview

This chapter introduces Part D of the book. Here the emphasis is on an examination of the nature, content and role of marketing communication activities as part of B2B marketing.

This particular chapter commences with a consideration of some of the strategic promotional issues and explores strategy from an audience perspective. Issues concerning the nature of strategy and planning are also considered before presenting a framework for the development of marketing communication plans.

Part of this chapter is devoted to marketing channel-based communications. This specialist area is often overlooked but if marketing channels are to operate successfully and interfirm relationships are to be developed for the benefit of all in the channel, then sound trade channel communications are crucial.

The chapter concludes with an examination of relationship-based marketing communication, and in particular, the nature, role and dynamics associated with client/ agency based relationships.

Chapter aims

The aim of this chapter is to explore issues concerning the role and strategic use of marketing communications in a B2B context.

Objectives

The objectives of this chapter are to:

1   Explain the role and principles of business-to-business marketing communications.
2   Examine the nature of strategy and planning in marketing communications.
3   Consider the characteristics of interorganisational and channel-based marketing communications.
4   Review a model of B2B communications.
5   Explore relationship-based marketing communications.
6   Examine interactive B2B marketing communications.

Introduction

Effective communication is critically important for all organisations. One of the reasons for this is the necessity to inform customers of their products and services but another, and perhaps even more important reason, is to establish and maintain suitable relationships with a wide array of stakeholders. Communication enables organisations to join up and to facilitate the development and maintenance of active, positive relationships with a range of stakeholders. To assist this linkage, organisations use a mix of communication methods that are examined individually in Chapter 11.

Marketing communications provides a means by which organisations and their brands can be presented to their audiences with the intention of stimulating a dialogue. It is anticipated that this interaction will assist the development and sustenance of a relationship, which will eventually lead to a succession of satisfactory transactions.

Essentially, marketing communication represents the promotion flow identified in Chapter 7 as an exchange between organisations, customers and other stakeholders. To a large extent the differences between many products (structure, composition and performance) have diminished to a point where the level of differentiation between products has become much more difficult to observe and communicate. This results in a decrease in the number of available and viable positioning opportunities. One way to resolve this problem is to use the parent organisation rather like an umbrella and to provide the near brand associations buyers need to understand the source of a message. In addition, use of the parent organisation in communication activities can provide greater support and leadership in the promotion of offerings and reduce the costs associated with supporting individual brands. Therefore, marketing communications are concerned with both the organisation and its products and services.

Many organisations focus on the needs of distributors and channel intermediaries. As determined earlier, organisations in the channel work together to satisfy their individual and collective objectives. The degree of conflict and cooperation in the channel network depends on a number of factors, but some of the most important factors are the form and quality of the communications between member organisations. This means that marketing communications must address the specific communication needs of members of the distribution network and those other stakeholders who impact on or influence trade channel performance.

This and the following two chapters explore some of the key issues and methods associated with business-to-business marketing communications. After first defining marketing communications, this chapter examines some of the roles and strategic issues associated with B2B marketing communications, the next chapter examines the principal tools and methods used by organisations to communicate with B2B audiences and the last provides a deeper insight into personal selling and key account management, two vitally important aspects of business relationship management.

Defining marketing communications

The conventional perspective on marketing communications is that it is an umbrella term embracing activities designed to convey information and persuade customers to purchase products and services. The focus of marketing communications has traditionally been product-orientated, and corporate communications have either encompassed all of an organisation's product and company image-based communications (van Riel, 1995) or just those communications associated with the organisation's image and reputation. This separation of communication activities reflects a silo or compartmentalised approach to communication. It is inward looking and considers the communication of information as one-way and hierarchical. Furthermore, it fails to encompass the variety of touch points customers, organisations and their staff have with other organisations and their products and services.

Business-to-business marketing communications are concerned with the way in which an organisation communicates with other organisations with regard to its products, services and its own desired organisational identity and associated reputation. Communication in this context is not about static, one-way information but about the meanings that are both intended (by the source organisation) and derived, as a result of interpretation, by the other audiences (organisations) in the communication process. Marketing communications are about participation and involvement and not exclusion or distance. Therefore, marketing communications should not be primarily about products, instruction and communication instruments, but rather concerned with audiences, involvement and meanings.

In order for marketing communications to work, they must be based on an understanding of the context and environment of the target audience, not that of the source organisation. This enables the development and presentation of relevant and timely messages, plus evaluation and reaction to responses received. The communication process should be symmetrical, such that both the audience and the originating organisation are willing and able to adjust their position, according to the messages received. The basis should not be power or price. With this in mind the following is presented as a working definition of marketing communications.

> Marketing communications is a management process through which an organisation converses with its various audiences. The aim is to influence the perception and understanding of the organisation, and/or its products and services, with a view to generating specific meanings and ongoing attitudinal and behavioural responses.

Implicit within this definition are three main dimensions: dialogue, relationships and cognitive processing.

Dialogue. Marketing communications enable organisations to converse with their audiences in such a way that multi-way communications are stimulated. Promotional messages should encourage members of target audiences to respond to the focus organisation (or product/brand). This response can be immediate through, for example, purchase behaviour or it can be deferred as information is assimilated and considered for future use. Even if the information is discarded at a later date, the communication will have prompted attention and consideration of the message and its meanings. With many B2B purchase decisions involving several people, various locations and often being diffused across considerable periods of time, marketing communications must encourage dialogue. In particular, it should encourage prompt questioning and curiosity within and about the source, in terms of both their products and the organisation itself.

Relationships. The initiation, development and maturation of interorganisational relationships should be rooted within consistent and relevant marketing communications. To influence perception and understanding of the organisation and its offerings requires a marketing communications approach that stimulates initial interest, curiosity and self-interest at the initiation stage. This should evolve through experience into trust, with an approach founded on mutual interest, involvement and commitment. Interorganisational relationships are often based on personal relationships, and marketing communications, through personal selling, should be orientated to developing trust, commitment and goodwill.

Cognitive response. B2B audiences should be regarded as active problem solvers, who use marketing communications to help them in their purchasing and organisation-related activities. Recognising that organisations actively seek out and process relevant information about many of their intended purchases and the organisations with which they are prepared to interact, makes it advisable to provide for these needs in the target audience. Therefore, marketing communications should be designed to carry sufficient relevant and credible information to enable organisations to review, consider and cognitively engage with the source. This may lead to attitudinal adjustments and/or behavioural responses.

The role of marketing communications

Marketing communications can fulfil four fundamental roles in B2B exchange networks. These are to **differentiate**, **reinforce**, **inform**, or **persuade** (DRIP) audiences to think and/or behave, in a particular way, about an organisation and/or its products. This may result from the meanings ascribed to the communications received. The DRIP framework provides a useful means of ascribing the key roles that marketing communications or a particular campaign is required to undertake.

Differentiate	organisations, products and services.
Reinforce	by reminding and reassuring current, lapsed and potential customers.
Inform	and educate customers and other stakeholders of organisational issues and product features and benefits.
Persuade	target audiences to think or act in a particular way.

At a basic level, marketing communications can **differentiate** products, services and organisations, particularly in markets where there is little to separate competing offerings. For example, waste disposal products, such as bags, sacks and liners for

CR TECHNOLOGY AND THEIR AUDIENCES

Many SMEs have limited knowledge of their market position, have difficulty forecasting business growth and have limited marketing/communications budgets. CR Technology, a manufacturer of X-ray and vision inspection equipment, identified these problems and appointed an agency, Kanatsiz Communications, or K-Comm, to help them move forward.

The agency discovered that their client held less than 5 per cent of the market share, generated revenues less than $8 million, and, most importantly, had little or no name or product recognition in the market. When interviewing editors from the electronics trade, 90 per cent had never heard of CR Technology. K-Comm also conducted in-depth assessments of CR Technology's competitors during trade shows and discovered many strengths and weaknesses which were soon applied to the overall communications campaign.

The campaign objectives that evolved from this context analysis were to:

- obtain substantial market share;

- generate qualified sales leads;

- increase name recognition;

- enhance product identification;

- be known as a leading manufacturer of X-ray and vision inspection equipment.

The strategies developed to achieve these goals were targeted at the media and competitors as well as established and potential customers. Public relations, advertising, direct mail, an Internet presence, a stronger affiliation with third-party organisations, a newly designed trade show booth and an in-depth marking analysis that was updated quarterly were developed through the campaign. Press releases and other public relations materials were disseminated through both traditional – mail, fax – and new media such as the Internet, email and Internet fax.

The campaign, which featured 110 news release placements, 14 feature story article placements, and 4 prestigious industry awards, generated huge numbers of qualified sales leads. As a result CR Technology's market share rose to 15 per cent, sales reached $18 million and profits went up 124 per cent within the year. Name recognition and understanding among the industry increased while editorial bookings at trade shows also ran at an all-time high. K-Comm secured an average of 45 editorial meetings and demonstrations during each trade show.

CR Technology needed to communicate with a variety of stakeholders and to achieve both tangible sales-related and intangible communication-related goals. Most notably the organisation had to build knowledge and understanding with customers, competitors, the media, intermediaries and internally with staff and employees, through a planned approach to marketing communications.

Source: Adapted from www.kanatsiz.com/case_studies.cfm (Accessed 4 January 2004.) Used with permission.

municipal, industrial, commercial and medical use are largely similar. It is the communications from the organisations that manufacture and distribute them that have helped create various corporate images, enabling customers to make purchasing decisions. In these cases, the images created by marketing communications, and the meanings that audiences derive from them, differentiate one organisation or product brand from another and position them so that customers' attitudes and purchasing confidence develops.

Communications can also **reinforce** perceptions and images associated with organisations and their products. This is an important aspect of relationship management as it can enable favourable perceptions to be established and refreshed. Reinforcement can work in one of two main ways – reminding or reassuring. Messages can work by helping audiences to recall previous messages, that is, to remind buyers of a need they might have or recall the benefits of past transactions and so convince them that they should enter into a similar exchange. Alternatively, reinforcement might work through comforting or reassuring audiences that purchase decisions they have made in the past are sound or, especially in the case of crisis situations, that the continuity of the organisation is assured and the relationship is to continue. This is a fundamental part of the customer retention process and, if used effectively, marketing communications can contribute to a more cost-effective customer management strategy.

An important aspect of B2B marketing communications is enabling stakeholders to learn, and become more knowledgeable, about products, services and related issues such as organisational policies and positions on a variety of social, corporate and ethical issues. In particular, marketing communications can be used to **inform** current, lapsed and potential customers of an organisation's offerings or issues.

Finally, communications may also attempt to **persuade** current and potential customers of the desirability of purchasing an organisation's offerings and thus lay down the foundation for an exchange relationship. Persuasion is the conventional, and in many respects the central interpretation, of marketing communications. It has already been established that interorganisational relationships evolve, very often from a price and product orientation. Persuasion can be a necessary element of discrete exchanges and, therefore, marketing communications have a potent role to play in bringing organisations, buyers and sellers, together. As exchanges become more frequent, established and regularised so the need for persuasion decreases and the dynamics of the relationship become predominant.

The IBM campaign featured in Snapshot 10.2 demonstrates aspects of the DRIP framework. IBM sought to differentiate itself from competitors through its expertise and range of innovative technological products. IBM have such strong awareness levels that the campaign had an element of reminding potential customers and reassuring current customers and business partners of the value of working with IBM. Undoubtedly the IBM campaign helped inform and educate the market about the importance of a suitable business infrastructure while it also served to persuade potential customers to consider IBM as the most credible business partner.

It should be noted that successful campaigns normally seek to achieve a couple of the DRIP goals, not all four. An attempt to achieve all four may result in confusion, a lack of clarity and then failure.

SNAPSHOT 10.2

IBM AND 'PLAY TO WIN'

The collapse of the dot.com era, the aftermath of 11 September and the economic downturn that followed, led IBM to launch a campaign that sought to re-establish themselves as the leading partner to help customers capitalise on the opportunities being created by the next phase of e-business.

Their worldwide campaign, 'Play to Win', was aimed at business leaders and tried to play to IBM's competitive strength (Oracle, Sun, etc.), that e-business is different from eCommerce and to establish in many customers' minds, that eBusiness infrastructure needs to be considered as a cohesive whole, not just a series of disparate products. It positioned eBusiness as the most important issue in business and identified IBM as the partner that helps you play to win. The concept was designed to work across all business units, all communication activities and all media.

The Play to Win campaign attempted to establish IBM's credibility as a strategic business partner and the importance of a responsive business infrastructure in the light of business demands, new strategies, ever-changing customer, supplier, partner needs, and 24/7 customer expectations.

Source: Adapted from IBM UK materials. Used with permission.

A model of B2B communications

Gilliland and Johnston (1997) published a model of B2B marketing communication effects, which has been reproduced at Figure 10.1.

In this model the buy task involvement (BTI) represents the degree to which individual members of the buying centre or decision making unit (DMU) feel personal relevance (involvement) with each purchase decision. They identify four main elements that can impact on an individual's level of personal involvement, as set out in Table 10.1.

The model follows a similar path to the elaboration likelihood model (ELM) (Petty and Cacioppo, 1983). Those involved with the purchase decision will be more attentive to well-argued messages and look for rational logical information in order to support their decision. In terms of the ELM, they process information via the central route. Those less involved in the purchase decision will not pay very much attention to the arguments or the information provided. They process information by the peripheral route and will be more concerned with the design and layout of an advertisement or the attractiveness of the expert sources used. The authors claim that attitude and behavioural change caused by central route processing tends to be longer lasting than that changed through peripheral cues.

Petty and Cacioppo also recognise that there are political dynamics associated with the roles each member of the DMU adopts. Indeed, there will be a degree of intergroup persuasion according to the degree of affiliation or identification with the products and brands being considered. The more positive the association and the higher the BTI, the more likely it is that an individual will seek more information and attempt to influence others.

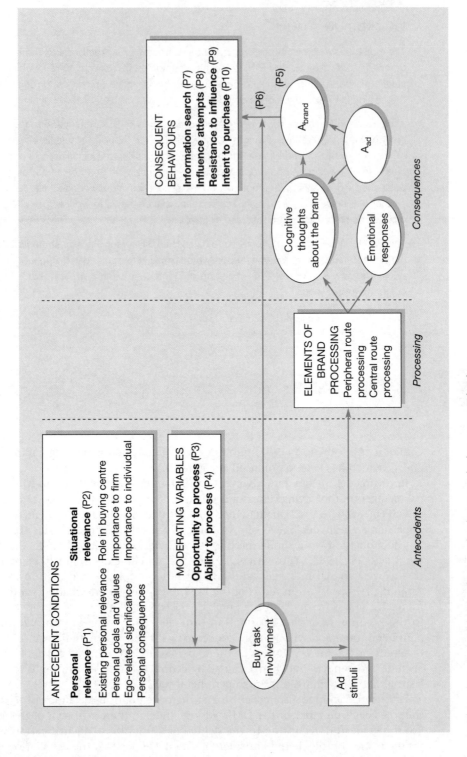

Figure 10.1 A model of business-to-business marketing communications

Source: From Gilliland and Johnston (1997). Used with permission

Table 10.1 The antecedents associated with BTI

Relevance factor	Explanation
Personal	Refers to personal goals, any ego-related significance and the perceived personal consequences of the purchase decision. The higher the personal relevance, the higher the BTI.
Situational	Refers to the importance of the decision to the individual and to the firm. The higher the situational relevance, the higher the BTI.
Opportunity to process	Refers to the level of distractions and noise that might impede exposure or prevent comprehension of a marketing message. The higher the number of opportunties to process information, the higher the BTI.
Ability to process	Refers to the knowledge an individual has about the product under consideration as the more the individual knows, the greater his/her ability to process information about it. The greater the ability to process information, the higher the BTI.

Source: Reprinted from Gilliland and Johnston (1997). Copyright © 1997. With permission from Elsevier.

The significance of this model is that it draws attention to both the importance of understanding buyer behaviour and the significance of emotion and feeling in B2B advertising messages. For a long time the focus of B2B advertising has been on producing informational advertisements and functional messages that present product-related information. This will be an effective appeal to those who have a higher BTI. However, there are many others involved with purchase decisions who have a low BTI but who may have a significant input to the decision process. There are also implications for the media schedule with more reason to use television and consumer print media in particular.

Strategy and planning MCs

Traditionally, marketing communications strategy has been considered to encompass a combination of activities in the communications mix. In other words, strategy is about the degree of direct marketing, personal selling, advertising, sales promotion and public relations that is incorporated within a planned sequence of communication activities. This approach is understandable but suffers from a fundamental flaw. It is based upon an internal, production orientation, one which focuses on and around the resource base. This contradicts the customer perspective and is not the essence of a sound marketing communications strategy, which should be market-orientated and, specifically, audience-centred.

Adopting an audience perspective from which to build a B2B marketing communications strategy necessitates efforts to understand the buying behaviour, characteristics and information needs of the different target audiences. As stated previously, organisational purchase decisions are characterised by group buying centres and can involve a large number of people, all fulfilling different roles in the process and receptive to different marketing communication messages. It is also important to remember that audiences are normally attentive to messages that either have a product or company focus. As a result it is possible to identify three main marketing communication strategies:

Pull strategies   designed to influence end-user customers (consumers and organisations); product focus;

Push strategies   designed to influence trade channel buyers; product focus;

Profile strategies   designed to influence a range of stakeholders; company focus.

These are referred to as the **3Ps** of promotional strategy and relate to the target audience and direction of the communication. **Push** communication strategies direct messages through members of the marketing channel, whereas **pull** communication strategies target end-user organisations, motivating them to seek out distributors (or the manufacturer). **Profile** communication strategies aim at a range of stakeholders and, normally, do not refer to specific products or services that the organisation offers (see Table 10.2).

Pull strategies

If messages are directed at target end-user customers, the intention is invariably to generate increased levels of awareness, inform and educate, change and/or reinforce attitudes, reduce risk, encourage involvement and, ultimately, to bring about a motivation within the target group. This stimulates expectation that the offering will be available to them when they decide to enquire, experiment or make a repeat purchase. The strategy thus encourages customers to 'pull' products through the channel network, or straight from the manufacturer where there is a direct channel. In the B2B context, this usually means that organisations approach distributors to enquire about a particular product and/or buy it, or undertake a similar transaction directly with the manufacturer, or an intermediary, through direct mail or the Internet.

To accomplish and deliver a B2B pull strategy, the traditional approach has been to use personal selling, direct marketing and, increasingly, the Internet. The decision to use a pull strategy has to be supported by a core message. This will vary according to the context analysis and the needs of the target audience. However, it is probable that the core message will seek to differentiate, or reinforce or inform or persuade the audience to think, feel or behave in a particular way.

Table 10.2 Marketing communications strategy options

Strategy	Target audience	Communication focus	Communication goal
Pull	Consumers	Product/service	Purchase
	End-user B2B customers	Product/service	Purchase
Push	Channel intermediaries	Product/service	Developing relationships & distribution network
Profile	All relevant stakeholders	The organisation	Building reputation

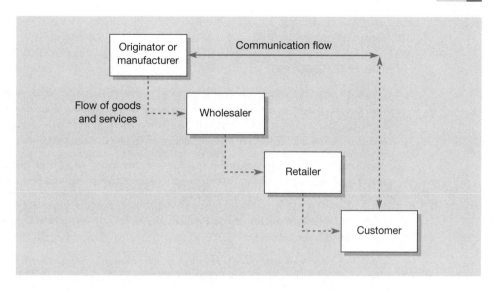

Figure 10.2 Direction of communication in a pull strategy

Push strategies

A second group, or type of target audience, can be identified, namely those organisations that buy products and services, perform some added value activity and move the product through the marketing channel network.

The 'trade' channel has received increased attention in recent years, as the strategic value of intermediaries has become more apparent. As channel networks have developed, so their increasing complexity has impacted on marketing communications strategies and tools. The expectations of buyers in these networks have risen in line with the significance attached to them by manufacturers. The power of multiple retailers, such as Tesco, Sainsbury's and Asda, is such that they are able to dictate terms (including the marketing communications) to many manufacturers of branded goods.

A push strategy involves communications that influence other trade channel organisations, encouraging them to take stock, allocate resources (for example shelf space) and become fully aware of key attributes and benefits associated with each product, with a view to adding value prior to further channel transactions. This strategy is designed to encourage resale to other members of the network and contribute to the achievement of their own objectives. This approach is aimed at 'pushing' the product down through the channel towards the end users for consumption (see Figure 10.3).

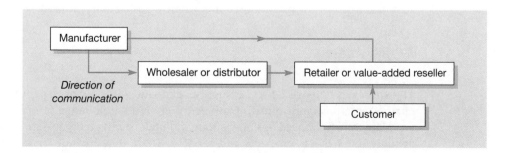

Figure 10.3 Direction of communication in a push strategy

HITACHI NOTEBOOKS

In order to enter the competitive US notebook market, Hitachi had to become a recognised top-10 player in order to have any chance of succeeding. Part of the strategy focused on developing relationships with key stakeholders, increasing representation and perception in the distribution channel and also raising the profile of the Hitachi brand.

To accomplish this a public relations strategy was developed which was geared to supporting advertising, tradeshows, events, web, collateral, direct mail and related sales and marketing programmes. In addition it aimed to:

- capture immediate awareness and market share-of-voice, using enduring messaging and strong sales support;

- create solid industry relationships with key 'influencers' to establish credibility, mindshare, and foster long-term interest for the company, products and key corporate executives;

- develop and communicate unique brand attributes, the corporate vision, customer promises, and market and product positioning points that create compelling reasons to buy.

A whole range of public relations activities were used but one was targeted at members of the various marketing channels. This involved creating and conveying channel news, related stories and features in order to generate widespread channel awareness.

Within six months of launch, Hitachi PC secured IDC and Dataquest rankings as a top-10 notebook company, secured key business and channel accounts with industry leaders, including: Ingram Micro, TechData, CompUSA and others and grew the channel reseller base to include over 2,000 Hitachi authorised resellers.

Source: Adapted from www.mhpr.com/Hitachi%20PC%20Case.htm (Accessed 14 December 2003.)

Marketing communications targeted at people involved in organisational buying decisions are characterised by an emphasis on personal selling. Trade advertising, trade sales promotions and public relations all have an important yet secondary role to play. Direct marketing has become increasingly important and the development of the Internet has had a profound impact on B2B communications and interorganisational relationships. However, personal selling has traditionally been the most significant part of the promotional mix where a push strategy is used.

Profile strategies

The strategies considered so far involve dialogue with customers (pull) and trade channel intermediaries (push). However, there is a whole range of other stakeholders, many of whom need to know about and understand an organisation rather than actually purchase its products and services. These may include financial analysts, trade unions, government bodies, employees or the local community. Different stakeholder groups can influence the organisation in diverse ways and thus need to receive (and respond to) varied types of messages. So, financial analysts need to know about financial and trading performance and expectations, the local community may be interested in employment and the impact of the organisation on the local environment, whereas the government may be interested in the way the organisation applies health and safety regulations and pays VAT, corporation and other taxes.

Traditionally, these organisationally orientated activities have been referred to as corporate communications, as they deal more or less exclusively with the corporate entity. Products, services and other offerings are not normally the focus of these communications. It is the organisation and its role, in the context of the particular stakeholders' activities, that is important. However, as more corporate brands appear, the distinction between corporate and marketing communications is becoming much less clear. Indeed, in the light of the development of, and interest in, internal marketing and communications, it may be better to consider corporate messages as part of an organisation's overall marketing communications activity.

Communications to satisfy this array of stakeholder needs and the organisation's corporate promotional goals are developed through what is referred to as a **profile** strategy, major elements of which are corporate branding and reputation management.

The awareness, perception and attitudes of stakeholders towards an organisation need to be understood, shaped and acted upon. This can be accomplished though continual dialogue, which will lead to the development of trust and commitment and enable relationships to grow. This is necessary in order that stakeholders act favourably towards an organisation, enabling strategies to flourish and objectives to be achieved.

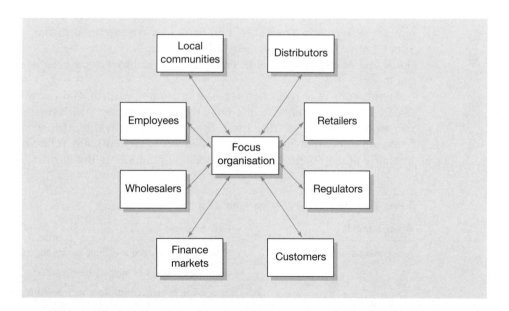

Figure 10.4 Direction of communication in a profile strategy

Within an overall strategy, individual approaches should be formulated to address the needs of a particular case. So, for example, the launch of a new office air-conditioning system will involve:

1 A push strategy to make distributors aware, educated, trained, motivated and stocked. The objectives would be to gain acceptance of the new system and to position it as an important source of new income streams for all distributors. Direct mail and personal selling, supported by trade sales promotions, web-based information plus service and support information will be the main promotional approaches.

2 A pull strategy to develop awareness about the system will then be needed, accompanied by appropriate public relations work in order to generate third-party credibility. Particular system (brand) associations will be created to position the brand in the minds of target audiences. Messages may be functional or expressive but they will endeavour to convey meanings, which encapsulate a brand promise. This may be accompanied, or followed, by the use of incentives to encourage presentations, demonstrations or a short trial of the product. To support the brand, third-party reference sites will need to be established plus product specification details, normally by way of both hardcopy sales literature and a web site.

B2B branding

Branding is a method commonly used in B2C markets to package information in order to provide differentiation, positioning opportunities and competitive advantage. The benefits that can accrue from branding have been articulated by many authors (Aaker, 1996 and Keller, 1998) and from an industrial marketing perspective (Shipley and Howard, 1993). Generally these distil into three main dimensions: functional and product use benefits, emotional and self-expressive benefits. These are set out in Table 10.3.

Brands consist of two main types of attribute: intrinsic and extrinsic (Riezebos, 2002). Intrinsic attributes are the properties of an offering, which if modified in some way would alter the offering itself. By way of contrast, the extrinsic attributes of a brand are those elements that if modified would not have any influence on the performance of the offering, in other words do not influence the intrinsic attributes. For

Table 10.3 Benefits derived from branding

Brand benefit	B2B example
Functional advantages	Product performance and high quality associations.
	Superior service and support associations.
	Specific application and/or location advantages.
Emotional advantages	Improved confidence and trust through a reduction in perceived risk.
Self-expressive advantages	Buyer-related personal and professional satisfaction.

example, the intrinsic attribute of a special lubricant used in a manufacturing process may be the constituent oils and its overall viscosity. The extrinsic attributes may be the name of the supplier or type of oil, the wording on, or the colours of, the containers in which the oil is delivered.

It has been alleged that B2B markets have been slow to develop brands and that product-based branding in them is a relatively underdeveloped area (Mudambi, 2002). This may stem from the nature of organisational decision making processes and associated group activities. Whatever the root cause, Mudambi states from her review of the literature and research that branding is not of equal significance to all organisational buyers, nor is it important in all B2B buying situations.

In comparison with consumer markets, the use of branding in B2B markets has appeared limited. However, work by Shipley and Howard (1993) and by Michell *et al.* (2001) suggests that brand strategies are used widely by industrial organisations, as product and corporate branding can be crucial contributors to successful performance. A partnership might develop whereby the brand, among other things, reassures a customer and the customer supports the brand by paying the price premium that the brand demands. As a result, brands can not only provide solutions on a continuous basis for certain customers but they may also become integral to a long-term relationship.

To build corporate brands, organisations must develop modern, integrated communication programmes with all of their key stakeholder groups. Stakeholders demand transparency, accountability and instant, often online, access to news, developments, research and networks. This means that inconsistent or misleading information must be avoided. As if to reinforce this, a survey reported by Gray (2000) found that CEOs rated the reputation of their organisations as more important than that of their products. However, the leading contributors to the strength of a corporate brand are seen to be their products and services, followed by a strong management team, internal communications, public relations, social accountability, change management and the personal reputation of the CEO.

Mudambi suggests that there are three types, or clusters, of B2B customers based upon the way they each perceive the importance of branding in the organisational purchase decision process. The highly tangible, brand receptive and low interest clusters reflect differing attitudes towards B2B brands. From this base, marketing communications can be developed more sympathetically and effectively. Note the link between segmentation and communications:

- the highly tangible cluster require messages that stress quantifiable and objective benefits of the product and company;

- the brand receptive cluster require messages that emphasise the support of a well-established and highly reputable manufacturer, the emotional and self-expressive benefits should be stressed;

- the low interest cluster are more likely to respond to brand-based communications that highlight the importance of the purchase decision and which are supported with processes and procedures that assist the ordering systems. Communications need to stimulate interest in the product and associated purchase decision, perhaps by using testimonials and mini-cases highlighting customers who have experienced similar purchase situations.

It is accepted by Mudambi that the research and data from which these clusters have been derived is not totally reliable, nor is the information based on anything other than judgement and experience. However, it is a useful step forward because Mudambi demonstrates that B2B branding opportunities are currently under-exploited.

Co-branding

Co-branding strategies provide organisations with an opportunity to promote their distinct corporate brands as one unique offering that represents superior customer value and is difficult to replicate (Prince and Davies, 2002).

Interesting aspects of co-branding are the processes and relationships associated with its evolution and development. Unlike strategic alliances, which commence with a formal contract, are usually long term and frequently involve substantial investment or equity adjustments, co-branding arrangements often start with informal information exchanges (Gundlach and Murphy, 1993). These arrangements progress to formalised contracts but only for a relatively short-term period, normally less than a year. Short-term contracts allow for renewal on a roll-over basis, but also offer each party an opportunity to either terminate or build the relationship. Co-branding arrangements can develop into strategic alliances as the relationship becomes established.

While there are a number of market-related factors that are important to the eventual success of a co-branding arrangement, choice of partner and the relative fit of the brands, as perceived by the market, is critical.

Planning B2B marketing communication activities

Planning is not the same as strategy, although the two terms are often used interchangeably. Promotional strategy is about the choice of audience and what is to be communicated. Planning is usually about the formalisation and articulation of the strategy. This process is necessary to ensure that activities are coordinated, coherent and can be delegated and implemented within available resource constraints.

SNAPSHOT 10.4

CO-BRANDING BY HERTZ AND BRITISH AIRWAYS

Hertz the car rental company and British Airways use a co-branding strategy in order to develop competitive advantage. British Airways regard the partnership as a means of adding value for their customers, simply because air passengers very often require car hire facilities and the partnership enables them to offer a seamless transport package. For Hertz there is access to the details of BA's 2 million frequent flyers, whose segment characteristics are remarkably similar to their own market.

As a result the partners share a database and jointly target particular groups of travellers offering distinct services and exclusive deals. Each organisation openly promotes the other as a brand partner. This creates more exposure and allows for each of the partner's brand values to be associated with the other.

Source: Adapted from Prince and Davies (2002).

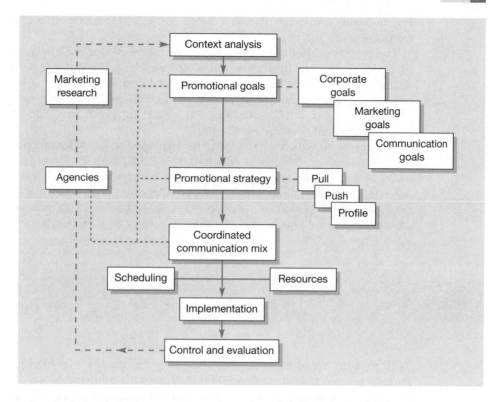

Figure 10.5 The marketing communications planning framework

Planning has an internal orientation. Marketing communications strategy has an external orientation, concerned as it is with the timing of, and approach adopted to, communication with customers and stakeholders. It must be formulated, in the context of overall business and marketing strategies, in order to encourage dialogue with selected stakeholders.

So, a marketing communications plan is concerned with the development and managerial processes involved in the articulation of an organisation's marketing communication strategy. There is little doubt that planning and strategy are interlinked but it is useful to consider strategy as something that is audience and externally centred and planning which is resource and internally orientated.

The marketing communications planning framework (MCPF) set out at Figure 10.5 brings together various marketing communications activities into a logical sequence of events. Working hierarchically, the rationale for promotional decisions is built upon information generated at previous levels in the framework. It also provides a checklist of activities that need to be considered.

The MCPF represents a way of understanding the different promotional components, appreciating the way in which they relate to one another and a means of writing coherent plans in order to communicate effectively with other organisations.

The MCPF embodies a sequence of decisions that marketing managers undertake when preparing, implementing and evaluating communication strategies and plans. It should not be taken to mean that this sequence represents an immutable reality; indeed, many marketing decisions are made outside any recognisable framework. However, as a means of understanding the different components, appreciating the way in which they relate to one another and bringing together various aspects for work, the MCPF can be useful.

The process of marketing communications, however, is not linear, as depicted in this framework, but integrative and interdependent. It requires a perspective that enables messages to be developed from an understanding of the real dynamics and characteristics of a relationship. To that extent, this approach recognises the value of stakeholder theory and the need to build partnerships with buyers and other organisations networked with the organisation.

The degree to which these plans are developed varies across organisations and some rely on their agencies to undertake this work for them. However, there can be major benefits from in-house planning, for example by involving and discussing issues internally and developing a sense of ownership. Many small and medium-sized organisations can benefit from developing their own promotional plans and avoid the costs associated with agencies undertaking this work on their behalf.

Strategic drift and balance

With so many variables, and an external environment that is subject to tremendous and often rapid change, promotional strategy within organisations can be seen to drift and move away from its central message. Conceptually, the only way to correct drift is to change the marketing communications strategy by an amount according to the degree to which messages have drifted. This might be best observed at Figure 10.6.

Line B suggests that if current marketing communications remain as they are then the size of the gap with the central theme of marketing communications will widen and any attempt to get back will become increasingly large and expensive.

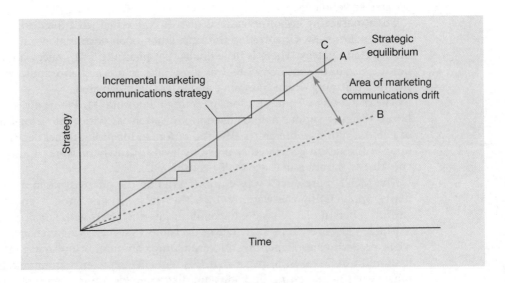

Figure 10.6 Drift in marketing communications strategy

Line C depicts a brand that has adapted its marketing communications on a more frequent basis (than B) and as a result follows an incremental strategy, one that results in a more consistent message. This concept might be interpreted in terms of positioning and repositioning brands and the changing of agencies in order to revitalise and change the direction of the communications strategy currently being pursued.

While the pull, push and profile strategies are important, it should be remembered that they are not mutually exclusive. Indeed, in most organisations it is possible to identify an element of each strategy at any one time. In reality, most organisations are structured in such a way that those responsible for communications with each of these three main audiences do so without reference to, or coordination with, each other.

Recognising these common organisational limitations, the 3Ps should be considered as part of a total communication effort. Figure 10.7 depicts how the emphasis of a total communication strategy can shift according to the needs of the various target audiences, resources and wider elements such as the environment and the competition. The marketing communications eclipse provides a visual interpretation of the balance between the three strategic dimensions. The more that is revealed of any one single strategy the greater its role in any campaign. Conversely, the less that is revealed the smaller the contribution. In any one campaign, one or two of the three strategies might be used in preference to another and will often reflect branding approaches.

The role of each element of the promotional mix is important in the implementation of promotional strategy. Each tool has different strengths and should be used accordingly. For example, direct marketing and personal selling are the more commonly used tools to reach B2B audiences used in conjunction with print and web-based media. A profile strategy designed to change perception and understanding of the organisation is more likely to utilise public relations and corporate advertising.

As a final comment on marketing communications strategy, it is necessary to recognise that different internal audiences and coalitions often have conflicting proposals. In other words there is a political element to be considered and there may also be a strong overriding culture that not only directs the communication strategy but may also hinder innovation or the development of alternative methods of communication.

In order that marketing communications campaigns be successful, good working relationships between all the parties involved with the campaign are necessary. These

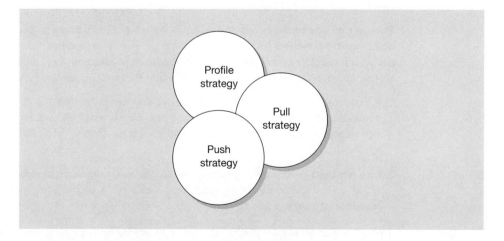

Figure 10.7 Marketing communications strategic eclipse

include strong managerial leadership, consultation and agreement between all the parties involved and a clear schedule and prioritisation of activities. The development of a marketing communications plan facilitates this process and enables the strategy to be articulated in such a way that the goals can be achieved in a timely, efficient and effective manner.

Interorganisational communication

The vital role that communication plays in determining the effectiveness of any group or network of organisations is widely recognised (Grabner and Rosenberg, 1969; Stern and El-Ansary, 1992). According to Mohr and Nevin (1990, p. 36), communication is 'the glue that holds together a marketing channel'. From a managerial perspective, it is acknowledged to be important because many of the causes of tension and conflict in interorganisational relationships stem from inadequate or poor communication. Likewise, good interorganisational relationships stem from appropriate communication between members. Communication within networks serves not only to provide persuasive information and foster participative decision making, but also provides for coordination, the exercise of power and the encouragement of loyalty and commitment, which might reduce the likelihood of tension and conflict.

Channel networks consist of those organisations with which others must cooperate directly to achieve their own objectives. By accepting that there is interdependence,

SNAPSHOT 10.5

FORD DEALERS ARE 'INTERNET APPROVED'.

Ford USA introduced a web-based programme designed to help customers with web research. Ford's 6,000 dealers were required not only to participate in the Ford Internet training programme but also dedicate an Internet manager resource at their dealership.

The intention was to create a digital resource, based on Ford's own rigorous standards, which enabled dealers to be 'Internet Approved'. Such dealerships would help customers search for cars, parts and even build custom-made vehicles. In addition, the Internet approved scheme has achieved a number of interesting strategic changes.

1 It encouraged dealers to help maintain customer relationships and assist with purchasing decisions, through customised web pages, email and instant messaging. This remote management of customer relationships has helped Ford collect and build relationships directly with customers while avoiding conflict with its dealer channel.

2 Ford has used its extensive dealership network to push customers to web transacting, allowing Ford to decrease operating costs, better track and forecast inventory and capture customer purchasing data.

Source: Adapted from Matta and Mehta (2001), www.141XM.com/white_paper/channel_conflict.html (Accessed 3 December 2003.) Used with permission.

usually dispersed unequally throughout the network, it is possible to identify organisations that have a stronger/weaker position within a network. Communication must travel not only between the different levels of dependency and role ('up and down' in a channel context) in bidirectional flows, but also across similar levels of dependency and role, that is, horizontal flows. For example, these may be from retailer to retailer or wholesaler to wholesaler.

Some specialised messages need to be distributed across a variety of networks, for example those proclaiming technological advances, business acquisitions and contracts won. It is also apparent that communication flows do not change radically over the short term. On the contrary, they become established and regularised through use. This facilitates the emergence of specialised communication networks. Furthermore, it is common for networks to be composed of sub-networks, overlaying each other. The complexity of an organisation's networks can be such that unravelling any or every one could be dysfunctional.

It is necessary to establish those elements that contribute to the general communications in a B2B situation, and a marketing channel environment in particular. The development of a planned, channel-orientated communications strategy, a push strategy, should be based on identifiable elements that contribute to and reinforce the partnerships in the network. A number of these can be identified, namely the movement of flows of information and, in particular, the timing and permanence of the flows (Stern and El-Ansary, 1992). It should also take into account the various facets of communication and the particular channel structures through which communications are intended to move (Mohr and Nevin, 1990). These will now be considered in turn.

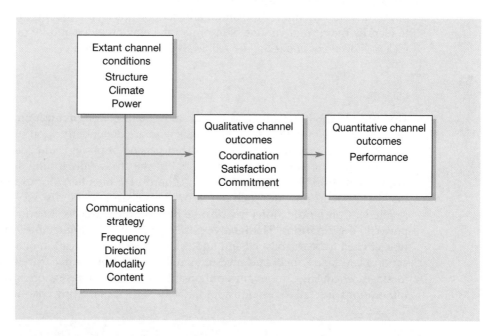

Figure 10.8 A model of communication for marketing channels

Source: Mohr and Nevin (1990). Used with permission.

Channel-based marketing communications

Mohr and Nevin suggest that that the success of a marketing channel is mainly a result of the interaction between the channel structure and the communications used between members. Figure 10.8 depicts the relationships between communication strategies and structure. Thus, by examining the constituent elements and moulding the variables to meet the channel conditions, it may be possible to enhance the performance/success of the network.

Communication facets

Communication strategy within a channel results from a combination of four facets of communication. These are frequency, direction, modality and content.

Frequency

The amount of contact between members of a network should be assessed. Too much information (too frequent, aggregate volume or pure repetition), can overload members and have a dysfunctional effect. Too little information can undermine the opportunities for favourable performance outcomes by failing to provide necessary operational information, motivation and support. As a consequence, it is important to identify the current volume of information being provided and for management to make a judgement about the desired levels of communication.

Direction

This refers to the horizontal and vertical movement of communication within a network. Each network consists of members who are dependent upon others, but the level of dependency will vary – hence the dispersion of power is unequal.

Communications can be unidirectional in that they flow in one direction only. This may be from a source of power to subordinate members (for example, from a major IT systems provider such as Cisco, to small and medium-sized distributors or resellers). Communications can also be bidirectional, that is, to and from equally powerful organisations. The relative power positions of manufacturer/producer and reseller need to be established and understood prior to the creation of any communication plan. Many small and medium-sized organisations suffer from unidirectional messages where larger more powerful organisational customers ignore incoming communications and fail to respond appropriately to their marketing channel partners.

Modality

Modality refers to the method used to transmit information. Mohr and Nevin agree that there is a wide variety of interpretations of the methods used to convey information. They use modality in the sense that communications can be either formal and regulated, such as meetings and written reports, or informal and spontaneous, such as corridor conversations and word-of-mouth communications, often carried out away from an organisation's formal structures and environment.

Content

This refers to what is said. Frazier and Summers (1984) distinguish between direct and indirect influence strategies. Direct strategies are designed to change behaviour by specific request (recommendations, promises and appeals to legal obligations). Indirect strategies attempt to change a receiver's beliefs and attitudes about the desirability of the intended behaviour. This may take the form of an information exchange, where the source uses discussions about general business issues to influence the attitudes of the receiver.

Channel structures

Communication facets can be seen in the light of three particular channel conditions: structure, climate and power.

Channel structure

Channel structure, according to Stern and El-Ansary (1988), can be distinguished by the nature of the exchange relationship. These are relational and discrete relationships. Relational exchanges have a long-term perspective and high interdependence, and involve joint decision making. Discrete or market exchanges are by contrast *ad hoc* and hence have a short-term orientation where interdependence is low (see Chapter 1).

Channel climate

Anderson, Lodish and Weitz (1987) used measures of trust and goal compatibility in defining organisational climate. This in turn can be interpreted as the degree of mutual supportiveness that exists between channel members.

Power

Dwyer and Walker (1981) showed that power conditions within a channel can be symmetrical (with power balanced between members), or asymmetrical (with a power imbalance). Table 10.4 shows the relationships between communication facets and channel conditions. This is the combination of elements identified above.

Two specific forms of communication strategy can be identified. The first is a combination referred to as a 'collaborative communication strategy' and includes higher frequency, more bidirectional flows, informal modes and indirect content. This combination is likely to occur in channel conditions of relational structures, supportive climates or symmetrical power. The second combination is referred to as an 'autonomous communication strategy' and includes lower frequency, more unidirectional communication, formal modes and direct content. This combination is likely to occur in channel conditions of market structures, unsupportive climates and asymmetrical power.

Table 10.4 The relationships between channel conditions and the facets of communication

Channel conditions	Communication facets			
	Frequency	Direction	Content	Modality
Structure				
Relational	Higher	More bidirectional	More indirect	More informal
Market	Lower	More unidirectional	More direct	More formal
Climate				
Supportive	Higher	More bidirectional	More indirect	More informal
Unsupportive	Lower	More undirectional	More direct	More informal
Power				
Symmetrical	Higher	More bidirectional	More indirect	More informal
Asymmetrical	Lower	More undirectional	More indirect	More informal

Source: Mohr and Nevin (1990). Used with the permission of the American Marketing Association.

Communication strategy should, therefore, be built upon the characteristics of the situation facing each organisation in any particular network. Not all networks share the same conditions, nor do they all possess the same degree of closeness or relational expectations. By considering the nature of the channel conditions and then developing communication strategies that complement them, the performance of the focus organisation and other members can be considerably improved, and conflict and tension substantially reduced. Where channel conditions match communication strategy, the outcomes are likely to be enhanced (Mohr and Nevin, 1990). Likewise, when the communication strategy fails to match the channel conditions, the outcomes are not likely to be enhanced (see Figure 10.9).

The shaded areas represent enhanced outcome levels, or where communication strategies fit channel conditions. The unshaded areas represent non-enhanced outcome levels, or where communication strategies do not fit channel conditions.

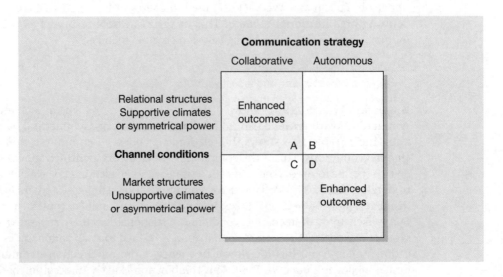

Figure 10.9 Proposed relationships between communication strategies and channel conditions

Source: From Mohr and Nevin (1990). Used with permission.

Timing of the flows

Message flows can be either simultaneous or serial. Where **simultaneous** flows occur, messages are distributed to all members so that the information is received at approximately the same time. Business seminars and dealer meetings, together with direct mail promotional activities and the use of integrated IT systems between levels (overnight ordering procedures), are examples of this type of flow. **Serial** flows involve the transmission of messages so that they are received by a preselected number of network members who then transmit the message to others at lower levels within the network. Serial flows may lead to problems concerning the management of the network, such as those concerning stock levels and production.

Permanence of the flows

The degree of permanence that a message has is determined by the technology used in the communication process. Essentially, the more a message can be recalled with-

---

SNAPSHOT 10.6

VIDEO CONFERENCING FOR SIMULTANEOUS COMMUNICATIONS

Video conferencing enables the same message to be communicated at the same time to audiences at any location. This provides for message effectiveness and minimises information discrepancy.

Coutant Lambda, a manufacturer of power supply equipment, uses video conferencing to demonstrate and discuss their designs and products with overseas suppliers and customers, as well as their own international offices. The company uses the facility to develop new products in partnership with overseas component manufacturers because it is easier for engineers to discuss product specifications, especially when multi-lingual discussions are involved.

The International Trade Development Centre in Taunton, a collaborative project between Somerset Training and Enterprise Council, Business Link Somerset and the Chamber of Commerce and Industry, provides video conferencing facilities for SMEs so that they can link up with the 'Somerset office' in Brussels and British embassies across the world. The major advantage for companies in the region is that they can have face-to-face contact with their own representative in Brussels, and quickly clarify the impact of EU legislation without the delays introduced by traditional lines of communication.

ActionAid is a charity that works from three UK locations. Through video conferencing it has become possible to hold daily staff meetings. Not only does this improve internal communications but the faster response rates being achieved reflect improved communication effectiveness.

Source: Adapted from Midland Communications, www.midlandcomms.co.uk/clients/casestudies/charity.shtml (Accessed 5 December 2003.) Used with permission.

out physical distortion of the content, the more permanent the flow. This would indicate that the use of machines to record the message content would have an advantage over person-to-person messages transmitted at a sales meeting. Permanence can be improved by recording the meeting with a tape recorder or by putting the conversation on paper and using handouts and sales literature.

Therefore, the nature and form of the cooperation and the interorganisational relationships that develop from the exchanges influence the nature of the marketing communication activities used. The degree of cooperation between organisations will vary and part of the role of marketing communications is to develop and support the relationships that exist between partner organisations.

In this sector organisations buy products and services and they use processes and procedures that can involve a large number of people. Fuller details about these characteristics can be found in Chapter 5. What is central, however, is the decision making unit and the complexities associated with the variety of people and processes involved in making organisational purchase decisions and the implications for suppliers in terms of the length of time and nature of the communication mix and messages necessary to reduce the levels of risk inherent in these situations.

Propensity to share information

A relatively new and interesting perspective on marketing channels concerns the quality of the communications and the success that might be attributed to the communication behaviours of the partners in any loose or tight networks.

Mohr and Sohi (1995) considered whether communication quality might be a function of the propensity of members to share information. The inclination among members to share information could be assumed to be positive in channels and networks where members show high levels of trust and commitment. Frequency of communication flows, the level of bidirectional communications in a network and the level of communication formality are assumed to be the main elements of the propensity to share information.

Another aspect considered by the researchers was the degree to which information might be withheld or distorted (deviance). Information deviance might be high when there is an absence of rules (norms) determining what information needs to be communicated. Informality may lead to vagueness or inattentiveness and higher levels of deviance.

The research sought to determine whether any (or all) of the three factors indicated that there was a link between the variables and the quality of information perceived by channel members. The results suggested that in the sample sector (computer dealers) the only significant variable was the frequency of information. The higher the frequency of communications received by channel members, the higher the perception of the quality of the communications. Issues concerning information overload and irritance are discounted.

Satisfaction levels appear to be correlated with higher levels of bidirectional communications. So, frequency impacts on perceived quality (and hence satisfaction) and the degree of bidirectional communications is significant in determining levels of satisfaction with the communications in a channel (network) environment.

Relationship-based marketing communications

From a relationship perspective, marketing communications can perform different yet significant roles as relationships evolve. Some of these are set out in Table 10.5.

At a higher level, the communication process not only supports transactions, by either differentiating, reinforcing, informing or persuading, but also offers intangible benefits, such as the psychological satisfactions generated by, for example, being associated with particular or prominent organisations. Communications can also be regarded as a means of perpetuating and transferring values and culture to different parts of society or networks, increasingly important for multi-national organisations and in situations of merger and acquisition. Internal marketing communications can be instrumental in developing organisational culture through not only the development of internal organisation identification but also externally through brand and product recognition and perception.

Other examples of these intangible satisfactions can be seen in the recognition of the need to communicate with various audiences about non-product issues. Communication concerning organisational ethics and corporate governance issues are becoming increasingly significant for a range of audiences. Part of the value that can be offered by organisations is in the quality and regularity of their communications together with their propensity to share information with various external audiences. Marketing communications, therefore, can be regarded as a means of gaining advantage by being 'of value' to audiences. A consequence of this could be a positive impact on corporate reputation.

It has been a established in this book, as elsewhere, that organisations do not exist in isolation from each other: each one is part of a wider system of corporate entities,

Table 10.5 The different relationship roles of marketing communications

Relationship stage	Role of marketing communications
Acquisition	Differentiation to establish position.
	Information about organisational credentials and product features.
	Persuasion to stimulate behavioural action.
Development	Differentiation and information provision predominate as organisations become increasingly open and reveal more about themselves. Increasing levels of trust emerge as the boundaries of the relationship become established.
Retention	The provision of knowledge and sharing of information becomes regularised and a common part of the relationship. Reinforcement messages, based on both reminding and reinforcing, are used to provide trust and commitment in order to support valued relationships.
Decline	Discrete relationships resort to persuasion in order to extract remaining value from the relationship.

where each enters into a series of exchanges to secure raw material inputs or resources and to discharge them as value added outputs to other organisations in the network. The exchanges that organisations enter into require the formation of relationships, however tenuous or strong. Andersson (1992) looks at the strength of the relationship between organisations in a network, and refers to them as 'loose or tight couplings'. These couplings, or partnerships, are influenced by the communications that are transmitted and received. The role that organisations assume in a network and the manner in which they undertake and complete their tasks are, in part, shaped by the variety and complexity of the communications in transmission throughout the network. Issues of channel or even network control, leadership, subservience and conflict are implanted in the form and nature of the communications exchanged in any network.

Agency/client relationships

One final area to be considered concerns the nature of the relationships formed between clients and their various marketing communications partner organisations, most notably advertising agencies, although the ideas that follow apply equally to a host of different marketing facilitators. These relationships have a service sector, buyer–seller orientation and so aspects of trust, commitment, conflict and relationship cycles, covered elsewhere in this book, apply here. However, the quality of agency/client relationships is influenced strongly by the nature of the interaction between the parties. Therefore, the behaviours of both parties and the performance of the agency in meeting the needs of the client frame the overall quality of the relationship and influence the disposition of the client towards either maintaining or dissolving the relationship (LaBahn and Kohli, 1997).

Wackman *et al.*, (1989) argue that productive interaction and relationships that are essentially harmonious lead to superior working relationships. A statement of the obvious perhaps, but research has shown that the most common reason for clients terminating agency agreements is dissatisfaction with performance and that normally means a failure of the creative design and implementation processes, as perceived by the client (Mitchell *et al.*, 1992). It follows therefore that a relationship characterised by productive interaction (for example positive meetings), and a willingness to share both formal and informal information are more likely to generate more creative solutions. When these factors are paired with diligent agency implementation and frequent feedback to the client, thus engaging the client in the process, higher levels of trust, commitment and overall perceived agency performance will emerge. When these positive, collaborative conditions exist it is likely that clients will view the costs associated with developing other, alternative agency relationships as suitably unattractive and will be more positively inclined to sustain current arrangements (Moorman *et al.*, 1992).

This emphasis on the nature and character of the working relationship and the importance of agency performance suggests that the use of IS&T might be beneficial. Global and multi-national advertising agencies work with a variety of clients generating

SNAPSHOT 10.7

B2B PORTALS FOR HAVAS

Havas, a large advertising agency operating across 131 countries developed a web-based system to improve internal and external interaction, collaboration and to manage the huge and increasing volumes of data and information. However, it found that it did not have the most effective tools to structure and manage the increasing levels of information, and navigation became problematic.

The organisation developed a B2B portal to enable them to manage their diverse and globally distributed agencies. The goal was to enable the agencies and their clients to work more closely together with improved rapport. The portal's features include content authoring and categorisation, threaded discussions, personnel directories, calendars, templates for campaign tracking, as well as document routing and management.

Source: Adapted from www.kandasoft.com/success_GEM2.html (Accessed 29 October 2003.) Used with permission.

high volumes and a broad variety of materials (for example storyboards, design and copy for print advertisements, media plans). Traditional methods of communications, such as telephone and mail, are often slow and inefficient. Faster alternatives, such as overnight delivery and couriers, can become expensive as projects pass through multiple review cycles. Even e-mail has limited application (see Snapshot 10.7).

Table 10.6 Key criteria for agency/client portals

Criteria	Explanation
Simplicity of creation and operation	Client portals need to be easy for the company's account teams. A template-based system can save time, reducing duplication of effort and bringing consistency to the construction and ongoing management of such sites.
Low maintenance	The system should have built-in capabilities to keep every portal site organised and running properly with minimal intervention.
Flexible and comprehensive	The system must accommodate graphical images, audio and video files and common office documents. In addition, multi-lingual capability is required.
Solid security	The system requires security features that instil confidence in the agency clients and guarantee that unauthorised personnel cannot see or access documents or collaborative areas.
Powerful and accurate searching	With the large number of documents, these systems require a powerful search capability for both document content and Meta data.

Source: Adapted from www.kandasoft.com/success (Accessed 29 October 2003.) Used with permission.

The development of a B2B portal for the advertising agency Havas, cited in Snapshot 10.7 required the identification of five criteria. These are set out in Table 10.6.

The success of B2B portals can be measured in terms of time savings and cost reductions. However, there are a range of other benefits associated with the ease of use and maintenance of a wide range of documents. In addition, there is improved collaboration and link management facilities, which are regarded as an important factor when attempting to improve agency performance and reduce client turnover. As part of the process of enhancing client interaction, a number of features and benefits accrue to the user and their networks. These can be seen at Table 10.7.

Havas claim their portal has increased efficiency and saved time and money. Turnaround times for client approval of creative work have been significantly reduced, by as much as 50 per cent. The ability to manage global research and creative materials within the agency's network has improved dramatically as has staff's willingness to share knowledge among account teams. As a result, account teams now have more time to focus on strategic planning and delivering greater value to their clients. The agency can now communicate rapidly and more efficiently with clients giving both the agency and their clients an improved quality of interaction and a positive working relationship. Through the use of IS&T this case demonstrates the opportunities to improve agency/client relationships and reduce client turnover.

Table 10.7 Features and benefits of using a portal within an advertising agency

Feature	Benefit
Content organisation	Workspace views, links to other web pages and news updates.
Productivity tools	Secure, threaded discussions to foster and enhance collaboration; directories with phone listings; calendar functions; and templates for campaign tracking.
Document routing and management	Expedites the review and approval process and improves workflow. This includes document version controls, distribution list maintenance and automated notification agents to alert clients and account teams when new content is added or modifications are made to existing content.
Server architecture	A distributed architecture that allows several GEM servers to function as a single server. This brings increased scalability, improved load balancing and distribution, and a higher degree of reliability to the agency's portal environment.
Administrative functions	Activity audit trail reports, user profile maintenance, user definitions and access privileges and default view definitions.

Source: Adapted from www.kandasoft.com/success (Accessed 29 October 2003.) Used with permission.

Summary

Marketing communications play an important strategic role within B2B marketing. All the tools of the promotional mix have a role to play, depending upon the context of the communications. Essentially, marketing communications should be used to differentiate, reinforce, inform or persuade target audiences to think or behave in a particular way about an organisation or its products, or issues that are pertinent to both parties.

The development of push, pull and profile strategies reflect an audience perspective for marketing communications. This is important if meaningful relationships are to be developed and sustained with various stakeholder audiences. At the heart of effective B2B promotional activities is a sound understanding of organisational buyer behaviour and the various types of people who can be involved in the buying process. This information is necessary not only for segmentation processes but also in terms of developing product offerings that represent significant values and in terms of the most effective way of reaching them through effective communications.

Understanding some of the ideas about marketing channel-based communications is critical to B2B marketing. Not only is this a specialised, sometimes neglected, area, channel-based communications concern a central aspect of interorganisational strategy, namely the management of significant relationships. From a network perspective, these relationships and the associated dialogues, in terms of what, when and how something is said, can determine the length of interorganisational associations. Co-branding represents a short-term approach to joint communications, whereas strategic alliances signify a more permanent relationship. Whatever the dimension or form of relationship, the success of B2B marketing communications are to a very large extent underpinned by the willingness of all parties to share information with one another.

Discussion questions

1 Explain each of the four aspects of the DRIP framework and find examples of B2B marketing communications that illustrate each of these elements.

2 Write brief notes explaining the differences between promotional strategy and planning. Without referring to the text, attempt to draw the marketing communications planning framework.

3 Discuss the extent to which interorganisational relationships can be influenced by marketing communications.

4 Critically appraise the Mohr and Nevin model of channel-based marketing communications.

5 Evaluate the terms, BTI, ELM and strategic eclipse.

6 Explain the three brand clusters identified by Mudambi and discuss the potential for branding in B2B marketing.

References

Aaker, D.A. (1996). *Building Strong Brands*, New York, NY: The Free Press.

Anderson, E., Lodish, L. and Weitz, B. (1987). 'Resource allocation behaviour in conventional channels', *Journal of Marketing Research*, (February), pp. 85–97.

Andersson, P. (1992). 'Analysing distribution channel dynamics: loose and tight coupling in distraction networks', *European Journal of Marketing*, 26, 2, pp. 47–68.

Dwyer, R. and Walker, O.C. (1981). 'Bargaining in an asymmetrical power structure', *Journal of Marketing*, 45 (Winter), pp. 104–15.

Frazier, G.L. and Summers, J.O. (1984). 'Interfirm influence strategies and their application within distribution channels', *Journal of Marketing*, 48 (Summer), pp. 43–55.

Gilliland, D.I. and Johnston, W.J. (1997). 'Towards a model of marketing communications effects', *Industrial Marketing Management*, 26, pp. 15–29.

Grabner, J.R. and Rosenberg, L.J. (1969). 'Communications theory in distribution channels', in L. Stern (ed.), *Distribution Channels: Behavioural Dimensions*, Boston, MA: Houghton Mifflin, pp. 227–52.

Gray, R. (2000). 'The chief encounter', *PR Week*, 8 September, pp. 13–16.

Gundlach, G.T. and Murphy, P.E. (1993). 'Ethical and legal foundations of relational market exchanges', *Journal of Marketing*, 57, 4 (October), pp. 35–46.

Keller, K.L. (1998). *Strategic Brand Management: Building, Measuring and Managing Brand Equity*, Upper Saddle River, NY: Prentice Hall.

LaBahn, D.W. and Kohli, C. (1997). 'Maintaining client commitment in advertising agency–client relationships', *Industrial Marketing Management*, 26, pp. 497–508.

Matta, E. and Mehta, N (2001). 'Turning channel conflict into channel cooperation: a roadmap for manufacturers', 28 March, www.ccgxm.com/white_paper/channel_conflict.html (Accessed 3 December 2003.)

Michell, P., King, J. and Reast, J. (2001). 'Brand values related to industrial products', *Industrial Marketing Management*, 30, 5 (July) pp. 415–25.

Mitchell, P.C., Cataquet, H. and Hague, S. (1992). 'Establishing the causes of disaffection in agency–client relations', *Journal of Advertising Research*, 31, pp. 41–84.

Mohr, J. and Nevin, J.R. (1990). 'Communication strategies in marketing channels', *Journal of Marketing* (October), pp. 36–51.

Mohr, J. and Sohi, R.S. (1995). 'Communication flows in distribution channels: impact on assessments of communication quality and satisfaction', *Journal of Retailing*, 71, 4, pp. 393–416.

Moorman, C., Zaltman, G. and Deshpandé, R (1992). 'Relationships between providers and users of market research: the dynamics of trust within and between organisations', *Journal of Marketing Research*, 29, pp. 324–28.

Mudambi, S. (2002). 'Branding importance in business-to-business markets: three buyer clusters', *Industrial Marketing Management*, 31, 6 (September) pp. 525–33.

Petty, R.E. and Cacioppo, J.T. (1983). 'Central and peripheral routes to persuasion: application to advertising', in L. Percy and A. Woodside (eds), *Advertising and Consumer Psychology*, Lexington, MA : Lexington Books, pp. 3–23.

Prince, M. and Davies, M. (2002). 'Co-branding partners: what do they see in each other?', *Business Horizons*, September–October, pp. 51–5.

Riezebos, R. (2002). *Brand Management*, Harlow: Pearson Education.

Shipley, D. and Howard, P. (1993). 'Brand-naming industrial products', *Industrial Marketing Management*, 22, 1 (February), pp. 59–66.

Stern, L. and El-Ansary, A.I. (1988). *Marketing Channels*, Englewood Cliffs, NJ: Prentice Hall.

Stern, L. and El-Ansary, A.I. (1992). *Marketing Channels*, 4th edn, Englewood Cliffs, NJ: Prentice Hall.

van Riel, C.B.M. (1995). *Principles of Corporate Communication*, Hemel Hempstead: Prentice Hall.

Wackman, D.B., Salmon, C.T. and Salmon, C.C. (1989). 'Developing an advertising agency relationship', *Journal of Advertising Research*, 26, pp. 21–28.

Chapter 11

The tools of B2B
marketing communications

Chapter overview

The Internet and related technologies have had a profound impact on the way in which organisations communicate with each other. However, this is not to suggest that the influence of the traditional offline communication tools has waned, indeed it can be argued that marketing communications have been augmented by the application of new technologies.

In this chapter a distinction is made between the promotional tools and the media used to convey messages. Consideration is given to the key characteristics and effectiveness of each of the primary tools used in B2B marketing communications. It also considers both offline and online tools and examines the application of new media from a communication perspective. In addition, an overview of the main media used in the sector is also provided. However, readers are advised that a deeper review of these subjects can be found in specialised marketing communication texts.

Chapter aims

The aims of this chapter are to explore the main characteristics of each of the tools of the promotional mix and to determine their significance in business-to-business marketing.

Objectives

The objectives of this chapter are to:

1 Examine the key characteristics of the tools of the marketing communications mix.

2 Consider the degree to which the tools can be used to support one another.

3 Examine the role and application of databases in B2B marketing communications.

4 Determine fundamental criteria associated with the selection and use of particular tools.

5 Explore the promotional tools in terms of their digital applications.

6 Review the effectiveness of the tools relative to the organisational purchase decision process.

7 Determine the types and key characteristics of the main media used in the sector.

Introduction

The previous chapter considered strategic aspects of B2B marketing communications. Part of the implementation process is the utilisation and deployment of the marketing communication (or promotional) tools and media. When bundled together in various configurations, they help organisations achieve particular marketing goals. Tools and media should not be confused as they have different characteristics and serve to achieve different goals.

There are five principal marketing communications tools: advertising, sales promotion, public relations, direct marketing and personal selling (see Figure 11.1). These tools are used in different combinations to achieve a variety of tasks. In B2B marketing there is a greater emphasis on personal selling and direct marketing than the other tools. Indeed, there has been a dramatic rise in the use of direct-response media as direct marketing becomes an integral part of the marketing plan for many organisations and products.

The media are used to convey messages to audiences. There are a variety of media available, from television and newspapers to billboards and petrol-pump nozzles. Each has particular characteristics that enable it to reach distinctive audiences. Developments in digital technology have given rise to a mass of different media and ways in which organisations can communicate with each other. The plethora of new media has resulted in media **fragmentation**, a term indicating that audiences for each vehicle have decreased. This, in turn, creates a great media **'noise'** through which it becomes more difficult to be seen, heard and understood. This clutter is not a major problem for B2B marketing, in contrast to B2C, but the diversity and range of available media should not be underestimated. The development of the Internet has been a major influence on the manner and content of B2B marketing communications. The Internet and digital technologies have enabled organisations to engage in new interactive forms of communication with customers and other stakeholders. Studies undertaken by Bush *et al.* (1998) and Leong *et al.* (1998) found that the Internet was seen as a primary means of providing product information in the B2B sector, although users at that time had doubts about its ability to provide competitive advantage. Greater consideration is given to B2B media later in this chapter.

Figure 11.1 The tools of the promotional mix

The characteristics of each of the main promotional tools are now considered in turn. Some of the derivative tools that are particular to B2B marketing are also explored, before examining some of the more prominent media used. The chapter concludes with a view of the collective impact and effectiveness of the promotional mix as a whole.

Table 11.1 shows the key characteristics and relative effectiveness of the promotional tools across three main criteria, namely the ability of each to communicate, the costs involved and the control that management is able to maintain over each promotional tool.

Advertising and B2B communications

Advertising is a non-personal form of mass communication and offers a high degree of control for those responsible for the design and delivery of advertising messages. However, the ability of advertising to persuade target audiences to think or behave in a particular way is suspect. Furthermore, the effect on sales is extremely hard to measure. It also suffers from low credibility, in that audiences are less likely to believe messages delivered through advertising than they are messages received through some of the other tools.

In consumer markets, advertising is used a great deal because of its ability to reach a national or mass audience and its flexibility in communicating with a specialised segment. However, in the B2B market this capacity is not important and, as the associated costs can be extremely large, advertising is not the most effective means of communication and is therefore not the primary tool of the communications mix.

Table 11.1 A summary of the key characteristics of the tools of marketing communications

	Advertising	Sales promotion	Public relations	Personal selling	Direct marketing
Communications					
Ability to deliver a personal message	Low	Low	Low	High	High
Ability to reach a large audience	High	Medium	Medium	Low	Medium
Level of interaction	Low	Low	Low	High	High
Credibility given by target audience	Low	Medium	High	Medium	Medium
Costs					
Absolute costs	High	Medium	Low	High	Medium
Cost per contact	Low	Medium	Low	High	Medium
Wastage	High	Medium	High	Low	Low
Size of investment	High	Medium	Low	High	Medium
Control					
Ability to target particular audiences	Medium	High	Low	Medium	High
Management's ability to adjust the deployment of the tool as circumstances change	Medium	High	Low	Medium	High

SNAPSHOT 11.1

IBM'S USE OF ADVERTISING

IBM's 'Play to Win' campaign featured in the previous chapter sought to establish their market leadership credibility and the importance of a sound business infrastructure. It was targeted at CEOs, senior marketing and sales executives plus those executives responsible for contributing to planning and implementation activities.

The campaign consisted of several phases. In the launch phase IBM used a broad-based media mix. Using television as 'air-cover' under which all the other, more detailed and targeted messages were delivered through four-page advertisements containing UK and WW [World Wide] customer references across broad-based media (e.g. national and business press).

The momentum phase featured double page advertisements in business and IT press (tailored copy for each) – one advertisement per customer reference. The web was used for information purposes and banner advertisements were also taken to drive site traffic.

The issues phase dealt with current hot topics by audience (IT/LOB [Line of Business]) and detailed the IBM solution to these issues.

The vertical expertise phase demonstrated IBM's deep understanding of each of their focus industries and again provided customer references. Product issues were targeted at IT executives and sought to promote particular IBM offerings.

Source: Material kindly supplied by IBM.

Perhaps the most important roles of advertising in the B2B context are to inform and remind, whereas differentiation and persuasion are delivered through other tools of the promotional mix, namely public relations, direct marketing and personal selling. Apart from an increasing use of online advertising, used to drive website traffic and develop name awareness, the most important form is print advertising in trade journals and newspapers.

The use of online advertising is predominantly geared to driving website traffic and providing product and corporate information. In an environment where the prime objective of customers is to seek information, the use of banner advertisements, pop-ups, microsites and superstitials or interstitials, has a supportive rather than a lead communication role. B2B advertisers prefer to emphasise the informational aspect rather than the emotional, particularly when purchase decisions evoke high involvement and central route processing. At present, the prime objective of organisational customers appears to be to seek information and, until this changes in the B2B context, the emotional and entertainment aspect of advertising messages will continue to have a low significance and online advertising a low profile in the communication mix.

Sales promotions and B2B communications

Sales promotion seeks to offer buyers additional value, as an inducement to generate action, often to make an immediate sale. In B2B marketing these inducements, normally referred to as trade promotions are targeted at three main audiences, intermediaries, end-user customers and the sales force.

Sales promotion is used for one of two main reasons: as a means to accelerate sales or to generate a change in attitude. Essentially, these are achieved by either rewarding current customers or encouraging prospective customers. The acceleration represents the shortened period of time in which a transaction is completed, relative to the time that would have elapsed had there not been a promotion. This action does not mean that an extra sale has been achieved. Indeed, B2B promotions are often aimed at moving buyers along the buying process rather than making a complete transaction. Therefore, gifts, free merchandise or premiums are used in the hope of generating a reciprocal action. For example, they are used at exhibitions to attract buyers to stand, they are left at the end of sales visits as a way of triggering name recall and as a form of residual value, and they are used as an insert in a piece of direct mail to stimulate interest and to provoke further action, such as an appointment. Apart from these there are a number of other reasons why sales promotions are used, some of which are set out in Table 11.2.

Sales promotion is an important promotional tool for organisations supplying low unit value products and where there is a high purchase frequency. Product differentiation within the grocery and office stationery markets, for example, is difficult to achieve and, in these circumstances, sales promotion provides a point of added value. Conversely, sales promotion can be of limited value in high technology markets and others where the unit value is high and purchase frequency low. In such circumstances buyers are able to discern many technical and service attributes that provide differentiation and added value, thus negating the use of sales promotion techniques.

Methods of B2B sales promotion

The main type of sales promotion used to motivate intermediaries is an **allowance**. Allowances can take many forms but some of the more common ones are buying, count and recount, buy-back allowances, merchandising and promotional allowances. Allowances are a means of achieving a short-term increase in sales. In the grocery sector they can be used defensively to protect valuable shelf space from aggressive competitors. By offering to work with resellers and providing them with extra incentives, manufacturers attempt to guard territory gained to date. The main types of Allowances are set out in Table 11.3.

There are a number of other techniques that can be used to achieve sales promotion objectives. These include dealer contests, which should be geared to stimulating increased usage. By encouraging resellers to improve their performance, growth can be fostered and the reseller's attention focused on the manufacturer's products, not those of the competition. Motivation and the provision of information are necessary

Table 11.2 Reasons for the use of sales promotions

Reach new customers	They are useful in securing trials for new products and in defending shelf space against anticipated and existing competition.
Reduce distributor risk	The funds that manufacturers dedicate to them lower the distributor's risk in stocking new brands.
Reward behaviour	They can provide rewards for previous purchase behaviour.
Retention	They can provide interest and attract potential customers and in doing so encourage them to provide details for further communications activity.
Add value	Can encourage sampling and repeat purchase behaviour by providing extra value (superior to competitors' brands) and a reason to purchase.
Induce action	They can instil a sense of urgency among consumers to buy while a deal is available. They add excitement and interest at the point of purchase to the merchandising of mature and mundane products.
Preserve cash flow	Since sales promotion costs are incurred on a pay-as-you-go basis, they can spell survival for smaller, regional brands that cannot afford big advertising programmes.
Improve efficiency	Sales promotions allow manufacturers to use idle capacity and to adjust to demand and supply imbalances or softness in raw material prices and other input costs, while maintaining the same list prices.
Integration	Provide a means of linking together other tools of the promotional mix.
Assist segmentation	They allow manufacturers to price discriminate among consumer segments that vary in price sensitivity. Most manufacturers believe that a high-list, high-deal policy is more profitable than offering a single price to all consumers. A portion of sales promotion expenditures, therefore, consists of reductions in list prices that are set for the least price-sensitive segment of the market.

at the launch of new products and at the beginning of a new selling season. To assist these objectives, dealer conventions, seminars and meetings are used extensively, often in conjunction with a contest. The informal interaction that these events facilitate between the focus organisation and its resellers can be an invaluable aid to the development and continuance of good relations between the two parties and at a horizontal level between resellers.

The use of trade-based promotions is an often understated aspect of marketing communications. However, trade promotions and interorganisational incentives are common and generally effective. Manufacturers use competitions and sweepstakes to motivate the sales forces of its distributors, as well as technical and customer support staff in retail organisations and as an inducement to encourage other businesses to place orders and business with them.

Table 11.3 The main types of B2B sales promotion and allowances

Type of B2B sales promotion	Explanation
Buying allowance	Reward for specific orders between certain dates, a reseller will be entitled to a refund or allowance of x per cent off the regular case or carton price.
	Used to encourage new stores to try the manufacturer's products or to stimulate repeat usage (restocking).
Count and recount allowance	Reward for each case shifted into the reseller's store from storage, during a specified period of time.
	Used to prevent stock outs and to encourage resellers to move old stock out of storage and into the store and so clear the way for a new or modified product to be introduced.
Buy-back allowance	Reward for purchases made after the termination of a count and recount scheme. Normally limited to the actual number of units exchanged under the count and recount scheme.
	Used to encourage stores to replenish their stocks with the manufacturer's product and not that of a competitor.
Merchandising allowance	Reward of extra free units delivered to a reseller once their order reaches a specific size.
	Used to open up new distributors and dealerships.
Promotional allowance	Reward against product purchases or a contribution to the cost of an advertisement or campaign in return for promoting a manufacturer's products.
	Used to encourage stocking, lock out competitors and to create shelf space for new products.
Gifts and premiums	Used to provoke reciprocal actions and to provide a longer lasting internal advertisement for the organisation or as an incentive to take further action (e.g. visit an exhibition stand or make an appointment).

Price-based promotions and delayed discounts are used to encourage organisations to place business. Another popular approach is to discount technical support and bundle up a range of support facilities. Whatever the package, the purpose remains the same, to add value in order to advance (or gain) a purchase commitment.

Online trade promotion activity is growing, although mainly restricted to incentivise current, rather than potential, customers. Although such schemes are often administered over the web, product and negotiation complexity restrict the scope of this form of online marketing communications.

Control and the use of channel incentives

Most of these methods involve a level of collaboration between parties and can serve to develop relationships in a constructive way. However, it should be noted that one of the main drawbacks associated with the promotional allowance and channel incentive programmes is that resellers often assume a degree of control over the process by rejecting the incentives on offer. This occurs because resellers do not have the capacity to hold all the stock across all of the suppliers in a sector and therefore each reseller has to make judgements not only about which supplier but also about which range of stock and hence which incentives to adopt (Gilliland, 2004).

Another way resellers assume control is through their use of inappropriate messages and use of media that may not be in the best interests of either party. Furthermore, some resellers have been known to submit fraudulent claims for advertising that either did not take place or duplicated a previous claim. Such behaviour is indicative of a poor relationship and can lead to conflict and deterioration in the quality of collaborative behaviour. For example, 'hostaging' is a process whereby a retailer/reseller is able to exert power over a manufacturer in order to pressurise or force them into providing trade promotions on a more or less continual basis. A less dependent firm may use influence strategies, such as requests and information exchange (Anderson and Narus, 1990). In contrast, a more dependent firm should seek to add value (or reduce costs) to the exchange for the partner firm, at a relatively small cost to itself.

The more dependent firm in a working relationship needs to protect its transactions-specific assets by taking various actions, such as close bonding with end-user firms. Strategies to avoid 'hostaging' would include reducing the frequency of trade deals, converting trade spending into advertising and consumer promotions and focusing on differentiating the brand with less reliance on price (Blattberg and Neslin, 1990). The relationship between an intermediary and manufacturer, where the former is responsible for distributing the manufacturer's sales promotions, can be made considerably more complex if there is an allegation of sales promotion abuse.

Many manufacturers provide extensive training and support for their resellers. This is an important communications function, especially when products are complex or subject to rapid change, as in IT markets. Such coordination means that a stronger relationship can be built and manufacturers have greater control over the messages that the reseller's representatives transmit. It also means that the switching costs of the reseller are increased, since the training and support costs will be incurred again if a different supplier is adopted. Coordination through training and support can be seen as a form of marketing communications.

Marketing communications between manufacturers and resellers are vitally important. Sales promotions play an increasingly important role in the coordination between the two parties. Resellers look for sales promotions to support their own marketing initiatives. Supplier selection decisions depend in part upon the volume and value of the communications support. In other words, will supplier X or Y provide the necessary level of promotional support, either within the channel or direct to the end-user customer?

SNAPSHOT 11.2

KENT EXPRESS AND TRADE PROMOTIONS

Kent Express markets competitively priced supplies to dental health practitioners. Customers buy direct from Kent Express, either online or over the phone. Having operated a successful loyalty scheme with over 1,000 active members across the United Kingdom, the company decided to increase sales through customer incentives. To do this they targeted their top spending accounts by launching a more 'exclusive' element to the programme that would go beyond acknowledging basic loyalty and that would provide a selection of high quality rewards plus the kudos that comes with being part of an exclusive club.

Kent Express understood that it needed a programme that would attract customer attention – and commitment – by offering a wide range of premium quality yet cost-effective rewards. Argos Business Solutions uses its online reward and incentive management system, 'the Hive', to support and control all aspects of Kent Express's loyalty and reward programme. Argos Business Solutions designs the branded 'Partner Points' catalogues, which are then published, printed and distributed by Kent Express. Participants order their choice of rewards online – via the Partner Points Hive site – or via telephone ordering. A call centre team handles all telephone orders and a help desk to deal with queries. By accessing 'the Hive' online portal, Kent Express's own customer service team can also respond to queries regarding a participant's Partner Point account.

The scheme increased customer retention on the top-tier accounts and differentiated the company from their competitors in terms of understanding customer aspirations.

Source: Adapted from www.argos-B2B.co.uk/reward_solutions/Case_studies/kent.asp (Accessed 3 December 2003.) Used with permission.

Public relations and B2B communications

According to the Institute of Public Relations, 'Public Relations practice is the planned and sustained effort to establish and maintain goodwill and mutual understanding between an organisation and its publics' (www.ipr.org.uk/). The use of this non-personal form of communication is increasing as it offers organisations a different way to communicate, not only with customers but also with many other stakeholders, including members of the supply chain and intermediaries.

Publicity involves the dissemination of messages through third-party media, such as magazines, newspapers or news programmes. There is no charge for the media space or time but there are costs incurred in the production of the material. The decision on whether an organisation's public relations messages are transmitted rests with those charged with managing the media resource, not the message sponsor. Consequently, it is difficult to control a message once placed in the media channels, but the endorsement offered by a third party can be very influential as it confers greater perceived credibility than those messages transmitted through paid media, such as advertising.

The degree of trust and confidence generated by public relations makes this tool important because it can reduce buyers' perceived risk. However, while credibility may be high, the amount of control that management is able to bring to the transmission of the public relations message is very low. For example, a press release may have been carefully prepared in-house, but as soon as it is passed to the editor of a magazine or newspaper, a possible opinion-former, all control is lost. The release may be destroyed (highly probable), printed as it stands (highly unlikely) or changed to fit the available space in the media vehicle (almost certain, if it is decided to use the material). This means that any changes to the copy have probably not been agreed with management, so the context and style of the original message may be lost or corrupted.

Table 11.4 Main types of public relations

Type of Public Relations	Explanation
Publicity Press releases	Press releases are a written report concerning a change in the organisation, which is sent (or posted on a website) to various media houses for inclusion in their media vehicles as an item of news.
Press conferences	Press conferences are used when a major event has occurred and where a press release cannot convey the appropriate tone or detail required by the organisation.
Interviews	Interviews with representatives of an organisation enable news and the organisation's view of an issue or event to be conveyed.
Events	Product, corporate or community activities designed to improve goodwill and understanding.
Lobbying	Helps ensure that the views of the organisation are heard in order that legislation can be shaped appropriately, limiting any potential damage that new legislation might bring.
Corporate advertising	One of the means by which stakeholders can identify and understand the essence of an organisation. This is achieved by presenting the personality of the organisation to a wide rage of stakeholders, instead of portraying particular functions or products.
Sponsorship	This is used to develop awareness in the target market and to enable them to make associations between the event (or sponsee) and the sponsor. Through such sponsorship activities it is intended that levels of credibility will be increased.
Crisis management	The increasing occurrence of crises throughout the world has prompted many organisations to review the manner in which they anticipate managing such events, should they be implicated. It is generally assumed that those organisations that take the care to plan in anticipation of disaster will experience more favourable outcomes than those that fail to plan.
Investor relations	Relationships with the money markets and financial stakeholders, are a vitally important part of an organisation's communication activities. The ability to maintain confidence in an organisation during periods of economic buoyancy and downturn can be crucial in delivering consistent shareholder value.

Types of public relations

While there is general agreement on a definition, there is a lower level of consensus over what constitutes public relations. This is partly because the range of activities is diverse and categorisation problematic. The approach adopted here is that public relations consists of a range of communication activities, of which publicity and event management appear to be the main ones used by practitioners. There are also other activities which are derived from public relations and these are set out in Table 11.4. The effectiveness of public relations in a B2B context should not be underestimated. The wide range of public relations tools and techniques enable credibility to be developed in an environment where the other promotional tools contribute in different ways.

Public relations can be involved with a range of organisational issues. This may be seen as a reflection of the potency of this form of communication. It is more than just a means of influencing other stakeholders through propaganda and/or publicity-based activities. Public relations can be used to mediate the different relationships that an organisation has with its environment and can perform a number of valuable roles, such as counsellor, diplomat and arbiter (Pieczka, 1996). For this to happen a

SNAPSHOT 11.3

PUBLIC RELATIONS AND HIGH TECHNOLOGY

A UK manufacturer of torque wrenches had seen a niche market for high-tech ultrasonic instruments that can measure the stress in a bolt or fastener far more accurately than by measuring the torque applied to the nut.

The campaign

First, a general new product release was put together and widely distributed, achieving good coverage for the launch of the original mains-powered meter. Soon after, a longer, more detailed technical article explaining ultrasonic stress measurement was written and made available to a small number of complementary publications. This too achieved in-depth coverage in the target publications, focusing attention on the technology of ultrasonic stress measurement in a different way from the product story. A programme of individual editor visits to the factory was then put in place, with each editor being briefed on the background to the development of the ultrasonic meters. These were then followed by the launch of the second meter in the range, a portable, battery-powered unit that brings ultrasonic stress measurement within reach of a new and much wider audience.

The results

In-depth articles explaining how the technique works and its advantages to users followed wide coverage of the launch of the original ultrasonic meter. This awareness-raising campaign has now been followed up with the launch of the second-generation instrument, a product that the manufacturer hopes will provide a solid future proof adjunct to production of its more traditional torque wrenches.

Source: Fisher Marketing; www.fishermarketing.co.uk/challengeswehavemet-fullstory.asp?ID=4 (Accessed 8 August 2004.) Used with permission.

number of environmental conditions need to exist, such as equitable information flows, a managerial predisposition to treat incoming information in an unbiased and apolitical manner, being power bases throughout the information network equally dispersed and the level of connectedness being relatively stable and suitable. If these conditions prevail, public relations may be able to perform the role of a communication conduit for internal and external stakeholders more effectively than under adverse conditions.

Many organisations use their websites to post press releases, to provide third-party endorsements, together with case studies. In high-technology markets, white papers and documentary evidence relating to both product and corporate reliability, integrity, performance and overall reputation are made available. This information can also be used to provide support for and links to strategically significant channel and business partners.

Whereas online event management poses certain practical difficulties, sponsorship is easily facilitated, and websites can make a fundamental contribution to providing information for a range of stakeholders during periods of crisis and uncertainty.

It is important to remember that the shift to a relationship management perspective effectively alters the way public relations is perceived and practised by organisations. Instead of trying to manipulate audience opinion so that the organisation is of primary importance, the challenge is to use symbolic, visual communication messages in combination with behaviour such that the organisation–audience relationship improves for all parties (Ehling, 1992). What follows from this is a change in evaluation, from assessing the decimation of messages to measuring audience influence and behavioural and attitudinal change or, as Ledingham and Bruning (2000) succinctly put it, from outputs to outcomes.

Gummesson (1996), cited by Farrelly *et al.* (2003), makes the point that relationship marketing is most suited to observe the role of sponsorship because it is concerned with the provision of value rather than goods and services. In this sense sponsorship reflects some of the qualities associated with relationship marketing, where trust and commitment to a long-term set of associations and partnerships is important. Their initial research suggests that the greater the level of commitment to a sponsorship-based relationship the more likely it is that the desired outcomes will be achieved.

Direct marketing and B2B communications

Direct marketing can represent a strategic approach to the market although some organisations use it as a tactical tool. Use of this tool signifies an attempt to actively remove channel intermediaries, reduce costs and improve the quality and speed of service for individual customers. The significance of B2B direct marketing is that it can be used to complement personal selling activities and in doing so reduce costs and improve overall performance. By removing the face-to-face aspect of personal selling and replacing it with either an email communication, a telephone conversation or a direct mail letter, many facets of the traditional sales persons' tasks can be removed, freeing them to concentrate on their key skills. In addition, the personalisation associated with direct marketing messages is compatible with a relationship marketing strategy (Chaffey *et al.*, (2002). Direct marketing is generally regarded as the second most important tool of the communication mix for most B2B organisations.

Direct marketing seeks to target individual customers with the intention of delivering personalised messages and building a relationship with them based on their responses. In contrast to conventional approaches, direct marketing attempts to build a one-to-one relationship, a partnership with each customer, by communicating with customers on a direct and personal basis. There are a growing number of direct marketing methods but essentially there are two main offline approaches, as shown in Table 11.5.

Direct mail

Direct mail refers to personally addressed advertising materials delivered through the postal system. It can be personalised and targeted with great accuracy, and the results precisely measured. Direct mail has been an important part of the B2B communication mix for some time, especially as it can be coordinated to support personal selling by building awareness, enhancing image and establishing credibility. The generation of enquiries and leads, together with the purposeful building of personal relationships with customers, are the most important factors contributing to the growth of direct mail. However, the intention to build loyalty is not always reflected in the statistics, as Ridgeway (2000) reports that mailings appear to be focused on customer acquisition, not retention. Direct mail can be expensive, at anything between £250 and £500 per 1,000 items dispatched. It should, therefore, be used selectively and for purposes other than creating awareness.

Voegle (1992) identified a number of stages through which a receiver of direct mail moves. These are the opening, scanning, (re)reading and response behaviours. Vriens *et al.* (1998) suggest that there are three main parts to the process, namely the opening behaviour, which is influenced by the attractiveness of the envelope and situational factors. Next, reading behaviour is influenced by the opening behaviour, the reader's situational characteristics and the attractiveness of the mailing and its contents. The final behaviour concerns the response generated, which is affected by the attractiveness of the offer, by the reading behaviour that preceded the response and the characteristics of the individual reader and their situation.

Wulf *et al.* (2000) used this framework to find ways in which to increase response rates to direct mail. They found that the attractiveness of the envelope did impact on opening behaviour but so did the envelope size, material, colour and even type of

Table 11.5 Main types of direct marketing

Type of direct marketing	Explanation
Direct mail	Used to support personal selling by building awareness, enhancing image, taking orders and establishing credibility, and it can provide levels of customer management.
Telemarketing	Used to facilitate customer enquiries, establish leads, make appointments, collect low value orders and even provide a direct sales channel.

SNAPSHOT 11.4

USING VIDEO FOR DIRECT COMMUNICATION

An increasing number of organisations of all sizes are making greater use of the corporate video (Middleton, 2002). Using light-weight cassettes, CD-ROMs, Laptop Computers, CD Business Cards, websites and even DVDs it is possible to use corporate video to take prospective customers, investors and employees on a tour of an organisation's facilities, to demonstrate products and to develop reputation without their having to move. In addition to direct mail campaigns videos are used at exhibitions, sales presentations, conferences, staff induction, in reception areas and at websites.

As Middleton argues, using video to feature case studies and testimonials from satisfied clients enhances credibility and provides further opportunities within other promotional activities. For example, these testimonials can be used as part of a standard sales presentation, put on CD cards or placed on the website to add a multimedia dimension to a client list.

Source: Adapted from Middleton (2002); www.wnim.com/archive/issue1303/index.htm (Accessed 31 December 2003.) Used with permission.

postage. Surprisingly the volume of direct mail each manager received had no impact on opening behaviour. With regard to reading behaviour it was the attitudes of the reader that were found to be significant not the situational factors. Finally, response behaviour appeared to be determined more by the reading behaviours of the individual rather than any other factor.

Telemarketing

Telemarketing can be used in both an inbound and outbound manner. When used outbound the goal is to generate leads, make appointments, close sales and to collect information about the market and particular customers. When used for inbound calls the role is to collect orders, provide support and information for both customers and the sales force and to coordinate sales activities.

By using telemarketing as a sales order processing system to collect routine low value orders, the sales force is freed up to concentrate on other more profitable activities. In particular, the use of an inside telemarketing department is seen as a compatible sales channel to the field sales force. A telemarketing team can accomplish the following tasks: search for and qualify new customers, so saving the field force from cold calling; service existing customer accounts and prepare the field force should they be required to attend to the client personally; seek repeat orders from marginal or geographically remote customers, particularly if they are low unit value consumable items; and finally, provide a link between network members that serves to maintain the relationship, especially through periods of difficulty and instability. Many organisations prefer to place orders through telesales teams, as it does not involve the time costs associated with personal sales calls. The routine of such orders gives greater efficiency for all concerned with the relational exchange and reduces costs. The complementary use of direct marketing and personal selling is explored further in Chapter 12. It should be noted, however, that many of the tasks accomplished through telemarketing have been overtaken or superseded by the use of the Internet and web-enabled services.

It has been established, in Chapters 6 and 9, that the creation of trust is vital if relational exchanges are to be developed. Trust is a multi-dimensional construct (Morgan and Hunt, 1994) and it is highly important to ensure this is recognised and accepted by parties where direct marketing is used (Fletcher and Peters, 1997). The development of permission and opt-in marketing has brought about a change in perspective, as contemporary approaches are now based on communications with people and organisations who have already agreed to receive them, very often when registering at a website.

The database

At the hub of successful direct marketing activities and a CRM programme, is a database. As described in Chapter 2, a computerised database is a collection of records that can be related to one another in multiple ways and from which information can be obtained in a variety of formats. Often, for marketing purposes, the data held is about prospects and customers. This can be analysed to determine appropriate segments and target markets, or used to stimulate and record individual responses to marketing communications. It therefore plays a role as a storage, sorting and administrative device to assist direct, personalised communications. Designed and used appropriately in a marketing context, the database can constitute the memory of a customer relationship (Blattberg and Deighton, 1991), preserving a record of every interaction between an organisation and each of its customers.

Data gathered from transactions undertaken with customers may not always provide sufficient information for marketing purposes, and further layers might be required. For example, additional information can be gathered from a list agency to refine further an organisation's data analysis. Response analysis can identify the best customers, and then another layer of data can be introduced to select those that are particularly responsive to specific forms of communication, for example, direct mail, telesales or email. The increasing sophistication of information retrieval from databases enables much more effective targeting and communications.

Databases provide a means by which a huge range of organisations, large and small, can monitor changes in customer behaviour, adapting their view of and contribution to various interorganisational relationships. Very importantly, database systems can be used not only to identify strategically important customers and segments but also to ascertain opportunities to cross-sell products. The purpose of cross-selling is to reduce customer churn and increase switching costs (Kamakura *et al.*, 2003). While increasing a customer's potential switching costs may not be compatible with relationship marketing principles, the result of successful implementation may be improved levels of customer retention and satisfaction where relationships are more discrete and transactional rather than collaborative in nature.

However, there are a number of tensions associated with the use of databases. For example, customers and governments have varying tolerances regarding privacy and the scope of information that database information systems can exploit. Consumer

SNAPSHOT 11.5

B2B INFORMATION SUPPLIER

Emap Glenigan provides information about construction, civil engineering and property management projects in the United Kingdom. By tracking the development of projects from the early planning stage right through the tender stage to the contracts being awarded, clients can obtain leads and target their business activities according to their needs.

Using a team of external full-time field researchers who visit local authority planning offices to view the plans submitted for planning permission, information about each application is then validated against various databases and checking procedures to ensure completeness and accuracy. The Emap Glenigan database is updated throughout every working day and in-house researchers then develop the detail and specifications on planned and current projects by talking directly to decision makers. The Emap Glenigan Research team make over 1 million telephone calls each year to ensure this huge database remains up-to-date, comprehensive and accurate.

This vast database of business-to-business activity in the United Kingdom is used, for example, by materials manufacturers for leads concerning plans at the submitted stage as this helps them to influence architects so that they specify their products from the start. Plant hire companies are more interested in projects at the main contract award stage in the planning process while telecommunications companies use the leads service to provide them with the expansion plans of various companies. Recruitment consultants use the leads to identify staff requirements, from office personnel, through IT consultants and even cleaning and security staff.

Source: Adapted from www.glenigan.com (Accessed December 2003.) Used with permission.

tolerance thresholds (Goodwin, 1991) are known to vary according to the nature of the data, how it was collected and even who collected it. Often data has been captured in a database because a customer entered into a transaction. Any business entity recording such transaction data has a moral duty, and sometimes a legal obligation, to declare that it will be stored, to acknowledge and respect confidential aspects, and to make explicit the context in which it might be sold or shared with third parties or otherwise exploited. Breaking privacy codes and making unauthorised disclosures of personal details might very well expose the tenuous relationship an organisation has with its 'loyal' customers.

Personal selling and B2B communications

Personal selling is the most important and most expensive tool of the communication mix used by B2B organisations. It is an interpersonal communication tool which involves face-to-face activities undertaken by individuals, often representing an organisation, in order to inform, persuade or remind an individual or group to take appropriate action, as required by the sponsor's representative. A salesperson engages in communication on a one-to-one (or one-to-group) basis where instantaneous feedback is possible.

This tool differs from the others in that, while still possibly lacking in relative credibility, the degree of control is potentially lower. This is because the salesperson is free at the point of contact to deliver a message other than that intended (Lloyd, 1997). Indeed, many different messages can be delivered by a single salesperson. Some of these messages may enhance the prospect of the salesperson's objectives being reached (making the sale), or they may retard the process and so incur more time and hence costs. Whichever way it is viewed, control is lower than with advertising.

Personal selling is very important in interorganisational markets, often because of the need to help build relationships with members of buying centres and the need to demonstrate and explain technicalities associated with the products and services being marketed. In support of the personal selling effort (and exhibitions), trade promotions, trade advertising, direct marketing and public relations all play important roles. Increasingly, the Internet provides not only new direct routes to customers and intermediaries but also a vibrant new communications medium.

There are three particular promotional activities derived from personal selling. These are exhibitions, field marketing and video conferencing. Each is discussed in the sections that follow, and Chapter 12 explores personal selling in greater detail.

Exhibitions and trade shows

According to Boukersi (2000) industrial fairs, that is exhibitions and trade shows, tend to be smaller, more specialised and of shorter duration than consumer-orientated general fairs. There are many reasons for their use, but the primary attractions appear to be opportunities to meet potential and established customers and to create and sustain relationships within the market, not to 'to make sales' or 'because the competition is there'. The main aims, therefore, are to develop partnerships with customers, to build upon or develop the corporate identity and to gather up-to-date market intelligence (Shipley and Wong, 1993). In addition, these events can be more about managing conflict rather than generating sales (Blythe, 2002). This implies that exhibitions and trade shows should not be used as isolated events, but that they should be integrated into a series of promotional activities. These activities can serve to develop and sustain buyer relationships. The reasons for attending exhibitions are set out in Table 11.6.

One of the main drawbacks associated with exhibitions is the vast and disproportionate amount of management time that can be tied up with their planning and

Table 11.6 Reasons exhibitors choose to attend exhibitions

To meet existing customers

To take orders/make sales

To get leads and meet prospective new customers

To meet lapsed customers

To meet prospective members of the existing or new marketing channels

To provide market research opportunities and to collect marketing data

implementation. However, good planning is essential if the full potential benefits of exhibition work are to be realised (Poorani, 1996). For example, the anticipated visitor profile must be analysed in order that the number of quality buyers visiting an exhibition can be determined. The variety of visitors attending an exhibition can be misleading, as the vast majority may not be serious buyers or indeed may not be directly related to the industry or the market in question.

The costs associated with exhibitions, if controlled properly, can mean that this is an effective and efficient means of communicating with customers although the quality of the audience can vary considerably. However, taking members of the sales force 'off the road' can also incur large costs. Calculating these costs is problematic and will vary according to the nature of the business and which direct and indirect costs are determined. Many organisations use costs per order taken as the main form of evaluating the success of an exhibition. This can paint a false picture, as the true success can never really be determined in terms of orders because of the variety of other factors that impinge upon their placement and timing.

Costs can be reduced through the use of private exhibitions, where the increased flexibility allows organisations to produce mini or private exhibitions for their clients at local venues (for example hotels). This can mean lower costs for the exhibitor and reduced time away from their businesses for those attending. The communication 'noise' and distraction associated with the larger public events can also be avoided by these private showings.

Exhibitions are an important means of gaining information about competitors, buyers and technical and political developments in the market, and they often serve to facilitate the recruitment process. Above all else, exhibitions provide an opportunity to meet customers on relatively neutral ground and, through personal

SNAPSHOT 11.6

GROWTH IN EXHIBITIONS

In terms of value the three most important B2B media are magazines, business newspapers and directories, all owned by publishers. In fourth place are exhibitions which publishers appear to be using in order to grow. In 2000–02, there were 2,200 UK B2B exhibitions, an increase of 17 per cent.

The Association of Exhibition Organisers claims that 91 per cent of exhibiting companies make contact with new customers, 90 per cent generate valuable leads and a staggering 87 per cent generate real sales. Exhibitions are a very direct and personal way of creating new business and like personal selling represent a completely different environment from that of electronic communications. Exhibitions have become media enablers, rather than basic marketplaces. Indeed, some see exhibitions as a superior 'media' (to other B2B media) in order for purchase decisions to be made.

However, this approach to the role of exhibitions reflects a customer acquisition perspective whereas the retention and relationship development are of less significance.

Source: Adapted from the Association of Exhibition Organisers website: www.aeo.org.uk/page.cfm/T=m/Action=Press/PressID=12 (Accessed 4 December 2003.) Used with permission.

interaction, develop relationships. Products can be launched, demonstrated, prices agreed, technical problems discussed and trust and credibility enhanced.

As a form of marketing communications, exhibitions enable products to be promoted, and brands built. They can be an effective means of demonstrating products and developing industry-wide credibility in a relatively short period of time. Attendance at exhibitions may also be regarded from a political dimension. For example, non-attendance may be seized as an opportunity by attendees to suggest weaknesses (Kerin and Cron, 1987).

In the B2B sector new products and services are often introduced at exhibitions, especially if there are to be public relations activities and events that can be spun off the launch. In other words, exhibitions are not independent of the other parts of the promotional mix. If used effectively they can be part of a coordinated communications campaign. Advertising prior, during and after a trade show can be dovetailed with public relations, sponsorship and personal selling. Sales promotions can also be incorporated through competitions among customers prior to the show to raise awareness, generate interest and to suggest customer involvement. Competitions during a show can be focused on the sales force to motivate and stimulate commercial activity and among visitors to generate interest in the stand, raise brand name attention and encourage focus on particular products (new, revised or revolutionary) and generate sales leads and enquiries.

Above all else, exhibitions are an important way of building relationships and signalling corporate identity. Trade shows are an important means of providing corporate hospitality and showing gratitude to all its customers, but in particular to its key account customers and others of strategic significance. Positive relationships with customers, competitors and suppliers are often reinforced through face-to-face dialogue that happens both formally in the exhibition hall and informally through the variety of social activities that surround and support these events.

Field marketing

Field marketing is a relatively new sector of the industry and seeks to provide support for the sales force and merchandising personnel along with data collection and research facilities for clients. The key to field marketing is the flexibility of services provided to clients. Sales forces can be hired on short-term contracts and promotional teams can be contracted to launch new products, provide samples (both in-store and door-to-door) and undertake a range of other activities that are not part of an organisation's normal promotion endeavours.

The decision about whether to own or to hire a sales force has to be based on a variety of criteria, such as the degree of control required over not only the salesperson but also the message to be transmitted. A further criterion is flexibility. Ruckert *et al*. (1985) identified that in environments subject to rapid change, which brings uncertainty (for example, because of shortening product life cycles or large technological developments), the ability to adjust quickly the number of representatives in the distribution channel can be of major strategic importance. A further criterion is cost; for some the large fixed costs associated with a sales force can be avoided by using a commission-only team of representatives.

A large number of organisations choose to have their own sales force, but of these many use the services of a manufacturer's agents to supplement their activities.

A number of pharmaceutical manufacturers use independent sales forces to supplement the activities of their own sales teams.

Field marketing is a response to market needs and is a development practitioners have pioneered to fulfil a range of customer needs that presumably had not been adequately satisfied.

Field marketing has undoubtedly expanded its role in recent years and in doing so has begun to establish itself as a core marketing support activity. Indeed, Moyies (2000) claims that field marketing should be cross-fertilised with direct marketing and sales promotion and that doing so would not only benefit clients but would add credibility to the industry.

Table 11.7 Essential features of field marketing activities

Core activities	Essential features
Sales	Provides sales force personnel on either a temporary or a permanent basis. This is for business to business and direct to the public.
Merchandising	Generates awareness and brand visibility through point-of-purchase placement, in-store staff training, product displays and leaflets.
Sampling	Mainly to the public at shopping centres and station concourses but also for business-to-business purposes.
Auditing	Used for checking stock availability, pricing and positioning.
Mystery shopping	Provides feedback on the level and quality of service provided by retail staff and the promotion of special offers.
Event marketing	Used to create drama and to focus attention at sports events, open-air concerts and festivals. Essentially theatrical or entertainment based.
Door to door (home calls)	A form of selling where relatively uncomplicated products and services can be sold through home visits.

Source: Adapted from McLuhan (2000) and Moyies (2000).

Video conferencing

The Internet is an impersonal medium and as such does not allow for direct personal communication. Face-to-face personal communications over the Internet for the purposes of buying and selling remain the one part of the promotional mix that the Internet cannot address. However, video conferencing does provide this facility and although costs, technical issues and user attitudes used to limit the practical application of this tool, costs have fallen, the technology is now much more reliable and of higher quality and attitudes have changed. Video conferencing is now much more accessible for a wide variety of organisations for both internal and external meetings.

There are currently two main types of video conferencing systems, PC-based and room-based. PC-based, or desktop, systems are suitable for a small number of people, for short periods of time. The cameras are usually fixed focus, with small field capability and the viewing screens tend to be small. Transmission speeds are limited by modem and telephone line capabilities. An advantage is that software applications and files can be shared and viewed jointly.

Room-based systems use large, sophisticated (pan-tilt-zoom) cameras and wide television screens. A greater number of people can participate. Transmission via ISDN

(Integrated Services Digital Network) including satellite links, facilitates better picture/sound quality. Sessions have to be pre-booked and are costlier than PC-based (www.videocom.co.uk, accessed July 2000).

Video conferencing can be used in marketing communications for research (audience polling), product promotion/launch, training, employee and/or channel member briefings and sales negotiations. The advantages of video conferencing include speed and convenience as travel costs are minimised, potential reduction in message ambiguity as there is joint and simultaneous viewing of materials and instant feedback.

One of the disadvantages is that all participants have to be available at the same time, which can be difficult across time zones. The connections are not always reliable and room time-slots often cannot be extended beyond the original booking. Some people are uneasy in front of cameras, which may impair effectiveness.

The use of video conferencing has increased because of major technical advances, which have improved the clarity and reliability of many commercial systems. This factor, combined with periods of major global crisis that have led to a rapid decrease in the volume of air travel, appears to have spurred the use of video conferencing.

Business-to-business media

Decisions about the choice of media can be complex, although realistically the range of media available to B2B marketers is somewhat limited compared to those for the consumer market. Of the many available media, six main classes can be identified. These are broadcast, print, outdoor, new, in-store and other media classes. Within each of these classes there are particular media types. For example, within the broadcast class there are television and radio, and within the print class there are newspapers and magazines. Within each type of medium there are a huge number of different media vehicles that can be selected to carry an advertiser's message. For example, in print, there are business-orientated magazines such as *The Economist* and there are also an expanding number of specialist magazines such as the *Timber Trades Journal* and *ThirdSector*. Therefore, there are three forms of media: classes, types and vehicles (see Table 11.8).

Organisations use a variety of media in order to deliver their planned messages to a number of target audiences. As a general rule business marketers use print rather than broadcast media, simply because of the informational nature of the messages they wish to convey and the size and geographic dispersion of their audiences. While choosing a single medium is reasonably straightforward, combining media and attempting to generate synergistic effects is far from easy.

One of the key tasks is to decide which combination of vehicles should be selected to carry the message to the target audience. First, it is necessary to consider the main characteristics of each media type in order that media planning decisions can be based on some logic and rationale. The fundamental characteristics concern the costs, delivery and audience profile associated with a communication and these are summarised in Table 11.9. It can be seen that each media type has a variety of characteristics that help or hinder the communication of an advertiser's message. In addition to this, each media vehicle has a discrete set of characteristics that will also influence the way in which messages are transmitted and received.

Table 11.8 Summary chart of the main forms of media

Class	Type	Vehicles
Broadcast	Television	*Brookside, Friends*
	Radio	*Virgin 1215, Classic FM*
Print	Newspapers	*Sunday Times, The Mirror, The Mail*
	Magazines	
	Consumer	*Cosmopolitan, FHM, Woman*
	Business	*The Grocer, Plumbing News*
Outdoor	Billboards	96 and 48 sheet
	Street furniture	Adshel
	Transit	London Underground, taxis, hot-air balloons
New media	Internet	Websites, email, Intranet
	Digital television	Skydigital
	Teletext	SkyText, Ceefax
	CD-ROM	Various: music, educational, entertainment
In-store	Point of purchase	Bins, signs and displays
	Packaging	The *Coca Cola* contour bottle
Other	Cinema	Pearl and Dean
	Exhibitions	Ideal Home, The Motor Show
	Product placement	FedEx in *Castaway*
	Ambient	Rubbish bins, golf tees, petrol pumps
	Guerrilla	Flyposting

Broadcast media is usually associated with consumer marketing activities but can be of use to reach a general business audience. Both Hewlett Packard and IBM have made extensive use of television and radio to launch campaigns and build corporate reputation. The use of outdoor posters on specific road and rail sites and at airports can be effective in reaching elusive buyers. In addition, small and medium-sized organisations can create general levels of awareness and reach buyers who are difficult to reach by other methods.

As mentioned above, print media is an important part of B2B communications. It enables reasonably detailed information to be conveyed to buyers and designers. Trade journals, business magazines and industry-based directories are common media. Web-based materials can also be downloaded and printed off.

Sales support literature is used extensively to follow up leads and to bolster the personal selling effort. Used early in the buying process, it can be an important means of clarifying features and benefits, and also differentiate an organisation as customers compare, contrast and draw up their shortlists of prospective suppliers. There are a number of different forms of sales support literature, each of which should be used to achieve specific goals.

Product brochures and catalogues not only provide detailed information but serve to add value to the communication process as they can be left after a sales visit. Normally these brochures contain information about standard ranges of products and equipment and can be used to prompt orders. These communication devices can be an integral part of a transactional relationship.

Table 11.9 A summary of media characteristics

Type of media	Strengths	Weaknesses
Newspaper	Wide reach High coverage Low costs Very flexible Short lead times Speed of consumption controlled by reader	Short lifespan Advertisements get little exposure Relatively poor reproduction, gives poor impact Low attention-getting properties
Magazines	High-quality reproduction which allows high impact Specific and specialised target audiences High readership levels Longevity High levels of information can be delivered	Long lead times Visual dimension only Slow build-up of impact Moderate costs
Television	Flexible format, uses sight, movement and sound High prestige High reach Mass coverage Low relative costs, so very efficient	High level of repetition necessary Short message life High absolute costs Clutter Increasing level of fragmentation (potentially)
Radio	Selective audience, e.g. local Low costs (absolute, relative and production) Flexible Can involve listeners	Lacks impact Audio dimension only Difficult to get audience attention Low prestige
Outdoor	High reach High frequency Low relative costs Good coverage as a support medium Location orientated	Poor image (but improving) Long production time Difficult to measure
New media	High level of interaction Immediate response possible Tight targeting Low absolute and relative costs Flexible and easy to update Measurable	Segment specific Slow development of infrastructure High user set-up costs Transaction security issues
Transport	High length of exposure Low costs Local orientation	Poor coverage Segment specific (travellers) Clutter
In-store POP	High attention-getting properties Persuasive Low costs Flexible	Segment specific (shoppers) Prone to damage and confusion Clutter

STRATEGIC PROMOTIONAL PORTFOLIOS

Many organisations, especially in the high-technology sector, develop specialised networks or portfolios of organisations, as a means of reaching specific market sectors.

Targeted at small and medium-sized companies, the Industry Solutions Portfolio has been set up by IBM for the wholesale distribution; fabrication and assembly; retail and financial services industries. This ISP programme represents a network of expertise which includes business partners and independent software vendors (ISVs), who together with IBM have to solve the issues specific to the target market. IBM claim that organisations who become involved will benefit from information and suppliers' solutions, thought leadership articles, case studies, ask the expert facilities, surveys, industry reports, newsletters and networking opportunities.

Another advantage of the Industry Solutions Portfolio from IBM is that it integrates the ISVs and business partners at a strategic level and helps forge an alliance. This programme is planning to expand to other industrial segments such as media and entertainment.

This portfolio approach seeks to provide high levels of credibility and trust based on the expertise and brand reputation of the partner organisations.

Source: Adapted from IBM materials. Used with permission.

Corporate-based brochures, which reflect on the supplier organisation and its overall capability, are more likely to be of use in situations where the customer has a specific problem and is looking for a partner or collaborator in a particular project. In addition to the overall technical capability of the supplier, its credibility is presented, often through the use of testimonials and third-party references. This can be supported through the use of technical data sheets, independent test reports and case histories. This approach is best used where the relationship between the organisations is more relational and hence collaborative.

A great deal of this information is now available at company websites where the prime advantages are that the information is instantly accessible and can be updated regularly.

The Internet and B2B marketing communications

In addition to the various traditional promotional tools being used online, as mentioned previously, the Internet is a medium that allows for interactivity, and is possibly the purest form of marketing communications dialogue outside of personal selling. Electronic communication is two-way and very fast, allowing businesses and individuals to find information and enter exchange transactions in such a way that some traditional communication practices and exchanges are being reconfigured. Evans and King (1999) listed several strengths and weaknesses associated with the

Web in business-to-business contexts. These are shown in Table 11.10 although it should be noted that some of the negative elements have already been overcome as technology has progressed since their paper was written.

The Internet combines many of the strengths of other media. For example, it bundles together, text (print), audio (radio), visual (television) and semiotics/display (outdoor). The Internet is therefore a hybrid of various media and it works as a composite promotional tool encompassing advertising, sales promotions, public relations, direct marketing and personal selling activities. However, there are specific promotional methods that are especially useful in B2B marketing, in particular the overall use of organisational websites and email communications.

Websites

When commercial websites were first developed the trend was to design them as online brochures. This static and passive approach changed as the opportunities afforded by interactivity became recognised and technically within reach of a wider

Table 11.10 Opportunities and obstacles associated with B2B websites

Opportunities	Obstacles
Numerous tools to assist managing the marketing mix	Transmission speeds (now of declining relevance)
Access to commercial research	Site and ISP congestion (too many visitors at some individual sites)
Competitive intelligence	Web culture (sites should be designed not to appear too promotional)
Customer service	Lack of internet organisation (may mean wasted time for some users)
Just-in-time inventory planning	Lack of security (some lack of policing but security improving)
Sales channel	Sub-optimal information control (users decide on site visits and the way they physically set their PC settings)
Channel partner support	Unwieldy URLs (can be long and difficult to memorise)
Image enhancement	HTML programming limitations (declining relevance)
Global reach	Global differences (e.g. can make pricing on the web impractical)
Hardware/software neutrality	Sceptical buyers (some buyers in the middle and later stages of the adoption process)
24/7 availability	Resistance to payment for web services (of declining importance)
Ability to target narrowly	Measurement challenges (becoming more sophisticated)
Cost effectiveness	
Up-to-date information	
Linkages to sites	
Interactive and multimedia capability	

Source: Adapted from Evans and King (1999).

range of organisations. As a result rich media content emerged, eCommerce sites flourished and bidirectional communications became established. Website design and the ability to enter into interactive communications now permits organisations to develop customised content and personal solutions for those customers who freely provide specific, individually orientated information.

A customer-orientated approach to the design of a website should improve its performance. For example, the ease with which a site is accessible and navigable will not only be a positive factor for site visitors but will also reduce information search costs (Hoque and Lohse, 1999). However, knowledgeable and experienced buyers may not find these attributes of particular relevance.

Website attractiveness is a function of many elements but one important one concerns the degree of interactivity and engagement that a site visitor experiences. The development of multimedia facilities that enable sound, music, graphics, text and video can help customers focus on relevant parts of a website's presentation. This in turn should reduce search costs and improve levels of interactivity. Ghose and Dou (1998) argue that media-rich content improves a site's attractiveness and, as B2B branding becomes more important, so this aspect may become more significant.

The content discovered on a website should be relevant, stimulating and contain something new to the visitor. In terms of the range of content, Karayanni (2000) argues that the content of B2B websites should emphasise the identity and reputation of the company and also assist customer-related information exchange. The company-related information helps reduce buyer risk while the exchange encourages customer participation in the communication flow and hence increases buyer control. Both of these elements were found to be significant drivers of web-based sales (Karayanni and Baltas, 2003).

E-mail

The use of email to attract and retain customers has grown in the past five years. Using appropriate email lists is a fast, efficient and effective way to communicate regularly with a market. While the potential through email-based communications is high and often quite legitimate when a user has registered their email address at a particular site, the risk of being accused of sending spam or junk mail is equally high and is perceived as unethical and intrusive.

Email-based marketing enables organisations to send a variety of messages concerning public relations-based announcements, newsletters and sales promotions, to distribute online catalogues and to start and manage permission-based contact lists. Many organisations build their own lists using data collected from their CRM system. By acquiring email responses and other contact mechanisms, addresses and contact details can be captured for the database and then accessed by all customer support staff.

The use of viral marketing, that is email messages conveyed to a small part of the target audience where the content is sufficiently humorous, interesting or persuasive that the receiver is compelled to send it on to a friend, is limited in the B2B market. However, apart from just preparing lists and messages, organisations must be equally prepared to manage responses. The majority of responses are likely to be received within a day of transmission and organisations must be prepared to act upon the requests of those responding by at least acknowledging their message. The next step may require the activation of some form of internal processing and fulfilment, very often offline and out-sourced.

USING RICH MEDIA AT GOTMARKETING

Gotmarketing wanted more of its web-marketer clients to sign up for their newsletter and also to try out their email campaign management software – Campaigner. They decided to use a rich-media approach and set up a viral marketing campaign which contained a video showing a funny yet meaningful marketing situation. It was designed that the embedded video and email would be forwarded to their friends. The video opened automatically for html users and was linked to a text version for others.

A pilot run was broadcast to approximately 3,000 opt-in subscribers and it became clear that not everyone could see the video in the email as they opened it and it was difficult to determine how many passed the email on to friends. However, the results indicated that 45 per cent of the people who got the email viewed the movie and 28 per cent of them clicked through to get more information. The unsubscribe rate is a rough measure of the campaign's effectiveness. A high unsubscribe rate can indicate high annoyance, a lack of value, technical difficulties or all three. For this campaign the unsubscribe rate was a normal 1 per cent.

By clicking on a link to indicate their feelings towards the question 'Do you think that rich media email is an effective marketing tool?' 43 per cent of the people who saw the video took the time to answer and 55 per cent of them voted yes!

Adapted from Partner (2001), www.optinnews.com/read-article.php?id=311 (Accessed 31 December 2003.) Used with permission.

Another approach is to identify affinity groups such as those used within the financial services industry. Given the increasingly goal-directed nature of much web activity, communicating to people through an affinity site can be more cost effective than trying to bring people to a site.

The use of the Internet should not be restricted to a series of independent, isolated communication activities. Through coordination with other tools and media the influence of the Internet can be considerably enhanced. The website lies at the heart of an organisation's Internet activities but it is necessary to use other tools and media to drive traffic to the site. Direct mail to generate leads and permission-based email lists plus print advertising for product and company awareness are effective at directing potential visitors and customers to a website. Once at the website the quality and relevance of the content will be paramount for retaining and developing interest.

A B2B communication strategy will often consist of a series of activities designed to ultimately influence the audience and persuade a percentage of them to take a particular action, very often to purchase the product/service itself. For example, a five-stage strategy to launch a new website for the purchase of office services might be:

1 To build brand name awareness among the target audience. This would involve both offline and online communications. The goal would be to drive site traffic and to encourage visitors.

2 To drive site registration and generate reasons for visitors to return to the site.

3 To convert registrations into purchasers. The use of online and offline sales promotions might be effective.

4 To ensure that a certain percentage of purchasers are retained and are encouraged to return to the site. Not necessarily loyalty but a retention facility based upon a points collection scheme could be useful.

5 To build into the communication strategy a means of personalising communications such that each buyer would receive special offers and notices of products and services that reflect their purchase patterns to date.

To support this strategy a creative proposition will need to be developed so that there is a central theme around which all communications are linked. This might be related to particular attributes such as product features, for example colour, size or speed of service. The benefits of the attributes might also be used, for example no production downtime or improved staff efficiency might be valid claims. In contrast, an emotional feeling might be generated through the use of a tag line, gimmick, slogan, music or perhaps a mood. In other words, some form of branding needs to be used to differentiate the website and create longer-lasting memories which can be easily recalled through the mention of the brand name or perhaps an attribute or central theme.

Coordinating promotional activities

Each element of the mix has a different capacity to communicate and to achieve different objectives. The effectiveness of each tool can be tracked against the purchase decision process. Here customers can be assumed to move from a state of unawareness through product comprehension to purchase. As a generalisation, advertising is better for creating awareness and personal selling is more effective at promoting action and purchase behaviour. These two tools have been used together for a long time by organisations but these tools are now being supplemented in B2B markets by the use of direct marketing and increasingly the Internet (Garber and Dotson, 2002).

Readers are encouraged to see the elements of the mix as a set of complementary ingredients, each drawing on the potential of the others. The tools are, to a limited extent, partially interchangeable and in various circumstances different tools are used to meet diverse objectives. For example, many B2B organisations use personal selling to complete the majority of activities in the purchase decision sequence. The high cost of this approach is counterbalanced by the effectiveness of the communications. However, this aspect of interchangeability only serves to complicate matters. If management's task was simply to identify problems and then select the correct precision tool to solve the problem, then the issue of the selection of the 'best' promotions mix would evaporate (see Figure 11.2).

These five elements of the promotional mix are supplemented by one of the most effective forms of marketing communication, **word-of-mouth** recommendation. Word-of-mouth recommendation ('word-of-mouse' online) is one of the most powerful supplements to marketing communications and, if an organisation can develop a programme to harness and accelerate the use of personal recommendation effectively, the more likely it will be that the marketing programme will be successful.

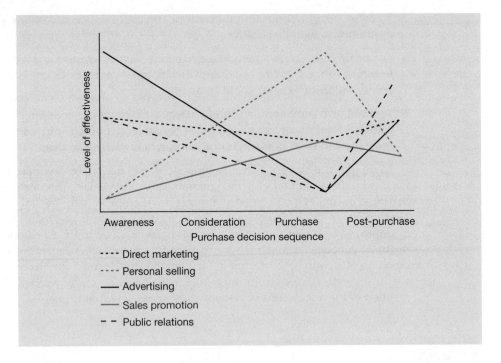

Figure 11.2 The relative effectiveness of the tools of the marketing communications mix

Word-of-mouth communications are embedded within the social networks that individuals, in this case organisational buyers, are involved. There is little doubt that word-of-mouth communications have strong levels of credibility attached to them and can be considerably more effective than personal selling or print media in inducing customers to switch suppliers. Money (2004) cites Raymond and Tanner's (1994) research that showed that use of referrals could be more than twice as successful as cold calling at generating new sales. Therefore, most B2B communication mixes should be deliberately orientated to generating and facilitating word-of-mouth communication.

When designing a B2B marketing communications programme, it should be remembered that there are generally only a few business customers in a single market, that they are geographically dispersed and they look for particular, specialised information. This means that messages must be appropriate for the individuals in the buying centre and the stage reached in the buying process. In addition, messages must be consistent so that whatever the point of contact, a customer will perceive the same message and reinforce previously learnt information about a supplier or set of products. The implication of this is that the tools and media used to deliver messages must be timed, capable of reaching the right targets and they must be based on a sound understanding of organisational buying behaviour and the particular characteristics of each individual customer.

Finally, B2B marketing communication programmes require finance. In order to determine the correct or the most appropriate level of investment various budgetary methods and techniques should be used. Readers interested in this topic area are referred to Fill (2002) where a detailed account of the various techniques can be found.

Summary

The prime marketing communication tool used in B2B markets is personal selling supported by direct marketing and public relations. Sales (or trade) promotions are significant in channel partner relationships and advertising is of least significance. Communications in B2B marketing are very personal, often requiring face-to-face interaction and this interactivity lends itself to tailored messages and rapid feedback.

The Internet and related digital technologies have had a very significant impact, changing the way business is conducted and the speed at which transactions can be undertaken and costs reduced. The Internet is of course both a new distribution channel and a communication medium. As a form of communication it can be deemed impersonal and more disposed to information search and retrieval than to delivering heavily branded and emotionally driven messages.

In an effort to increase the productivity of the sales force and to use their expensive skills more effectively, direct marketing has evolved such that it can enable organisations to improve their interorganisational relationships and levels of corporate and product performance.

Discussion questions

1 Using examples to illustrate your points compare and contrast the roles of B2B sales promotions and public relations.

2 Identify the stages associated with receiving direct mail.

3 Find details on the Internet of an exhibition and examine the information provided about the visitor profile. Why might organisations wish to attend this exhibition as an exhibitor and as a visitor?

4 Critically evaluate the role of the database in B2B marketing communications.

5 Using an organisation (or product range) with which you are familiar, examine the different media used to reach organisational buyers and consider the effectiveness of this media mix. How might you improve it?

6 To what extent are the tools of the marketing communication mix enhanced when a deliberate attempt is made to promote word-of-mouth communication?

References

Anderson, J.C. and Narus, J.A. (1990). 'A model of distributor firm and manufacturer firm working partnerships', *Journal of Marketing*, 54 (January), pp. 42–58.

Blattberg, R C. and Deighton J. (1991). 'Interactive marketing: exploiting the age of addressability', *Sloan Management Review*, 33 (Fall), pp. 5–14.

Blattberg, R.C. and Neslin, S.A. (1990). *Sales Promotion: Concepts, Methods and Strategies*, Englewood Cliffs, NJ: Prentice Hall.

Blythe, J. (2002). 'Using trade fairs in key account management', *Industrial Marketing Management*, 31, 7 (October), pp. 627–35.

Boukersi, L. (2000). 'The role of trade fairs and exhibitions in international marketing communications', in S. Moyne (ed.), *The Handbook of International Marketing Communications*, pp. 117–35, London: Blackwell.

Bush, A.J., Bush, V. and Harris, S. (1998). 'Advertisers' perceptions of the Internet as a marketing communications tool', *Journal of Advertising Research*, 38, 2 (March–April), pp. 17–27.

Chaffey, D., Mayer, R., Johnston, K. and Ellis-Chadwick, F. (2002). *Internet Marketing*, Harlow: Financial Times/Prentice Hall.

Ehling, W.P. (1992). 'Estimating the power of public relations and communication to an organisation', in J.E. Grunig, D.M. Dozier, P. Ehling, F.C. Repper and J. Whits (eds), *Excellence in Public Relations and Communications Management*, Hillsdale, NJ: Lawrence Erlbaum, pp. 617–38.

Evans, J.R. and King, V.E. (1999). 'Business-to-business marketing and the world wide web: planning, managing and assessing web sites', *Industrial Marketing Management*, 28, pp. 343–58.

Farrelly, F., Quester, P. and Mavondo F. (2003). 'Collaborative communication in sponsor relations', *Corporate Communications: an International Journal*, 8, 2, pp. 128–38.

Fill, C. (2002). *Marketing Communications: Contexts, Strategies and Applications*, 3rd edn, Harlow: Pearson Education.

Fletcher, K.P. and Peters, L.D. (1997). 'Trust and direct marketing environments: a consumer perspective', *Journal of Marketing Management*, 13, pp. 523–39.

Garber, Jr, L.L. and Dotson, M.J. (2002). 'A method for the selection of appropriate business-to-business integrated marketing communications mixes', *Journal of Marketing Communications*, 8, 1, (March), pp. 1–17.

Ghose, S. and Dou, W. (1998). 'Interactive functions and their impacts on the appeal of Internet presence sites', *Journal of Advertising Research*, 38, 2 (March/April), pp. 29–44.

Gilliland, D.I. (2004). 'Designing channel incentives to overcome reseller rejection', *Industrial Marketing Management*, 33, 2 (February), pp. 87–95.

Goodwin, C. (1991). 'Privacy: recognition of a consumer right', *Journal of Public Policy and Marketing*, 10, 1, pp. 149–66.

Gummesson, E. (1996). 'Relationship marketing and imaginary organizations: a synthesis', *European Journal of Marketing*, 30, 2, pp. 31–44.

Hoque, A. and Lohse, G. (1999). 'An information search cost perspective for designing interfaces for electronic commerce', *Journal of Marketing Research*, 36, 3 (August), pp. 387–94.

Kamakura, W.A., Wedel, M., de Rosa, F. and Mazzon, J.A. (2003). 'Cross-selling through database marketing: a mixed factor analyzer for data augmentation and prediction', *International Journal of Research in Marketing*, 20, 1 (March), pp. 45–65.

Karayanni, D.A. (2000). 'An integrated model of communication strategies for business network alliances, antecedent conditions and business performance, using the Internet as the mediating communication means', PhD thesis, Athens University of Economics and Business.

Karayanni, D.A. and Baltas, G.A. (2003). 'Web site characteristics and business performance: some evidence from international business-to-business organisations', *Marketing Intelligence and Planning*, 21, 2, pp. 105–14.

Kerin, R.A. and Cron, W.L. (1987). 'Assessing trade show functions and performance: an exploratory study', *Journal of Marketing*, 51, 3 (July), pp. 87–94.

Ledingham, J.A. and Bruning. S.D. (2000). *Public Relations as Relationship Management: A Relational Approach to the Study and Practice of Public Relations*, Mahwah, NJ: Lawrence Erlbaum Associates, Inc.

Leong, E.F.K., Huang, X. and Stanners, P.J. (1998). 'Comparing the effectiveness of the web site with traditional media', *Journal of Advertising Research*, 38, 5 (September–October), pp. 44–52.

Lloyd, J. (1997). 'Cut your rep free', *Pharmaceutical Marketing*, (September) pp. 30–2.

McLuhan, R. (2000). 'Fighting for a new view of field work', *Marketing*, 9 March, pp. 29–30.

Middleton, P, (2002). 'The corporate video revival', *What's New in Marketing*, 13 (December–January) www.wnim.com/archive/issue1303/index.htm (Accessed 31 December 2003.)

Money, R.B. (2004). 'Word of mouth promotion and switching behaviour in Japanese and American business-to-business service clients', *Journal of Business Research*, 57, 3 (March) pp. 297–305.

Morgan, R.M. and Hunt, S.D. (1994). 'The commitment–trust theory of relationship marketing', *Journal of Marketing*, 58 (July), pp. 20–38.

Moyies, J. (2000). 'A healthier specimen', *Admap*, June, pp. 39–42.

Partner, L. (2001). 'The rich media challenge', *Opt-In News*, Friday 13 July, www.optinnews.com/ read-article.php?id=311 (Accessed 31 December 2003.)

Pieczka, M. (1996). 'Public opinion and public relations', in J. L'Etang and M. Piezka (eds), *Critical Perspectives in Public Relations*, London: International Thomson Business Press.

Poorani, A.A. (1996). 'Trade-Show Management', *Hotel and Restaurant Administration Quarterly*, (August), pp. 77–84.

Raymond, M.A. and Tanner, J.F. (1994). 'Maintaining customer relationships in direct sales: stimulating repeat purchase behavior', *Journal of Personal Selling Management*, 14, 4 (Fall) pp. 67–76.

Ridgeway, J. (2000). 'DirectWatch in 2000', *Marketing*, 21 December, pp. 24–5.

Ruckert, R.W., Walker, O.C. and Roering, K.J. (1985). 'The organisation of marketing activities: a contingency theory of structure and performance', *Journal of Marketing*, (Winter), pp. 13–25.

Shipley, D. and Wong, K.S. (1993). 'Exhibiting strategy and implementation', *International Journal of Advertising*, 12, 2, pp. 117–30.

Voegle, S. (1992). *Handbook of Direct Mail. The Dialogue Method of Direct Written Sales Communication*, New York, NY: Prentice Hall.

Vriens, M., van der Scheer, H.R., Hoekstra, J.C. and Bult, J. (1998). 'Conjoint experiments for direct mail response optimization', *European Journal of Marketing*, 32, 3/4, pp. 323–39.

Wulf, K.D., Hoekstra, J.C and Commandeur, H.R. (2000). 'The opening and reading behaviour of business-to-business direct mail', *Industrial Marketing Management*, 29, 2 (March), pp. 133–45.

Chapter 12
Personal selling and key account management

Chapter overview

The importance of personal selling in the B2B promotional mix should not be underestimated. Although all of the tools can play a significant part in an organisation's overall marketing communications activities, personal selling, delivered through a sales force is the most potent. A key theme throughout this book has been the development of relationships, principally between customers and suppliers. Meaningful collaborative relationships can only be established and nurtured through personal contact and selling.

In this final chapter consideration is given to the role and characteristics of personal selling and to when it should play a lead role in the promotional mix. However, the main thrust is centred on the impact of selling on interorganisational relationships and how the other promotional tools can be blended to provide cost and communication effectiveness. In addition, issues concerning the management and organisation of the sales force are explored before examining the role of technology in selling and in particular sales force automation. The chapter concludes with an examination of key account management.

Chapter aims

The main aims of this chapter are to consider some of the key characteristics of personal selling and to examine how this promotional tool can best be used to influence the nature and shape of relationships between organisations and individual buyers and sellers.

Objectives

The objectives of this chapter are to:

1 Consider the role and tasks of personal selling.
2 Examine the characteristics of this promotional tool and determine when it should be a major part of the mix.
3 Evaluate the contribution sales force activities can and should make to the development of interorganisational relationships.
4 Appraise the effective mix of promotional tools for selling through multiple channels.
5 Appreciate the range of issues impacting on sales force managers.
6 Explore the impact of technology on the performance of the sales force with particular emphasis on sales force automation.
7 Determine the role and key characteristics of key account management.

Introduction

Personal selling is different from the other forms of communication mainly because transmitted messages represent dyadic communication. This means that there are two persons involved in the communication process. Feedback and evaluation of transmitted messages is possible, more or less instantaneously, so that these personal selling messages can be tailored to be much more personal than any of the other methods of communication.

Since personal selling brings buyers and sellers into close proximity it is possible to induce a change in behaviour. This occurs because information can be provided quickly and with conviction, in the context of the buyer's environment. In addition to product demonstration, information is provided in the setting of the transaction and can be used to overcome objections and encourage buyers to place orders.

Given that the costs associated with personal selling are high, it is vital that sales staff are used effectively. To that end, many organisations seek methods to decrease the time that the sales force spends on administration, travel and office work and to maximise the time spent in front of customers, where they can use their specific selling skills.

Organisations adopt a mixture of personal selling activities, often based on the proven methods appropriate to their type of business. Indeed, there is evidence that the activities undertaken by a sales force are strongly related to the overall marketing strategies that an organisation seeks to implement (Cross *et al.*, 2001). It is normally assumed that the sales force collect and bring into the organisation orders from customers wishing to make purchases. This aspect of personal selling can be typified in four ways:

Order takers are salespersons to whom customers are drawn at the place of supply. Reception clerks at hotels and ticket desk personnel at theatres and cinemas typify this role.

Order getters are sales personnel who operate away from the organisation and who attempt to gain orders largely through the use of demonstration and persuasion.

Order collectors are those who attempt to gather orders over the telephone or through email. The growth of telesales operations as a sales support programme is designed to save the time of both the buyer and seller. Telesales are used to gather repeat and low value orders, reduce costs, speed transaction time, improve cash flow and free valuable sales personnel to seek new customers and build relationships with current customers.

Order supporters are all those people who are secondary to salespersons in that they are involved with the order once it has been secured, or are involved with the act of ordering, usually by supplying information. Order processing or financial advice services typify this role.

These types of personal selling are to some degree superficial as they all represent people who have a customer-facing role and who are expected to engage in customer interaction. It is the depth of customer contact that provides the real measure of customer interaction.

Personal selling cannot work effectively in isolation from the other elements in the promotional mix. For example, members of the sales force are literally **representative** of the organisation for which they work so, in one sense, they can be deemed a mobile form of public relations. Stakeholders view them and partly shape their perception of the organisation they represent based on, for example, the way in which they dress, speak and handle questions, the type of car they drive and the level of courtesy they display to support staff.

The role and tasks of personal selling

It is generally agreed that personal selling is most effective at the later stages of the buying process, rather than at the earlier stage of awareness building. It follows that each organisation should determine the precise role the sales force is to play within their communication mix. Personal selling is the most expensive element of the communications mix, so the use of a sales force should be a very carefully considered element of an organisation's promotional activities. In terms of the DRIP framework (see Chapter 10), personal selling may fulfil different roles. Where the relationship between organisations is new or basically discrete in nature, information and persuasion will tend to be the predominant roles. Where the relationship is established and more collaborative, information and reinforcement will be the more prominent roles.

In B2B markets it is often assumed that sales personnel operate at the boundary of the organisation. They provide the link between the needs of their own organisation and the needs of their customers and in this sense they perform an important representational role. This linkage is absolutely vital, for a number of reasons that will be discussed shortly, for without personal selling communication with other organisations would occur through impersonal, electronic or print media, probably to the detriment of relationships. However, the notion that there is a boundary between organisations who operate within a close network or within a collaborative relationship is both tenuous and contradictory. Boundaries may exist where discrete exchanges predominate but in situations where trust, commitment and reciprocity are fundamental, it is unlikely that a boundary could, or should, be identified.

When these factors are brought together, the salesperson is not only expected to act as a manager of customers (Wilson, 1993) but increasingly also as a person responsible for, among many other elements, the development of customer relationships (Marshall *et al.*, 1999). Strong personal interaction with clients, based upon either a collaborative or transactional (problem–solution) perspective to buyer needs, can provide a source of sustainable competitive advantage for organisations.

SNAPSHOT 12.1

ROLE OF THE SALES FORCE

The Robert Mondavi company employs over 1,000 people worldwide and generates annual sales of $450 million. The company relies on a worldwide sales force of over 130 to promote 21 different brands and has established partnerships with wineries in Australia, Italy and Chile.

Robert Mondavi employs a conventional, indirect marketing channel using distributors to sell into retailers, who then sell to consumers. The key role of the sales force therefore is to ensure that distributors sell wine into the retail channel, a classic push strategy scenario.

Part of the role is to provide distributors access to promotions to enable them to push products through the channel more effectively, thereby improving productivity of the distribution chain. To accomplish this task the sales force have various sales tools which include product fact sheets and logos, which retailers use to create in-store merchandising opportunities, press clippings and harvest reports used to promote the brands. Because this information changes rapidly, it is imperative that the sales force has access to the most up-to-date marketing. To help achieve this the company uses an extranet, called Partner Connect, which enables more than 200 distributors to access real-time information on stock, pricing and promotions.

Source: Adapted from www.vignette.com/contentmanagement/0,2097,1-1-31-1665-1756-2653,00.html (Accessed 14 December 2003.)

Salespersons do more than get or take orders and organisations should decide which tasks it expects its representatives to undertake. The list in Table 12.1 is an adaptation of the work by Guenzi (2002). These tasks provide direction and purpose, and also help to establish the criteria by which the performance of members of the sales force can be evaluated.

Table 12.1 Tasks of personal selling

Activity	Explanation
Selling	Leading prospects (and established customers) to a successful close.
Prospecting	Finding and using leads to create new customers.
Inbound information	Reporting information to the organisation about customers and associated stakeholders.
Outbound information	Reporting organisational information to customers and associated stakeholders about products and organisational issues.
Market research	The analysis and forecasting of market trends and related activities.
Sales team coordination	Developing strong internal links with sales support teams.
Customer relationship management	Developing mutually satisfying relationships with customers.
Sales service	Pre-sales support to encourage buyer engagement and trust prior to any transaction. Post-sales support to provide reassurance and formative collaborative gestures.

Source: Adapted from Guenzi (2002).

Personal selling is often referred to as interpersonal communication and from this perspective Reid *et al.* (2002) determined three major sales behaviours, namely, getting, giving and using information.

Getting information refers to sales behaviours aimed at information acquisition. For example, gathering information about customers, markets and competitors.

Giving information refers to the dissemination of information to customers and other stakeholders. For example, sales presentations and seminar meetings designed to provide information about products and an organisation's capabilities and reputation.

Using information refers to the sales person's use of information to help solve a customer's problem. Associated with this is the process of gaining buyer commitment through the generation of information (Thayer, 1968, cited by Reid *et al.* 2002).

These last authors suggest that the using information dynamic appears to be constant across all types of purchase situations. However, as the complexity of a purchase situation increases so the amount of giving information behaviours decline and getting information behaviours increase. This finding supports the need for a sales-person to be able to recognise particular situations in the buying process and to then adapt their behaviour to meet buyer's contextual needs.

However, salespeople undertake numerous tasks in association with communication activities. Guenzi (2002) determined that some sales activities are generic simply because they are performed by most salespeople across a large number of industries. These generic activities are selling, customer relationship management and communicating to customers. Other activities such as market analysis, pre-sales services and the transfer of information about competitors to the organisation, are industry specific. Interestingly he found that information-gathering activities are more likely to be undertaken by organisations operating in consumer markets than in B2B, possibly a reflection of the strength of the market orientation in both arenas.

The roles and tasks of the sales force have been changing because the environment in which organisations operate is shifting dramatically. These changes, in particular those associated with the development and implementation of new technologies, have had repercussions on the activities of the sales force and are discussed later in this chapter.

Characteristics of personal selling

There are a number of characteristics, seen as strengths and weaknesses, associated with this promotional tool. It is interesting to note that some of the strengths can in turn be seen as weaknesses, particularly when management control over the communication process is not as attentive or as rigorous as it might be.

Strengths

Dyadic communications allow for two-way interaction, which, unlike the other promotional tools, provide for fast, direct feedback. In comparison with the mass media, personal selling allows for the receiver to focus attention on the salesperson, with a reduced likelihood of distraction or noise.

There is a greater level of participation in the decision process by the vendor than in the other tools. When this is combined with the power to tailor messages in response to the feedback provided by the buyer, the sales process has a huge potential to solve customer problems.

Weaknesses

One of the major disadvantages of personal selling is the cost. As reach is limited, costs per personal contact are normally high. Costs include salaries, commission, employment costs, expenses including travel, accommodation and subsistence. This means that management must find alternative ways of communicating particular messages and improve the amount of time that sales personnel spend with prospects and customers. Reach and frequency through personal selling is always going to be low, regardless of the level of funds available.

The amount of control that can be exercised over the delivery of messages through the sales force can be low. This is because each salesperson has the freedom to adapt messages to meet changing circumstances as negotiations proceed. In practice, however, the professionalism and training that members of the sales force often receive and the increasing accent on measuring levels of customer satisfaction, mean that the degree of control over the message can be regarded, in most circumstances, as very good, although it can never, for example, be as high as that of advertising.

The potential disadvantage of message inconsistency can lead to confusion (perhaps a misunderstanding with regard to a product specification), the ramifications of which can be enormous in terms of the cost and time spent by a variety of individuals from both parties to the contract. The quality of the relationship can, therefore, be jeopardised through poor and inconsistent communications.

When personal selling should be a major part of the promotional mix

In view of the role, advantages and disadvantages of personal selling, when should it be a major part of the communications mix? The following is not an exhaustive list, but is presented as a means of considering some of the important issues: complexity, network factors, buyer significance and communication effectiveness.

Complexity

Personal selling is very important when there is a medium to high level of relationship complexity. Such complexity may be associated with either the physical characteristics of the product, such as computer software design, or with the environment in which the negotiations are taking place. For example, decisions related to the installation of products designed to automate an assembly line may well be a sensitive issue. This may be due to management's attitude towards the operators currently undertaking the work that the automation is expected to replace. Any complexity needs to be understood by buyer and seller in order that the right product is offered in the appropriate context for the buyer. This may mean that the buyer is required to customise the offering or provide assistance in terms of testing, installing or supporting the product.

When the complexity of the offering is high, advertising and public relations cannot always convey benefits in the same way as personal selling. Personal selling allows the product to be demonstrated so that buyers can see and, if necessary, touch and taste it for themselves. Personal selling also allows explanations to be made about particular points of concern to the buyer or about the environment in which the buyer wishes to use the product.

Buyer significance

The significance of the product to the buyers in the target market is a very important factor in the decision on whether to use personal selling. Significance can be measured as a form of risk, which is associated with benefits and costs.

The absolute cost to the buyer will vary among organisations. The significance of the purchase of an extra photocopier for a major multinational organisation may be low, but for a new start-up organisation or for an established organisation experiencing a dramatic turnaround, an extra photocopying machine may be highly significant and subject to high levels of resistance by a number of different internal stakeholders.

The timing of a product's introduction may well be crucial to the success of a wider plan or programme of activities. Only through personal selling can delivery be dovetailed into a client's schedule.

Communication effectiveness

There may be a number of ways to satisfy the communication objectives of a campaign, other than by using personal selling. Each of the other communication tools has strengths and weaknesses; consequently, differing mixes provide different benefits.

One of the main reasons for using personal selling occurs when advertising alone, or any other tool or medium, provides insufficient communication. The main reason for this inadequacy surfaces when advertising media cannot provide buyers with the information they require to make their decision. For example, a fleet car buyer may well observe and read various magazine and newspaper advertisements, often as a consumer. The decision to buy on behalf of their organisation, however, requires information and data upon which a more rational decision can be made. This rationality and experience, through face-to-face negotiations, visits, road reports and test drives, balances the former, more emotional, elements that shaped their earlier thoughts.

The decision to buy capital assets normally evokes high involvement, and motivation occurs through the central route of the elaboration likelihood model (ELM) previously considered in Chapter 10. Therefore, manufacturers tend to provide a wealth of factual information in various formats, from which prospective buyers seek further information, experience and reassurance, usually via a salesperson, that is, a personal point of contact.

Personal selling provides a number of characteristics that make it more effective than the other elements of the B2B promotional mix. As discussed, the complexity of many products requires salespeople to be able to discuss with clients their specific needs; in other words, to be able to talk in the customer's own language, to offer source credibility through expertise and hopefully trustworthiness, and build a relationship that corresponds with the psychographic profile of each member of the DMU. In this case, mass communications would be inappropriate.

There are two further factors that influence the decision to use personal selling as part of the communications mix. When the customer base is small and dispersed across a wide geographic area it makes economic sense to use salespersons, because advertising in this situation is inadequate, ineffective and inefficient.

Channel factors

If the communication strategy combines a larger amount of push, rather than pull, activities then personal selling is required to provide the necessary communications for the other members of a network. Following on from this is the question of what information needs to be exchanged between members, in what form and with what timing. Handling objections, answering questions and overcoming misconceptions are also necessary information exchange skills.

When the number of members in a network is limited, the use of a sales force is advisable, as advertising is inefficient in these circumstances. Furthermore, the opportunity to build a close collaborative relationship with channel members may enable the development of a sustainable competitive advantage. Cravens (1987) has suggested that the factors in Table 12.2 are important and determine when the sales force is a significant element of the communications mix.

Table 12.2 When personal selling is a major element of the communications mix

	Advertising relatively important	Personal selling relatively important
Number of customers	Large	Small
Buyers' information needs	Low	High
Size and importance of purchase	Small	Large
Post-purchase service required	Little	A lot
Product complexity	Low	High
Distribution strategy	Pull	Push
Pricing policy	Set	Negotiate
Resources available for promotion	Many	Few

Source: Adapted from Cravens (1987).

However, although personal selling may be the most persuasive single tool of the promotional mix, combining it with advertising results in the most potent combination of communication elements. Their strengths serve to complement each other. Advertising is more effective at the initial stages of the response hierarchy, but the later stages of inducing trial and closing the order are the strong points of personal selling.

To illustrate the potency of this combination, Levitt (1967) reported that organisations that invest in advertising to raise awareness are more likely to create a favourable reception for their salespeople than those organisations that do not undertake such activities. However, those that had invested were also expected to have a better trained sales force. Morrill (1970) found that selling costs were as much as 12 per cent lower if the customer had been made aware of the salesperson's organisation prior to the call. Swinyard and Ray (1977) determined that, even if a purchase was not made for reasons other than product quality, further use of advertising increased the probability of a future sale. All these findings suggest that, by combining advertising with personal selling, costs can be reduced, reach extended and the probability of a sale considerably improved.

Personal selling is a major tool of the B2B promotional mix and a significant part of marketing management (Anderson, 1996) in business markets. One of the reasons for this is the responsibility sales people have to manage customer relationships.

Personal selling and managing relationships

One view of personal selling is that the sales force is responsible for selling, installing and upgrading customer equipment. Another is that they are responsible for developing, selling and protecting accounts. The interesting point from both views is that responsibilities, or rather objectives, are extended, vertically upstream, into offer design, or vertically downstream, into the development and maintenance of long-term customer relationships. It is the last point that is becoming increasingly important. In the B2B sector the sales activity mix is becoming more orientated to the need to build and sustain the relationships that organisations have, or want, with their major customers.

Many authors consider the development, organisation and completion of a sale in a market exchange-based transaction to be the key part of the personal selling role. The focus of activity is on closing the sale and very much transaction orientated. Little attention is given to customer expectations of the sales process and whether a buyer will be a source of future business (Keillor *et al.*, 2000). Sales personnel provide a source of information for buyers so that they can make the right purchase decisions. In that sense they provide a good level of credibility, but they are also perceived, understandably, as biased. The degree of expertise held by the salesperson may be high, but the degree of trustworthiness will vary, especially during the formative period of the relationship, unless other transactions with the selling organisation have been satisfactory.

Once a number of transactions have been completed and product and service quality established, trustworthiness may improve. Indeed, a more relational perspective can start to emerge based around customer needs concerning the sales process, the

SNAPSHOT 12.2

THE ALLIEDSIGNAL SALES FORCE AND CUSTOMER RELATIONSHIPS

In 1995 American Airlines was forced to use AlliedSignal as a parts supplier because there were no alternatives. Unfortunately the service given by AlliedSignal to American, and to many other customers, was reportedly very poor. In fact, the problem became so acute that many customers moved to low-cost, inferior quality suppliers and the reputation of the company plummeted.

The root of the problem lay within the four AlliedSignal Aerospace business units. The units did not have a common systems infrastructure and they could not share information about sales opportunities, the status of maintenance requests or the products customers had on their aircraft. With 40 independent product lines, it was quite usual for several salespeople across the aerospace division to contact the same customers, during the same week or even on the same day, without knowing they were doing so. Large customers sometimes had as many as 50 points of contact with the company.

The effort taken to improve the company's customer service reputation was enormous. It required a major rethink of sales and service practices and the implementation of new CRM software. However, very few Allied salespeople wanted to use the CRM system having seen two past sales force automation (SFA) efforts fail. They wanted to stick with their own databases and actively resisted initial attempts to convert.

To overcome the resistance, Honeywell created a new post, a manager of CRM business processes, to work with each sales unit in order to create a new, single sales process tied into the CRM system. The team overcame legacy loyalty by transferring data from existing databases into Atlas, the new system and then shutting down salespeople's old databases.

Now the unified CRM system is widely used, customers and the sales force are comfortable with the high levels of service and, as a result, after-market sales have doubled.

Source: Adapted from Levinson, M. (2003), www.cio.com/archive/040102/takeoff.html (Accessed 1 January 2004.) Reprinted through the courtesy of CIO. Copyright © 2003 CXO Media Inc. All rights reserved.

quality of the overall buyer–seller interaction and the wider network implications and expectations of the participants.

Research indicates that for salespeople to be successful within a relational context there are three particular characteristics that can influence outcomes. These are a **customer/selling orientation** (Saxe and Weitz, 1982: Kelly, 1992), **adaptability** (Morgan and Stoltman, 1990) and a **service orientation** (Cronin and Taylor, 1992) (see Table 12.3).

Keillor *et al.* found the customer/selling orientation to be significantly related to salesperson performance, which has implications for sales training, although these authors did not find any significant relationship with the other two variables.

Table 12.3 Categories associated with developing relational sales activities

Category	Explanation
Customer orientation	By discovering customer needs and working to satisfy them by providing products and services that will provide customers with benefits, a long-term approach is adopted and short-term sales may be forsaken for longer-term goals.
Adaptability in the sales process	A salesperson's ability to adapt their sales approach in order to maintain a dialogue and continued interaction with the client. Adaptability should be seen as superior to both self- and task-orientated approaches. Listening, probing, questioning and detecting a variety of client clues are all signs of an adaptable approach.
Service orientation	This refers to the perception a buyer has of a salesperson's enthusiasm to engage in both selling and non-selling tasks, throughout the buyer–seller relationship.
	Service quality is an antecedent to customer satisfaction, which in turn has a positive impact on purchase intentions (Cronin and Taylor, 1992).

The behaviours most associated with relational selling have been identified as the intensity of the interaction, the mutual disclosure of information and cooperative intentions (Guenzi, 2002). There is also some general agreement that these behaviours do not necessarily impact on sales performance but do influence the quality of the relationship and the inherent trust between partner organisations. Indeed, trust, a concept examined in Chapter 9, appears to increase as the selling task adopts a deeper relationship orientation (Wilson, 1995). Customer perception of the levels of **trust** (in a salesperson and the organisation represented) and **expertise** constitute two crucial sales attributes. When these attributes are positive it is more likely that long-term interorganisational relationships will develop (Liu and Leach, 2001). Not surprisingly, sales training programmes should, according to Guenzi, be designed to highlight the importance of developing and maintaining customer trust and emphasise the benefits of adaptive relational behaviours.

Sales managers are broadly seen to be responsible for the management and achievement of the sales goals set for a particular salesperson, team and/or regions. They are, as Mehta *et al.* (2002, p. 430) put it, 'trainers, motivators, coaches, evaluators and counsellors for their sales people'. They perform many other roles but one, that appears to be identified as significant yet understated, concerns marketing channels. Initial work by these researchers indicates that many sales managers are increasingly acting as channel managers and take on the task of managing customer relationships across an increasing number of channels. They point out the implications of this development in terms of the range and type of training that sales managers need in view of the strategic significance of channel strategy and customer relationships.

Multiple channel selling

As discussed earlier in this book, many organisations have restructured their sales operations, partly in an attempt to reduce costs and partly to meet the future channel needs of their customers. With the huge variety of sales channels that are available there is also an increased complexity. These channels include the basic electronic and direct marketing channels at one end of the spectrum and at the other multi-functional, global, personal sales teams (Ingram *et al.*, 2002).

The restructuring of sales channels has often taken the form of introducing multiple sales channels, where the simple objective is to use less expensive channels to complete those selling tasks that do not require personal, face-to-face contact and which are typified by transaction-orientated relationships. In contrast, collaborative relationships tend to be better supported by personal, face-to-face selling efforts.

This principle can be best observed within a simple matrix, based on the dimensions of potential account attractiveness and strength of relationship. Attractiveness refers to the opportunities a buying organisation represents to the supplier while the strength of relationship maps the extent to which two organisations are experienced and actively engaged in transactions with each other (see Figure 12.1).

For reasons of clarity, these scales are presented as either high or low, strong or weak. However, they should be considered as a continuum, and with the use of some relatively simple evaluative criteria, accounts can be positioned on the matrix and strategies formulated to move them to different positions, which in turn necessitates the use of different sales channel mixes.

Using the approach of Cravens *et al.* (1991), appropriate sales channels are superimposed on the matrix in order that optimum efficiency in selling effort and costs be managed (Figure 12.2). Accounts in Section 1 vary in attractiveness, as some will be assigned key account status. The others will be very important and will require a high level of selling effort, which has to be delivered by the field sales force.

Accounts in Section 2 are essentially prospects because of their weak competitive position but high attractiveness. Selling effort should be proportional to the value of

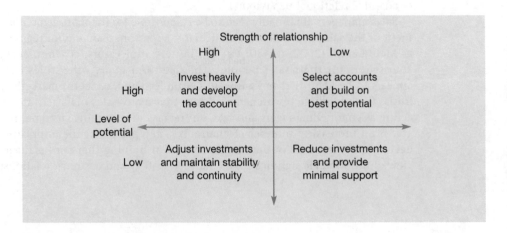

Figure 12.1 Account investment matrix

SNAPSHOT 12.3

DIRECT MARKETING FOR THE SALES FORCE

The BUPA Wellness Dental Service, part of the BUPA group and Inbox Media worked together to promote BUPA's in-house dentistry service for the corporate market.

The objectives of the campaign were to make contact with the key decision makers within major organisations (heads of HR within medium to large corporates), to introduce the main benefits of the dental service and to generate highly qualified sales appointments for the sales team at BUPA Wellness.

Inbox's first task was to build a database of target organisations and decision makers and then get the permission of the recipient to receive interactive email.

The Inbox email dynamically used the recipient's individual details to personalise each movie. This enabled thousands of high impact, personalised television-style advertisements to be delivered, direct to key decision makers, that promoted the BUPA Wellness on-site dental service. Each email was tracked and integrated into the telemarketing campaign. This meant that all click-throughs were followed up, in real time, by the Inbox telemarketing team, who were dedicated to the campaign and who had been fully trained on the range of BUPA Wellness products.

This campaign was considered one of the first of its kind to use rich media, be truly personalised, interactive and be fully integrated with telemarketing. The qualified leads that resulted from this campaign enabled the sales team to follow up in the knowledge that the prospect was fully aware of the product and the BUPA brand, thus improving trust and credibility.

Source: Adapted from www.inbox.co.uk/htmlv/News.asp?ID=2 (Accessed 1 January 2004.) Used with permission.

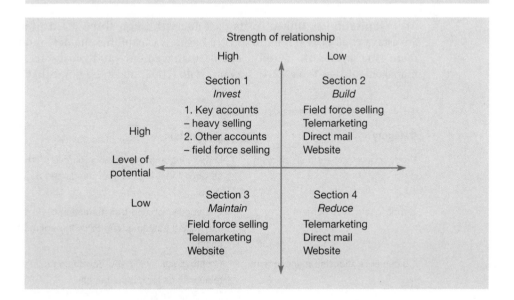

Figure 12.2 Sales channel mix allocation
Source: Adapted from Cravens *et al.* (1991).

the prospects: high effort for good prospects and low for the others. All the main sales channels should be used, commencing with direct mail to identify prospects, telesales for qualification purposes, field sales force selling directed at the strong prospects and telesales for the others. As the relationship becomes stronger, so field selling takes over from telesales. If the relationship weakens then the account may be discontinued and selling redirected to other prospects.

Accounts in Section 3 are not particularly attractive and, although the relationship is strong, there are opportunities, according to Cravens *et al.*, to switch the sales channel mix by reducing, but not eliminating, the level of field force activity and to give consideration to the introduction of telesales for particular accounts. Significant cost reductions can be achieved with these types of accounts by simply reviewing the means and reasoning behind the personal selling effort. Accounts in Section 4 should receive no field force calls, the prime sales channels being telesales, direct mail and catalogue selling.

Establishing a multiple sales channel strategy based on the matrix suggested above may not be appropriate to all organisations. For example, the current level of performance may be considered as exceeding expectations, in which case there is no point in introducing change. It may be that the costs and revenues associated with redeployment are unfavourable and that the implications for the rest of the organisation of implementing the new sales channel approach are such that the transition should either be postponed or rejected. However, experience has shown (Cravens *et al.*, 1991) that costs can be reduced through the introduction of a multiple sales channel approach and that levels of customer satisfaction and the strength of the relationship between members of the network can be improved considerably.

Sales force management and organisation

An organisation is linked to its customers through three main processes which Srivastava *et al.* (1999) refer to as core business capabilities, namely product development management, supply chain management and customer relationship management (see Table 12.4). Ingram, *et al.* (2002) make the point that the centrality

Table 12.4 Core business capabilities

Category	Explanation
Product development management	Developing and maintaining suitable products and services to meet customer needs and provide customer value.
Supply chain management	The acquisition and transformation of resources (inputs) into valued customer offerings, throughout the supply chain.
Customer relationship management	Creating, sustaining and developing customer relationships for mutual benefit.

Source: Adapted from Srivastava *et al.* (1999).

of the customer to the organisation highlights the crucial role of sales strategy with regard to the organisation's overall customer interaction process.

In order to decide on an appropriate sales strategy, the nature of the desired communication needs to be examined. Are there to be salespersons negotiating individually, or as a team with a single buyer or buying team? Is a sales team required in order to sell to buying teams or will conference and seminar selling achieve the desired goals? What is the degree of importance of the portfolio of accounts, and how should the organisations be contacted?

The primary, and traditional, sales channel is the field sales force. These are people who are fully employed by the organisation and are referred to as the direct sales force. Salespersons, like any other unit of resource, should be deployed in a way that provides maximum benefit to the organisation. Sales organisation effectiveness results from the performance of salespeople, organisational factors and various environmental factors (Baldauf *et al.*, 2002).

Grant and Cravens (1999) suggest that the effectiveness of the sales organisation (or unit) is determined as a result of two main antecedents – the sales manager and the sales force itself. The content of these antecedents is shown at Figure 12.3.

The performance of salespeople is a measure of both their work- or task-related, behaviours and the results of their activities and inputs. Therefore, a sales management control strategy should refer to the degree to which sales managers actively manage the inputs as well as reward against targeted outcomes (sales, market share and so on).

From this it is possible to identify two main sales management approaches, behaviour-based and outcome-based control systems (Baldauf *et al.*, 2002). Essentially, control through behaviour-based systems is based on managing the inputs or processes to a salesperson and rewarding with a high fixed salary and low commission. Conversely, control through outcome-based approaches is characterised by a focus on

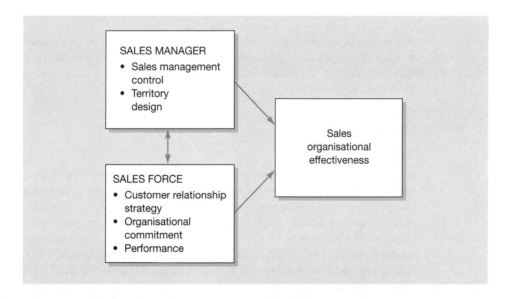

Figure 12.3 Antecedents of sales organisational effectiveness

Source: Grant and Cravens (1999). Published with permission, Emerald Group Publishing Limited, www.emeraldinsight.com

results, little managerial supervision and direction, and high levels of commission as an incentive to perform.

Many organisations use a hybrid approach but research by Baldauf *et al.* indicates that sales managers appear to utilise a 'coaching rather than command and control management styles' (p. 591). The emphasis appears to be on the long term and the value of developing relationships. The performance of salespeople is therefore enhanced by sales management strategies that are based on generating positive behaviour. However, results from previous work undertaken by Piercy *et al.* (1998) supported many previous findings that salespeople with high levels of behaviour performance also exhibit high levels of outcome performance. This implies that sales managers should spend a greater amount of their time selecting, training and developing salespeople rather than just selecting, directing and measuring results.

From this brief overview of sales management responsibilities it can be concluded that managers are responsible for five broad activities associated with salespeople:

- selection and recruitment;

- training and coaching;

- deployment;

- motivation and supervision;

- evaluation, control and reward.

Sales force ownership, size and shape

Assuming the decision has been made that some form of personal selling is required in the communications mix, one of the first questions to be addressed concerns the type of sales force to be used The direct sales force is one solution, another is the manufacturer's representative.

Manufacturers' representatives

Manufacturer's representatives (reps) are outsourced sales people. They can be considered as a contract sales force hired to perform specific duties. They sell other, often complementary yet non-competitive, products and services into distributors, OEMs and end-user customers (McQuiston, 2001). The reasons for adopting this approach, according to McQuiston, is to enable the direct sales force to concentrate on larger, strategically more significant accounts. The independent reps, who often have a strong and detailed knowledge of the market, are then targeted to work with the smaller accounts.

The level of dependency between the manufacturer and the rep is interesting in that, in a transaction-based environment, the manufacturer needs reps to open new accounts and shift product. With a move to more collaborative relationships, information

SNAPSHOT 12.4

USING MANUFACTURERS' REPRESENTATIVES

A major pharmaceutical manufacturer with a strong portfolio of alternate care products wanted to expand its access to and overall provision of customer service in its home market. With an annual growth rate of over 10 per cent it was seen as important to provide the resources to meet customers service and training needs.

A major part of its new strategy was to build a national network of independent manufacturers representatives. This new team would complement the established direct sales force whose main responsibility was for servicing the larger metropolitan areas. It was planned that the independent reps would cover all other areas.

Adding approximately 30 independent manufacturers reps to supplement their direct sales force enabled the organisation to provide greater geographical coverage in the marketplace. The Alternate Care sales team was organised into five regions, each headed by a regional manager responsible for both the independent reps and the direct sales force.

becomes specifically integral to the success of the relationship and hence the rep is dependent upon the manufacturer for detailed product specifications and application knowledge.

McQuiston reports research aimed at identifying the constructs or core values which are judged to be critical for the success of relationships between manufacturers' reps and the organisations (or principals) they represent. These are shown at Figure 12.4.

As depicted in Figure 12.4, McQuiston's six core values are supplemented by four supporting factors. Added to this should be two further factors, namely suitable strategic and selling skills (Weinraunch *et al.*, 2001). The 'interlocking' nature of these constructs reflects previous research in the field. However, the important aspect appears to be that the model can be used positively to develop relationships. Through an auditing process parties can identify their relationship strengths and weaknesses and determine how their affiliation should proceed.

Team selling

For organisations that offer relatively complex products the decision to employ their own direct sales force is a straightforward necessity. However, it is becoming increasingly common to assign a team of salespeople to meet the needs of major customers. A variety of different skills are necessary to meet the diversity of personnel making up the DMUs of the larger organisations. Consequently, a salesperson may gain access to an organisation, after which a stream of engineers, analysts, technicians, programmers, training executives and financial experts follow.

For example, when car manufacturers plan a new model, they often invite current suppliers to contribute to the development process. The supplier's salesperson will provide an initial communication link between the two organisations. Soon, a project team evolves, consisting of engineering, manufacturing, purchasing, production and quality

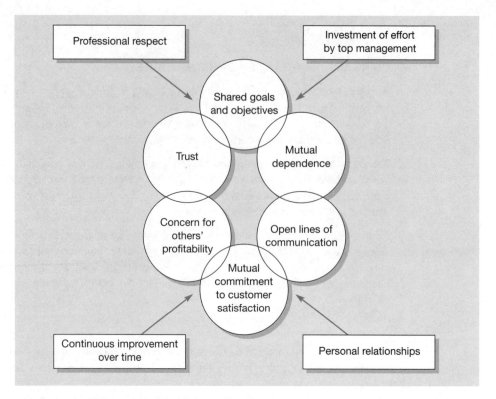

Figure 12.4 A conceptual model for building relationships between manufacturers' reps and their principals
Source: McQuiston (2001). Copyright © 2001. With permission from Elsevier.

staff, all working to satisfy the needs of their client. Some organisations use the same project code number as the client to provide improved clarity and reduced ambiguity. It also helps to build the relationship and identification between the partners.

In the past, some leading IT-based organisations sold hardware and then left the customer to work out how to use it. Team selling is now used by Hewlett-Packard, IBM and most other leading organisations, to provide customised combinations of hardware, software and technical support as solutions to their customers' business problems. This requires teams of salespeople and technical experts working closely with the customers' DMUs throughout the sales/purchasing cycle and beyond.

The sales team approach requires high levels of coordination and internal communication if it is to be successful and sell across product lines from various locations (Cespedes *et al.*, 1989). The costs associated with cross-functional team selling are large, which is one of the reasons why this approach is restricted to key accounts.

Sales force structure

There are a number of ways in which an organisation can structure the sales force, but there are three broad approaches (geographic, product and market/customer), which most organisations have used. These are set out in Table 12.5.

Table 12.5 Types of sales force structure

Type of structure	Explanation
Geographic-based sales force	Sales people are assigned separate geographic areas and each are responsible for all the activities necessary to sell all products to all potential customers in the region or area in which the territory is located.
	Used by new companies in situations where customers buy a range of products, where there is little difference in the geographic spread of the products and when resources are limited.
Product-based sales force	Uses different sales teams, each carrying a particular line of products. Often used by organisations with large and diverse product lines, with highly technical and complex products which require specialist knowledge and particular selling techniques.
Market-based sales force	Organising a sales force by market or customer type is an activity complementary to the marketing concept.
	This form of sales force organisation has increased in popularity, as it allows products with many applications to be sold into many different markets and hence to different customers.

The form of structure that any organisation adopts is a function of a number of variables. There are no fixed rules that determine how businesses should organise their sales force. However, due to the high costs associated with running a sales force, one overriding factor is the level of financial resource available. Some large organisations use a mixture of methods in order to best complement customer needs, market conditions and their own resources and competitive advantages. Some organisations use temporary or field force sales teams in addition to their own direct sales force in order to reach particular markets and to help launch new products.

Sales force size

Once the preferred structure has been established it is necessary to calculate the size of the sales force and the right number of salespeople required to deliver the marketing objectives.

The size of the sales force should be determined on a regular basis because the environments in which sales forces are operating change rapidly. The decision regarding the optimal size of the sales force presents a dilemma. Increasing the size of the sales force will increase the sales revenue, but it will also increase costs. A balance needs to be achieved, and according to Govoni *et al.* (1986) the decision is a blend of the following factors: the number of potential customers, the sales potential of each of these accounts, the geographic concentration of the customers and the availability of financial resources.

There are many different approaches to the determination of the appropriate sales force size. Some of the more recent ones are based upon sophisticated software, but these are derived essentially from three main approaches: the **breakdown**, **workload** and **sales potential** methods.

NEW SALES REGIONS AT JELD-WEN

The largest manufacturer of windows, doors and stairs in the United Kingdom announced that it had restructured its merchant sales force. Its previous two sales areas were reconfigured into six new sales regions.

Each region is now run by an appointed regional sales manager supported by four sales representatives. The move had two main aims. The first was to provide greater support to merchant branches and the second was to give greater focus to their key customers and help develop more sales opportunities with them.

The new sales regions were :

■ Scotland, Ireland and north east England;

■ A1/M1 corridor from Leeds to Peterborough;

■ North west, north Wales and west Midlands;

■ East Anglia and south east;

■ South Wales and south west;

■ London and south east.

A new national technical support team was to be developed to provide more customer assistance by taking special responsibility for measuring stairs orders and giving technical support to end users.

Source: Adapted from www.jeldwen.co.uk/press_release.asp?Action=LevelOne&PressReleaseID=27 (Accessed 30 November 2003.) Used with permission.

The breakdown method

This is the simplest method. Each salesperson is viewed as possessing the same sales productivity potential per period. Therefore, divide the total anticipated sales by the sales potential and the resultant figure equates to the number of salespeople required:

$$n = \frac{sv}{sp}$$

where n is the number of salespeople required, sv is the anticipated sales volume and sp is the estimated sales productivity of each salesperson/unit.

This technique is flawed because it treats sales force size as a consequence of sales, yet the reverse is probably true. A further difficulty concerns the estimate of productivity. It fails to account for varying levels of potential, abilities and levels of compensation. Furthermore, there is no account taken of profitability as it treats the estimated sales figure as an end in itself.

The workload method

Underlying this next method is the premise that all salespeople should bear an equal amount of the work necessary to service the entire market. The initial task is to determine the frequency and duration of calls to different types of customers. The ABC Rule of Account Classification holds that the first 15 per cent of customers account for 65 per cent of sales (A accounts), the next 20 per cent will produce 20 per cent of sales (B accounts) and the final 65 per cent will yield only 15 per cent (C accounts). This leads to the number of hours necessary to cover a market area, which, when considered in the light of the selling time available, makes it possible to derive the total number of sales people required.

While this technique is relatively easy to calculate, it does not allow for differences in sales response among accounts that receive the same sales effort. It fails to account for servicing and assumes that all salespersons have the same contact time. This is simply not true. One further shortcoming is that the profitability per call is neglected.

Sales potential method

Semlow (1959) was one of the earliest to report the decreasing-returns principle when applied to sales force calculations. The principle recognises that there will be diminishing returns as extra salespeople are added to the sales force. For example, one extra salesperson may generate £120,000, but two more may only generate a total of £200,000 in new sales. Therefore, while the first generates £120,000, the other two only generate £100,000 each.

Semlow found, for example, that sales in territories with 1 per cent potential generated £160,000, whereas sales in territories with 5 per cent averaged £200,000. Therefore 1 per cent potential in the second territory equates to £40,000 (200,000/5) and £160,000 (160,000/1) in the first. The conclusion reached was that a higher proportion of sales per 1 per cent of potential could be realised if the territories were made smaller by adding salespeople. This begs the question, touched on above, of deriving an optimum number of salespersons, given that costs rise as more salespeople are added.

Semlow's work provides the basis for some of the more sophisticated techniques and derivatives of the incremental or marginal approach. It is relatively simple in concept, but exceedingly difficult to implement. The conclusion, that a salesperson in a low-potential territory is expected to achieve a greater proportion of the potential than a colleague in a high potential territory is attractive (Churchill *et al.*, 1990).

Sales force automation

There is overwhelming evidence to show that organisations have used technology to enhance the effectiveness of their selling activities (Engle and Barnes, 2000). Driven by the attraction of lower selling costs, improved communication effectiveness and enhanced market and customer information, various forms of technology have been employed. Widmier *et al.* (2002) argue that such technology includes sales force automation, communication technology and customer relationship management (CRM). These authors used the literature to determine six main sales-related functions, namely organising, presenting, reporting, communicating, informing and supporting transactions. These are set out in Table 12.6.

Table 12.6 The use of technology in sales

Sales function	Use of technology
Organising	Call schedules, route plans, contacts, sales plans
Presenting with	Portable multimedia presentations, customised proposals
Reporting on	Call reports, expense claims, monthly performance
Informing about	Prospecting, product performance and product configuration information
Communicating via	Mobile phones, pagers, internet, email, personal organisers, fax machines
Supporting transactions	Order status and tracking, stock control, stock availability

Source: Adapted from Widmier *et al.* (2002).

Research by these authors shows that technology is used extensively to assist all of the selling functions but is used least by salespersons when in the field for actually supporting transactions (for example order status and stock enquiries and qualifying customers). It also indicates that technology is more likely to be used by salespersons in the office (preparing presentations, proposals, route planning, scheduling and reporting) than in the field.

Sales force automation (SFA) refers to hardware, software and telecommunication devices used by salespersons in their work-related activities. As Morgan and Inks (2001) suggest, there is no exact configuration or system that can be called SFA. However, through the linkage and integration of these various and growing number of devices, increased productivity through lower costs, or improved number and quality face-to-face buyer–seller interactions, should be realised.

The deployment of SFA varies among organisations and its effectiveness will, to a large extent, be dependent upon appropriate implementation, proper utilisation by the sales force and suitable support processes. Indeed, Morgan and Inks report SFA failure rates between 25 and 60 per cent, a large proportion of which can be accredited to poor management of change and sales force resistance to change. The factors that relate to the successful implementation of SFA will vary according to industry and organisation and perhaps even individual sales people. Research by Morgan and Inks identified four main elements associated with the successful implementation of SFA: management commitment; training; user involvement; and accurate expectation setting. They also determined that implementation will be less than satisfactory when there are fears of technology, of interference in an individual's selling activities, or a loss of power (over the information they have on their customers), as well as where there is a general resistance to change (see Table 12.7).

Table 12.7 Factors likely to influence the adoption and rejection of SFA

Factors for the adoption of SFA	Factors likely to affect the rejection of SFA
Accurate expectations	Fear of technology
User influence	Fear of interference
Training	Loss of power
Management commitment	General resistance to change

Source: Adapted from Morgan and Inks (2001).

It would appear logical that the adoption of SFA should lead to substantial productivity gains. Engle and Barnes (2000) suggest that this may not be the case. They report that one of the earlier adopters of SFA was the pharmaceutical industry. However, despite initial optimism, doubts ensued about whether there were real productivity gains as a result of adopting SFA. High implementation costs, sales force resistance and under utilisation have been cited as some of the key reasons for the failure to substantially increase productivity. This apparent conflict of views should be considered in the light of varying industry characteristics, operational circumstances and different definitions of SFA and technology. To date, there is little research evidence to show the impact of SFA on relationships.

There can be little doubt that most salespeople use technology much more in their work than their counterparts of 15 years ago. However, the impact of SFA will increase with experience, and care must be taken to help and encourage its acceptance through appropriate management leadership, training, accurate expectations and the influence and encouragement of users themselves (Morgan and Inks, 2001).

SNAPSHOT 12.6

SFA AT CHARLES WELLS BREWERY

Charles Wells is a family-owned brewery which employs 400 people. Some of its products are well known in the United Kingdom, beers such as Bombardier real ale and lager such as Red Stripe. These products are cask-conditioned, which means they require three weeks to brew and consumption must be within two weeks. The use of technology has always been a part of the brewery's competitive strategy, especially with larger breweries. Their adoption of Wireless LAN technology to improve the efficiency of its customer service was a natural progression.

The brewery employs 40 field sales reps who travel the country selling beer to pub chains and restaurants. Because orders used to be fed into the company's planning systems from the rep's home or when reps visited head office, orders could be delayed for several days which then impacted on forecasting, production and stock control.

Through the use of laptops and mobile phones, the sales force can now enter orders in real time, which allows the brewery to improve customer service while reducing stock levels, working capital and wastage. In addition to these tangible benefits staff can access information much more quickly, and productivity is improved because they can use their laptops from any location.

Source: Adapted from O'Halloran (2003).

Key account management

The increasing complexity of both markets and products, combined with the trends towards purchasing centralisation and industrial concentration, mean that a small number of major accounts have become essential for the survival of many organisations. The growth in the significance of key account management (KAM) is expected to continue and one of the results will be the change in expectations of buyers and sellers, in particular the demand for higher levels of expertise, integration and professionalism of sales forces.

It has long been recognised that particular customer accounts represent an important, often large proportion of turnover. Such accounts have been referred to variously as national accounts, house accounts, major accounts and key accounts. Millman and Wilson (1995) argue that the first three are orientated towards sales, tend to the short term and are often only driven by sales management needs. However, Ojasalo (2001) sees little difference in the terminology KAM, national account marketing (NAM) and strategic account management (SAM).

Key accounts may be of different sizes in comparison with the focus organisation, but what delineates them from other types of 'account' is that they are strategically important. Key accounts are customers who, in a business-to-business market, are willing to enter into relational exchanges and who are of strategic importance to the focus organisation.

There are two primary aspects of this definition. The first is that both parties perceive relational exchanges as a necessary component and that the relationship is long term. The second aspect refers to the strategic issue. The key account is strategically important because it might offer opportunities for entry to new markets, represent

SNAPSHOT 12.7

KEY ACCOUNT COMPLEXITY AT COMPSYS

INTEC is a division of COMPELEC, a Swedish manufacturer of computer hardware, software and services. INTEC has two subsidiaries COMPSYS and COMPSERV.

COMPSYS provides complex, bespoke products and services with approximately 50 per cent of turnover derived through a KAM structure. This has four key account teams, each of three people, who manage 40 customer accounts which are aligned on a vertical industry basis (financial services, general manufacturing and so on).

COMPSERV provide more standardised products and emphasise customer service but this is all delivered through a network of virtually autonomous dealers.

The complexity of the relationships is highlighted when one of COMPSERV's dealer engineers works on equipment sold through one of the key accounts of COMPSYS. Key accounts therefore involve more than a single dyadic relationship and conflict remains inherent in KAM structures.

Source: Adapted from Spencer (1999).

access to other key organisations or resources, or provide symbolic value in terms of influence, power and stature.

The importance of the long-term relationship as a prime element of key account identification raises questions about how they are developed, what resources are required to manage and sustain them, and what long-term success and effectiveness results from identifying them. Essentially this comes down to, who in the organisation should be responsible for these key accounts? Generally there are three main responses: to assign sales executives, to create a key account division or to create a key account sales force (see Table 12.8).

Key account managers

Abratt and Kelly (2002) report Napolitano's (1997) work which found that, to be successful, a KAM programme requires the selection of the right key account manager. This person should possess particularly strong interpersonal and relationship skills and be capable of managing larger, significant and often complex customers. Key account managers act as a conduit between organisations, through which high value information flows, in both directions. They must be prepared and able to deal with organisations where buying decisions can be protracted and delayed (Sharma, 1997).

Table 12.8 Three ways of managing key accounts

Category	Explanation
Assigning sales executives	Common in smaller organisations that do not have large resources. Normally undertaken by senior executives who have the flexibility and can provide the responsive service often required. They can make decisions about stock, price, distribution and levels of customisation.
	There is a tendency for key accounts to receive a disproportionate level of attention, as the executives responsible for these major customers lose sight of their own organisation's marketing strategy.
Creating a key account division	The main advantage of this approach is that it offers close integration of production, finance, marketing and sales. The main disadvantage is that resources are duplicated and the organisation can become very inefficient. It is also a high-risk strategy, as the entire division is dependent upon a few customers.
Creating a key account sales force	This is adopted by organisations who want to differentiate through service and they use their most experienced and able salespersons and provide them with a career channel.
	Administratively, this structure is inefficient as there is a level of duplication similar to that found in the customer-type structure discussed earlier. Furthermore, commission payable on these accounts is often a source of discontent, both for those within the key account sales force and those aspiring to join the select group.

KEY ACCOUNT MANAGERS AT COFUNDS

Cofunds is a fund supermarket that only serves intermediaries. As at June 2003 they offered more than 680 funds from 50 fund managers through the Cofunds platform, to which intermediaries have access. Over 3,500 registered intermediary firms currently administer in excess of £1 billion of funds on behalf of over 92,000 investors by using the platform.

Cofunds is 100 per cent committed to intermediaries. They publicly state that they do not deal with private investors nor do they deal directly with intermediaries' own clients. By not offering their own investment funds Cofunds are able to be truly independent and focus totally on supporting the intermediary.

Part of their strategy and strong market position is that they are underpinned by the backing of IFDS, the UK's leading fund administrator, and four of the country's major fund managers, Gartmore, Jupiter, M&G and Threadneedle. This support provides a high level of reassurance for their clients, an important issue in this market.

Cofunds operate a regional sales team responsible for managing relationships with UK intermediaries across six sales regions. However, the strategic importance of the four major fund managers is recognised by the use of a key account team whose responsibility is to manage the relationships with the fund management groups.

Source: Adapted from www.cofunds.co.uk/content.asp?PN=Background (Accessed 30 December 2003.)

Benedapudi and Leone (2002) agree that the key account manager is vitally important to the success of a KAM relationship but they also consider the relationship differences between the organisations as distinct to the interpersonal relationships between the customer firm's contact person and the supply side firm's key account manager, or contact employee as they refer to them. These relationships will vary in strength and there are differing consequences for the KAM relationship should the contact person leave the supply side organisation.

Among the key success factors, Abratt and Kelly report that, in addition to selecting the right key account manager, the selection of the right key account customers is also important for establishing KAM programmes. Not all large and high volume customers are suitable for KAM programmes. Segmentation and customer prioritisation according to needs and an organisation's ability to provide consistent value should be used to highlight those for whom KAM would not be helpful.

In addition, particular sales behaviours are required at this level of operation. As the majority of key account managers are drawn internally from the sales force (Hannah, 1998, cited by Abratt and Kelly) it is necessary to ensure that they have the correct skills mix. It is also important to take a customer's perspective on what makes a successful KAM programme. Pardo (1997) is cited as claiming that the degree of impact a product has on the customer's business activity will determine the level of attention offered to the supplier's programme. Also, the level of buying decision centralisation will impact on the effectiveness of the KAM programme.

Abratt and Kelly found six factors were of particular importance when establishing a KAM programme. These are the 'suitability of the key account manager, knowledge and understanding of the key account customer's business, commitment to the KAM partnership, delivering value, the importance of trust and the proper implementation and understanding of the KAM concept' (p. 475).

One final point can be made concerning key account managers. The inference is that one, multi-talented individual is the sole point of contact between the supplier and customer. This is not the case as there are usually a number of levels of interaction between the two organisations. Indeed, there could be 'an entire team dedicated to providing services and support to the key account' (Ojasalo, 2001, p 109). Therefore, it is more appropriate to suggest that the key account manager should assume responsibility for all points of contact within the customer organisation.

Key account relationship cycles

A number of researchers have attempted to gain a greater understanding of KAM by considering the development cycles through which relationships move. Millman and Wilson (1995) offer the work of Ford (1980), Dwyer *et al.* (1987) and Wotruba (1991) as examples of such development cycles (see Table 12.9).

Millman and Wilson have attempted to build upon the work of the others (included in Table 12.9) and have formulated a model which incorporates their own research as well as that established in the literature. McDonald (2000) has since elaborated on their framework providing further insight and explanation.

The cycle develops with the **exploratory** KAM level where the main task is to identify those accounts that have key account potential, and those that do not, in order that resources can be allocated efficiently. Both organisations are considering each other; the buyer in terms of the supplier's offer in terms of its ability to match their own requirements and the seller in terms of the buyer providing sufficient volume, value and financial suitability.

The next level is **basic** KAM, where both organisations enter into a transactional period, essentially testing each other as potential long-term partners. Some relationships may stabilise at this level while others may develop as a result of the seller seeking and gaining tentative agreement with prospective accounts about whether they would become 'preferred accounts'.

Table 12.9 Comparison of relational models

Ford (1980), Dwyer *et al.* (1987)	Wotruba (1991)	Millman and Wilson (1995)	McDonald (2000)
Pre-relationship awareness	Provider	Pre-KAM	Exploratory
Early stage exploration	Persuader	Early KAM	Basic
Development stage expansion	Prospector	Mid-KAM	Cooperative
Long-term stage commitment	Problem solver	Partnership KAM	Interdependent
Final stage institutionalisation	Procreator	Synergistic KAM	Integrated
		Uncoupling KAM	Disintegrated

Source: Updated from Millman and Wilson (1995). Used with permission.

At the **cooperative KAM** level more people from both organisations are involved in communications. At the basic KAM level both parties understand each other and the selling company has established their credentials with the buying organisation, through experience. At this next level, opportunities to add value to the relationship are considered. This could be encouraged by increasing the range of products and services transacted. As a result more people are involved in the relationship.

At the **interdependent KAM** level of a relationship both organisations recognise the importance of the other to their operations, with the supplier either first-choice or only supplier. Retraction from the relationship is now problematic as 'inertia and strategic suitability', as McDonald phrases it, holds the partners together.

When the two organisations view the relationship as consisting of one entity where they create synergistic value in the marketplace **integrated KAM** is achieved. Joint problem solving and the sharing of sensitive information are strong characteristics of the relationship and withdrawal by either party can be traumatic at a personal level for the participants involved, let alone at the organisational level.

The final level is **disintegrating KAM**. This can occur at any time due to a variety of reasons, ranging from company takeover to the introduction of new technology. The relationship may return to another lower level and new terms of business are established. The termination, or readjustment, of the relationship need not be seen as a negative factor as both parties may decide that the relationship holds no further value.

McDonald develops Millman and Wilson's model by moving away from a purely sequential framework. He suggests that organisations may stabilise or enter the model at any level, indeed he states that organisations might readjust to a lower level. The time between phases will vary according to the nature and circumstances of the parties involved. The labels provided by McDonald reflect the relationship status of both parties rather than of the selling company (for example 'prospective') or buying company (for example 'preferred supplier'). While the Millman and Wilson and McDonald interpretations of the KAM relationship cycle provide insight they are both primarily dyadic perspectives. They neglect to consider the influence of significant others, in particular those other network member organisations who provide context and interaction in particular networks and who do influence the actions of organisations and those key individuals who are strategic decision makers.

Some final aspects of KAM

In mature and competitive markets, where there is little differentiation between the products, service may be the only source of sustainable competitive advantage. Key account management allows senior sales executives to build a strong relationship with each of their customers and so provide a very high level of service and strong point of differentiation.

This approach enables an organisation to select its most experienced and able salespersons and, in doing so, provide a career channel for those executives who prefer to stay in sales rather than move into management. Administratively, this structure is inefficient as there is a level of duplication similar to that found in the customer-type structure discussed earlier. Furthermore, commission payable on these accounts is often a source of discontent, both for those within the key account sales force and those aspiring to join the select group.

The development and management of key accounts is complex and evolving. Key account relationships are rarely static and should be rooted within corporate strategy, if only because of the implications for resources, which customers seek as a result of partnering in this way (Spencer, 1999).

Summary

The role of personal selling is changing. As organisations move to more relational exchanges, so the sales force has to adapt and work with the other tools of the promotional mix and adopt a more complementary role. This role necessitates the execution of tasks such as managing customers, developing long-term customer relationships and managing the activities of marketing channels.

The sales force should be deployed in a way which optimises the resources of the organisation and realises the greatest possible percentage of the available sales and profit potential that exists in the defined area of operation. This will result in a continuance of the growth of key accounts.

The use of the field sales force as the only means of personal selling is unlikely to remain. Technological advances and the need for increasing levels of promotional effectiveness and accountability, together with tighter cost constraints, indicate that the more progressive organisations will employ multiple sales channels. This may mean the use of the Internet, telemarketing and direct mail to free the sales force from non-selling activities, which will allow management to focus the time of the sales force on getting in front of customers and prospects, with a view to using their particular selling skills.

Finally, the use of key account management programmes signals the identification of, and intention to provide, specific and customised sales support for particular, strategically important customers. Key accounts, which can be built largely upon interpersonal or interorganisational relationships, evolve through various stages and suitable management action needs to be undertaken to realise the potential inherent in each key account.

Discussion questions

1 Describe the role of personal selling and highlight its main strengths and weaknesses.

2 Make a list of those factors that need to be considered when determining the size and role of personal selling in the promotional mix.

3 Explain the three methods used to determine the optimal size of the sales force.

4 Evaluate the way in which direct marketing might be best used to assist personal selling activities.

5 Suggest four ways in which technology could be used by a sales force to improve its performance.

6 Appraise the role of the key account manager and evaluate the extent to which they are just sales people responsible for very important accounts.

References

Abratt, R. and Kelly, P.M. (2002). 'Perceptions of a successful key account management program', *Industrial Marketing Management*, 31, 5 (August), pp. 467–76.

Anderson, R.E. (1996). 'Personal selling and sales management in the new millennium', *Journal of Personal Selling and Sales Management*, 14, 4 (Fall), p. 17–32.

Baldauf, A., Cravens, D.W. and Grant, K. (2002). 'Consequences of sales management control in field sales organisations: a cross-national perspective', *International Business Review*, 11, 5 (October), pp. 577–609.

Benedapudi, N. and Leone, R.P. (2002). 'Managing business-to-business customer relationships following key contact employee turnover in a vendor firm', *Journal of Marketing*, 66, (April), pp. 83–101.

Cespedes, F.V., Doyle, S.X. and Freedman, R.J. (1989). 'Teamwork for today's selling', *Harvard Business Review*, (March/April), pp. 44–55.

Churchill, G.A., Ford, N.M. and Walker, C. (1990). *Sales Force Management*, Homewood, IL: Irwin.

Cravens, D.W. (1987) *Strategic Marketing*. Homewood, IL: Irwin.

Cravens, D.W., Ingram, T.N. and La Forge, R.W. (1991). 'Evaluating multiple channel strategies', *Journal of Business and Industrial Marketing*, 6, 3/4, pp. 37–48.

Cronin, J. and Talyor, S. (1992). 'Measuring service quality: a reexamination and extension', *Journal of Marketing*, 56 (July), pp. 55–68.

Cross, J., Hartley, S.W., Rudelius, W., and Vassey, M.J. (2001). 'Sales force activities and marketing strategies in industrial firms: relationships and implications', *Journal of Personal Selling and Sales Management*, 21, 3 (Summer), pp. 199–206.

Dwyer, F.R., Schurr, P.H. and Oh, S. (1987). 'Developing buyer–seller relationships', *Journal of Marketing*, 51, pp. 11–27.

Engle, R.L. and Barnes, M.L. (2000). 'Sales force automation usage, effectiveness and cost benefit in Germany, England and the United States', *Journal of Business and Industrial Marketing*, 15, 4, pp. 216–42.

Ford, I.D. (1980). 'The development of buyer–seller relationships in industrial markets', *European Journal of Marketing*, 14, 5/6, pp. 339–53.

Govoni, N., Eng, R. and Galper, M. (1986). *Promotional Management*, Englewood, NJ: Prentice Hall.

Grant, K. and Cravens, D.W. (1999). 'Examining the antecedents of sales organisation effectiveness: an Australian study', *European Journal of Marketing*, 33, 9/10, pp. 945–57.

Guenzi, P. (2002). 'Sales force activities and customer trust', *Journal of Marketing Management*, 18, pp. 749–78.

Hannah, G. (1998). 'From transactions to relationships – challenges for the national account manager, *Journal of Marketing and Sales* (SA), 4, 1, pp. 30–3.

Ingram, T.N., LaForge, R.W. and Leigh, T.W. (2002). 'Selling in the new millennium', *Industrial Marketing Management*, 32, 7 (October), pp. 559–67.

Keillor, B., Parker, R.S. and Pettijohn, C.E. (2000). 'Relationship orientated characteristics and individual salesperson performance', *Journal of Business and Industrial Marketing*, 15, 1, pp. 7–22.

Kelly, S. (1992). 'Developing customer orientation among service employees', *Journal of the Academy of Marketing Sciences*, 20, 1, pp. 27–36.

Levinson, M. (2003). 'Cleared for takeoff', *CIO Magazine*, 1 April 2003; www.cio.com/archive/040102/takeoff.html (Accessed 1 January 2004.)

Levitt, T. (1967). 'Communications and industrial selling,' *Journal of Marketing*, 31 (April), pp. 15–21.

Liu, A.H. and Leach, M.P. (2001). 'Developing loyal customers with a value adding sales force: examining customer satisfaction and the perceived credibility of consultative salespeople', *Journal of Personal Selling and Sales Management*, 21, 2 (Spring), pp. 147–56.

Marshall, G.W., Moncrief, W.C. and Lassk, F.G. (1999). 'The current state of sales force activities', *Industrial Marketing Management*, 28, pp. 87–98.

McDonald, M. (2000). 'Key account management – a domain review', *Marketing Review*, 1, pp. 15–34.

McQuiston, D. H. (2001). 'A conceptual model for building and maintaining relationships between manufacturers' representatives and their principals', *Industrial Marketing Management*, 30, 2 (February), pp. 165–81.

Mehta, R., Dubinsky, A.J. and Anderson, R.E. (2002). 'Marketing channel management and the sales manager', *Industrial Marketing Management*, 31, 5 (August), pp. 429–39.

Millman, T. and Wilson, K. (1995). 'From key account selling to key account management', *Journal of Marketing Practice: Applied Marketing Science*, 1, 1, pp. 9–21.

Morgan, A.J. and Inks, S.A. (2001). 'Technology and the sales force: increasing acceptance of sales force automation', *Industrial Marketing Management*, 30, 5 (July), pp. 463–72.

Morgan, F. and Stoltman, J. (1990). 'Adaptive selling insights from social cognition', *Journal of Personal Selling and Sales Management*, Fall, pp. 43–54.

Morrill, J.E. (1970). 'Industrial advertising pays off', *Harvard Business Review*, (March/April), pp. 159–69.

Napolitano, L. (1997). 'Customer–supplier partnering: a strategy whose time has come', *Journal of Selling and Sales Management*, 17, 4, pp. 1–8.

O'Halloran, J. (2003). 'Telecoms and network technologies for SMEs: serving up the best with a wireless brew', *Computer Weekly*, Tuesday 28 October, www.computerweekly.com/articles/ (Accessed 29 November 2003.)

Ojasalo, J. (2001). 'Key account management at company and individual levels in business-to-business relationships', *Journal of Business and Industrial Marketing*, 16, 3, pp. 199–220.

Pardo, C. (1997). 'Key account management in the business-to-business field: the key accounts point-of-view', *Journal of Selling and Sales Management*, 17, 4, pp. 17–26.

Piercy, N.F., Cravens, D.W. and Morgan, N.A. (1998). 'Salesforce performance and behaviour-based management processes in business-to-business sales organisations', *European Journal of Marketing*, 32, 1/2, pp. 79–100.

Reid, A., Pullins, E.B. and Plank, R.E. (2002). 'The impact of purchase situation on salesperson communication behaviors in business markets', *Industrial Marketing Management*, 31, 3, pp. 205–13.

Saxe, R. and Weitz, B. (1982). 'The SOCO scale: a measure of the customer orientation of salespeople', *Journal of Marketing Research*, 19 (August), pp. 343–51.

Semlow, W.E. (1959). 'How many salesmen do you need?', *Harvard Business Review*, (May/June), pp. 126–32.

Sharma, A. (1997). 'Who prefers key account management program? An investigation of business buying behaviour and buying firm characteristics', *Journal of Personal Selling and Sales Management*, 17, 4, pp. 27–39.

Spencer, R. (1999). 'Key accounts: effectively managing strategic complexity', *Journal of Business and Industrial Marketing*, 14, 4, pp. 291–310.

Srivastava, R.K., Shervani, T.A. and Fahey, L. (1999). 'Marketing, business process and shareholder value: an organizationally embedded view of marketing activities and the discipline of marketing', *Journal of Marketing*, 63, pp. 168–79.

Swinyard, W.R. and Ray, M.L. (1977). 'Advertising–selling interactions: an attribution theory experiment', *Journal of Marketing Research*, 14 (November), pp. 509–16.

Thayer, L. (1968). *Communication and communication systems*, Homewood, IL: Irwin.

Weinraunch, J,D., Stephens-Friesen, M. and Carlson, R.L. (2001). 'Improving the viability of manufacturers' representatives with industry-based sales training initiatives', *Journal of Business and Industrial Marketing*, 16, 3, pp. 183–98.

Widmier, S.M., Jackson, Jr, D.W. and McCabe, D.B. (2002). 'Infusing technology into personal selling', *Journal of Personal Selling and Sales Management*, 22, 3 (Summer), pp. 189–99.

Wilson, D.T. (1995). 'An intergrated model of buyer–seller relationship', *Journal of the Academy of Marketing Science*, 23, 4, pp. 335–45.

Wilson, K. (1993). 'Managing the industrial sales force of the 1990s', *Journal of Marketing Management*, 9, pp. 123–39.

Wotruba, T.R. (1991). 'The evolution of personal selling', *Journal of Personal Selling and Sales Management*, 11, 3, pp. 1–12.

Index

Note: Figures and Tables are indicated by *italic page numbers* and Snapshot boxes by **emboldened numbers**